Germany in the
Nineteenth Century

PETER LANG
New York • Washington, D.C./Baltimore • Bern
Frankfurt am Main • Berlin • Brussels • Vienna • Oxford

Eda Sagarra

Germany in the Nineteenth Century

History and Literature

PETER LANG
New York • Washington, D.C./Baltimore • Bern
Frankfurt am Main • Berlin • Brussels • Vienna • Oxford

Library of Congress Cataloging-in-Publication Data

Sagarra, Eda.
Germany in the nineteenth century:
history and literature / Eda Sagarra.
p. cm.
Includes bibliographical references and index.
1. Germany—History—1789–1900. 2. Germany—Economic conditions—19th century.
3. Germany—Social conditions—19th century. I. Title.
DD203 .S22   943'.07—dc21   00-036839
ISBN 0-8204-4065-5

Die Deutsche Bibliothek-CIP-Einheitsaufnahme

Sagarra, Eda:
Germany in the nineteenth century: history and literature / Eda Sagarra.
−New York; Washington, D.C./Baltimore; Bern;
Frankfurt am Main; Berlin; Brussels; Vienna; Oxford: Lang.
ISBN 0-8204-4065-5

Cover design by Dutton & Sherman Design

The paper in this book meets the guidelines for permanence and durability
of the Committee on Production Guidelines for Book Longevity
of the Council of Library Resources.

© 2001 Peter Lang Publishing, Inc., New York

All rights reserved.
Reprint or reproduction, even partially, in all forms such as microfilm,
xerography, microfiche, microcard, and offset strictly prohibited.

Printed in the United States of America

for Mireia

Acknowledgments

I would like to thank the many people who have helped me in various ways with *Germany in the Nineteenth Century*, especially Ilse Samuel (born in Berlin 1909, died in Blackburn 1993) and her husband Herbert Samuel (born in Rostock 1907, died in Blackburn 1992), Mireia Sagarra, and Sheila Floyd.

Eda Sagarra Dublin, April 2001

We are grateful for permission to reproduce photographs:

Amerika-Gedenkbibliothek Berliner-Zentralbibliothek,
 from *Liederbuch des Deutschen Michel*, 1843: page 27

Bildarchiv Foto Marburg: pages 178, 186

Bildarchiv Preußischer Kulturbesitz, Berlin: pages 5, 12, 16, 34, 36, 58, 78, 110, 121, 165, 168, 183, 194, 227, 248, 265, 268

Facsimile Querschnitt durch den Simplicissimus,
 Scherz Verlag, München, 1963: pages 218, 230, 253, 276

Schloss Charlottenburg, Staatliche Schlösser und Gärten, Berlin: page 166

Staatliche Museen zu Berlin, Nationalgalerie: pages 107, 152

Staatsgemäldesammlungen, München: pages 97, 175

Contents

List of Illustrations xi

Preface.. xiii

Note on Currency Values xv

Chapter 1 Germany and Napoleon 1

Chapter 2 Authority and the Subject: Metternich's System 1815–48 19

Chapter 3 The German Economy in the First Half of the Century 31

Chapter 4 German Society 1815–48 43

Chapter 5 The German Revolution of 1848–9 71

Chapter 6 The Development of the German National Movement 97

Chapter 7 The Growth of Prussian Hegemony in Germany 1850–71 115

Chapter 8 The German Writer and the Literary Market 133

Chapter 9 German Women and Their History in the Nineteenth Century .. 151

Chapter 10 The Army, the Parties, and the State after 1871 183

Chapter 11 Politics, Government, and the Masses 1890–1914 207

Chapter 12 Developments in the German Economy 1850–1914 233

Chapter 13 German Society in the Later Nineteenth Century 247

Chapter 14 Germany in 1900—A State to Be Proud of? 273

Some Suggestions for Further Reading 281

Index 291

Illustrations

The "horse thief" of Berlin 5
Professor Henrik Steffens calls on his students 12
The Rhenish Courier 16
Satiric reference to the pigtail 27
The Lauchhammer Works 34
The political ambition of the citizen advances at a snail's pace 36
The *Zollverein* and the Tax Union (1834) 38
German Railways 41
The German Confederation 45
Parade Unter den Linden by Franz Krüger 58
Death of a young student 78
Italia and Germania by Friedrich Overbeck 97
Portrait of Heinrich Hoffmann von Fallersleben 107
Proclamation of the Emperor in Versailles 110
Unveiling the Victory Column 112
Bismarck in 1871 121
The evolution of Bismarck's Germany 129
The number of books published in nineteenth-century Germany ... 139
Frau Wilhelmine Begas 152
The German woman lecturer of the future 165
Queen Louise of Prussia 166

The German woman student of the future 168

At the window by Ferdinand Waldmüller 175

Panorama from the Werdersche Church by Edward Gärtner 178

Troops entering Berlin, June 1871 183

Portrait of an officer 186

Bismarck laying the foundation stone for the new Reichstag 194

Skit on Wilhelm II's love of travel 218

The Iron Foundry by Adolph von Menzel 227

Bismarck and Bebel from *Simplicissimus* 230

German Society as seen by *Kladderadatsch* 248

Der – Die – Das – from *Simplicissimus* 253

Strikers at their employer's 262

Employment agency for domestic servants 265

Father's birthday 268

"The English sword" from *Simplicissimus* 276

Preface

Germany in the Nineteenth Century is an account of the country in which German writers and their contemporaries grew up. Germany in the nineteenth century was very different from what we know as the Federal Republic of Germany today. Above all, it was far larger, extending deep into eastern Europe. Substantial territories of modern Poland were then an integral part of Germany. The river Oder, today the border between the Federal Republic and Poland, was then a "German" river. East Prussia on the Baltic coast, which now is part of Poland and of Russia, once held a special place in the minds of loyal Germans, since it was there that the kings of Prussia had traditionally gone to be crowned. Nineteenth-century Germans thought of the cities in these eastern regions, such as Breslau (Wrocław), Silesia's capital, or Königsberg (Kaliningrad), as of equal importance to Hamburg, Frankfurt, Munich, or other west German cities.

Perhaps even more significant historically was the position of Austria. Up to 1866, when Prussia defeated Austria and her federal allies, Germany also included the Austrian portion of the Austro-Hungarian monarchy, that is, the territory of the present Austrian Republic, as well as most of the present-day Czech Republic and part of modern Italy, Slovakia, and Slovenia. For centuries, Austria had been the dominant power in Germany. This all changed following the 1866 war, in which Prussia expelled her from Germany. From 1867 forward, until the Nazi era, the political history of Germany diverged from that of Austria, despite a multiplicity of cultural and other links between the Austrian Empire and, from 1871, the newly founded German Empire.

For Germans who lived through the middle decades of the nineteenth century the unification of the German state was the most important event of their lifetimes. Not everyone felt happy about its form, namely unification under Prussian leadership. Many Germans, especially in the south and among the smaller central German states, would have preferred a solution which included Austria. But the main point for them was that Germany at last had shaken off the great disadvantage under which she had so long labored by comparison with her western and northern neighbors: she was now, at last, a nation state.

For nineteenth-century Germans, theirs was a century of astonishing change and of remarkable achievements, in politics and scientific inquiry, in technology, industry, and culture. One German novelist, Theodor Fontane, set himself the task to capture in imaginative form the changes which national unity and the industrial revolution had wrought in his country. For him, the changes in human consciousness were even more fascinating than the physical changes all around him. Fontane was an almost exact contemporary of Bismarck, about whom he frequently wrote. He is of particular interest to the historian of nineteenth-century Germany, because he reflected the changing temper of the century in his oeuvre. He wrote about his century in novels and lyric poetry, in patriotic and social critical ballads, in travelogues, political journalism, art and theater criticism, autobiography, and letters. Fontane's letters are among the best in the German language. The extraordinary range of Fontane's work and his acute awareness of the impact of change on society and the individual makes him an ideal occasional companion for the interested reader. In what follows, developments in Germany's political, social or economic history are frequently exemplified by reference to Fontane's novels and stories. The reader will find that these offer quite remarkable and many-faceted insights into contemporary processes, events, and personalities. This is especially true of his most profound work, the novel *Der Stechlin*, which was published in 1898, the year in which he, like Bismarck, died.

Note on Currency Values

Currencies were, until the founding of the German Empire in 1871, a potent symbol of German disunity. In the same way, from about the middle of the century onwards, the gradual advance of the Prussian taler signaled the coming hegemony of Prussia in Germany.

At the beginning of the nineteenth century, Germany had some five currency systems, of which the three versions of the taler (Prussian, Saxon, and Mecklenburg) were dominant in the north and parts of central Germany and the gulden or florin in the south and in some central German states. Hamburg and Lübeck used what was known as Lübeck currency, but Hamburg and Bremen also employed other coinages.

Currency reforms in south Germany in 1837 and in Dresden in 1838 attempted to introduce some standard practices. In particular, the Dresden agreement of 30 July 1838 established conversion rates of 3½ gulden = 2 Prussian talers, with the result that the one-taler piece became effectively the standard currency in north Germany and the one-gulden piece in the south. By the time of the Vienna Coinage Treaty of 24 January 1857, the last major reform before the introduction of the mark in the German Empire in 1873, the taler had begun to extend its sphere of influence into the south, at the cost of the gulden.

After 1870, the Prussian taler, subdivided into 30 Groschen and 360 Pfennig, replaced the gulden, and in fact became widely accepted in central Europe as well. The (Reichs)mark became the official German currency in 1873, valued at about one half of the taler, though the latter continued in circulation for some years.

1 taler = 30 groschen = 360 pfennig = 20¢ or approximately 0.20 Euro

1 gulden or guilder = 1 florin (French name for gulden) = 2/3 taler

1 (Reichs)mark = c. half a taler or c. 0.10¢

10 marks = 1 gold crown (Krone)

20 marks = 1 Doppelkrone = c. one English gold sovereign

Chapter 1
Germany and Napoleon

The French revolutionary wars and Germany

When in the year 1792 the French armies invaded the territory of the Holy Roman Empire, Germany was a geographical and a cultural concept, but not a political one, at least not in the modern sense of the term. *Deutschland, wo liegt es?* asked Johann Wolfgang von Goethe (1749–1832), *Ich weiß nicht zu sagen*. (Where is Germany? I simply don't know.) In the years which followed the invasion, neither the establishment of the short-lived Jacobin Republic of Mainz of 1792–3 nor the French annexations on the left bank of the Rhine, neither the destruction of the Holy Roman Empire in 1806 by Napoleon Bonaparte (1769–1822) nor even the French conquest and humiliation of Prussia in 1806 and of Austria in 1809, altered this situation. At the beginning of the nineteenth century, the people of Germany were subjects of secular and ecclesiastical rulers governing more than 300 sovereign political units. Some further 1,500 territories could be described as having semisovereign status, a rich source, surely, of that regional and local culture and even local patriotism which still informs many parts of Germany today. In 1800 the ecclesiastical rulers, among them the powerful prince archbishops of Cologne, Mainz, and Trier, ruled over almost one sixth of the entire territory of the Empire. Some states of the Empire, such as Austria or Prussia, were substantial European powers. Very many others were no larger than an English gentleman's country estate. Indeed, a person traveling up the right bank of the Rhine in 1800 from Cologne to Mainz would cross more than a dozen state frontiers—and it could take him or her up to three days to get there.

The political boundaries were only one obstacle on the traveler's path. Internal customs barriers on roads and waterways, a variety of coinages existing alongside the 'official' currencies, of taler, florin, gulden, and so on, and a truly bewildering number of weights and measures provided the commercial counterpart of the checkered map of the Holy Roman Empire. Nor did this unwieldy structure embrace all the territories ruled over by its princes and its free cities. Switzerland had 'left' the Empire in 1648; East and West Prussia had never formed part of it. Nor was the Holy Roman Empire a purely German affair. The southern Netherlands (modern Belgium) and Luxembourg formed part of it, while the Danish king was one of the princes of the Empire by virtue of his capacity as hereditary ruler of the duchy of Holstein. It was a Dane, Ludvig Holberg (1684–1751), who perhaps best described the hybrid nature of the German polity. Author of the popular comedy on parish-pump politics under the title of *Der politische Kannegiesser* (1723), much admired by Germans, he once remarked that should anyone care to inquire about the type of government in Germany, the answer must be: "Germany is governed in the German manner."

The political divisions of Germany were not the only barrier to the creation of a sense of nationhood in the political sense. Germany's social structure on the eve of the nineteenth century was reminiscent of an earlier age. Essentially, Germany was still a *Ständestaat*, a society based on traditional feudal orders. The nobility enjoyed privileged legal, political, social, and fiscal status. In the western parts of Germany peasants, though legally free men, labored under many onerous obligations, often to more than one lord—rent to one, labor dues to another, tithes to a third. In the manorial lands east of the river Elbe, in Prussia and in Mecklenburg, where towns were few and far between, the peasantry was largely bound to the soil, owing service and dues, dependent on the landlord for permission to marry, subject to his jurisdiction. Furthermore, and in contrast with the United States or with France, Britain, the Low Countries or Northern Italy, Germany lacked a large indigenous mercantile class. True, Hamburg and Bremen, with their well-developed overseas trade (soon, too, in emigrants), and Leipzig, center of the growing book trade, gave the lie to the older view of middle-class Germany as an almost wholly bureaucratic institution. But by 1800, many of Germany's great medieval and early modern towns were but a shadow of their former selves. This was the case with Lübeck and Danzig, the one on the western, the other on the eastern shores of the Baltic sea, and it was true of Nuremberg in the south, where the great sixteenth-century artist Albrecht Dürer (1471–1528) had lived and worked. Most German towns of any size in 1800 owed their character to the fact that the prince resided there. "One cannot even buy a pair of gloves here," lamented a Scottish traveler of early nineteenth-century Karlsruhe. Yet this southwest German city was the seat of one of Germany's more enlightened and energetic princes, Frederick Karl, margrave of Baden (1746–1811), whose forebears had designed the town in imitation of Versailles, and whom Napoleon would soon make a grand duke, quadrupling the size of his state in the process.

More recent German historiography has persuasively challenged the traditional view of the quiescent nature of Germany's intellectual class on the eve of the French invasion. The extraordinary vigor of German philosophical inquiry and of literary production in Germany in the period of Napoleon's life and active career is ample proof that such a class did exist. The rapidity with which institutions like the clubs, reading societies, and lending libraries spread across northern and central Germany in the late eighteenth century, and the speed with which French publications were translated into German, is further evidence of the existence of a vigorous intellectual debate. What was never in dispute is that Germans had far greater problems in gaining access to the political decision-making process, because their country lacked the kind of public sphere which the United States, France, or Britain could take for granted. This deficiency was part of the fragmented nature of Germany and the bureaucratic and paternalist traditions by which it was governed. It was by no means unknown for princes to employ middle-class advisers, but in general the gifted sons of officials, pastors, teachers, and master craftsmen found little outlet for their talents, as Gotthold Ephraim Lessing (1729–81), author of the bourgeois tragedy of princely corruption, *Emilia Galotti* (1772), knew all too well. The experience of Goethe's hero in the novel, *The Sorrows of Young Werther* (1774), who found himself as a public servant passed over in favor of scions of noble houses, was a generational experience. It was replicated in the lives of the following generation, namely Napoleon's German contemporaries. A fundamental feature of Germany in 1800 was that she had no capital city. And because she lacked such a natural focus, most of the discussion on the future role and function of the middle ranks of society took place, not in the coffeehouses, salons or parliamentary chamber, as was the case in Paris or London, but rather in the often short-lived learned journals and literary periodicals published in the provinces, which are such a feature of the years between about 1770 and 1830, known as the *Sattelzeit* (or saddle years separating early modern from modern Germany). Equally significant, in terms of the intellectual ferment of late eighteenth-century Germany, was the extensive correspondence between reflective minds living far away from each other and often never destined to meet in person. For so many, this was the only practical alternative to the missing public sphere. In the towns, trade was still largely regulated by guilds, which survived longer in Germany than elsewhere. Though politically ineffective, they exercised a strong social and economic influence in the townships of the Holy Roman Empire, usually as an obstacle to change. Their firm opposition to technical and product innovation, their restrictive practices, designed to exclude 'unfair' competition and ensure their members a reasonable living, encouraged a defensive, highly conservative mentality, and also contributed to the proliferation of 'illegal' craftsmen who produced inferior goods for lower prices. It has been estimated that two-thirds of town dwellers in the southern state of Württemberg and two-fifths in Brandenburg fell into this latter category.

The impact of Napoleon on Germany

It was the historic role of the French revolutionary wars and Napoleon to have acted as the catalyst of polity and society in Germany on the eve of the nineteenth century. Not only did Napoleon rationalize the map of Germany in the wake of conquest, reducing its sovereign states to scarcely more than one-tenth of their former number; he also gave a powerful impulse to finding an answer to Goethe's rhetorical question by helping to create a nation of Germany in the political sense. The profound changes which resulted from the Napoleonic era were both direct and indirect. Direct were the consequences of administrative and economic reordering of the territory annexed by the French in the Rhineland or through the conditions imposed on the initial sixteen (ultimately over thirty) German satellites of France which constituted Napoleon's *Rheinbund* or Confederation of the Rhine of 1806–13. Indirect, but no less powerful in their impact on the future history of Germany, were the reform measures introduced by German governments to try and cope with defeat and occupation, and with the war indemnities and troops demanded by the French to satisfy Napoleon's imperial ambitions. No less important were those reforms which were *not* introduced: the failure of Austrian officials to pioneer the kind of far-reaching reforms implemented by Prussia or by the southern states, such as Bavaria, Baden, Württemberg, and Hesse-Darmstadt, was to have profoundly adverse effects on Austria's capacity to continue to function as the major player in Germany that she had so long been.

Economically, the French occupation stimulated the rise of capitalist enterprise in the Rhineland, now open to the French market, in what was to become Germany's key industrial region. Napoleon's continental blockade of England gave useful if brief protection to young German enterprises struggling to maintain themselves against British competition. The removal of that protection which followed Napoleon's defeat and the subsequent exposure of German manufacture to English competition was to prove disastrous for many German craftsmen. Similarly, in those western territories of Germany which had experienced the benefits of the Napoleonic Code, memories of the days of the French were by no means as negative as subsequent German nationalist mythmaking liked to suggest. Among those who looked back with regret were many of those German Jews in the former French-occupied territories of western Germany, whom Napoleon had emancipated. One was Heinrich Heine, author of the nostalgic poem on the loyalty of the two French grenadiers to Napoleon (*Die Grenadiere*); another, was the critic Ludwig Börne (1786–1837) from Frankfurt, who had had ambitions to become a civil servant, but who now, in 1815, as an unbaptized Jew, was barred from entry.

The "horse thief" of Berlin (Napoleon steals the horses from the top of the Brandenburg gate). Contemporary caricature (c. 1814).

Like Heine, he emigrated to Paris, where he wrote the scathing critique of post-Napoleonic Germany, his Letters from Paris (*Briefe aus Paris*, 1833).

Political nationalism

Napoleonic rule in Germany is credited with having created a totally new phenomenon, political nationalism. Nascent nationalism, as Slav and Celtic examples have shown, defines itself more easily if directed against a powerful neighbor. When, as in the case of Germany, her French neighbor had left countless monuments to earlier aggression in the national territory, such as the ruined Heidelberg castle, which later German nationalists carefully refused to rebuild, and had also been in recent or living memory an occupying power, it is not difficult to understand that German nationalism should have expressed itself in chauvinistic attacks on France.

For it was not the invasion of the Holy Roman Empire by the French in 1792, nor even the annexations in 1802, which were responsible for widespread German rejection of the ideas and ideals of the French Revolution. Rather it was the experience of the realities of Napoleonic occupation for over a decade. As the great theoretician of modern warfare, Carl von Clausewitz (1780–1831), put it, "The people themselves became participants in the war." The concepts of revolution, emancipation, equality of the citizen inevitably became associated for many with conquest, exploitation, and national humiliation. Just as the French revolution changed the political vocabulary of Europe, so too the Napoleonic years in Germany were fertile in German nationalist mythmaking. The propagation of myth was facilitated by the tendency of writers at that time to address the public as if speaking personally to them. Examples of such dialogue with the reader or listener include the inflammatory *Reden an die Deutsche Nation* by the philosopher Johann Gottlieb Fichte (1762–1814) which he gave in 1807–8, only a stone's throw from the French army garrison in Berlin; the *Political Catechism* (1809) of Heinrich von Kleist (1777–1811) on the devilish character of Napoleon, and the intellectually subtle but emotionally so fulfilling sermons of Friedrich Schleiermacher (1768–1834) which drew crowds of thousands to his Berlin church. Nor should we forget the impact on awakening German national consciousness of the public lectures in the new royal universities of Berlin and Breslau, founded in 1810, and which attracted such a galaxy of talent, among them, the philosopher Georg Wilhelm Friedrich Hegel (1770–1831). But the moral leaders of the nationalist opposition to the French were neither Immanuel Kant (1724–1804) nor Goethe nor Friedrich Schiller (1759–1805). Rather were they the romantic writers, many of them brilliant and original minds, all of them talented in multiple ways. Among them were the philosopher Fichte, Berlin University's first rector; one of Germany's greatest dramatists, Heinrich von Kleist; and the lyric poets Clemens Brentano (1778–1842) and Achim von Arnim (1781–1831), who recorded with imaginative ingenuity the folk songs of the people. Nor should one forget the contribution of scholars, most notably, perhaps, the brothers Jacob (1785–1863) and Wilhelm (1786–1859) Grimm, authors of Germany's most famous collection of folktales. Nor should the popularizers be forgotten, Ernst Moritz Arndt (1769–1860), son of a Mecklenburg serf and author of hugely successful patriotic lyrics, and *Turnvater* (father of gymnasts) Friedrich Ludwig Jahn (1778–1852), self-styled apostle of Germanic physical culture. They and others, such as the influential conservative theorist, Adam Müller (1779–1829), rejected the political implications of the notion of human equality, because of its associations with the French Revolution. The *Code Napoléon*, the benign legacy of Napoleonic occupation, was actually included in the ritual book-burning carried out by university students, the chief spokesmen of the nationalist movement after Napoleon's defeat. It is hard to judge their act on its own terms, overlaid as it is today by the incomparably more vicious and premeditated outrage of 10 May 1933 by book-burning students under the direction of Hitler's Storm Troopers. But Nazism could still draw on the powerful myth that identified Jewish emancipation in Germany with the 'stigma' of revolution. For it was the French, not the Germans, who had first removed disabilities from the Jews in occupied territories. Yet the Nazis with their selective memories could equally conveniently forget that it was a Prussian, Wilhelm von Humboldt (1767–1835), who had successfully introduced the *Edict of Tolerance* into Prussian law during the Napoleonic occupation in 1812. However, in the illiberal climate of post-Napoleonic Germany after 1815, von Humboldt failed to persuade king Friedrich Wilhelm III (1797–1840) to extend it to the rest of Prussia.

There was, however, another vigorous intellectual tradition in Germany, which looked back to the French Revolution and the Declaration of the Rights of Man for its legitimacy. It was represented in the nineteenth century most forcefully by poets such as Heinrich Heine, born in the Rhineland and living and working for most of his life as a writer in Paris, and by the generation of writers born about the end of the Napoleonic era, which included Karl Marx (1818–83) and Friedrich Engels (1820–95), as well as the Young Germans and the Young Hegelians. The dramatist Georg Büchner (1813–37) belonged to the same tradition; his first play, *Dantons Tod* (1835) was actually set in revolutionary France.

Territorial changes

In 1801 Napoleon consolidated his victorious campaign against the Empire in the Treaty of Lunéville, the principal provisions of which were the ceding of the left bank of the Rhine to France. According to the treaty, secularization of ecclesiastical territory in the rest of Germany was to provide compensation for German and other princes who had lost their lands. (Napoleon, son of the atheistic French revolution, paid no heed to the ancient rights of the ecclesiastical princes.) In 1803, Napoleon drove a further wedge between the secular and ecclesiastical princes of the Empire, and by so doing actually abolished one of the three estates of that institution. Of eighty-one ecclesiastical princes, only three remained after 1803: the once mighty archbishop of Mainz, who had owned vast tracts of land in what is today the state of Hessen, as well as territories along the Rhine and in Central Germany; and the grand masters of the ancient religious orders of the Teutonic Knights,

---

[1] The three estates were the church, the nobility, and the burghers.

whose seat had been in East Prussia, and the Knights of St. John. The poor leave few monuments to their history. Had they been able to, they might have produced a defense of a number of the ecclesiastical territories and the monasteries, now secularized. They might have reminded nationalist historians that beggars and those on the margins of society have more to expect from a theology which affords them some function in the salvation of the better-off than they could hope for from secular states before the advent of a system of social welfare. But of course it was a fundamental axiom of Napoleon's secularization, as of the Enlightenment, that the state, and not the church, be responsible for the well-being of its citizens. The gradual intrusion of the state into ever-increasing areas of human life was to be the key feature of nineteenth-century history, particularly in Germany. A further victim of the Napoleonic rationalizing impulse were the free cities, which since medieval times had given the Holy Roman Empire so much of its character. From the original number of fifty-one, only five, Hamburg, Bremen, and Lübeck in the north, Frankfurt on the river Main in the center, and Augsburg in the south, survived Napoleon. The imminent demise of the thousand-year-old empire itself was anticipated when Napoleon proclaimed himself Emperor of the French in 1804. Shortly after, the "Corsican adventurer" came in his regalia to Mainz, purporting to establish his succession to Frederick Barbarossa (1152–1189) when, on a legendary day in 1184, this greatest of medieval German emperors had held court there, making that lovely city near the juncture of the rivers Main and Rhine the center of high literary culture. In 1805–6 Napoleon wooed and bullied the princes of south and west Germany to gain support for the next stage of his wars. Territorial compensations were an attractive bait. Friendship, a two-edged affair as events would prove, was cemented between France and the German princes who formed the Confederation of the Rhine in July 1806. Baden, for example, gained the university town of Freiburg and the rest of *Vorderösterreich*, the Austrian possessions in Baden and the territory of the bishop of Konstanz, while the Bavarian and Württemberg rulers became kings by the grace of Napoleon (and would retain their titles until 1918). The creation of the Confederation of the Rhine was but the preliminary to the final dismantling of the Holy Roman Empire scarcely a month later, in August 1806. Few lamented its passing; many failed to notice it. In terms of its longevity, the empire belongs in the same league as the kingdom of the pharaohs of ancient Egypt or the Ming dynasty in China. But in 1806, 1006 years after its foundation by Charlemagne, it was no longer a tangible reality for many of those who had lived so long under its protection. It had been a force for peace in central Europe, an area so exposed to, and so experienced in conflict over the centuries. However, the sense of identity it had offered Germans, even in the last century of its existence, had all but disappeared under the impact of events which visited Germany since the French Revolution.

Jena: the collapse of Prussia and its revival

The year 1806 is perhaps less important as marking the demise of the Holy Roman Empire than because it marked the collapse of the old order, created by Friedrich Wilhelm I (1688–1740) and Frederick (Friederich) II of Prussia (1740–86), and the beginning of Prussia's association with the national movement, whose leadership in due course she would assume.

For it was almost at the precise moment of the creation of the Confederation of the Rhine and the abolition of the old Empire, that the vacillating Friedrich Wilhelm III, king of Prussia from 1797 to 1840, chose, ill-advisedly, to reenter the war against Napoleon. Prussia had preserved her neutrality since 1795, when the king's predecessor had negotiated peace with the French. In September 1806, Prussia declared war on France. Scarcely a month later, Napoleon was master of Prussia. The battle of Jena in October 1806 brought not merely the military annihilation of Prussia but also her moral collapse. In the peace of Tilsit 1807 Prussia lost all her territories west of the river Elbe to Napoleon, who created the puppet kingdom of Westphalia for his brother Jérome (1784–1860). Prussia also lost those lands she had acquired in the Polish Partitions of 1793 and 1795. She was required to pay a massive war indemnity and to contribute substantially to the costs of French occupation of the territory remaining to her. In the following years of Prussia's humiliation, she was also required to supply men and money for Napoleon's further campaigns, including the Russian campaign of 1812. Both events, Prussia's defeat and her resistance, would inspire Germany's greatest nineteenth-century novelist, Theodor Fontane (1819–98) with the subject of one of his finest novellas, *Schach von Wuthenow* (1882) and of his first novel *Vor dem Sturm* (1878); the latter work manages to be both a novel about the Napoleonic campaign and Prussia's revival and also, by analogy, a critique of the Second German Empire, following victory in war.

Jena is one of the turning points in nineteenth-century Prussian history, in fact and in myth. The response of the Prussian nation to this, its most overwhelming defeat, illustrates the resilience of this remarkable state. The rout of the Prussian army, which according to its ruling classes had embodied the ethos of state and nation, the panic shown by its officers and the craven surrender of fortresses to Napoleon, were followed by a degree of servility shown by Prussia's leaders to the conqueror, which inflamed opinion in intellectual circles. The whole *raison d'être* of the Prussian state had disintegrated in 1806. Yet within weeks of defeat, the Prussian king pledged to dedicate himself to the regeneration of his people and the state. He was supported in this by his queen, Louise, a woman of warm personality, who after her early death in 1810 was destined to become a powerful icon of Prussian and German nationalism. More importantly, Prussia had at this stage of her history the good fortune to attract several men of talent from outside the state to her service. These politicians, soldiers, and administrators were men of ability, character, and imagination who thought strategically. To them fell the task of reorganizing government, society, and the army in the following years. Many of Prussia's administrators in central and regional government had been trained at the Hanoverian university of Göttingen, where through its English connection (the elector of Hanover was also the English king), they encountered the writings of Adam Smith. They were impressed with the notion that if greater liberty were given to the individual, this would be conducive to greater national productivity. One of Prussia's most prominent administrators and a national leader of resistance to Napoleon, Baron Stein of Nassau (1757–1831), had his personal copy of Smith's *The Wealth of Nations* underlined at the point where Smith observes: "It appears, accordingly, from the experiences of all ages and nations, that the work done by free men is cheaper in the end than that done by slaves."

Faced with the daunting fiscal problems of Prussia following her defeat and occupation, government ministers and civil servants embarked on a course of reform which has been given the name of the Prussian liberal era. The reform program was diverse in its aspirations and generally more successful in its economic, administrative, and fiscal measures than in its social and political provisions. Both in concept and execution, however, it represented a vital contributory factor to establishing Prussia's hegemonial position in Germany later in the century.

Stein's vision, which Karl August von Hardenberg (1750–1822), uncle of the great Romantic poet Novalis (1772–1801), helped to implement, was inspired by the ideals of the age of classical humanism. It was a vision which Wilhelm von Humboldt, diplomat and scholar, brother of the explorer and scientist, Alexander (1769–1859), had helped to form. It inspired his reform of the Prussian secondary school system and the creation of the new university of Berlin which now bears his name and which has been well described (Saul 1997) as translating the age's theoretical humanism into institutional fact. Among their colleagues in the promotion of far-reaching structural reforms were the charismatic officers Gerhard Scharnhorst (1755-1813) and August Neithardt von Gneisenau (1760-1831), who were responsible for the humane reform of Prussian army discipline and the introduction of conscription. A number of the reformers were convinced that if the individual were to be freed from the restrictions on his initiative imposed by traditional feudal obligations, he would cease to regard himself merely as a subject of the prince, become a citizen of the state, and contribute meaningfully to its welfare, prosperity, and defense. Before his brief period in office between 1807 and 1808—Napoleon would demand and get his dismissal—he had described his own aims as being "to breathe life into the spirit of the community, to make citizens conscious of their powers, to exploit dormant or misapplied skills, to make use of talents now lying idle, and to revive sentiments of patriotism, self-reliance and national honor."

The Prussian reform program included the emancipation of the serfs, municipal self-government, abolition of restrictions on personal mobility, the sale of land, and the pursuit of trade, and abolition of cruel and degrading punishment for infringing military discipline. It was in his famous municipal ordinance of 1808, which gave self-government to the towns of the Prussian provinces, that Stein came nearest to realizing his ideals. Freedom to trade how and where one would was introduced in 1810 and aroused considerable opposition from vested interests. The traditional prohibition on the sale of manorial estates to non-nobles was also lifted, encouraging mobility of land as well as of people. Many such estates were in fact already in bourgeois hands, but the legalization gave encouragement to large-scale investment in land and to the development of capitalist enterprise, such as was already an established feature of the grain trade in East Prussia. Rural entrepreneurs benefited from the unexpected consequences of the agrarian reforms, the creation of a large pool of landless rural laborers. For Stein's emancipation of the peasantry had not transformed the serf, in a way imagined by Johann Heinrich Voß (1751-1826) in his poems *Die Leibeigenen* (The serfs: 1775, 1776, 1800) from brutalized victims into a sturdy peasant class. Only those with a viable amount of land and stock in general managed the transition; others lost the security of manorial protection in hard times and, by and large, also lost their land. As in Ireland, this new rural underclass contributed disproportionately to the demographic boom in the decades after the Napoleonic wars and to the specter of pauperism which would dominate the minds of government officials, social reformers, and political philosophers in the 1830s and 1840s.

Professor Henrik Steffens calls on his students at Breslau to join the volunteers. Lithograph of a painting by A. Kampf (1813).

The wars of liberation

During the early years of Napoleon's occupation of Prussia, that is, from about 1807 to 1811, national morale in Prussia was very low. The suicide of the poet Heinrich von Kleist in 1811 was interpreted by many intellectuals as a symbolic act of despair at the continued humiliation of the nation. The decision by Austria in 1809 to challenge Napoleon once more proved abortive. Austria was decisively defeated at Austerlitz in 1809. She was humiliated in peace, as Prussia had been, though in a different manner. She lost the southern Netherlands (modern Belgium) which she had acquired in 1714, when the Spanish Habsburgs died out. Far more hurtful to her pride was the diplomatic marriage negotiated between a daughter of the ancient Habsburg dynasty, who had ruled the Holy Roman Empire for nearly four centuries, and the son of a Corsican peasant. Napoleon married Marie Louise (1791–1847), daughter of Emperor Francis I of Austria (1804–35), in 1810. Napoleon had been emperor of the French for just six years. Popular resistance to the French was quickly crushed. Most notable in terms of later national legend were the rising led by the Tyrolean peasant leader Andreas Hofer (1776–1810) in 1809, for which he was publicly executed by the French in Mantua, and the abortive attempt by the Prussian officer Ferdinand von Schill (1776–1809), also in 1809, to seize the fortress of Magdeburg, garrisoned by the French. Following Schill's death and the execution of a dozen of his officers, 500 participants in the rising were condemned to the French galleys.

The defeat of Napoleon in Russia in 1812, where so many Germans forced to fight for Napoleon had lost their lives, gave a decisive impetus to the nascent national movement. Stein himself had become a symbolical figure for German nationalists, not least because of his forced dismissal and exile from Prussia on Napoleon's orders. Stein's famous phrase, coined in a letter dated 1811, that "I have only one fatherland and that is Germany," inspired poets, artisans, students, lawyers, and landowners, especially in Prussia. Henrik Steffens (1773–1845), Danish philosopher and professor in the new royal university of Breslau (Wrocław) joined the volunteer movement and brought his students with him; women surrendered their jewels and pastors preached a crusade against the 'godless' Napoleon; many students joined the Lützow Free Corps whose colors, black, red, and gold, are those of Germany's national flag today.

The actual significance of the contribution of the patriots to the military outcome of the so-called wars of liberation has been challenged by modern historians. What is not in dispute is the wars' contribution to national mythology, later enforced in school textbooks, anthologies, commemorative festivals and speeches, and in the texts sung by male choirs. And Prussia's central role in the national movement was placed beyond doubt when a reluctant king finally agreed to summon all Germans to arms against the usurper Napoleon in March 1813.

In August 1813 the Austrian foreign minister Clemens von Metternich (1773–1859) declared war on France. The coalition of Austria, Prussia, and Russia was led by the Austrian prince, Karl von Schwarzenberg, whose equestrian statue today stands opposite that of that legendary Austrian general Prince Eugene of Savoy, both dominating the center of Vienna, the *Heldenplatz* (heroes' square) beside the imperial palace. Almost seven years to the day after Prussia's defeat at Jena, the allies proved victorious at the battle of Leipzig, later named "the battle of the nations." The Confederation of the Rhine and the Napoleonic states in northern Germany were dissolved. The southern states hastened to protect themselves by signing treaties with Austria. Metternich was more concerned to contain Russia in the east than with nationalist concerns at home—he had come to regret the second and third partitions of Poland of 1793 and 1795 as robbing both Austria and Prussia of the Polish buffer between themselves and Russia's unpredictable hegemonial ambitions. Metternich might have been content to make peace with France, leaving her the left bank of the Rhine (and his own ancestral lands). It was Napoleon and not the German patriots who decided otherwise.

The war continued until the French defeat at Fontainebleau in April 1814. The numerous and complex questions facing Europe's statesmen after nearly a quarter of a century of war were to be decided at an international congress. The congress met at Vienna in 1814 and sat until the following June, interrupted by Napoleon's escape from Elba, followed by his final defeat at Waterloo in 1815, just one week after the massive protocol of the Congress of Vienna had been signed by all the powers. In the meantime, Beethoven (1770–1827) had scratched out the name of Napoleon as the dedicatee of his "Eroica" or Fifth Symphony.

The Napoleonic wars lasted, with interludes, for a whole generation. In that time, Germans experienced constant change, changes of territorial allegiance and political status, and also, though not everywhere, severe economic dislocation. War levies, the quartering of troops, high taxation, plunder, and requisitioning by troops who lived off the land, left their mark on people's minds as well as their pockets. The violent repression and often wanton destruction of the last years of the Napoleonic occupation, notably in Hamburg, cast long shadows. Yet the loss of a familiar if antiquated framework in which Germans had lived for centuries, along with the extent and duration of the war, and the imaginative response to it by Germany's poets, conferred on Germans a new sense of their identity. Napoleon, often remembered as the son of the French Revolution and the son-in-law of the Caesars, is also the father of German nationalism.

Germany and the Revolution

Almost equally important for the future history of Germany was the way in which the French revolutionary wars, and their attendant political, social and economic upheaval, came to be seen by the authorities and by other opinion makers as a direct consequence of the French Revolution. The favorite images used in speeches by the Austrian chancellor Metternich, the dominant figure in German politics from 1815 until 1848, when he was expelled by Viennese revolutionaries, were of conflagration, eruption, tempest, and storm. We encounter revolution as a central myth in the language and thought of German politicians and political thinkers throughout the nineteenth century, in Metternich and Otto von Bismarck (1815–98), in her leading political thinkers from Karl Marx to Jakob Burckhardt (1818–97), and in many of her great poets, most notably Heine. A whole generation of Germans were in fact traumatized by the era of the French wars. To the disorientation and insecurity of those years, ones which were followed by years of bad harvests, disease, and hunger, came the folk image of political and social change. It came to be associated in the public mind as the work of 'foreign' intervention, and hence to be regarded instinctively with suspicion and fear.

The association of defeat, occupation, and national humiliation with the revolution, and of major political and social change as the work of 'foreign' intervention was reinforced by state policy and propaganda, if one may use such a term, as well as by poets, in the post-Napoleonic era. This policy prejudiced German attitudes for generations against their own revolutionary or radical traditions. The evidence of revolutionary activity in Germany in the 1790s was forgotten or suppressed by historians. Such activity did occur in regions as disparate as the Rhineland in western Germany, Saxony in the southeast, and Mecklenburg to the north, offering close parallels with peasant uprisings in France. Most Germans associated freedom not so much with liberation from tyranny (as embodied for the French in the storming of the Bastille), or protection of the individual from the power of the state, as with security for ordinary citizens to live their lives in peace. And it was to the state, in the years after the Napoleonic wars, that they looked for such guarantees.

Napoleon and the Germans

The Napoleonic occupation of Germany was responsible for the creation of a German national identity in a political sense. But the response to Napoleon's person was not without ambiguity. During and after the war he exercised a powerful spell on the imaginations of Germans generally. Those who, either by experience of the war or in the process of reflection on it, became aware of their country's anomalous position among other European nation-states, could not but be fascinated by the notion of a single human being altering the destiny of his own nation and that of countless others besides. The person and myth of Napoleon exercised a peculiar fascination on Germany's writers, both during and after his lifetime. Kleist in his aforementioned *Catechism*, written during the French occupation of Prussia, made Napoleon the focus of a new aggressive nationalism.

Others, such as Heine, were moved by the idea of a man overturning the habits of minds and the prejudices of a whole society by the impact of the French occupation on his own native region, the Rhineland. His highly stylized account of Napoleon's entry to Düsseldorf in *Ideen: Das Buch Le Grand* (1822), reads like a sacramental act, modeled with typical Heinesque irony on Christ's entry into Jerusalem on the eve of His passion and death.

Heine's older contemporary, the Austrian playwright Franz Grillparzer (1791–1872), set a monument to Napoleon's endeavors and to the transience of human achievement in his historical drama of 1825, *König Ottokars Glück und Ende*, though he strenuously denied the parallel between the two rulers. In one of the most original plays of the day, the tortured genius Christian Dietrich Grabbe (1801–36) wrote his *Napoleon oder die Hundert Tage* (1831) to demonstrate the power of the mob, slaves of their bestial appetites, to destroy

The Rhenish Courier loses everything on his way from the Leipzig Fair (1813–14). Contemporary satire on Napoleon's defeat at Leipzig in 1813 and its consequences.

the work of individual genius. The response of German governments was almost equally diverse and ambivalent. Many separated the person of the French emperor from the revolution which had brought him forth. The majority accepted Napoleon's legitimacy as ruler of France and erstwhile lord of much of Germany. Even the public censor felt called upon to intervene in many parts of Germany after 1815 to forbid public criticism of Napoleon in the interests of "the monarchic principle." Over the nineteenth century as a whole, the pervasive influence of the Napoleonic era was evident in the stimulus it offered to the German economy by way of political and social change. Marx was to term Napoleon's harsh but systematic rationalization of the map of Germany as his "cleansing of the German Augean stables."

Engels declared that Napoleon was the creator of the German bourgeoisie. Certainly in the Rhineland, which benefited in so many ways from the French, this is true. But perhaps the most pervasive fascination in nineteenth-century Germany for the person of Napoleon, as reflected in her thought and literature, was the evident capacity of the individual to change history. It was Heine, a pupil of Hegel, the philosopher whose historical thinking had arguably the most powerful formative influence on his contemporaries, who described Napoleon as *der Weltgeist zu Pferde* (the world spirit itself, but on horseback).

Chapter 2
Authority and the Subject: Metternich's System 1815–48

"It is no little achievement to have governed a continent for nearly half a lifetime," remarked Bismarck with reference to Prince Metternich, Austria's foreign minister and chancellor for a period of almost forty years. But Metternich was much more than just an Austrian statesman. He was a major player on the diplomatic stage of Europe for over a generation, and helped to create the nineteenth-century concept of the "Congress of Europe," that is, the notion of the collective responsibility of the major European powers for preserving the balance of power, and therefore maintaining peace in Europe. Furthermore, Metternich was a principal architect of the German Confederation, founded at the Congress of Vienna on 9 June 1815, little more than a week before the battle of Waterloo and Napoleon's final defeat. The chief *raison d'être* of the Confederation in Metternich's view was to fill the power vacuum in central Europe left by the collapse of the Napoleonic order. A complicated series of territorial exchanges and annexations was worked out at the Congress of Vienna. Of these, undoubtedly the most important was Prussia's expansion into western Germany by her acquisition of the Rhineland and Westphalia. The particular significance of these territories for the future of Prussia and of Germany as a whole, lay in their mineral riches and their commercial traditions. In 1815 Prussian territorial aggrandizement was supported both by Metternich and by the British foreign secretary, Robert, Viscount Castlereagh (1769–1822), because they believed it would help contain France and guarantee European security. The subsequent history of Europe up to the 1860s suggested that they were correct. In the event, the actual German Confederation was a rushed job, largely because Germany's future seemed relatively unimportant to the European powers, taking decisions under the impact of Napoleon's escape from Elba and his triumphal progress in the early summer of 1815 through France. Moreover, both England and Austria were concerned to conciliate the volatile and ambitious Tsar Alexander I (1801–25), while at the same time resolutely impeding his plans for Russia's westward expansion. The Federal Act (*Bundesakte*), the founding document of the German Confederation, was not in fact drawn up until 10 June, a whole day after the long protocol of the Congress had been duly signed and several delegates had already left Vienna.

The German Confederation thus cobbled together proved enduring. It lasted until 1867, when, after Prussia had defeated Austria and her allies in the Confederation, Bismarck made it a condition of the peace that Austria leave Germany. Between 1815 and 1819 Metternich successfully opposed the creation of any form of unitary state in Germany, which had been the dream of the patriots who fought Napoleon. In the years that followed, he blocked development of the federal institutions which had been foreseen in the Federal Act. For over a generation he resisted both the nationalist and the constitutional aspirations of Germans, who contrasted their own lack of political freedom with the constitutional monarchies of western and northern Europe and rightly attributed the source of their frustration to the policies of the chancellor of Germany's leading power. For over thirty years, from the end of the Napoleonic wars to the "March days" of the Revolution of 1848, it was Metternich who was primarily responsible for imposing on the peoples of the German Confederation a system of political and social control which associated his name with an epoch and a system. After 1819, the year of the so-called Karlsbad Decrees, the Metternich system relied heavily on the instruments of tyranny, such as police spies, trials behind closed doors with fortress detention for offenders, prohibition of political associations, discrimination in the workplace, rigorous censorship of the printed word, and proscription of the public spoken word. It was a measure of Metternich's influence, and his readiness to use federal troops to put down public unrest, that the more constitutionally minded states, such as Baden, Württemberg, Bavaria, and Saxe-Weimar, Goethe's home for sixty years, were frequently forced to withdraw or dilute their liberal policies.

For the Confederation was by no means monolithic. Its forty-one states, later amalgamated to thirty-four, included the four city-states of Hamburg, Frankfurt, Bremen, and Lübeck, and those ruled by sovereign princes. They differed vastly in size, resources, and degree of modernization. There were nominally some forty-one legal systems, forty-one armies, and forty-one sets of diplomatic representatives; in practice the larger states sent their representatives abroad or to each other's courts, but the right to do so was not systematically exercised. Some states, such as Baden, Bavaria, and Württemberg in the south, became constitutional states in the years following the peace settlement; Nassau, home of Baron Stein, had already anticipated them in 1814. After the 1830 Revolution, Saxony followed suit, as did Hanover. However, in 1837 the new English king of Hanover, Ernst August (1771–1851), unilaterally abrogated the constitution in his territory, giving rise to the famous protest by the Hanoverian university professors at Göttingen, which included the brothers

Grimm and Friedrich Dahlmann (1785-1860); all were dismissed and sent into exile. Neither of the two largest and most powerful states, Austria and Prussia, had a constitution in the Metternich era. Prussia's reforming chancellor Hardenberg did attempt to put pressure on his king, Friedrich Wilhelm III, to implement his frequent promise to his subjects to introduce one. Not only was Hardenberg foiled in this by Metternich's active intervention, but he, along with other reforming ministers, such as Wilhelm von Humboldt and the liberal minister of war, Hermann von Boyen (1771-1848), were dismissed as a result in 1819.

The years 1815-48 are also known in German history as the Restoration era, though we now tend to apply the term more particularly to the years between the Congress of Vienna and the July Revolution of 1830, and to adopt the German term, the *Vormärz*, for the period between the July and March Revolutions of 1830 and 1848.

Restoration means, quite literally, the restoration of the German princes to their territories. It was a considered decision of the European powers, notably of Britain, Russia, and Austria at the Vienna Congress. Some of the territories, such as Prussia's west German possessions, had been confiscated by Napoleon. Others had been deserted by their princes during the Napoleonic wars. (No tradition here of the captain going down with his ship!) The Restoration meant that those kingdoms which Napoleon had created in Germany in 1806 would continue in existence. These included the former electorates of Bavaria and Saxony, and the duchy of Württemberg. It gave international recognition to the Austrian Empire founded in 1804 without popular or international legitimacy by the then Holy Roman emperor Francis II (1792-1806), who now styled himself emperor Francis I of Austria. At the same time it was accepted by the powers (but not by many south and west German populations) that the Holy Roman Empire which Napoleon had destroyed would not be restored, and that the ecclesiastical states would not be compensated for their losses. (The secular princes, such as the king of Bavaria, had been the main beneficiaries of that arrangement.) It is a characteristic feature of nineteenth-century German history that the monarchic system was enshrined at Vienna as the "natural" form of government, and that the hierarchical social system, on which the monarchic order was based, was the "proper" form of social organization. Certainly such views were challenged, but never successfully, during the century that followed, particularly during the Revolution of 1848 and in the so-called Constitutional Conflict (1862-67) between the Prussian king and parliament in the first years of Bismarck's administration. There was no "Glorious Revolution" in Germany, as there had been in Britain in 1688, in which parliament imposed powerful restrictions on the royal prerogative.

Nor did Germany succeed in emulating the American Revolution of 1776, though 1776 became and remained a model and an aspiration for important, if small, groups of Germany's intellectuals. Article 13 of the *Bundesakte* or Federal Act of the German Confederation promised representative assemblies or *Landstände* to the peoples of the constituent states. In practice, these assemblies, where implemented, as in Prussia, proved to be merely a revived (restored) form of corporate estate. The Prussian novelist Theodor Fontane reminds his modern readers how enduring such thinking was, in his last novel, *Der Stechlin* (1898), a kind of mirror of nineteenth-century Prussian and German history, in which his hero, Dubslav Stechlin, appears at the dinner in chapters 3 to 5, dressed in his uniform as member of the *Landstände*. True, individual rulers, such as the grand dukes of Baden in the southwest or of Saxe-Weimar in central Germany, were sensible of their people's aspirations to constitutional government, but their freedom of movement was circumscribed by the operation of the Metternich system. This is well exemplified in the case of the highly respected university professors, Karl Rotteck (1775–1840) at the University of Freiburg im Breisgau in Baden and Robert von Mohl (1799–1875) at Tübingen in Württemberg. It did not help Rotteck, who was also a member of the Baden parliament and co-author with Karl Welcker (1790–1867) of the immensely influential liberal encyclopedia of the social sciences, the *Staatslexikon* (1834–5), nor Mohl, one of Germany's leading constitutional lawyers, that they were citizens of constitutional states. Both were dismissed, like so many other academics in the Metternich era, from their university posts, for publicly criticizing the political system. Most German princes and their nobilities shared the attitude of the restored Bourbon dynasty, namely that they had forgotten nothing, remembered nothing, and learned nothing. Constitution or no constitution, Mohl's sovereign, King William I (1816–64) of Württemberg, could declare frankly during the 1848 Revolution that his subjects could of course wrest concessions from him by force, but once that force no longer operated, he would be entitled to go back on his word. And that he would do so.

The monarchic system as implemented at Vienna renewed the pre-French-revolutionary alliance between crown, nobility, and church. The notion of a God-given hierarchy in the social organization of the human race, a veritable cliché in upper-class circles for decades to come, was based allegedly on blood and on the collective achievement in past times. Thus the nobility's claim to privilege and power was based on their "defense of the realm"; what they saw as their prescriptive right to the higher commands in the army, which lasted in practice even beyond the fall of the monarchy in 1918, was also predicated on that claim. In fact privilege was a matter of power, of control over inherited property and extensive legal, political, and social privileges, carefully regulated, as with all enduring elites, in the interest of self-preservation. Its justification became more difficult in a century of industrialization and mobile capital. Tellingly, the parvenu landowner von Gundermann in Fontane's novel, *Der Stechlin*, is represented as much more wealthy than his Junker neighbors. Yet the defense of privilege was much more successful in central and southern Europe than in the western nation-states. In Germany (including of course Austria), there were a variety of forces and factors at work to place obstacles in the way of evolutionary change. The Metternich system proved remarkably enduring and it was followed in the postrevolutionary years (known as the *Nachmärz*) by an even more repressive police society.

A key instrument of support for the system was the role of the churches, known in Restoration Europe generally as the "alliance between throne and altar." The Christian churches gave collective legitimacy to the monarchic order; their role in underpinning hierarchical society in nineteenth-century Germany, psychologically as well as practically, should therefore not be underestimated. The churches socialized their congregations, teaching them that obedience was a prime civic as well as a religious virtue. There was of course a fundamental difference in this regard between the Roman Catholic Church and the Lutheran churches. While the ruler was the head of the Protestant church in his territory, German Catholics living in a state with a Protestant ruler, such as Baden and Prussia, proved ready to engage in acts of civil disobedience, where the state claimed authority over their church. Protestant rulers had a greater source of patronage for their ambitious clergy than was the case with the Catholic territories, following the disappearance of virtually all the wealthy ecclesiastical states and their once richly endowed monasteries during the Napoleonic era. The nineteenth-century German Catholic church no longer offered ambitious noblemen the opportunity for lucrative sinecures, as it had done before 1803, whereas senior appointments in the Protestant churches were effectively still in the gift of the secular princes. Catholic priests came increasingly from the middle and lower ranks of society, yet this was an age when the Catholic church in Germany, as in most of the rest of Catholic Europe, became increasingly clerical, and the influence of the laity counted for less. But the more humble social origins of their parish clergy helped the Catholic church to develop social policies which proved to be much more in tune with the social and economic realities of the century of pauperism and proletarianization than was the case with the established Protestant churches. In political outlook and practice, however, the Catholic church was, if anything, an even more conservative force than her Protestant counterparts.

In one respect German rulers after 1815 had changed. Advised by their civil servants and faced with the need to meet massive debts incurred by the wars, the princes showed themselves aware of the need to provide some popular legitimacy. One of the lessons they had learned from the French revolutionaries was the power of image and symbol over the minds of the governed. In a manner unimagined before 1789, the rulers (or their ministers) sought the imaginative support of the people (*das Volk*). For one thing, many princes of newly acquired territories needed to integrate populations of different culture and even religion from their own. Catholic Bavaria, for example, had acquired Franconia, where people spoke a very different dialect and, at least in upper Franconia, were mainly Protestants; furthermore, it had gained the Bavarian Palatinate, with its historic capital of Heidelberg, whose inhabitants had enjoyed for a generation the benefits of French rule. The case of Saxony was different again. Because he had remained loyal to Napoleon longer than his fellow monarchs, the king of Saxony had lost substantial territory to Prussia at the Congress of Vienna. The king therefore decided to dispense with his former flag, now associated with failure and defeat, and instead adopt the optimistic color combination of white and green, which are still today the colors of the federal state or Free State of Saxony. Patriotic verses set to familiar tunes, such as the Austrian *Kaiserhymne* (or *Gott erhalte unsern Kaiser*—God save our Kaiser, sung to Haydn's tune of *God save the Queen*) or Prussia's militaristic hailing the monarch crowned with victory (*Heil dir im Siegerkranz*) focused attention on the person of the prince as the incorporation of his people. King Ludwig I of Bavaria (1825-48), by contrast, courted popular approval by promoting as a 'national' anthem verses (*Gott mit dir, du Land der Bayern*), which addressed his subjects' strong sense of local identity anchored in landscape. The residence of the prince was designed to enhance his patriotic appeal and to direct minds away from the notion of popular sovereignty. Ludwig I rebuilt his capital in the grand manner and in neoclassical style, eliciting contemporaries' mocking description of the somewhat provincial Munich as "Athens on the [river] Isar," but it was a comment which hid grudging admiration. The rebuilding of Berlin in the harmonious neoclassical style of the Brandenburg architect Karl Schinkel (1781-1841) belongs to the same period. Friedrich Wilhelm III gave Schinkel full opportunity to display his talents in such enduring monuments as the New Museum and the pavilion erected to the memory of his queen Louise in the palace of Charlottenburg. Louise, of whose outgoing personality contemporaries spoke with much warmth, was retrospectively mythologized as a patriotic queen and as the ideal of German femininity and motherhood, since she was mother of several children, including the future kings Friederich Wilhelm IV and Wilhelm I (1861–88), the first German emperor.

The German dynasties in the Restoration era generally proved dexterous in putting across the impression that it was the princes rather than the people who had liberated Germany from Napoleon. The popular term *Freiheitskriege* (wars of liberty), which appeared to ascribe a key role to the talents and energies of the patriots in throwing off Napoleon's yoke, was gradually replaced in public discourse by *Befreiungskriege* (wars of liberation), liberation being construed as 'by the princes.' As 1813 receded into the past, the volunteer movement, whose participants had included the poet Joseph von Eichendorff (1788–1857), the natural philosopher Henrik Steffens, and the dramatist Karl Immermann (1796–1840), who had seen themselves as the seed of a future citizen militia-style army, was now represented by the authorities as breachers of the law and as such morally ambivalent. Particularly in south Germany, which was more socially homogeneous but less modern than the north, dynastic loyalty remained strong. Such loyalty allowed for a degree of decorous familiarity. After all, the king of Bavaria and the Austrian emperor spoke German with a pronounced local accent and shared the interests of their subjects, as diverse as music, the arts, mountain climbing and hunting; the last two they pursued dressed, like any commoner, in the local costume. It should be remembered that German (and Austrian) princes and wealthy noblemen commonly allowed the public access to the parks and gardens of their residences. Yet paradoxically, it was in the southern constitutional states that the religious origin of monarchic authority continued to be acknowledged in the formula that the person of the monarch was "sacred and inviolable." At the same time, Germans liked to see their rulers out walking in their capitals, with his spouse in her poke bonnet on their arm; Germans enjoyed the opportunity to salute their majesties and have their greetings graciously acknowledged. It made them feel of consequence. Intellectuals, too, were impressed at the learning of the Saxon king, Johann (1801–73, king from 1854 to his death), author of a fine translation of Dante's *Divina Commedia*. Theater enthusiasts liked to think that a bourgeois writer of humble origins, Ludwig Tieck (1773–1853), could hold Johann enthralled by his reading aloud of German and European drama. In Berlin, even critics of Friedrich Wilhelm III, who had so disappointed the hopes of the patriots and constitutionalists, approved the lack of conspicuous consumption at the royal court and the way he visited the theater regularly, going home like them to tea and early bed. People enjoyed reading about the way the future Tsar Nicholas I of Russia (1825–55), when he visited the Prussian capital with his young Prussian royal bride, the king's daughter, in 1821, was entertained by the Prussian royal family to charades, based on the oriental romance, *Lalla Rookh*, by the Irish poet Thomas Moore (1779–1852); the future Kaiser played the hero's part. It was just the sort of entertainment the ordinary burgher and his family might try their hand at.

    The chief author and agent of the political system of the Restoration era in Germany, the former count and now prince Metternich, was anything but bourgeois in lifestyle and inclinations. Rather was this cynical aristocrat in many ways a son of the Enlightenment. When the Austrian historian Srbik wrote his monumental biography of Metternich, following the collapse of the Danube monarchy in 1918, his focus was on Metternich the international statesman and on Metternich's successful defense of Austria's primacy in the German Confederation for almost two generations. For Srbik and his contemporaries were all too aware of the dangers to European peace created by the power vacuum in Central Europe. As far back as 1809, the year in which Napoleon inflicted a crushing defeat on Austria at Austerlitz, Napoleon's highly astute French foreign minister, Charles Maurice de Talleyrand (1754–1838) remarked that the "conglomeration of states" that constituted Austria must not be destroyed, that it was essential for the future well-being of the civilized world "that Austria be preserved." Bismarck would reiterate that judgment three quarters of a century later, and the experience of the twentieth century would seem to have proved them right. Modern historians, on the other hand, tend to be much more conscious of the domestic aspect of Metternich's regime, and their impact on the history of Austria and of Germany in the nineteenth century. For the educated and ambitious, the Metternich era was deeply problematical; for the individual it could be disastrous. The experience of two writers of different generations can illustrate the situation in practice. The dramatist Franz Grillparzer, the "Shakespeare of Austria," was an ill-paid junior civil servant of twenty-eight when he visited Rome in 1819. During his visit, which included an audience with the pope, Grillparzer wrote a poem for private circulation on the Coliseum, regretfully recalling its classical Roman past and without making reference to its Christian martyrs. It was published without his consent and unleashed on the unfortunate writer the full force of the imperial displeasure. Emperor Francis saw to it that Grillparzer received a personal rebuke, coupled with a veiled threat of dismissal in case of a future similar 'offense.' The affair dogged him for the rest of his career, adversely affecting his promotion prospects, and undermining his self-confidence. Grillparzer's younger contemporary, Fritz Reuter (1810–74), perhaps Germany's greatest humorous novelist, took part in 1833 in a student demonstration in Prussia, and was incarcerated for seven years, even though the Prussians had no right to do that to a Mecklenburg subject. Of course students and intellectuals are the natural victims of repressive regimes, and in this the German Confederation was no different from its twentieth-century successors. Yet despite the paternalism promoted by the rulers and their advocates along the lines of "everything for the people, nothing by the people," there was little protection of citizens' rights. To German writers, so vulnerable in their person in a system which regarded free speech as undermining public order and social stability, and equally threatened in their capacity to earn a living in the underdeveloped German economy, state paternalism offered no legal protection (see chapter 8).

A symbol of the often humiliating subordination of public servants to the authoritarian monarchical regime was the queue or pigtail, once the symbol of royal absolutism and now, following its reintroduction after 1815, regarded as a sign of "proper loyalty" to authority. In the stories of the Romantic writer, E. T. A. Hoffmann (1776–1822), these pigtailed bureaucrats appear as quaint philistines, the butt of ironic or even demonic wit for their underlings. But there is no doubt who is master in Hoffmann's grotesque fantasies—this gifted musician and satirist was, after all, a Prussian civil servant, though not by choice.

The first serious challenge to the Metternich system of internal control came in 1830. Once more, it was France which provided the motor. "The Gallic cock crowed, and even in Germany the light of day dawned," wrote Heine a year after the event, using imagery that would become increasingly popular in the cartoons and broadsheets that preceded and accompanied the Revolution of 1848. In the July Revolution of 1830, the French overthrew their restored monarchy in the person of the French king Charles X (1824–30), younger brother of Louis XVI (1765–93), who had died at age thirty-nine under the guillotine. German rulers got a severe shock, not so much at the violence, which was relatively muted, but at the notion that revolution was happening

Satiric reference to the "queue" or pigtail.

a second time, and that the "Restoration" might now be under permanent threat. "That was when it all began," reflected Metternich in later years. Fontane, who was an eleven-year-old schoolboy at the time, later created of the July Revolution an emblem of nineteenth-century history, both in his novel, *Der Stechlin*, and in his remarkable autobiography, *Meine Kinderjahre* (1894). Both Heine and Fontane were at one in seeing the real importance of the 1830 Revolution in Germany as having been in the change in public consciousness, and not in any real change in the political system. Awareness that change was, in fact, possible, the politicization of public discourse, the use by writers of humor, especially irony and satire, to operate on people's consciousness, technical developments in the print media—all these are features of the post-1830 situation in Germany which had not obtained earlier. Once more, Germany had followed where France had led, though at least in terms of political action, German revolutionaries had not gone very far. The repressiveness of the Confederation hampered her reformers and her radicals at every turn. But as Heine was constantly reminding his readers (writing from the safety of French exile), the German revolutionaries provided the ideas, and others must and would implement them. Take even the motto for one of the most revolutionary texts of the 1830s, the seditious tract about the oppressed peasants of the grand duke of Hesse-Darmstadt, *Der hessische Landbote* (1834), produced and distributed by a courageous young medical student and playwright from Gießen, Georg Büchner, with his collaborator, a Lutheran pastor. It was a Frenchman who in the 1790s had coined the motto used by them and which read: *Friede den Hütten, Krieg den Palästen!* (Peace to the hovels, war to the castles!) The iconography of revolution in German literature of the time, such as we encounter in Heine's prose writings of the 1830s and his political poetry of the 1840s and of German cartoonists in the *Vormärz*, also owed much to French models, notably Henri Daumier (1808–79). Predictably, political repression of writers and intellectuals became more onerous after the failed revolution of 1830. A series of decrees issued between 1832 and 1834 included one setting up a new federal authority to wipe out political protest. Among its infamous secret clauses were ones proscribing all forms of political association, with additional censorship of books of over 320 pages (previously exempted under the Karlsbad Decrees). Under this legislation, 390 students were sentenced to death allegedly for subversive activities, though their sentences were later commuted to life imprisonment; one student got a five-year sentence for reading Aristotle to a study group. The Confederation was now, in the words of a later historian, a "general police insurance against its own people."

Paradoxically, post-1830's repressive policies contributed to the vigorous politicization of German society which in due course proved to be a fundamental cause of the nationwide character of the 1848 Revolution in Germany.

The authorities were obsessed with revolution in a way that was neither justified by the facts nor, indeed, the actual course of the mid-century revolution. No one caught better the absurdity of the Metternich system on the eve of its demise than Ludwig Tieck, once a major Romantic poet and now a much revered prose writer. In the opening paragraph of his novella, *Des Lebens Überfluß* (An abundance of life), published in 1839, he conveys with exquisite irony and lavish use of the subjunctive mood—known in German as the *irrealis*, the unreal, the sheer pointlessness of the political repression of the German people, particularly when, at a time of growing economic hardship, government required more than all else a contract with the governed.

Chapter 3
The German Economy in the First Half of the Century

Agriculture

A fundamental difference between the modern German economy and that of the early and mid-nineteenth century concerns the role of agriculture and the rural world in people's lives. In 1800, three-quarters of Germans lived on and from the land; in the Austrian dominions more than four-fifths did so. That proportion only changed marginally over the next few decades. It was not until the last quarter of the century that the primary sector, agriculture, ceased to provide the greater part of Germany's gross national product. That radical change was the outcome of a long and complex process of agrarian reform which was begun in eighteenth-century royal council chambers and in the cabinets of reflective bureaucrats.

Under Empress Maria Theresia (1740–80) and her sons Emperor Joseph II (1765–90) and Leopold II (1790–2), Austria led other German state governments in the drive to raise the productivity of the land and ameliorate the lot of the peasantry. However, under their successors, the process was arrested for over half a century, and it was in Prussia under Baron Stein and Chancellor Hardenberg that the most energetic and, by and large, effective program of agrarian reform was introduced and implemented. Most other German states either followed suit or had already initiated their own reforming programs, which varied according to local conditions. However, if the impact of reform was profound, the results were often different from those envisaged. Land prices had risen significantly in the late eighteenth and early nineteenth centuries, and land now became increasingly a commodity with a commercial value. Few reformers were able to realize their vision of a healthy rural economy and contented, productive peasants. In general, the main beneficiaries of the program were the big estate owners and the larger farmers, not those at the bottom of the social scale. Many of the large landowners and farmers consolidated their holdings with peasant land since many of the peasants were unable to maintain themselves and found themselves forced to sell up. True, in western Germany nobles lost up to one-fifth of their land and faced significant losses of rent and other traditional benefits. In Westphalia and Bavaria, for example, with their established family farms, and in parts of Saxony, peasants benefited from the abolition of onerous labor obligations. By contrast, in Prussia's eastern provinces, opposition from the estate owners to the emancipation of their serfs was so vigorous that the state reached a compromise which greatly favored the landlord over the peasant. With an increasing proportion of manorial estates east of the Elbe in bourgeois ownership and landowners looking for commercial profit from their estates, seasonal laborers began to be employed in place of the former serfs. In any case, under the terms of the Prussian agrarian reform, only those peasants who owned a team of animals capable of tilling the soil were given land in return for cash payments.

The crisis years of post-Napoleonic Prussia resulted in many of these peasants having to default on their payments and being forced to lose their land. While some peasants prospered, and in the good years from 1825 onward began to farm commercially, a major and largely unforeseen consequence of the agrarian reform in Prussia and in other parts of Germany was to create a large pool of landless laborers. In hard times they could now no longer look to the local lord for succor. Moreover, in the rationalization of land use which was part of the reform movements, the rural poor had lost their traditional rights to graze their animals on the common land or to gather fuel in the local forest. It was in these strata, as in the economically hard-pressed artisan class, that the massive increase of population between 1815 and 1848 occurred, creating the greatest social problem of the age, pauperism.

But it would be wrong to overlook the positive long-term results of the structural changes associated with the agrarian reform movement, particularly when seen in association with state-sponsored improvements in road and water transport in the Restoration era. It became increasingly possible for farmers to supply their produce to markets outside their immediate locality. With the railways this range became greater and allowed for specialized farming. The impact of the numerous local learned societies' interest in improved methods of cultivation began to take effect. Moreover, the amount of land under cultivation increased dramatically between 1800 and 1850, especially in the populous eastern provinces. The amount of stock rose steadily, as did yields generally, stimulated by more rational crop rotation, and in particular by increasing root crops, for which the sandy soil of the north German plain was so suited. Food production rose significantly, though not yet in line with the massive increase in population. The lower strata of society suffered disproportionately in these years. In the 1830s and early 1840s an estimated 60 percent of the total population of Prussia lived below the poverty line. It was in these years that Germans, like the Irish, developed such a pronounced taste for the potato. This was a particularly suitable crop in areas of participle inheritance, that is, where all sons inherited their share of the farm. One such area was south Baden. The fact that a small plot planted with potatoes could provide for the nutritional needs of a whole family, encouraged large families, as in Ireland. And, as in Ireland, the dependence on a single crop proved catastrophic, as occurred in the years of the potato blight in the Hungry Forties. But, by and large, the potato proved a highly useful plant in Germany. By the beginning of the twentieth century Germany would in fact become the biggest producer of potatoes in the world. In other parts of Germany the introduction of new crops, rich in nitrogen, improved the fertility of the soil. As would be the case for industry in later decades, German agriculture became the beneficiary of university-based scientific inquiry with a well-developed applied dimension. Germany pioneered the application of chemical fertilizers to farming, associated with the names of Albrecht Thaer (1752–1828) and Justus Liebig (1803–73).

Early or protoindustrialization

Germany was slow to industrialize, and the industrial revolution proper belongs to the second half of the nineteenth century. But already in the century's first half, many regions had begun to experience what is known as protoindustrialization. The textile industry was the motor of early industrialization in this period of Germany's history, as it had been in Britain and would be elsewhere. A key development in preparing for Germany's later industrial revolution was the gradual changeover from the use of charcoal to coal in mining and in metal work. Protoindustrialization in Germany was in one sense the beneficiary of the very problems created by structural changes in agriculture. Thousands of landless peasants seeking ways of feeding themselves and their families found an additional source of income in the so-called putting-out industry, where they received raw materials from a merchant's agent and worked up the finished product. Typical products of the putting-out system were in textile manufacture, such spinning, weaving, and dyeing. Family labor was a key factor in maximizing earnings in some of Germany's poorer regions, such as the southwest, and across the border in Alsace in France and in northwest Switzerland. The putting-out system employed growing numbers from the late eighteenth century onward in Bohemia, Silesia, and parts of the Rhineland. It was still a widespread practice in the late nineteenth century in the mountainous regions of southeast Saxony. Because the system was highly labor-intensive and unskilled, even small children could be employed. This encouraged early marriage and large families, compounding social problems in bad times, particularly when food prices rose, as they so often did in the years between the end of the Napoleonic wars and the Revolution of 1848.

The Lauchhammer Works in 1800. Contemporary lithograph.

Many of Germany's major poets wrote in these years about the vulnerability to weather of a society which was still based on the primary sector. The Swiss novelist Jeremias Gotthelf (1779–1854) is probably the greatest epic genius of natural catastrophe, as recorded in his powerful allegorical novels *Die Wassernot im Emmenthal* (1838) on floods, *Geld und Geist* (1843–4) on fire following prolonged drought, and, in his best known work, the novella *The Black Spider* (1842), which evokes the specter of the plague. Less overtly but with equal power, the Austrian Adalbert Stifter (1805–68) conveyed in his short story *Granit* (in *Bunte Steine*, 1853) the age's ever-present fear of epidemics which overnight could wipe out a whole community of adults. But even as Gotthelf and Stifter were writing their works, the market and the state were promoting revolutionary changes in the spread of the factory system and, above all, in the growth of a nationwide system of communications between communities, which would in time provide the ultimate answers to cyclical catastrophes.

Communications

It was poets who first recorded the changes to the landscape and to the human imagination which new inventions brought about. It was the 1830s which first witnessed those developments in technology and interstate collaboration which would change the face of Germany. In 1832–33, barely two years after the Revolution of 1830, which changed little politically but a great deal in contemporaries' perceptions, the first optical telegraph was erected in Prussia. It linked Berlin to Cologne, providing sixty-one stations en route. It was, however, not open to commercial users, which helps to explain the keen interest shown by contemporaries in the electrical telegraph, which emerged in 1847, symbolically, perhaps, on the eve of the Revolution. A revolution in communications, the necessary first step to economic modernization of Germany, took place between the late 1820s and the expulsion of Austria from Germany in 1866. It began with the gradual improvement of Germany's legendary bad roads and of her waterways, and was followed by state investment in new ones. The reduction of tolls on rivers, highways, and canals was a further key element of the process. The statistics are impressive, though we have to remember that they have a very low baseline. Even before the advent of the railways in the mid-1830s, a number of German states had shown remarkable initiative in fostering better communications. Thus in Prussia alone the road network almost doubled between 1825 to 1835, to a little over 10,000 miles. In Germany as a whole, an additional 25,000 miles were added in this period. In 1815 the German Confederation had possessed scarcely more than 11,000 miles of roads on which one could actually use wheeled transport.

German geography is characterized by its many rivers suitable for transport, notably the Rhine, Weser, Elbe, and Oder flowing northward, and the Danube flowing southeastward. In 1818 the first steamships appeared on a number of Germany's rivers, on the Rhine and the Weser in western Germany, and on the Spree near Berlin. By 1831, the Rhine was made navigable as far as the sea, and the steamships, the first ones bought from Britain, gave considerable stimulus to commerce. They also helped to create the tourist industry in the Rhineland. Its earliest and most faithful customers were the British, savoring the delights which Lord Byron (1788-1824) had painted in 1816 in his epic poem *Childe Harold*, and which provided younger writers, such as William Thackeray (1811-63) or Charlotte Brontë (1816-55) with such abundant copy. Canals, however, by contrast with eighteenth-century Britain or in the United States, were slow to develop. The Rhine was linked with the Danube between 1836 and 1845, but it was not until the 1880s and 1890s that the major canal German network, so suitable to the country's physical geography, was planned and implemented. However, the 1840s saw the beginnings of Germany's shipping industry, based initially in the North Sea ports of Hamburg, where the Hapag (Hamburg-America line) was founded in 1847, and Bremen, which soon developed into a major center for emigrants to the New World.[1]

However in some respects major obstacles to effective communication remained untouched in this period. Even for short journeys, passports were required. Most towns closed their gates at night and prohibited exit or entry

---

[1] As early as 1840, Heinrich Heine writes graphically (in *Ludwig Börne*) about the sight of German emigrants being herded into ships for the transatlantic voyage.

after dusk. When the civil servant responsible for the department of trade in the Prussian ministry of Finance, Karl Georg Maaßen (1769–1834), prepared in 1818 to introduce a modified standard tariff, Prussia had sixty-seven distinct customs areas. And even though the German Confederation had fewer than forty sovereign states, where a few years earlier there had been several hundred, such was the fragmentation of territory, even in post-Napoleonic Germany, that a traveler going from Hamburg to Berlin would cross several dozen customs frontiers. In 1819 the economist Friedrich List (1789–1846), who had spent formative years in the United States, petitioned the Diet of the Confederation to promote trade by removing these internal frontiers. He declared that "thirty-eight [sic] customs boundaries cripple inland commerce and produce much the same effect as ligatures, which prevent free circulation of the blood." His dictum, often quoted in the early years of the German Federal Republic (1949–), that "if goods do not cross frontiers, armies will do so," must have struck a chord in those of his fellow countrymen, who had just been through half a lifetime of war. In subsequent years, List argued forcefully for the creation of a centralized German railway system, and even edited a journal, the *Eisen-*(iron)*Journal,* to foster public awareness of the economic potential of his proposal. Its full title was "Iron Journal and National Magazine to Promote Progress in Trade, Commerce and Agriculture." List is rightly regarded today as one of the spiritual ancestors of the present-day European Union.

But progress toward List's goal was all too slow, occurring piecemeal across the country. Standardization of the currency, for example, did not take place until well into the second half of the century. Meanwhile, the Rhinelanders continued to have their florins, Prussians their talers, Austrians their gulden;

"While the political ambition of the citizen advances at a snail's pace, the industrial development rushes by on wheels." Caricature (1848).

only in 1873 did Germany go on the gold standard. There was considerable and, certainly to a stranger, extremely confusing regional or even local variation in weights and measures. What this could mean in practice can be best gauged by imagining the outcome for a young bride from Saxony, who attempted to please a disapproving Bavarian mother-in-law by making a cake from her recipe, but who failed to appreciate the quite different calculations required by the Bavarian as against the Saxon ounce.

The Customs Union of 1834

The two innovations which most readily captured the imagination of the public in the 1830s were the Customs Union and the first railway. They occurred in successive years, the first in 1834, the second in 1835. At midnight between 31 December 1833 and 1 January 1834, eighteen states, with a population of well over twenty million, raised their colorful customs poles—black and white for Prussian frontiers, blue and white for Bavarian, and so on. What this meant in practice was that all internal tariffs were abolished between participating states, and a liberal external tariff adopted. Austria, which favored protectionism, and a number of northern states did not join. Prussia had succeeded in her bold initiative despite the strenuous opposition of Austria and the states of the northwest.

The Austrian delegate to the Federal Diet or Bundestag at Frankfurt declared portentously in December 1833 that the whole affair was "one of the chief nails in the coffin of the Confederation." It was a prophetic phrase. For, although the Customs Union was not a major step on the road to industrialization or German unification under Prussia, as nationalist historians once thought, the Customs Union did capture contemporaries' imagination. It also helped them to begin see Prussia in a new, more positive light. At the same time, the dexterity with which Prussia promoted the Customs Union, the experience she gained in interstate negotiations over the next thirty years, as well as her readiness to sacrifice financial to political gain, won grudging acknowledgment from both participant states and from those outside the Union. Over the next decades, most German states became members, apart from Austria, the two Mecklenburg states, and the Hanseatic city-states of Hamburg and Bremen. Between 1849 and 1853 Austria determined to join, but her efforts foundered on her own insistence on the need for a much higher protective tariff for her industries than Prussia was prepared to accept.

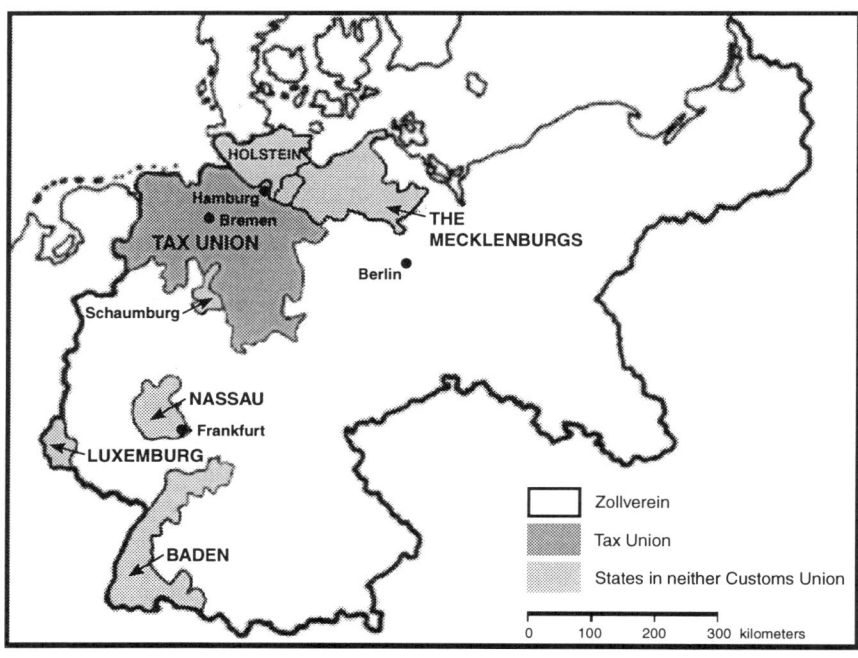

The *Zollverein* and the Tax Union (1834).

It was not until the 1860s that the correlation between economic and political leadership in German affairs was demonstrated when Prussia unexpectedly defeated Austria and expelled her from Germany. The south German states, most of whom had been Austria's allies in the so-called six weeks war of 1866, proceeded to sign military agreements with their recent foe, Prussia, not least in order to retain their profitable economic links with the Union. Despite the infant state of German industry, the Customs Union tariff was one of the most liberal in the world. Yet the volume of goods traded increased rapidly from 1834 forward: by 1845 revenues to the member states had risen by 90 percent, the population by some 21 percent. This increase in revenue—each member kept a share of the total, calculated on the basis of population—proved irresistible even in times of mutual hostility. Thus, paradoxically as it might seem, the revenue continued to be distributed between member states, even when several federal states were actually at war with Prussia in 1866.

The railways

The stimulus offered by the railways to the modernization and, above all, the industrialization of Germany is much more evident. The building of the railways linked peripheral areas of German territory which were vital to the development of her economy, and, perhaps even more importantly, with industrially and commercially developed regions beyond her frontiers, such as the Low Countries and northern France. The railways transformed business. Moreover, they provided an important stimulus to the developing market in agricultural produce, bringing ever wider markets within reach. Initially, railways were used to transport passengers, but soon took freight as well. Although at mid-century they only carried one-third of the volume of goods which went by water, less than twenty years later the position was reversed. The railways' demand for steel and coal inevitably acted as a powerful stimulus on these key industries of the industrial revolution, as well as helping to create a native machine tool industry. Between 1850 and 1890 about half of the steel produced in Germany and one-third of its coal went to the railways. The first railway in Germany[2] was the seven-kilometer track opened in 1835 between Fürth, which had a thriving Jewish community, and Nuremberg, where today the magnificent German transport museum is situated. The Berlin-Potsdam railway followed in 1837; by the early 1840s this line was carrying 2,000 passengers daily. Among other early lines was that from Brunswick to Wolfenbüttel in northern Germany, one of the few early state-owned railways. Something of the contemporary enthusiasm for this technological wonder was captured in the work of a local craftsman in Wolfenbüttel. On the cups and saucers of a delicate Biedermeier coffee set, which is displayed today in the Herzog August Museum, the former palace of the dukes of Brunswick-Wolfenbüttel, he painted the first railway station, its first locomotive, and various contemporary scenes depicting the local population welcoming their new trains.

More significant from the point of view of the economy was Germany's first long line, covering the seventy or so miles between the commercial capital of Saxony, Leipzig, and the state capital and residence of the king, Dresden (1837). This was followed by industrially important lines in the Ruhr Valley and the Rhine. By 1840, Germany had some 340 miles of rail track; ten years later this figure had increased almost tenfold; by 1860 Germany had almost

---

[2] While 1835 traditionally ranks as the date of the first German railway, in fact the first in the Confederation was the line from Linz in Upper Austria to Budweis (Czeské Budejovicé) in southern Bohemia, built in 1828.

7,000 miles. Between 1846 and 1867 the number of workers employed on the railways increased more than tenfold, from 7,000 to 74,000. In 1859 a great railway bridge was opened which spanned the Rhine. It connected the Roman city of Cologne with Deutz on the other side of the river, where once the Celtic tribes had been forced to settle. Now this bridge established a continuous rail link between Aachen, where Charlemagne had once reigned (768–814), and Memel (Klaipeda, chief port of modern Lithuania) close to the Russian frontier. On the eve of the First World War Germany had over 37,500 miles of rail track.

Initially, it was private enterprise and not the state which supplied both the impetus and the capital for the railways. British rolling stock was used in the early stages, but by mid-century, German manufacture was beginning to supply the home market. Returns on investment in railway bonds in the boom periods of the railway construction age were very high indeed, as much as 40 percent per annum. The shareholders of what was to prove one of the most lucrative, the Leipzig-Dresden line, raised sufficient funds in a single day for the entire enterprise. The boom in railway investment continued into the 1870s, by which time the principal lines had been built, and the prime economic and social function of providing cheap transport of goods and people achieved. The fall in costs was significant: from 17 Pfennig per kilometer (1 km = c. five-eighths of a mile) in 1848, to 6 Pfennig per passenger by 1872. In 1896 it was less than 4 Pfennig. By the 1880s, more and more Germans were taking holidays and using the railways to do so. In everyday life, as in the railway carriages, social distinctions and divisions were clearly marked (see page 248). In the last decades of the century, progressive nationalization of the railways took place. They had already established their military importance in the wars of unification, against Denmark in 1864, Austria in 1866, and especially against France in 1870–1. Indeed, Prussia's great general Helmut von Moltke (1800–91) had observed prophetically as early as 1843 that a few million invested in the railways would be more profitable strategically than the same amount spent on fortresses. Under Bismarck the railways would form part of government policy of social engineering, most notably in the granting of preferential tariffs to east Elbian landowners transporting their grain, and to heavy industry.

The revolution in communications profoundly affected the way people thought about themselves and their environment. In the early years of railway-building, poets rather than engineers first grasped the impact of the railways on the human mind. It was they who intuitively understood that the imagination was shaped through changing experience of time and space.

The German Economy in the First Half of the Century

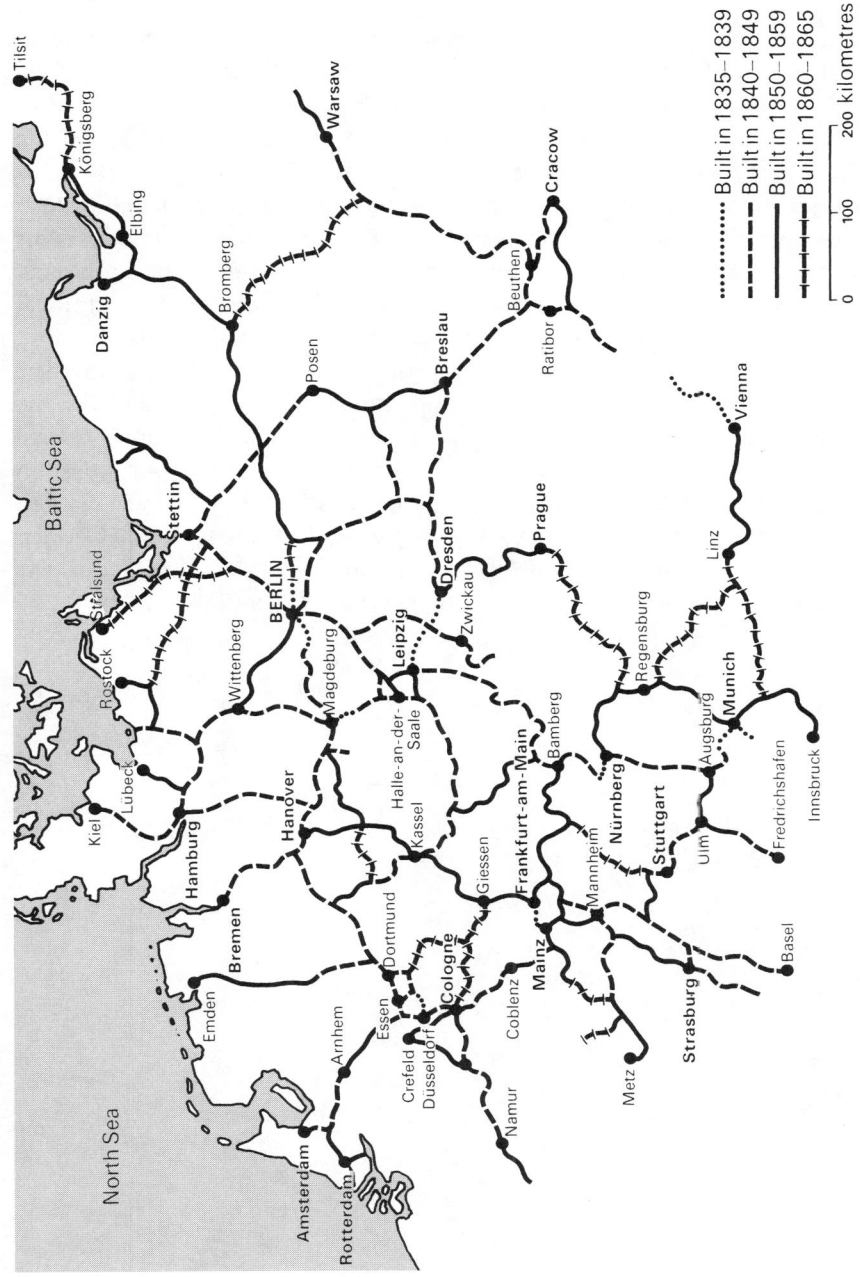

German Railways (1835–65).

One of the earliest and most original expressions of that experience is a poem by the former French Huguenot émigré to Prussia, Adelbert von Chamisso (1781–1836), entitled "steam horse" or *Dampfroß*. The poem was written in 1830, twelve years after his return from a three-year sea voyage around the world, during which the author personally recorded his sense of dislocation, as the expedition traversed what we today call timezones. Chamisso, best known for his remarkable novella, *Peter Schlemihl* (1814), about a man who loses his shadow, dramatizes in his poem the impact of the new invention on human beings' sense of time. Global time, he declares, makes nonsense of traditional chronology. Other poets, notably Nikolaus von Lenau (1802–50), lamented in more elegiac tones the death of nature at the hands of this steel-clad invader. Liberals, by contrast, exulted in man's capacity to harness nature and saw the railway as a symbol, not just of human progress, but of Germany's elusive national unity. Certainly, the railway age, which coincided with an explosion of the print media, thanks to the ongoing capitalization of the literary market, contributed in its own way to the outbreak and progress of German revolution (or revolutions) of 1848–9. Before turning to that topic, let us first look at the kind of society Germany was between 1800 and 1848.

Chapter 4
German Society 1815–48

The world of German society between the Napoleonic wars and the age of industrialization was in many respects profoundly different from our own. A fundamental difference is our totally distinctive sense of time. Before the railway age was established, people thought of time as measured by the bells of their local church. Not many people, and certainly few women, owned a watch. Mobility shapes people's sense of time, and in those days most people's mobility was determined by the distance a person might travel by foot in one day. Artisans, Jews, and students traveled by foot. Noblemen and merchants traveled on horseback or by coach. Most of the rest stayed at home. Another difference lay in the manner and function of dress. An early nineteenth-century German's dress, before clothes began to be mass produced, was less an expression of their personality than an indicator of social status and profession. One dressed, and one was expected to dress, according to one's station. No one in early nineteenth-century German society could possibly have confused a university professor in his leisure dress with a laborer, as we well might do today. People wore particular clothes for particular occasions, and excited much negative comment if they did not. Thus it was virtually obligatory for a woman to wear "deep mourning," that is, unrelieved black, for up to a year following the death of her husband or close family member. A man would wear a black crepe band on his arm or in his hat. After a stated time, a woman in such a situation would wear "half mourning," that is to say, she could wear a gray dress or even a white blouse for a further stipulated time. Such customs endured in rural Germany and Austria well into the second half of the twentieth century.

As far as literature is concerned, many other related differences operated. Literary conventions, for example. Poets did not just write about any member or group in society. They concentrated on the middle and upper echelons, though this would change in the period under discussion. Early nineteenth-century representation of contemporary life focused almost exclusively on those who had property and status in their community, on those who had received an education, and omitted the rest. However, by the 1830s and 1840s or *Vormärz*, some pioneering German writers were beginning to draw portraits of men and women on the margins of society. Virtually all such works were written by the well educated who had failed to get into a 'respectable' profession, people who observed others different from themselves. It is not accidental that many of these authors of life "on the margins" were themselves Jewish. Thus in the work of the Jewish peddler's son Berthold Auerbach (1812-82) from southwest Germany, we meet Jewish peddlers, poor peasants from the overworked land of participle inheritance in Baden, forced to emigrate to the New World, we encounter the criminalized and even the handicapped. In his ghetto tales of the Austrian Empire, Leopold Kompert (1822-86) from Bohemia introduces us to the harsh reality of the Jewish hawker's life, while in their poems on the Silesian weavers' revolt of 1844, Heinrich Heine and the Saxon writer, Louise Otto (1819-95), feature the victims of capitalist oppression and the brutality of the authorities. In his poem (*Die schlesischen Weber*, 1844) Heine actually focuses on what contemporaries regarded as the most significant problem of the society of his age, termed by a contemporary "the bleeding wound of our age—mass pauperism." In his image of the *blechende Zähne* or bared teeth of the starving weavers, who briefly rose against their oppressors, Heine brilliantly encapsulates contemporaries' dread of the consequences of pauperism for the social order in which they lived. Bared teeth can signify the threat of revolution by the oppressed or it can simply operate as a description of what happens to the mouth and lips of those who are so undernourished that they lose the fine layer of fat which helps contour the human face. In Heine's poem it means both simultaneously. But even in Heine, and in other works of poetic literature which deal with grave social problems, those on the margins of society appear only as a collective or as social types. They scarcely ever merit consideration as individuals. A significant exception is Büchner's *Woyzeck* (written in 1837), an eponymous play about a schizophrenic soldier so poor that he submits to appalling dietary experiments at the hands of his masters, just to support his girlfriend and their child.

Yet even for members of the upper and middle classes, broadly defined, life was lived in Restoration Germany much more in the collective than would be the case a century and a half later. The reasons for this were both socio-economic and ideological. Children, except perhaps for some royal children, did not have their own rooms. Adolescents, separated by gender, normally had to share a bedroom with their sisters or brothers until marriage. (In poverty-stricken families, in the new urban slums of Berlin in the 1840s, or in the cabins of the rural poor, whole families, including the parents, might sleep in the same bed.) Until marriage, upper-class children did not leave the parental home, though those who needed the money—and they were the majority—sent their children out to work at a very young age, as indeed is still the practice for many very poor children of today's Third World.

German Society 1815–48

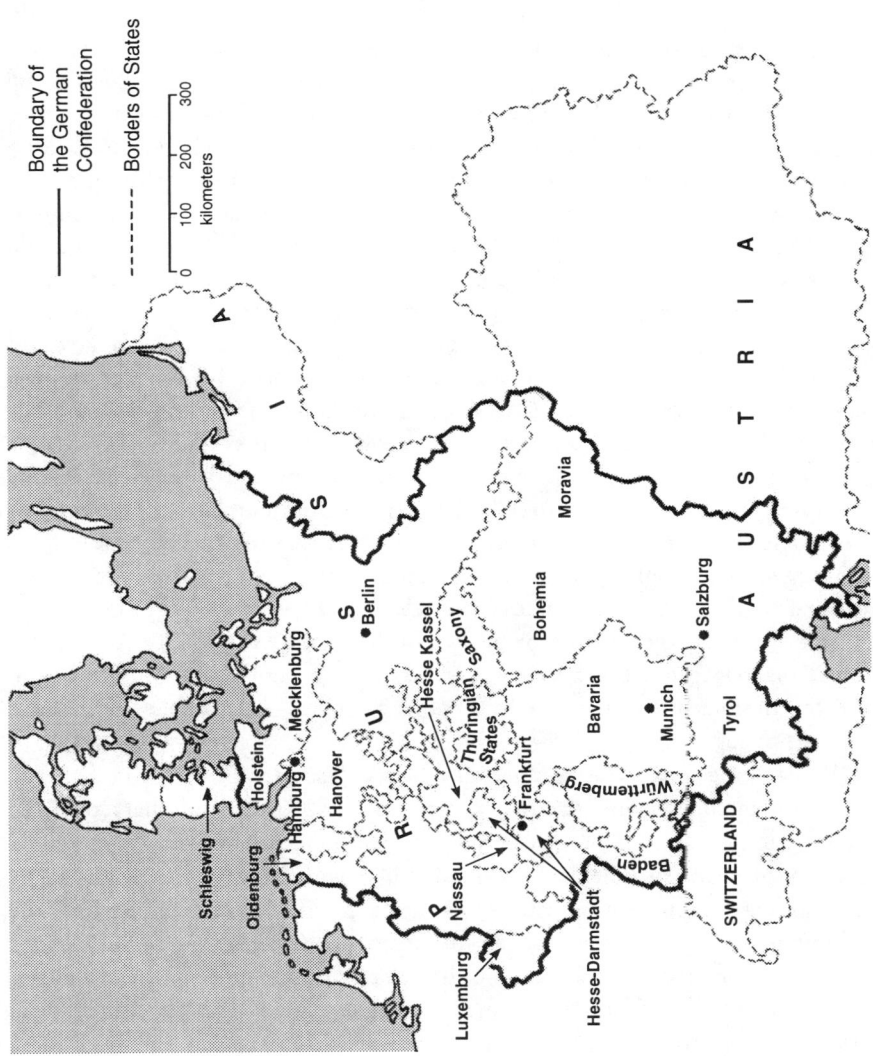

The German Confederation (1815).

Early nineteenth-century German society, which had the highest rates of literacy in the world, discovered the delights of reading, since books and journals had become accessible through the lending libraries (see chapter 8, beginning on page 133). Yet young people in middle-class homes could not just go and read in their room of the evening. In a society which was forced by relative poverty, even in the middle ranks of society, to be thrifty, one candle was the norm, and that was in the living room. One member of the family or group read aloud to the rest, who got on with whatever handiwork lent itself to be done without direct light. Bedrooms were not heated, except perhaps for the sick.

For women in particular, it was unusual to be alone—and not thought good for them. The higher up the social scale, the less freedom of movement a girl or young woman might expect. Unmarried women were accompanied virtually everywhere, for it was vital for their reputation, and hence for their prospects of marriage, that they were never the object of gossip, as they would have been had they been seen by a neighbor talking, however innocently, to a member of the opposite sex. Marriage in traditional societies was an affair more of economics than the heart, and economic factors certainly played a far greater role in marriage than we can easily imagine today. Karl Marx, for example, was continually forced to postpone his marriage to Jenny von Westphalen, the daughter of a civil servant, because his mother cut off his allowance: she thought it would make him at last get a "proper job." One did not marry in middle- and upper-class circles before one could support a wife. Fontane was engaged to his bride Emilie Rouanet-Kummer for five years before marriage, much to her chagrin.[1] Fontane had not got a secure job and, like the dramatist and poet Friedrich Hebbel (1803–63), he had illegitimate children to support.

Perhaps the most striking difference between society as we know it today and German society of that time, was the latter's hierarchical character. The intervention of the market and the state, which James J. Sheehan has identified in his book *German History 1770–1866* (1989) as the key influences on social development in nineteenth-century Germany, modified that character over the following decades. During this time education, greater wealth, a better diet for most, and immensely increased mobility created opportunities which had not existed before. But these developments changed rather than abolished social stratification, with contract only gradually replacing custom and traditional rights, and property in the form of capital increasingly determining the social pecking order.

---

[1] Fontane's courtship and marriage is documented in a unique correspondence with his wife, Emilie (1824–1902), spanning over 54 years of the century (1844–98), published in three volumes in Berlin in 1998 by Gottfried and Therese Erler.

In what follows, the reader is invited to examine German society in the first half of the century, not in abstract terms, but through concrete examples, namely in terms of the social origins and subsequent careers of writers, born or active in the first half of the century.

German society in this period is commonly considered under four general headings, namely according to the traditional categories of nobility, middle classes, and peasantry, but with the addition of what historians nowadays refer to as the "fourth class." This highly diverse social group was a new phenomenon of post-1815 Germany, the consequence of fundamental changes, over a period of two or more generations, in the way society was organized and in the way people thought about its purpose. The emergence of such a "fourth class" marks the changeover from what was known as corporate society, based on estates, to modern class society. In the past, in theory at least, society was seen as a (traditionally God-ordained) hierarchy, based on privileged estates, each of which had a defined function. Thus the nobility, by far the most privileged, derived their status from their defense of the realm (the old term was *Wehrstand*,[2] the estate that defends) and continued to try and legitimize their privileges on that now outdated basis. They had the right to bear arms and they rode on horseback, whereas ordinary people walked. In medieval times, the clergy, the only members of society who could read and write, constituted the second estate. Their more exalted members, such as bishops and members of cathedral chapters, continued to sit in local assemblies. Over time, the inhabitants of towns and cities, who were property-owners, merchants, and master craftsmen, members of guilds, or men of learning charged with the education of the next generation, were regarded as constituting the second rank. These were the *Bürger* (English *burgher*), that is, citizens of their town. Early anthropologists used the term *Lehrstand* or "teaching estate," that is, those who needed to be literate in order to pursue their profession and conduct their business. The third, and numerically by far the largest estate, were the peasants, the *Nährstand*, that is, those who supplied the rest with food (and provided the foot soldiers and cannon fodder for Germany's numerous wars).

In the old corporate society, there were many who did not fall into any of the three recognized groups. These were those who were in a position of dependency and therefore lived in the household of a member of society. Among these were household and rural servants, the latter including farm laborers, apprentices, and the young, and, broadly speaking, women also, who on marriage went from a position of dependency on their fathers or male guardians to being dependants of their husbands. The rest of the country's

---

[2] This was a secular variant on the traditional feudal classes of nobility, clergy, and burgher.

inhabitants, who belonged neither to a particular estate nor were members of other people's households, were not regarded as forming part of 'society' in the old dispensation. Those who were unfortunate enough to fall into that category—namely beggars, gypsies, unmarried mothers, the destitute (through no fault of their own), as well as actors playing for traveling companies—existed on the margins of society and were forced to live as best they could. In crisis years and especially after wars, their numbers increased, as did vagrancy and petty criminality.

A further category outside a society which still defined itself as Christian, was the Jews; in a precapitalist age, they had traditionally been employed by the authorities as rudimentary bankers and used by the populace to supply them with goods. Before the late eighteenth century they enjoyed little tolerance or security. In the East they lived in Jewish settlements or villages—the Yiddish word *stetl* means "little town"—regulating their own affairs under the general protection of a local territorial ruler, and speaking their own language, Yiddish, an early modern German dialect interspersed with Hebrew words. On the eve of the nineteenth century, as part of the general influence of Enlightenment thinking, the idea of the (partial) emancipation of the Jew was mooted, notably in Prussia and in Austria. As in the case of the servile peasantry, the civic amelioration of the lot of the Jews in Germany was less concerned with altruism than with the economic advantage of the state. The immense contribution of German and eastern Jews to German culture and thought in the nineteenth century requires the student of German to pay particular attention to this social group (see chapter 13). In the eastern provinces of the Austrian Empire and of Prussia, another marginalized social group was marked by its own language, *Rotwelsch* ("the strange red language") and by the victimization of its members by settled society. These were the gypsies or Romanies, discovered by literature in the opening years of the century, notably by the Romantic poets, Clemens Brentano and Heinrich von Kleist.[3]

Most of Germany's writers in the period under discussion came from the middle ranks of society or from the lower nobility. Very many were the sons and daughters of professional men, of men of private means, as was Goethe, or of lawyers, as were the Austrian dramatist Grillparzer and the actor-playwright Johann Nestroy (1801–62). A number of leading German writers and critics were the sons of Lutheran parsons, as were the brothers Schlegel in the Romantic era and Friedrich Nietzsche (1844–1900) in the second half of the century. Very few writers came from peasant stock; one of these was Voß, who, besides his greatly admired satiric and family idylls, was also the

---

[3] An example is Kleist: *Michael Kohlhaas* (1811).

translator of Homer into German verse. He had profited from the fact that university study in certain faculties was cheap. In the theological faculties scholarships were available for well-recommended clever boys in poor circumstances, whom their teachers felt had the makings of future clergymen. Voß became a schoolmaster, supplementing his income by editing and writing for popular almanacs. Considerable numbers of German writers in the age of Romanticism and the Biedermeier came from the ranks of the (lesser) nobility. They had met their peers at one of Germany's numerous universities, such as Berlin, Jena in central Germany, or Heidelberg in the south, which had a celebrated law school. Thus the poet Novalis, a relation of Prussia's later chancellor, von Hardenberg, was part of an intimate group of friends which included the Schlegels and Tieck. The Silesian poet, Eichendorff, son of a feckless landowner who had forfeited the family estates, was a university friend of Achim von Arnim, a landowner from Brandenburg, who in turn was the collaborator of his closest friend at university, Clemens Brentano, in the famous collection of German folksongs, *Des Knaben Wunderhorn* (1805–8). In Germany, unlike in Britain, all noblemen's sons inherited their father's title and noble status. But the majority could not live on the family lands, and being forced to find work, required an education to aspire to positions in the state service befitting their rank. In late sixteenth- and early seventeenth-century Germany, educated men of middle-class origin had found a career open to their talents in the service of a prince (or city government). With the age of absolutism (c. 1648–1789), German rulers began to buy the loyalty of their nobility in exchange for privileged access to positions in the service of the prince, as in the army and the church; at the same time, city government became more or less the hereditary preserve of a few privileged families.[4]

One of the most important impulses for the creation of a national literature in the last decades of eighteenth-century Germany was poets' critical reflection on the inequities of a system which denied non-noblemen of education and ability access to interesting careers in the public sector. Thus in their bourgeois tragedies, Lessing (son of a parson) in *Emilia Galotti* (1772) and Schiller (son of an army barber-surgeon) in *Kabale und Liebe* (1784) present angry portraits of the disadvantage of middle-class birth and the demoralizing effect on society of the corruption of the German courts. Both authors had had plenty of personal experience of social exclusion and disadvantage. In the same dramas, Lessing and Schiller show how the system corrupts those few successful middle-class

---

[4] These privileged families became a rich topic of prose fiction among bourgeois writers of the later nineteenth century, such as Theodor Storm, and the inspiration, based of course on personal experience, of Thomas Mann's novel *Buddenbrooks* (1901).

applicants to princely service: Marinelli in *Emilia Galotti* and the hero Ferdinand's father, along with chancellor Wurm in *Kabale und Liebe*, buy their position at the price of moral deformation. They are corrupt, venal, and a danger to society. Indeed a sociohistorical reading of Goethe's famous and in its time so successful novel, *The Sorrows of Young Werther* (1774), might attribute the real origins of the hero's melancholy to the limited career opportunities open to talented young men of middle-class background and to the humiliations to which Werther found himself submitted because of his birth. In traditional societies, such as late eighteenth- and early nineteenth-century Germany, meritocracy was virtually unknown. Instead, patronage played a key role in gaining employment or getting promoted once there, and patronage lay almost exclusively in the hands of the aristocracy or local notables. Even in England of that time, as Jane Austen (1775–1817) reminds us in her novel, *Mansfield Park* (1814), it was essential for an ordinary person to have connections. The talented young sailor William Price, sister of the heroine Fanny, would probably never have become a lieutenant, had not the scheming Henry Crawford arranged it through the connections of his uncle, the Admiral, in order to ingratiate himself with Fanny. Hence, one of the most far-reaching reforms of the radically minded Austrian Emperor Joseph II was to open up the developing imperial state service to men of all nationalities and, ideally, of all backgrounds. In that event, only those of some means could afford to take such posts, as they were forced to live for a number of years without any pay until a permanent position became vacant. But over time, the Austrian civil service became one of the great stabilizing forces in central Europe.

Turning, then, to a survey of Germany's social organization in the first half of the nineteenth century, and her writers' location within it, we start with contemporaries' view of what constituted the zenith of the social pyramid, the *Hochadel* or high nobility.

The high nobility encompassed the sovereign rulers, such as the Austrian emperor, or the Prussian, Saxon, Württemberg, or Bavarian kings, the grand dukes and dukes of medium and smaller territories and those who lost their sovereignty when Napoleon suppressed the Holy Roman Empire and its institutions between 1803 and 1806. These were the so-called mediatized princes or *Standesherren* (the word means gentlemen or lords of rank), numbering about eighty families of princes and counts. Despite their loss of sovereignty, they were regarded as equal in rank, though not in wealth and power, with the sovereign princes; they were specifically identified in the founding document of the German Confederation of 1815 as the most privileged class in the state. They could and did intermarry with royal families. The *Standesherren* retained their former political privileges, namely the hereditary rights to seats in the upper house of state parliaments, where these existed, and they always displayed a strong sense of their worth, even where the economic base for this was lacking. Thus the anecdote is told of the late nineteenth-century count of the former sovereign territory of Erbach in Hesse, who, riding out on horseback, was passed by the driver of a new-fangled motor car. He immediately fell into a towering rage and declared: "I, and nobody else, decides who overtakes me in Erbach!" Few members of the high nobility were active as writers, though many were patrons of letters as well as of the theater and music. However, an exception was Johann, brother of the king of Saxony and himself later king (1854–73), who made the Dresden court a cultural center in the 1830s and 1840s, and who under the pseudonym of Philalethes was much admired by contemporaries for his accurate translation of Dante's *Divine Comedy*. A few of Germany's nineteenth-century writers did enjoy something of the patronage of their eighteenth-century predecessors, such as Friedrich Klopstock (1724–1803).

But patronage in the Restoration tended to be insecure, as the *Vormärz* poet Georg Herwegh soon found, when he tested the munificence of Friedrich Wilhelm IV of Prussia. Emboldened by the new king's reputation for accessibility, he sought and secured an audience with the monarch, where he demanded "liberty for the people." The politically naive young poet was unceremoniously escorted to the nearest Prussian border under armed guard. Heine, who did not share the view of Herwegh and the Young Germans that politically correct sentiments guaranteed the worth of a poem, made himself unpopular by writing a mischievous but extremely witty verse about the whole affair, under the title *Die Audienz* (1853). Princely patronage could also be eccentric, as in the court circle of the Bavarian king, Maximilian II (1848–64), which Fontane vainly hoped to join in the 1850s. Maximilian "headhunted" poets, mainly from northern Germany, to give his rather provincial court some glamour. Unfortunately his taste was not very good, and although the poets enjoyed themselves, they produced little of lasting value. For princely patrons in the nineteenth century tended to sun themselves in the talents of minor poets. They were much better at spotting musical talent. The mediatized princes were in general not normally in a position to offer patronage to writers, though some gave a helping hand to individuals. One of these fortunate writers was Herwegh's colleague, Ferdinand Freiligrath. He was given a post as librarian on the Silesian estates of prince Hohenlohe-Ratibor when his political poetry got him into trouble with the authorities. Most *Standesherren* were forced to earn their living, but they could expect preferment in the service of other German princes. Thus prince Kraft von Hohenlohe-Ingelfingen (1827–92) made a successful career in the Prussian army, and wrote informative memoirs of army and court life in Berlin and Vienna. The last imperial chancellor of the century, Chlodwig von Hohenlohe-Schillingsfürst (1894–1900), born in the same year as Fontane in 1819 and a former prime minister of Bavaria and governor of Alsace-Lorraine, was a *Standesherr* and brother of Freiligrath's employer; another brother was made a cardinal. Embedded in the subtext of Fontane's remarkable novel, *Der Stechlin*, are many and diverse references to the Hohenlohe family, who had estates both in south Germany and in Silesia and, through marriage, in Tsarist Russia. The author uses the Hohenlohes as a contrast to the less attractive representatives of the Prussian Junkers, who are generally portrayed as authoritarian yet provincial and self-regarding. By contrast, Graf Barby, father of Melusine and Armgard, shares distinct characteristics with the urbane, well-connected and humorous Chlodwig Hohenlohe.

Court and service nobility (*Hofadel* and *Dienstadel*)

Many members of the court or service nobility, who, or whose ancestors, derived their noble titles from service to the prince, were considerably wealthier than the mediatized princes. The diplomat and commander-in-chief of the Austrian troops against Napoleon at the battle of Leipzig in 1813, Karl von Schwarzenberg (1771–1820), came from the family of great estate-owners in Bohemia who could trace their pedigree back to the twelfth century; his nephew was emperor Franz Joseph I's (1830–1916) first chancellor, Felix von Schwarzenberg, in whose house the young Adalbert Stifter lived in the 1840s. The service nobility was also stratified internally according to rank; successful service of the monarch could bring elevation to higher rank within the group, promotion, as it were, from count to prince. In the eighteenth and nineteenth centuries, members of the lesser nobility might be rewarded by being elevated to the ranks of the court and service nobility. Thus Metternich was made a prince of the Austrian Empire in 1813, following Napoleon's defeat at Leipzig, and the former Junker Bismarck became an imperial German prince, after the unification of Germany under Prussia in 1871. Austria was particularly munificent in this cheap form of social recognition to its public servants who might include such people as the director of a local hospital or a prison governor or an army officer. However, there was a strong dividing line between this large latter group and the "first society" to which the old court nobility belonged and the "first society's" few new recruits, such as prince Metternich.

Perhaps unsurprisingly, the service or court nobility was not well represented among nineteenth-century authors writing in German. An exception were two of the century's best known women writers, Annette von Droste-Hülshoff (1797–1848) and Marie von Ebner-Eschenbach (1830–1916). Droste was the daughter, and Ebner the step-daughter, of ancient families, the one from the landed nobility of Westphalia, the other linked through the third marriage of her father, Count Dubsky, with one of the leading families in Austria, the Kolowrats. In their lives as writers, both women experienced major psychological and personal problems with their families, who regarded it as a form of class betrayal that their relatives should write about, let alone reflect critically on the ancient institutions of aristocracy, church, family, and marriage. Ebner, in particular, was guilty of the latter charge. Writing, according to the caste code, was a perfectly creditable occupation, for a woman as for a man, but it was expected to be affirmative, and in the case of women, edifying or devotional. Droste's grandmother was very pleased to learn that her talented young granddaughter Annette was writing spiritual sonnets for the Sundays and feasts of the year. She was horrified when she got a closer acquaintance with the metaphysical doubts and personal anguish expressed by the poet in her great cycle of poems, published only after her death under the title, *Das geistliche Jahr* (1851). Annette was dutiful, but as an unmarried woman living in the family she had little choice. After this incident she kept rebellious thoughts largely to herself, as she tells us in one of her most impassioned poems, "Standing at the turret" (*Am Thurm*, 1844), which in its poignant last lines relates how she secretly undid her hair and allowed it to wave in the wind: "*heimlich lösen mein Haar und lassen es flattern im Winde.*" Ebner was punished for 'showing off' as a child when she shyly showed her first poems to her family. She published her satirical portrait of the Austrian aristocracy, *Sechs Epistel aus Franzensbad*, anonymously in 1858, but never lived down the anger she aroused among those who felt her target. Later, she was bitterly upbraided by her husband, Moritz, a field marshal in the Austrian army and fifteen years her senior, for "defaming his good name," after her dramas received a bad press on performance in the Vienna *Burgtheater* in the 1860s.

Minor Nobility (*Kleinadel*)

By contrast, the minor nobility, much the most populous and not always well-to-do sector of Germany's first estate, attracted many men and women of literary talent in the years between the French Revolution of 1789 and the First World War of 1914–18. This was a most diverse class, composed, among others, of former Holy Roman imperial knights, of the East Elbian Junkers, of ennobled officials, such as the eighteenth-century Saxon publishers, the Hohenthals, or the Hessian landowners and Rhenish entrepreneurs, such as the brothers Heinrich (1799–1848) and Friedrich von Gagern (1794–1848), who would play such a prominent role in the 1848 Revolution. One of the features of the growing influence of the nineteenth-century German state in the regulation of people's lives was the need to employ more people to administer the process. Members of the lesser nobility looked to the service of the state, as did their middle-class contemporaries, and now came equipped with useful technical qualifications or a university education. Early in the century, the Romantic poet Novalis was a mining engineer who worked for his short career in Freiberg, in central Germany, and wrote in his spare time. Eichendorff spent a long and not very happy career as a Catholic in the overwhelmingly Protestant Prussian civil service; the burdens of office were many, but they allowed him time, not just for his poetry and prose fiction, but also for a long history of German poetic literature (1857) and polemical writings. A different kind of state service seemed to be the promised lot of the scion of an old Prussian military family when Heinrich von Kleist joined the army in 1792 at the age of fifteen. After seeing military action in the war against France and being promoted to sublieutenant, he applied to leave the service, though had to wait two years before being released in 1799. Kleist's junior by four years, Achim von Arnim, studied law but chose instead of the state service to write his novellas and farm his family estates in Brandenburg—the latter not very successfully, as it turned out. His wife, Bettine, sister of his university friend Clemens Brentano, fortunately proved a rather better economic manager than he. She combined writing with raising seven children, running a household and, after Achim's death, editing his as well as her own works. A generation later, Ferdinand von Saar (1833–1906), the son of an Austrian bureaucrat ennobled just before his own death and his son's birth, made the army his career and began writing mainly to pay his debts. The legendary hero of Prussia's wars of unification, Helmut von Moltke, had a more basic reason for looking for money through writing: he was promoted to the general staff of the Prussian army in the 1840s and needed the money to pay for his horses and new uniforms. His letters and diaries of the following years speak eloquently of the sheer drudgery of translating Gibbons' *Decline and Fall of the Roman Empire* to meet the bills.

The urban patriciate

The urban patriciate comprised the ruling families of those few major German towns which had a long and unbroken commercial tradition and substantial inherited wealth behind them. They were regarded in some regions as members of the aristocracy in the sense that intermarriage was possible, theoretically at least, between them and the landed or court nobility. Goethe's family fell into this category: his father lived on his inheritance and his mother, that splendid letter writer Catherina Textor (1731–1808), was the daughter of a former mayor of their native city of Frankfurt. When Goethe went at the age of sixteen to study law at the then fashionable University of Leipzig in 1765, he enjoyed a monthly allowance of 1000 gulden, which was more than double what many respectable middle-class fathers of families earned. Yet when in 1775 he joined the service of duke Karl of Saxe-Weimar, then an insignificant duchy in central Germany, he was not permitted to dine at court, because he was "only a bourgeois." It was only after the duke ennobled Goethe in 1786 that this was "rectified." In due course he ennobled Schiller also, a gesture that did not help him financially, but did benefit his family in all sorts of ways, not least after Schiller's early death in 1805. After all, as was wittily observed in 1833, a year after Goethe's death, by the author of a celebrated study of Germany's so very different neighbor to the West, the republican Netherlands: "All Germans can be divided into two classes, the von's and the non-von's."[5]

The middle classes

"Conceptually elusive because they were historically disparate" (Sheehan 1989, 522), the nineteenth-century German middle classes encompassed a socially and regionally very diverse section of society, ranging from the commercial and educated bourgeoisie, and including middle-ranking officials, to the very numerous *Kleinbürgertum* or petty burghers. The bourgeoisie was a prominent and influential social group in France and in England, in the 1830s and 1840s, their lives and values attracting the talents of great novelists such as Honoré de Balzac (1799–1850), Charles Dickens (1812–70), or Thackeray. This was not the case in Germany before the second half of the century. Despite the number and variety of towns in Germany, there were only a handful of larger cities. Of these, Vienna, the largest, numbered just over a quarter of a million in 1800, though it grew to over 430,000 fifty years later; the corresponding figures for Berlin are 170,000 at the beginning of the century and 390,000 in 1846. German cities, with the exception of Hamburg and one or two more, were administrative centers, not hubs of commerce. Towns such as Königsberg in the eastern Baltic, Lübeck in the western Baltic, or Nuremberg or Augsburg in Bavaria, which had been rich and powerful in the Middle Ages and early

---

[5] This was the American historian, John Lothrop Motley (1814–77), who wrote his celebrated *History of the Rise of the Dutch Republic* in 1856.

modern times, were now shadows of their former selves. Karlsruhe, Munich, and Stuttgart, capitals of Baden, Bavaria, and Württemberg, respectively, owed their status simply to the fact that the prince had his residence there. Commerce played a minimal role in defining their character. Yet very many families of very modest income across the towns and larger villages of the diverse German regional landscape enjoyed the status of belonging to the 'middle ranks of society,' as contemporaries liked to phrase it, based on their capacity to educate their sons, to own books and even a musical instrument, and to dress in an accepted manner.

The commercial bourgeoisie

Like the philosopher Arthur Schopenhauer (1788–1860), Clemens Brentano, who came from a Frankfurt merchant's family, was destined to follow in his father's footsteps, but it was clear that he inclined to poetry rather than gold. He undoubtedly used his brief experience of life at a desk in his harsh fictional portraits of his own kind. Both parents of the philosopher Schopenhauer came from rich mercantile families in Danzig in East Prussia (now Polish Gdansk), who in their heyday had trade connections all over northeastern Europe, from Leipzig to Russia. But Danzig's prosperity was already in decline by the time Arthur was born, badly hit by the wars of Frederick II (1712–86) of Prussia.

During the Napoleonic wars, the Schopenhauers moved to Hamburg, where Arthur began the unhappiest years of his life in the family business. He learned enough of his trade to salvage something of the family inheritance for himself, when the business crashed in the postwar depression, leaving his mother Johanna (1766–1839) and sister Adele (1797–1849) in straitened circumstances. Johanna proved both resourceful and relatively successful, moving adroitly to Weimar, not least to use Goethe's hoped-for patronage to market her writings, travel books, and prose fiction; Adele shared her mother's minor talent as a writer, but neither Johanna's cheerful nature and business flair nor Arthur's intellectual capacity. Indeed, the history of early nineteenth-century Germany contains numerous examples of women writers on the margins of the literary market in Adele's position, without a career to save them from depression and penury. The opposite career path from that of Brentano and Schopenhauer was chosen by Abraham, son of Moses Mendelssohn (1729–86), the great Jewish Enlightenment philosopher. Father of Felix Mendelssohn-Bartholdy (1809–47), Abraham went into banking in Hamburg and was able to afford the best tuition for his gifted composer son and his daughter, Fanny. Another wealthy Hamburg citizen resident who supported the artistic ambitions of his relations was the financier Salomon Heine, uncle of the poet Heinrich Heine.

Salomon did so reluctantly, it is true, as Heine was extravagant and ungrateful. Heine's own father had been a textile merchant in a small way in their native city of Düsseldorf.

Other German writers from this period with a background and career in commerce included Friedrich Engels and his fellow Communist, Georg Weerth (1822–56), as well as Ferdinand Freiligrath, who worked as a banker during his long English exile. Both Engels and Weerth came from the new manufacturing industry. Engels' father, a factory owner in the Ruhr valley, opened an office in Manchester and sent his son to learn the textile trade there. Here the young Friedrich wrote *The Condition of the Working Class in England* (1845). Engels described his junior by two years, the textile merchant Georg Weerth, as the first major poet of the proletariat. Born in Cologne, Weerth worked in the English center of the woolen industry, Bradford in Yorkshire, and in the United States and Central America. At the same time he managed to produce several poems on the plight of the poorest workers, as well as two entertaining novels on German commercial life. One of these, *Humoristische Szenen aus dem deutschen Handelsleben* (1847–8), was the first German novel to be serialized in a newspaper, in Karl Marx's *Neue Rheinische Zeitung*. A year earlier, their contemporary, Louise Otto, made early factory life the subject of the best known of her some fifty novels (*Schloß und Fabrik*, 1846). The connections of the radical feminist Louise Aston (1814–71) with mid-century commercial life were closer still: she was unhappily married to Samuel Ashton, an English factory owner based in Magdeburg in central Germany. She duly divorced him, embarking on a career that led to poetry, a novel, an autobiography, hard-hitting journalism and, in 1848, on to the barricades.

A vitally important enterprise in the development of nineteenth-century German literature was the commercially successful publishing house, for publishers came to replace the prince as patrons of major and minor poets. Three of the most important in the years 1815–48 were Cotta, Brockhaus, and Campe. Friedrich (later Baron) Cotta (1764–1832) was the publisher of Goethe, Schiller, Annette von Droste, Nikolaus von Lenau, Eduard Mörike (1804–75), and many more. Friedrich Arnold Brockhaus (1772–1823) became a household name through his marketing of the popular encyclopedia, the *Brockhaus*. Julius Campe (1792–1867) of Hamburg was the courageous patron of radical political writers, including Heine and the Young Germans, such as Karl Gutzkow and Heinrich Laube (1806–84). Many struggling writers, such as Therese Forster-Huber (1764–1829), twice married to men who gave her more children than income, had reason to be grateful to Cotta's magazine, the *Morgenblatt* (or *Morning paper for the educated classes*), whose literary section she edited for some

Parade Unter den Linden. Detail of painting by Franz Krüger (1837). Many famous contemporaries, including the actress Stich-Crelinger and her daughters and the opera singer Mantius, are shown.

years. The *Morgenblatt* and other literary ventures by Cotta provided writers of lyric verse and novellas with an outlet for their talents, and above all a means of supplementing their incomes. Brockhaus, whose 15-volume *Conversationslexikon* was continually updated over the century (and beyond), was continually looking for contributors, while his much-imitated almanacs, such as *Urania*, marketed German classics which might otherwise never have been published in their authors' lifetimes. They include Droste's *Die Judenbuche* (1842) and Grillparzer's *Der arme Spielmann*, published in Budapest in 1848. Campe was something of a unique figure in the German literary scene between the revolutions of 1830 and 1848. Not only was he prepared to take commercial and political risks in publishing the work of dissidents, such as the Young Germans and Heine—though censorship in Hamburg was somewhat more lenient than in most German states—he was also ingenious in designing his distribution system to evade police vigilance in the Confederation. (see chapter 8).

Civil servants and educated middle classes employed by the state

The career of a public official was attractive to the educated middle class on two main grounds. The first was the lack of alternative; the second, in states such as Prussia, Hanover, Bavaria, Baden, or Württemberg, was the association of officialdom in the Napoleonic age and its aftermath with the modernization of society and the state. The reality, however, did not always match the image, notably in Austria. Franz Grillparzer's mother had been left a widow with four sons to educate, when Franz, the eldest, was only eighteen. Yet when he entered the imperial state service as a clerk in 1811, having graduated in law at the University of Vienna, Grillparzer initially received no pay at all. In his *Autobiography* (written in 1853), he described his efforts to secure a patron in the court aristocracy, to help him to secure a permanent position, and later promotion. The manner in which even the emperor could become personally involved in a minor official's career brings home the extraordinary paternalism of the whole organization. Henry Simon (1805-60), a Jewish lawyer from Breslau, Silesia, in the southeast of the German Confederation, joined the Prussian civil service as a young graduate. If he wanted a holiday (no one automatically received holidays in those days), he had to submit a personal request to the king, Friedrich Wilhelm III, who would grant or refuse it in a handwritten letter. Probably the most celebrated Prussian writer-civil servant was the Romantic author, Hoffmann, poet, conductor, opera composer, literary and music theorist, and graphic artist. He had trained as a lawyer in his native Königsberg, entered the Prussian service, and was dismissed in 1806; he returned reluctantly for economic reasons after the war. It was ironic that he, Romantic artist par excellence and master of irony, should have been put to work on drafting the Karlsbad Decrees of 1819, which were specifically designed to shackle the creative writer. Perhaps it was the grotesqueness of his personal situation in those last years of his life that inspired him to write his most original work, the fragmentary *Views on Life by the Tomcat Murr* (1820-2), a postmodernist novel written in premodern times, and unfinished when he died.

Many writers were either themselves or were the sons of those who in Britain or the United States would have been, by virtue of their training and employment, members of the independent professional classes, but who in Germany were counted as state officials. These included many lawyers, such as the district court judges Karl Immermann, author of influential novels on early industrialization and the destruction of the peasant culture,[6] and Theodor Storm (1817-88), the poet and short story writer. Not only grammar school teachers but also university professors were public servants in Germany (and still are); in the period between the war and the 1848 Revolution, many of them were prominent in the national movement. One of the most popular, both as a poet and as a person, was Ludwig Uhland (1787-1862), a professor at the university of Tübingen. He actually took the initiative himself to resign his post in the Württemberg civil service when he was refused leave to attend the local parliament to which he had been elected. Another such group who in Germany were beholden to the state were Protestant clergymen. Clergy in Germany were paid by the state, and the state exercised control (shared in some cases by landowners) over appointments to office in the Protestant churches. When the state sought to extend this control to Catholic clergy, the result was a series of celebrated clashes between church and state which were a feature of the middle decades of the century. The importance of the Protestant clergyman as a cultural institution has long been recognized by literary historians—so many great names in German literature were, in the old-fashioned phrase, "sons of the manse." In the Romantic era, Friedrich Schleiermacher, theologian, philosopher, charismatic preacher, and father of hermeneutics, was a Lutheran pastor; so too in the Biedermeier era were Gotthelf and Eduard Mörike. Many of the radical poets and writers of the *Vormärz* had begun their studies as students of theology, because this was the only way they could afford to attend university. They included the philosopher of materialism, Bruno Bauer (1809-82), who became a lecturer in theology at both Bonn and Berlin universities but had his license to teach revoked on account of his radical Bible criticism. Another was the art historian and 1848 revolutionary, Gottfried Kinkel (1815-82), whose spectacular escape, with the aid of his musician and novelist wife Johanna (1810-59), from his Prussian prison for his part in the revolution so impressed contemporaries.

On account of clerical celibacy in the Roman Catholic church, there was no such equivalent on the Catholic side, but many priests exercised a formative if often forgotten influence on the lives and minds of their fellow countrymen, just as their Protestant colleagues did, by identifying clever boys of poor back-

---

[6] *Die Epigonen* (1836) and *Der Oberhof*, part of his last work, *Münchhausen* (1838-9).

ground and using their contacts to send them to grammar school. In fact, a Protestant, Friedrich Rückert (1788–1866), the Orientalist, master of German metrics, and author of the text of Gustav Mahler's *Kindertotenlieder*, attributed his knowledge of metrics to the local Catholic priest. Among the most influential Catholic priests of the century were the charismatic father of modern pastoral theology, Michael Sailer (1751–1832), translator of Thomas à Kempis and friend and mentor of many Romantics, and Christoph Schmid (1768–1854), the century's most successful children's author. Schmid, a peasant's son from Bavaria, was ennobled in 1837 for his efforts; his stories, which reached sales of a million copies over the century and had numerous English translations in the United States and Britain, remained the staple diet of German Catholic children until the Nazi era.

The Jewish rabbi was no less important a mediator of learning and culture to his community, as so many late eighteenth- and nineteenth-century autobiographies attest. Non-Jewish authors wrote about him: thus Gutzkow rewrote his short story *Der Sadduzäer von Amsterdam* (1843) as a tragedy *Uriel Acosta* (1846). Jewish writers on the subject include Heine, whose impassioned protest against Christian intolerance, *Der Rabbi von Bacherach* (1840), took its author more years to complete than almost any other of his works. A few years earlier, in 1837, Berthold Auerbach, a Jewish peddler's son who had wanted to be a rabbi, but was barred on account of his political activities, published his eponymous novel about Spinoza. A much more influential political activist descended from a long line of learned rabbis had, however, no interest in such a career. This was Karl Marx. But it would be wrong to overlook the influence of rabbinical learning and orthodox Jewish altruism as an indirect yet important influence on the humanist ethic informing Marx's political philosophy.

To the post-Romantic generation, born during or just after the Napoleonic wars, and which included the Biedermeier and realist writers, such as Stifter, Mörike, Gotthelf, Gottfried Keller (1819–90), Storm, and Fontane, it was both economically necessary and socially desirable to have a "bourgeois" profession to support oneself. The literary market was not sufficiently developed before the last third of the nineteenth century to provide for the professional writer. Successful writers, such as Heine, or more accurately (since Heine had his rich uncle Salomon), Karl Gutzkow, are the exception. But to have a bourgeois profession was also a sort of guarantee of worth. Keller found this to be the case, after he had unsuccessfully tried his hand as a freelance artist and writer and finally settled down in his native Zurich to combine the post of secretary to the city council with his prose fiction and lyric poetry.

Many of Germany's freelance middle-class intelligentsia were members of this social group, as it were, against their own will: either they were not acceptable to the authorities as political subversives or they did not succeed in getting inside what the Young German poet Heinrich Laube described with reference to the late 1820s as the "fence surrounding jobs in the civil service." According to Laube's fellow Young German, Gutzkow, 97 of every 100 university students hoped to find a safe haven as a civil servant or clergyman. Because Theodor Fontane's pharmacist father was an inveterate gambler and had to sell his business in Fontane's native Neuruppin and again in Swinemünde (the scene of Fontane's most famous novel, *Effi Briest*), the fourteen-year-old was not sent to grammar school but to a trades school. This effectively excluded the young Theodor from the *Abitur* or high school-leaving examination and university. In 1834 in Prussia the *Abitur* became the qualifying examination to enter the middle ranks of the civil service. This remained a lifelong source of grievance to Fontane, who at sixteen reluctantly followed in his father's footsteps, but now without much hope of ever owning his own pharmacy.

Yet in mid-century Berlin, failure to enter the professions or civil service did not mean social exclusion, unlike in later decades, where work became more professionalized and urban society so much more compartmentalized. Whereas Vienna was traditionally notorious for its social exclusivity, both toward strangers and within its own different social strata, early and mid-century Berlin offered many opportunities for contacts between men of different rank, wealth, and education. In the early part of the century, it was the Jewish salons, notably that of Rahel Levin (1771–1833), which afforded the best chance for the different strata to mix. Here a person of middle-class background could meet a scion of the Prussian royal house, the composer and officer, prince Louis Ferdinand (1772–1806),[7] or the diplomat and minister, Wilhelm von Humboldt. Rahel herself, who was Jewish, middle-aged, and, even her best friends would agree, neither beautiful nor pretty, ended up married to the Prussian diplomat Karl August Varnhagen von Ense (1785–1858), who remained fascinated with his intelligent wife. In mid-century the literary clubs played a somewhat similar role to the salons. Thus when Fontane was a penurious apothecary's apprentice, he experienced no difficulty in being admitted to membership of the club known as the *Tunnel over the River Spree*. Here he made contacts with members of the aristocracy and the university-educated elite. These included his later lifelong friend, the Prussian Junker lieutenant Bernhard von Lepel (1818–85), and the Prussian civil servant,

---

[7] Fontane offers a vivid fictional portrait of this diverse society in his novella *Schach von Wuthenow* of 1883.

Wilhelm von Merckel (1803-61), who got him a job to enable him to marry, acting subsequently as a kind of protector of the young couple. The group met weekly, and soon he was on good terms with the painter, Adolph (later von) Menzel (1815-1905), and with a number of members who were to become famous academics; Frank Kugler (1808-58), professor of art; and Max Müller (1823-1900), later professor of Sanskrit at Oxford University. Relatively few writers of this period had medical connections. Georg Büchner, himself a doctor's son and a medical student about to graduate when he died, caricatured the army doctor mercilessly in his tragedy of the "little man," *Woyzeck*, written in the year before his death. It was not until very much later in the century, not least thanks to much improved training, that the medical profession belatedly acquired a similar status among professional men to that traditionally afforded the law or the church.

On the margins of the educated middle class were those who, as it were, served their time as tutors to the better-off, like the poet Friedrich Hölderlin (1770-1843) from Swabia or the novelist, storyteller, and weaver's son, Adalbert Stifter from south Bohemia. Stifter, with the help of his aristocratic employer, managed to get into the Austrian schools service, but Hölderlin, like so many more, never succeeded in establishing himself in permanent employment.

Lower middle classes (*Kleinbürgertum*)

In the largely agrarian landscape of Metternich's Germany, where some 70 percent of the population derived their living predominantly from the land and lived in communities of less than 2,000 (in Austria over 80 percent), by far the largest component of the middle ranks of society were the *Kleinbürger*, craftsmen and small traders, petty officials, primary school teachers. These men felt themselves as middle class, regarded themselves as the backbone of society. They believed in self-education yet saw themselves in the crisis years between 1816 and the 1840s cast by forces outside their control into a marginal, if not actually proletarian, existence. One of the main sources of poverty in the *Vormärz* was the inability of so many small craftsmen to follow the time-honored path to status in the local community and a modest substance via apprenticeship and journeyman to master of one's own business. The comedies of the Viennese singer, actor, and brilliant playwright, Johann Nestroy, such as *Der Talisman* (1840) or *Einen Jux will er sich machen* (1842), provide a comic version of this process. In the face of competition and falling prices for their goods, the guilds of master craftsmen, in those states, such as Austria or Saxony, which had not introduced liberal trading laws, closed rank in self-protection. The masses of aspirants, like the former barber's apprentice

Titus Feuerfuchs in *Der Talisman*, seemed to be condemned to a perpetual life on the road. They were often forced to do menial work just for *a' Brot*, merely to feed themselves, as Titus says to the goose-girl Salome, who is the lowest on the social ladder of the village hierarchy. Protracted periods as a journeyman without real promise of a future inevitably politicized social groups who had traditionally epitomized the conservative element in society. The early socialist theorist and tailor's apprentice, Wilhelm Weitling (1808–71), the typesetter Stephan Born (born Buttermilch) (1824–98), who proved to have such brilliant organization talents in the 1848 Revolution, and the turner's apprentice and later long-time leader of the Social Democratic party in the Second Empire, August Bebel (1840–1913), were all at one time journeymen. Bebel left an evocative account of his life on the road in mid-century Germany in his vivid memoirs, *Aus meinem Leben*, published over half a century later.

The peasants

At the beginning of the nineteenth century, the German peasantry were a privileged estate in very few regions of Germany. The peasant had been the idealized object of admiration among Enlightenment writers such as the Göttingen scientist and poet Albrecht von Haller (1708–77), as depicted in his epic poem, *Die Alpen* (1732), or Salomon von Gessner (1730–88) in his extraordinarily successful idylls (1756), which were translated into twenty languages. In Frisia in northwest Germany, there was a strong tradition of independent yeoman farmers, while in the Austrian Tyrol, peasants actually sat in the local assemblies. But in most of Germany, the lot of the German peasant in the eighteenth and early nineteenth centuries was anything but enviable. He and his family were bound to the soil in the manorial lands east of the Elbe and in parts of the Austrian empire: he might not marry without his lord's permission, and he and his family owed his master onerous labor services. In some parts of western Germany, the obligations in form of taxes and labor dues might be even more onerous because the peasant was literally the servant of more than one master. In the late eighteenth century, in the literary movement of protest known as Storm and Stress (*Sturm und Drang*), writers such as Johann Heinrich Voß turned their attention to the oppressors of the peasantry. This was the age in which radical changes in the legal and socioeconomic status of Germany's peasants were initiated as part of the major reforming program of the princes and their officials; their main motive was greater economic efficiency. The process proceeded at a different pace in the different regions of Germany. Prussia led the way in the first decade of the century, while Austria, initially an innovator, at least on crown lands, failed to abolish the *robot* or forced labor services until the revolution of 1848; in Hanover, Saxony, and Württemberg agrarian reform had occurred in the 1830s. Overall, the effect was to benefit the more prosperous peasants. Those who lost out swelled the ranks of the new "fourth class." For it was among this disparate social group that the massive population increase was concentrated, that single most important feature of German society between 1815 and 1848.

It is understandable, given the lack of mobility in rural life before Germany became covered with a network of roads and railways in the twentieth century, that we find very few writers of peasant origin. The period between 1815 and 1848 was notable for the popularity of literature *about* peasants, but neither then nor, apart from a few exceptions, later did there exist a literature *by* peasants. The *Dorfdichtung* or village tale, whose most successful authors were Auerbach and Gotthelf, was an immensely popular genre in many parts of Germany. These tales contained many realist elements depicting the hardship and power struggles facing peasants and landless laborers. But its utopian message, designed to win popular support for state help for the conservative elements of society, the very qualities which made this type of literature popular among its middle-class readers, was at odds with the deep structural crisis which was gripping rural life in so many parts of Germany in the 1830s and 1840s. It was not until later in the century, that an author of impeccable peasant origin made a name and a highly successful career for himself. This was Peter Rosegger (1843–1918), born in the Styrian mountains of southeastern Austria, whose early tales in stylized dialect contained vivid portraits of the grim side as well as the attractions of the small peasant world from which he came.

The "fourth class"

The notion of what contemporaries in the years 1815–48 called the "fourth estate" derives, by analogy, from the French term for those members of society, *le tiers état*, the third estate, 'below' the aristocracy and the upper clergy. This third estate, roughly corresponding in the preclass society eighteenth-century France to what we now broadly refer to as the middle class, became the main proponents of the radical rethinking about society associated with the French Revolution of 1789. In early and mid-nineteenth-century Germany, it was from the ranks of the fourth estate that property owners and the authorities feared that the revolution would erupt. The fourth class was particularly diverse, because the massive population increases at the lower end of society, the rise in food prices and the depression, through oversupply of workers, of real wages, forced large numbers of former members of the lower middle urban and rural classes into pauperism and, in some cases, criminality. It is striking that writers as markedly different as the aristocrat Droste (in *Die Judenbuche*) and the communist Marx should each write about that clear indicator of social distress, wood theft.

In the first chapter of *The German Revolution of 1848–1849*, Wolfram Siemann identifies as belonging to the "fourth class" some six groups: un- or underemployed journeymen; the miners; the wage earners and freelancers, factory workers, day laborers, and servants. Those *Vormärz journeymen* who by the 1830s and 1840s could have little hope of joining the ranks of master craftsmen were a substantial and growing section of society. In the 1830s and 1840s many spent overlong periods "on the road" for want of secure employment at home. Even in normal times, journeymen had traditionally covered, on foot, extraordinary distances across Europe. Now, in the *Vormärz*, they became highly politicized, not just as individuals but as a social group, through their contacts with others in the journeymen's hostels where they spent the night, and, more particularly with militants in Switzerland and in France, in Paris and in the Rhone valley, notably in or around the textile city of Lyons. Back at home, small craftsmen, often working on their own for a shrinking or inadequate local market, were depressed into this class. They were resentful at what they saw as the lack of protection given them by the state and were particularly angry at the role of some states, notably Prussia, as modernizer. They regarded as unfair competition those new measures and trade ordinances which removed restraints on trading and undermined the power and control of the guilds.

The *miners*, by contrast, retained their strong corporate identity and tradition of self-help in the crisis years of Metternich's age, and did not suffer, either economically or in terms of loss of status, as much as the other groups. Subsequently, as coal mining became one of Germany's largest and a highly mechanized industry, the social composition of the group altered. But they still retained their characteristically strong corporate identity. This was made very evident, for example, in the history of the major strikes which hit the industry during the reign of Kaiser Wilhelm II (1888–1918) and which were put down with great ruthlessness.

The *freelancers and wage earners* comprised a group which has been estimated to have increased between 1800 and mid century by some 50 percent from its basis of about one million in 1800. These people were major victims of economic and social dislocation, whereas the *factory workers*, which in the 1840s constituted as yet only a small percentage of workers, tended to be drawn from the more skilled workers.

The *day laborers* could be employed (or left without sustenance) by a wide variety of employers; their womenfolk played a significant role in keeping the family going, often as servants, such as wet nurses, washerwomen, or in laying out the dead. Wilhelm Raabe (1831–1910) drew a portrait of many of these very poor in his first and most successful novel, *Die Chronik der Sperlingsgasse* (1856). The literature of the Metternich age is full of portraits of *servants*, though they are portrayed very largely within the tradition of the comic stage servant such as Figaro in the operas of Mozart and Rossini. However, in a little-known story of 1843, Otto Ludwig's (1813–65) *Die Emanzipation der Domestiken*, the author associates the emancipation of that diverse social group with the movement to emancipate, as the butler puts it, "the Jew, the negro and even the Irish," and thus prophetically anticipates the participation of servants in the German revolution only five years later.

The fourth class became the stuff of literature in the *Vormärz* era, but attention tended to be focused mainly on one category, the journeymen, and on representatives of two other groups, the freelancers and the factory workers, who were seen as the victims of the destruction of the craftsman class. Perhaps the best-known and certainly aesthetically one of the finest examples of this process is Heine's inflammatory poem *Die schlesischen Weber* (1844) on the Silesian weavers, once-proud craft workers. Rural poverty was much treated by bourgeois writers, such as Heinrich Zschokke (1771–1848), a German living in Switzerland, as in his novel, *Die Branntweinpest* (1817), on alcoholism born of destitution. In *Käthi die Großmutter* (1847), the Swiss parson Jeremias Gotthelf wrote a novel of a grandmother in a poverty-stricken area of rural Switzerland who starves herself so that her grandchild can survive to grow up. Generally, however, the overly didactic and even idealizing tendency of such literature allows the reader to overlook the harshness and scale of grim reality. Ernst Willkomm drew attention to the plight of early factory workers in his much-publicized novel *Die Sclaven* (1845). Yet in the *Vormärz*, when Willkomm and Aston were writing, factory workers constituted only a small proportion of manual workers (an estimated 4 percent in Prussia), and were generally more skilled and probably better paid than most. Louise Otto was surely much closer to contemporary reality when she singled out for portrayal in her poetry and in the articles of her (later banned) *Frauen-Zeitung* of 1849–52 the pieceworkers, such as the lacemakers of the Erzgebirge on the borders between Saxony and Bohemia, and the Silesian weavers.

Of all German writers who in mid-century enjoyed reputation and economic success, the dramatist Friedrich Hebbel, married to a celebrated actress at the leading Viennese theater, the *Burgtheater*, had the most humble social origins.

His mother was a washerwoman in Holstein in northern Germany; he himself lived off the earnings of his mistress, a seamstress, who bore him two sons. Hebbel made truly Herculean efforts to get himself a university education and succeeded, but the years of struggle left their mark on the obsessiveness of nearly all the main characters of his dramas, including his heroines, Judith in his eponymous tragedy of 1840, Mariamne (in *Herodes und Mariamne* (1849), and the queen in *Gyges und sein Ring* (1854).

Pauperism, and the fear that the sheer volume of the numbers of the destitute in the population would bring about the destruction of civil society, haunted society up to the time of the 1848 Revolution. In 1835 the Bavarian social philosopher Franz von Baader (1765–1841) coined the term "proletariat" to describe a new type of poor, the product of social dislocation brought about by the very liberal reforms, such as the emancipation of the serfs, designed to consolidate society, and accelerated by the long years of war and the disastrous harvests and epidemics in its wake. In the years in which Karl Marx was elaborating the principles of the class society and the new order, which was brilliantly glossed by Heine in the first section of his *Germany: A Winter's Tale* (1844), the Rhenish rolling mill owner and philanthropist Friedrich Harkort (1798–1873) provided a definition of contemporaries' understanding of the new phenomenon. The proletariat, he said, were those without a proper home, proper parents, without school or anything they could call their own.

It was the educated and not the victims who drew society's attention to the implications of what was happening in Germany in the decades between the revolutions of 1830 and 1848. Many of those who did so were journalists, many of them would-be poets who could not make a living by their literary writings. Indeed, the journalist became a popular fictional character in the 1840s. One of the most entertaining is Ultra, the journalist-hero of the revolution in the fictitious village of Krähwinkel in Nestroy's farce *Freiheit in Krähwinkel* (1848).[8] The journalist's name reflects the dislike and suspicion of journalists by the authorities: it is Ultra (=extreme). The years immediately preceding March 1848 had seen prodigious expansion and diversification in the German media. Similar in this respect to the pamphleteering in the years preceding the outbreak of revolution in France in 1789, pamphlets became a favorite form of agitation in Germany in the 1840s. In 1841, an unlikely candidate joined the pamphleteers' ranks. Bettine von Arnim, a grandmother and widowed for a decade, wrote a substantial polemical book challenging the king of Prussia himself over social policy. In her spirited *Dies Buch gehört dem König* (This Book Is

---

[8] Krähwinkel is, of course, the 'village' of Vienna, capital of the Habsburg Empire.

for the King to Read), she castigated the authorities for tolerating the kind of human wretchedness she encountered among the poor immigrants to Berlin, and which the journalist Ernst Dronke (1822–91) was to analyze more systematically and with specific reference to the appalling housing in his *Berlin* (1845). Heine, von Arnim, and Dronke were joined by numerous political poets who depicted the lot of workers, both men and women, freelancers, factory hands, laborers in the Rhenish and Moselle hillside vineyards, and stokers on the Rhenish steamships,[9] all as victims of "the system." Understandably, few of those who suffered wrote about it. Perhaps the nearest we can get to an authentic portrait of proletarian misery from mid-century is in Karl Gutzkow's wonderfully vivid memoir of childhood in a one-roomed flat in Berlin, *Aus der Knabenzeit* (1852). Yet Gutzkow's father, an employee in the Prussian royal stables, would not normally be regarded as a proletarian. It is only with the socialist movement and more particularly around 1900, with the direct encouragement of socialist publishing organs, that working men and women began to write or to record their memories and so gradually to produce a body of literature of a representative nature. Unlike Gutzkow's memoir, political poetry and related forms of protest literature in the 1840s were written primarily to promote radical political and social change at a time when this carried serious risk to the author, publisher, and seller of the work. Small wonder that when in March 1848 the revolution finally broke out in Germany, it won the immediate support of the writers, along with politicized officials, academics, students, and artisans.

---

[9] The most famous is Freiligrath's poem, 'Von unten auf!,' spoken by the stoker who prophesies the revolution, in the collection *Ça ira* of 1846.

Chapter 5
The German Revolution of 1848–9

Few periods of Germany's history exemplify more cogently the historicist dictum of Leopold von Ranke (1795–1866) that *jede Epoche ist unmittelbar zu Gott* (every age is to be understood on its own terms)—that is, any attempt at an objective portrait of an epoch is invariably colored by the hopes and fears of those who write about it. Not only the judgment on the achievements and failures of the revolution of 1848–9 but even the emphasis on the salient issues has differed widely according to the perspective of the writer's own time. The stimulus given by historians of the German Democratic Republic to the study of the social and economic history of the revolution, not least at the local level, has been fruitful. Although their emphasis on these aspects led to more exaggerated claims for the influence of Communist groups on events than they actually possessed, their work assisted western historians to see the period of the revolution more precisely in the context of the time. In most recent years, valuable work has been done on the topic by German and international scholars. The thrust of that work has been to emphasize the comparative and European context of what was happening in Germany. Detailed studies of the regions and of particular social groups have, for all their individuality and diversity, served to underline common features in the German and European experience. At the same time historians have broken new ground in emphasizing the degree to which the middle ranks of German society had been politicized before the revolution through membership in an extraordinarily widespread and diverse network of cultural, athletic, economic, and religious associations, which existed despite the authorities' repression of all forms of overtly political activity.

The revolution of 1848–9 was one of the most important events of Germany's nineteenth-century history, as much for what it failed to achieve as for what it did actually achieve. It brought some important reforms, such as the liberation of the Austrian peasantry from forced labor. It also gave Germans the experience of parliamentary government. But only in a few German states did the constitutional government of the summer of 1848 outlast the counter-revolutions of the autumn. More importantly, it did not bring Germans the national unity they now so greatly desired.

Origins of the Revolution

While the 1846 revolt in Galicia in the northeast territory of the Austrian Empire and widespread, violent expressions of social unrest in Germany in 1847, including bread riots, had provided a curtain-raiser for the European revolutions of 1848, the actual outbreak of revolution in Germany in March 1848 was activated by events in Paris in the last week of February. The news of the forcible abdication of the "bourgeois king," Louis Philippe, in Paris on 24 February reached the southwestern state of Baden by courier on the evening of Saturday 26 February. It was an actor who brought the news to an inn in Karlsruhe, capital of Baden on the southwest border with France. That "the mother of revolutions" had once again shown Europeans the lead, had an electrifying effect on the already widely politicized middle ranks of society. The news spread rapidly in the following days across Germany. It sent Karl Marx and Friedrich Engels hurrying back across the German border from exile in London. The publication of their *Communist Manifesto*, in London in late February, coincided with the outbreak of the European revolution of 1848. Marx, in particular, drew on his direct observation of the German revolutions for years to come. The causes of the German revolution, or, to be more accurate, given its diverse theaters, of the German revolutions, can be best described as a coincidence of both short- and long-term socioeconomic problems, by middle-class anger at their continued exclusion from political influence and by the fiscal problems experienced with particular acuteness by Austria and Prussia in the 1840s. It was, for example, Prussia's need for greatly increased revenue to fund Prussia's military defense and the integration of her scattered territories by way of the East-West railway which finally persuaded a very reluctant king, Friedrich Wilhelm IV, to concede in 1847 the summoning of a United Diet of the eight provincial assemblies. The Diet brought together liberals from every part of Prussia; their conversations and discussions both inside and outside the chamber acted as an equally powerful stimulus to raising political expectations. Indeed, the very fact that the Diet had taken place at all reinforced in the public's mind Prussia's possibly superior credentials over Austria as a leader of Germany's liberal and national aspirations. In Austria, the fiscal and political problems were far more acute, since a massive injection of finance was needed merely to keep Metternich's system of control in place. By the 1840s Metternich faced the dilemma that there was little likelihood of such supplies being conceded without the kind of concessions which must undermine his entire system. However, in March 1848 it was not economic and social issues, but political grievances which were uppermost in the minds of those who became the Revolution's leaders.

Since the abortive revolution of 1830, German governments had increasingly lost their popular legitimacy. They were not, with significant exceptions, guilty of widespread, flagrant abuse of power. The Confederation represented a considerable advance on the irresponsible government of many eighteenth-century German princes. Moreover, the paternalism of state governments in the Restoration era offered material advantages for the population which they had broadly appreciated. A number of German governments were often more aware of the problems of rural pauperization and of early industrialization than any other agency. However they had not demonstrated their capacity to deal with them, and their continued refusal to concede a free press was in part motivated by the attention which would be drawn to their mismanagement of, or incapacity to deal with, widespread social misery. True, the scale of socioeconomic distress caused by the massive population increases since 1815 and the dislocations caused by long-term structural change would have taxed the most enlightened rulers. The sufferings of those living on the margins of society worsened radically in the mid-1840s. Literary treatment of the Silesian weavers' revolt of 1844, beginning with Heine's great poem of the same year, has given it exemplary status. Yet it was but one instance in a whole catalogue of human wretchedness. But the long-established tradition of state paternalism in Germany which so long acted to pacify the populace also raised people's expectations of their rulers' capacity (and duty) to care for them. In the period known now as the *Vormärz* between 1830 and March 1848, the feeling grew that governments had lost touch with the governed; this sense was an important cause of popular disturbance in 1848. Moreover, from about 1840 onward governments' evident own loss of confidence in their capacity to deal with the problems of German society became a powerful impetus to revolt.

The sense of social exclusion was a major force of discontent for those—notably the artisan class—who had lost, or felt they had lost, their economic basis of life and their status in society. It was they who would be the revolution's principal victims. An occupational analysis of those killed in the Viennese and Berlin revolutions of March 1848, and in the resistance to the counter-revolution in October 1848, shows the vast majority to have come from the ranks of the artisan class, including journeymen and apprentices. For the educated classes on the eve of the revolution, their sense of grievance at being marked out from their western neighbors in Britain, France, and the Low Countries by their rulers' refusal to acknowledge in any way their political maturity, acted as a potent recruiting agent for protest. Because of the flagrant disregard of human rights by the rulers during the *Vormärz*, trial by jury, along with freedom of the press and rights of assembly, figured prominently in the so-called "March demands." The articulation of these brought people together in the opening weeks of the revolution and created the temporary solidarity of the very diverse groups which went to make up the "revolutionary classes." For both the officials and the intellectuals, and other groups also, such as the growing entrepreneurial class, the desire for political unity was a further contributory cause. It was fed by a variety of streams, romantic-nostalgic, liberal-rationalist, practical-commercial.

A large proportion of state officials, who would later play an active part in the parliaments and assemblies of the revolutionary year, were drawn from the intelligentsia and property-owning classes. A significant number of these officials had been disciplined or even imprisoned for political activities. For German princes did not hesitate to impose prison sentences on senior figures. The case of the Göttingen Seven had attracted widespread publicity in 1837. Those dismissed for courageously challenging the king of Hanover's right to set aside the constitution had included not just the Grimm brothers, but also Friedrich Dahlmann (1785–1860), a leading historian and later prominent advocate of the unification of Germany under Prussia, rather than Austria, at the Frankfurt Parliament. Even the author of the 1831 constitution of Hesse-Kassel, Sylvester Jordan (1792–1861), had received a six-year prison sentence eight years later for alleged political activity; in Hesse-Darmstadt, Heinrich von Gagern had been dismissed from his post in the ministry in 1833 for his liberal sympathies. The list of public officials driven from office in the *Vormärz* was a long one, and it included a large number of professors and lecturers in the new university subject of *Germanistik*, the study of the mother tongue. One of these was a professor of German at Breslau University, Heinrich Hoffmann von Fallersleben (1798–1874), the author of the *Deutschlandlied*, which in due course would become the German national anthem; another was Gustav Freytag (1816–95), who wrote Germany's best-selling nineteenth-century novel, *Soll und Haben* (1855). By their punitive actions the authorities forged an involuntary link between the rights of the citizen and the national cause. German civil servants had more contact with and understanding of contemporary socioeconomic problems than the princes and ministers. However, they lacked a channel of protest, and it was their sense of frustration at their inability to rectify justice which brought so many of their numbers to join the revolution.

The social and economic grievances of the populace had a major influence on the course of the revolution but were not the immediate cause of the outbreak. The middle years of the decade, notably 1845 and 1846, had been famine years, with bread riots in almost every German state, but the summer of 1847 brought a bumper harvest and with it new problems: a collapse in prices for peasant producers. These producers helped to trigger the agrarian uprisings in 1847 and again in February 1848; these continued sporadically and in a variety of different regions across the country for the next thirteen months to May 1849. Many of the rural disturbances took place alongside rather than within the general revolutionary movement. They formed part of the age-old popular revolt against oppression, residual feudal dues, the burden of debt on the peasantry. It was a feature of 1848 that, when legislation by governments or assemblies rectified immediate grievances, the peasantry and their spokesmen tended to lose interest in the revolution. Nor was proletarianization as such a direct cause of revolt. But the influence of the social question on the middle ranks of society, and their fear of what might lie ahead, should not be underestimated as an impulse toward political radicalization. Ideology was in fact a direct and powerful influence on events, helping to channel a widespread sense of grievance into direct and specific demands on the rulers, though by no means all in the direction of modernization. In his mock heroic epic, *Deutschland: Ein Wintermärchen* (1844), which tells of a journey through Germany on the eve of the revolution, Heine plotted the relationship between ideology and revolutionary violence. He does so in the persona of the poet and his companion, a lictor, who walks behind him with a cudgel to smash the objects of the poet's wrath. Robespierre (1758–94), Heine had provocatively written almost a decade earlier in *Zur Geschichte der Religion und Philosophie in Deutschland* (1834), had not in fact been the real source of revolutionary terror in the French Revolution. That had been the man who inspired it all: Jean Jacques Rousseau (1712–78). In the mid-1840s Heine was friendly with Marx and wrote his epic during his own brief Communist phase. But the fear of proletarianization was activating the artisan class, not any anxiety about the power of the proletariat. No worker, in fact, attended the secret Communist meetings organized by Friedrich Engels in the textile town of Elberfeld where his father had his factory. Supporters came from the lower end of the middle class or *Mittelstand*. It was the artisans who had been the main victims of the structural crises of mid-century, of overpopulation and the economic disasters of the most recent past. In general, then, the revolution or revolutions of 1848–9 were less the work of those forced to endure severe deprivation by famine and pauperization than of two other broadly based groups: on the one hand those whose livelihoods and status in the community were threatened by cyclical crisis, and, on the other, those who observed both the powerful moral issue of individual liberty and the deep structural problems of the age, and strove to find remedies for both.

The European context

The German Confederation, set up in June 1815 at Vienna, was itself the product of the intervention of the European powers in German affairs, and it should not therefore surprise us not just that the 1848 Revolution was keenly observed in the capitals of the other European states, but that its outbreak and course in Germany were dependent on factors operating in other parts of Europe. Lenin would in time attribute a key importance to Germany in the process of his anticipated world revolution, and even in 1848, the geographical location of Germany in central Europe gave international significance to events there during the revolutionary year of 1848-9. However, the fact that within a short space of time, most European rulers[1] were preoccupied with revolt at home, prevented their rulers from coming to the aid of the German princes. Not only the major players, Austria and Prussia, but all the German rulers, in Saxony and Bavaria, Hanover, Württemberg, and the two Hesses, and in the smaller states too, were thoroughly aware of this. The revolutionary leaders in Germany retained a real or apparent freedom of movement as long as the great powers most nearly concerned with events in Germany were prevented, for domestic political reasons, from intervening. This period ran from March until the late autumn of 1848. Furthermore, events in France stimulated a genuine fear of French invasion among many German rulers and made them, at least initially, more ready to conciliate popular opinion. After all, it was only eight years since the 1840 war scare over French ambitions to seize the Rhine had galvanized national opinion right across the social spectrum in Germany.

Moreover, the princes were more influenced by historical analogies than their subjects. Having based their policies of repression since 1815, or, more particularly since the Karlsbad Decrees of 1819, on the expectation of imminent revolution, the events of the spring of 1848 inevitably aroused memories of the 1789 French Revolution and its consequences for the monarchic order. Alexis de Tocqueville's (1805-59) dictum, that the German rulers yielded at the sight of, rather than under the onslaught of, the revolutionaries, is to be understood in this context. The princes had a clear understanding that they could preserve their position only as long as the European powers were in a position to support the status quo. Yet in 1847-8 the whole continental system set up under the Vienna Treaties of 1815 came under attack, a system which gave the self-appointed European Congress of powers the right to intervene in the internal affairs of states in order to preserve the stability of the whole. The immediate concern of most was to buy

---

[1] Only England, the Low Countries, and Scandinavia (apart from Denmark) escaped revolution.

time, by concessions. In Prussia a number of the king's advisers even saw the concessions as a way to buttress Prussia's authority in Germany, and also as serving to drive a wedge between the moderates and the radicals. This is precisely what happened. But it would be incorrect to present the rulers of Germany's thirty-nine states, from the kings and grand dukes to the city fathers of states such as Hamburg or Frankfurt am Main, as a monolithic body in 1848. A (small) number of them, such as the Duke of Saxe-Coburg-Gotha, brother of Prince Albert of England, favored a greater liberalization of their administration, as the king of Württemberg had wished in the matter of censorship years earlier, but they had not had the capacity or the will to stand up to Metternich's authority in the confederation. Such rulers now proved ready to yield to the wishes of their subjects.

The course of revolution

The "glorious revolution weather," as one eyewitness, Theodor Fontane, described it, brought demonstrators out into the streets in the first weeks of March 1848. These and the following weeks saw the granting and implementation of the "March demands" and the appointment of liberal ministries across Germany. But even before the first revolutionary acts, the *Bundestag*, the only functioning federal institution of Metternich's Germany, attempted to anticipate events by taking the initiative on a number of issues. As early as 8 March, the *Bundestag* accepted the banned colors of liberal Germany as the national colors: black, gold, and red, which since 1949 have constituted Germany's flag. Within the following two weeks, mass petitions, demonstrations often ending in attacks on symbols and institutions of state power, barricades, and street fighting almost throughout Germany forced concessions from the state governments. Vienna, where radical students fought alongside the burghers, took the lead. On 13 March Metternich resigned and fled into exile. So too did the hated police chief, at whose hands Austria's greatest dramatist, Franz Grillparzer, had suffered so long. In Berlin the Prussian king ordered his troops to withdraw and gave a citizen militia responsibility for public order in Berlin; on 20 March Ludwig I of Bavaria abdicated.

The rapidity and ease with which most German princes seemed to capitulate to the demands of demonstrators and petitioners was remarkable, especially to the revolutionaries themselves. Vienna and Berlin apart, relatively little violence occurred on either side. Even in Berlin, where an overprecipitate response by the military on 18 March to petitioners surrounding the royal palace resulted in 303 civilian deaths, among them eleven women, subsequent events gave an almost paternalistic air to the initial stages of the revolution there. The king showed himself almost overly anxious to conciliate, ordered the army to withdraw from the city, and appeared on the streets wearing the black, red, and gold of the revolution. He was actually seen to bare his head at the funeral of the fallen, commemorated one year later in the famous painting of the funeral of the victims by Adolph Menzel, *Die Aufbewahrung der Märzgefallenen*. Much comment was aroused by the public's being given permission to smoke on the streets, and Fontane noted that collection boxes for the wounded and for the relatives of the dead had been placed outside the most potent symbol of Prussian military power, the Arsenal (*Zeughaus*) on the central street

Death of a young student on the barricades in Berlin on 18 March 1848. Engraving of a drawing by J. Kirchhof.

of the capital, *Unter den Linden*. However, despite the citizen militia, the revolutionaries failed, here as elsewhere, to gain control of the key instrument of successful revolutions: the army. To be true, the Prussian army had been ordered to withdraw under its now deeply unpopular commander, Prince Wilhelm, the king's brother (and later German Emperor), but it remained loyal to the king.

A German national parliament

Elections to a national parliament at Frankfurt, where for centuries future Holy Roman Emperors had traditionally come first to be crowned as "King of the Romans," were the work of April and May. The national parliament was to be charged with the task of drafting a national constitution, for a new, united Germany. Parallel to this, and indicative both of the scale of political activity in this extraordinary year, as well as the variety and complexity of its chronology, were the elections to constituent assemblies in the two largest states of Austria and Prussia. The initiative to summon the parliament to Frankfurt came mainly from activists in the south and west, where for nearly a generation state officials, lawyers, teachers, businessmen, and even clergymen had identified themselves with the movement to win constitutional government. As early as 5 March some fifty-one liberals and democrats had met as self-appointed spokesmen of the German nation at Heidelberg on the Rhine to institutionalize the revolution through the convening of a national parliament. They convened as a "Pre-Parliament" in the Frankfurt Paulskirche from 31 March to 3 April to prepare the arrangements for implementing the Frankfurt Parliament.

Historical hindsight makes it easy to exaggerate the clarity of political alignments, to see how the fateful differences between moderates and radicals began to impede progress even in the very first weeks of the revolution. The differences were ideological, psychological, and social in origin; they expressed themselves in different strategies and in day-to-day tactics, but they were fundamentally political in nature. Prior to 1848, those opposing the regime included very disparate elements, from civil servants and professional men to unemployed craftsmen and anarchist students, but they possessed a cohesion simply from being in opposition. The *Vorparlament* at Frankfurt early in April brought a split in the ranks. The energetic young lawyer, Friedrich Hecker (1811–81), and his associate Gustav von Struve (1805–70), son of an official in the Russian service (who, incidentally, owned the apothecary where Fontane was employed in 1842), determined to turn it into a French revolutionary-type convention. Having failed to do so, or even win seats for themselves on the Committee of Fifty, which was set up to oversee the elections to the national parliament, they decided to take direct action.

The Baden rising

One week later, on 12 April, they led an uprising in Baden, declaring Germany a Republic, and were joined by a legion of Germans from Paris, led by the popular poet Georg Herwegh (1817–75) accompanied by his energetic wife, Emma; a host of Polish exiles swelled their numbers. They proved an ill match for federal troops, called in from their garrisons by the Baden government. This was but the first example of the new liberal German ministries relying on the troops of the old Confederation to maintain their authority. The Baden uprising was crushed almost within a week, but not before General Friedrich von Gagern (1794–1848), commanding the troops of the German Confederation, had been killed. He was a brother of the later president of the Frankfurt Parliament and himself the author of a work entitled *On the Need for German Unity and the Means to Achieve It*. The sight of a member of a distinguished liberal family being killed in defense of the now liberal Confederation by what could be seen as a power-hungry splinter group, filled many supporters of Germany's national revolution with foreboding. Yet the exemplary sentences handed out to insurgents, many of whom were imprisoned in the federal fortress of Rastatt, drew radicals' attention across Germany to the dangerous lack of solidarity among German revolutionaries. Moreover, this sorry episode also highlighted a key problem of the revolution, then as later—namely that, despite the concession of the liberal "March ministries" or state governments, no real transfer of power had taken place. What had been granted by the princes under threat, to buy time, could be and was revoked as easily as it was granted. Furthermore, when the central government was set up in June, it, too, was caught between the need to be seen capable of asserting its authority and maintaining public order, and appearing master of developments by promoting the goals of the revolution: it was constantly to find itself having to have recourse to the federal troops.

Popular uprisings

The issue of public order was complicated by the divisive influence of the nationality question, notably in Austria and in the eastern provinces of Prussia. In the early summer months, there occurred a spate of popular uprisings of ethnic minorities within the Confederation, such as the Polish revolt in the Prussian province of Posen in May and in that of the Czechs in Bohemia's capital, Prague, in mid-June. Whereas the radical wing of the German revolutionaries tended to side with the leaders of ethnic revolt, the deputies at the Frankfurt Parliament tended to see these as attacks on the integrity of the Reich. Inevitably this widened the split between those who sought a constitutional monarchy, and the democrats, who demanded a genuine democratization of the institutions of government, including a citizen army, and a republican form of government. Events would prove the latter right, but at no stage did the democrats command anything like a majority, neither in the constituent assemblies nor in the country at large.

The Frankfurt Assembly meets

A further problem for the liberals became evident during the elections to the national parliament which took place on 1 and 8 May. These were based, not on universal manhood suffrage, but varied according to the electoral laws of the various states, many of which used the notion of financial and legal independence as a qualifier, and so effectively excluded large numbers of revolutionaries, such as working men, servants, and students. The use of an out-of-date population census to determine electoral districts in Prussia and Saxony, whose population had increased massively since 1816, led to substantial underrepresentation of the lower orders. In the absence of party political structures, electors tended to return deputies on the basis of their personal qualities and also for their local associations. Thus Heinrich Laube, Young German poet and later director of the Viennese *Burgtheater*, who lived in Leipzig, was returned for the spa of Karlsbad in Bohemia, where he had frequently taken the waters. The Frankfurt Parliament was no gathering of "men of the people." Of those who sat there over the thirteen months from May 1848, 764, or almost 96 percent, had attended grammar school, and as many as 657, or over 80 percent, had received a university education. The fact that there was but a handful of craftsmen but no manual workers is more anomalous to twentieth-century commentators than it seemed to contemporaries. However, about one-fifth of the representatives of the professions and the business world were men of humble social origins who had risen through their own efforts. The high proportion of civil servants at Frankfurt derived in part from the fact that these men had been among the opponents of the prerevolutionary regimes. Most of the deputies were in the prime of life, between thirty-five and fifty, and they included many poets and scholars, among them the immensely popular poet Ludwig Uhland, whose ugliness surprised his lady admirers; the philosophers Arnold Ruge (1802–80) and Frederick Theodor Vischer (1807–87); as well as former and future victims of princely absolutism, the brothers Jacob and Wilhelm Grimm, and the historians, Friedrich Dahlmann, Johann Gustav Droysen (1808–84), and Georg Gottfried Gervinus (1805–71).

The Frankfurt or German National Assembly sat at Frankfurt from May 1848 until June 1849, when its radical rump, which had fled to safety in Stuttgart, was forcibly disbanded by Prussian troops. It opened on 18 May in an atmosphere of intense awareness of the historical moment whose memory, evoked in the autobiographies of the participants and observers over many decades, still manages to communicate the atmosphere of that marvelous day, when the bells rang throughout the city and the black, red, and gold flag of liberal Germany bedecked all public buildings. The members processed to the Paulskirche (Church of St. Paul) on the banks of the river Main for the first session, to a gallery filled with excited witnesses, including a large number of women. "A fine and imposing circular building, the choir supported by pillars, opposite which stands a dais," enthused the thirty-seven-year-old novelist Fanny Lewald (1811–89), "the presidential tribunal stands now where once pulpit and altar stood ... the German flags now flutter where once the image of the Crucified hung."

The first task of the Frankfurt Parliament was to create its own procedures. Only the Baden members had genuine experience of parliamentary session, while the "north German passion for long speeches" (Friedrich Theodor Vischer) and the radicals' bent for turning every item into a question of principle hampered the dispatch of business. The discussion of the basic rights of the German people, the first item on the program, threatened to occupy the members for the next two years, complained one commentator, but under Heinrich von Gagern's efficient presidency, special committees were appointed for various tasks, and the work of the assembly began to proceed systematically, if with excessive deliberation. By June a Regent (*Reichsverweser*) had been elected and he had arrived to take up his duties. The choice was a felicitous one: the Habsburg Archduke Johann of Austria (1782–1859), whose statue stands today at the center of Graz, the capital of his much-loved Styria, was a genuine man of the people. By early August, a provisional central government was in office, composed of men from all parts of the country. Their status, the responsible attitude of parliamentary procedure, the lack of violence at Frankfurt and its firm repression elsewhere, gave the Frankfurt Parliament nationwide authority in these first months. But subsequent events, starting with the problem of Schleswig-Holstein and brought to a head by the ensuing September riots, showed how little real power the parliament actually possessed. It had no army of its own, but was forced to rely on the federal troops of the old regime; it had no treasury. Yet from the perspective of contemporaries—including the princes—both the Frankfurt Parliament and, to a lesser extent, the two assemblies which met at Berlin from May to

December 1848, and at Vienna from June to December, certainly appeared to possess sufficient influence to institutionalize the reforms won in the spring of 1848, the so-called March achievements (*Märzerrungenschaften*).

However, the purpose for which the Frankfurt Parliament had been summoned was a dual one: the creation of a constitution and the unification of Germany. In the view of contemporaries these tasks were inseparable, and it is therefore inappropriate to argue, as some have done, that the liberals should have concentrated on the one or the other. Those who had suffered for their political beliefs and activities under Metternich and those who had merely theorized, were equally aware that the different historical traditions, ranging from the still semifeudal duchies of Mecklenburg to the relatively liberal constitutional state of Baden, would make nonsense of a constitution unless a unified form of state was set up to implement it. Moreover, liberals were painfully aware of how easy it was for foreign princes to intervene in the affairs of the German Confederation, as currently constituted. The deputies hoped to prevent this by creating a unified German state, but they paid insufficient regard either to the vested interests of the European powers in Germany—such as England and Denmark in Schleswig-Holstein, or Russia in the Polish provinces, or to the relationship between their own assembly and the existing institutions of the Confederation, notably the Federal Diet. The Diet was, prior to the Revolution, and again from 1850 to the dissolution of the Confederation in 1867, an assembly of ambassadors from the thirty-nine constituent states. It had been much modified by the events of March and now included many prominent liberals appointed by the March governments, such as the former companion-in-exile of the Italian revolutionary Giuseppe Mazzini (1805–72) and later Baden parliamentary deputy, Karl Mathy (1806–65). The Diet welcomed the deputies to Frankfurt in an address in May, but their discourteous refusal to read it out, and the tactically and psychologically foolish decision to abolish the Diet in June, robbed them of a useful liaison office and source of important information. Moreover, it challenged state governments. In their determination to institute their own central government, the politicians of the Frankfurt Parliament tended to lose sight of how much they needed the support of the existing state governments for their work. This was particularly true of Prussia, which remained much more directly involved in the German situation in 1848 than did Austria, since Austria was faced with simultaneous revolutions in its Italian, Hungarian, and Czech possessions.

The course of the Revolution in Austria

Even if less directly affecting the proceedings of the Frankfurt Parliament, the complex history of Austria during the revolutionary year of 1848–9 exercised a constant influence in all its permutations on the course and outcome of the German revolution. Vienna provided perhaps the one genuinely metropolitan center which all national revolutions need. The 1848 Revolution in Vienna was much more radical than elsewhere in the Confederation. It also, until the violent counter-revolution of the autumn 1848, effected a more complete transformation of power than in any other German state. For centuries the Austrian ruler had been Holy Roman Emperor. From 1815 Austria—that is, the western part of the Habsburg monarchy, excluding Hungary, but including Bohemia and Moravia—formed part of the German Confederation and had held its presidency. In this capacity the Austrian emperor had to be party to the decisions taken at Frankfurt. This was duly acknowledged by the deputies' choice of Archduke Johann, younger brother of emperor Francis I and uncle of the reigning emperor Ferdinand (1835–48), as Regent and by the appointment of an able Austrian, Anton von Schmerling (1805–93), later Austria's prime minister, as minister of the interior in the provisional government. But the Austrian authorities had from the outset given far less support to the Frankfurt Parliament than had other state governments. More than two-thirds of the constituencies in Bohemia and Moravia (more or less the equivalent of the modern Czech Republic) effectively boycotted the elections in 1848. The first Viennese revolution of 13 March, which had led to Metternich's flight and the appointment of a liberal government, was followed on 25 April by an imposed constitution which satisfied no one, not least the radicals. Three days before the opening of the Frankfurt Parliament, on 15 May, a further Viennese revolt broke out, precipitating the flight of the court to Innsbruck, followed by yet a further rising on 26 May. The opening of the Pan-Slav Congress in Prague on 3 June under the direction of the sage Czech historian, František Palácky (1798–1876), the Prague rising from 12–16 June, and its suppression by Alfred Fürst zu Windischgrätz (1787–1862) on the orders of the provisional central government at Frankfurt had far more immediacy to Austrians than the debates about the constitution. Moreover, Germans in Austria were increasingly preoccupied with their relationship to other ethnic groups, and supported the German cause in order to protect their own hegemony in the Danube monarchy. The leaders of the revolution in Vienna were both more able and more radical than those in Berlin, but they aroused the resentment of the rural population, which had been appeased by the emperor's decision to accept the Viennese assembly's decision, on 22 July 1848, to abolish servile relationships and especially the robot or statutory labor services. Other factors stimulated local grievances against the revolution: the absence of the court from Vienna between May and August brought unemployment to the city. Furthermore, in the course of the debates of the summer, it gradually became clear to the Germans of Austria that they stood to lose far more than Prussia or other states, such as Hanover, Saxony, Baden, Württemberg, or Bavaria, with their purely German populations, if a liberal constitution granted equal rights to ethnic minorities. The essential dilemma of Austria in 1848-9 was characterized by the Prussian diplomat, Gustav von Usedom (1805-84) in his *Politische Briefe* (1849) as follows: "Austria can do nothing for the organic development of the state or for the freedom of peoples without disintegrating; so she decrees immobility in the rest of the world on these issues."

The course of the revolution in Prussia

The Berlin National Assembly met in the capital on 22 May and remained in session until December. In terms of its social composition, it was much more representative of the populace as a whole than the Frankfurt Assembly, and it proved much more consequential in the power political issues underlining its central task of agreeing on a constitution with the king. At the same time Berlin and Prussia became the focus of interest of German nationalists. The alternative to Austria as leading power in Germany was Prussia. This was now the view of many liberal politicians from different parts of the country. They included the Baden deputies Karl Mathy and Friedrich Daniel Bassermann (1811-55), the historian Johann Gustav Droysen from Schleswig-Holstein, and Heinrich von Gagern from Hesse-Darmstadt. Admittedly, Friedrich Wilhelm IV, Prussia's unpredictable king, had disappointed the hopes placed in him in the early days of the revolution. But the fact that the Prussian army under General Friedrich von Wrangel (1784-1877) was playing a prominent part in the war being waged throughout the spring and summer of 1848 between federal troops and Denmark in Schleswig-Holstein, won Prussia much sympathy among supporters of the German cause. It was during these months that the vital importance of Prussian leadership in Germany's economic affairs became evident to many Germans and that the term was coined of a *kleindeutsche Lösung* (or little German solution) as to how Germany would be unified: Germany without Austria.

The problem of Schleswig-Holstein and its symbolism

The problem of the Elbe duchies exemplified the multifaceted nature of the German revolutionaries' task. While Holstein was almost wholly German in population and had formed part of the Holy Roman Empire and of the German Confederation, the opposite was true in Schleswig, which had a large Danish minority. The duchies were united under the personal rule of the king of Denmark, who, two years before the revolution, had declared his intention to integrate Schleswig into the Danish kingdom. The decision provided a focus and a cause for the German national movement at a time when it was creating its own grassroots organization. This took the form of middle-class associations, such as singing or athletic festivals, whose supporters used the new method of railway travel to come together and infect each other with enthusiasm for the "national cause." The symbolic nature of the Schleswig-Holstein affair as a barometer of German national self-confidence was amply demonstrated during the critical summer months of the German revolution. Danish troops had begun to advance into Schleswig only days after the outbreak of revolution in Berlin. Prussia intervened on its own initiative—and could in later years claim "nationalist" credentials for so doing. By mid-April resistance to the Danes was launched as a federal war. It won strong support from the new central government at Frankfurt and in the process took on something of the character of a national crusade. The Danish blockade of north German harbors triggered an appeal for money for a German fleet which met with immense enthusiasm and a flow of contributions. (Heine's brilliant satire in his poem on the German fleet earned him few friends and much opprobrium from later chauvinistic nationalists.) British diplomatic support for the Danes and the success of the Danish blockade persuaded the Prussian king to sign an armistice with Denmark at Malmö on 26 August 1848. His failure to consult either the Frankfurt Parliament or the central government provoked a storm of anger. The intervention of the European powers had been crucial, since England and Russia were guarantors of the status quo in the duchies under international law. The experience by German nationalists of their own impotence in the face of such intervention, helps to explain why Bismarck's policy of pursuing German unity from strength two decades later, without regard to the wishes of the great powers, was greeted with such enthusiasm by the vast majority of politically minded Germans. Meanwhile the August armistice was rejected by the Frankfurt Parliament and an attempt was made to carry on the war with federal troops, but without Prussia. The campaign ended in ignominious failure, prompting in the press a host of cartoons highly unflattering to the revolutionaries. In mid-September the

Frankfurt deputies voted by a narrow majority to accept the armistice. Anger and frustration that events were bypassing the revolution, that the historic moment to unify the country was being lost, caused violence to erupt right across Germany. Resentment at the central government and the Frankfurt Parliament as tools of the European and German princes, brought to the very streets of Frankfurt violence whose suppression by force alienated the population. Among its first victims were members of both Parliament and central government, lynched a stone's throw from the Paulskirche by the mob. From a longer perspective the real victim was the German revolution itself.

The autumn crisis and the counter-revolution

The Prussian and Austrian garrison troops from the nearby federal force at Mainz were called in by the central government to restore order, as they had been so often by the princes in Metternich's time. The Frankfurt Parliament never recovered its prestige or indeed its unity of purpose following those fateful weeks. By and large, the politically articulate middle classes responded to the autumn violence with anger and fear. Fanny Lewald, at this stage in her life a militant champion of democracy and women's rights, declared contemptuously that anyone with property had come to long for a return to absolutism, right down to the last gendarme. All they wanted now, she alleged, was to be able to promenade in peace along the Berlin boulevard *Unter den Linden*. There was some truth in the comment. The beginning of the counter-revolution in the late autumn of 1848 won the tacit approval of much of the populace outside Vienna. Yet it was in Vienna that the first moves against the revolution began in early October. Prince Windischgrätz, who had suppressed the Prague uprising in June, was appointed commander-in-chief of the counter-revolutionary forces by the emperor. On 4 October *Freiheit in Krähwinkel*, the brilliant satire on the contradictions of revolution by the Viennese comic dramatist, Johann Nestroy, which had played to capacity audiences in the Viennese Carl Theater since its premier on 1 July 1848, was performed for the last time. Two days later, in response to the command to the Vienna grenadiers to suppress the Hungarian revolution, the Vienna populace lynched the minister of war and stormed the arsenal. The revolutionary troops in Vienna numbered some 100,000. However, with the aid of the Croat leader, Joseph Jellacic (1801–59), Vienna was surrounded and almost 1,000 civilians were killed. By 1 November Windischgrätz was master of the city. The Austrian authorities wreaked a bloody revenge on the insurgents, executing many, including even the charismatic Saxon delegate from the Frankfurt Parliament, Robert Blum (1807–48), who vainly pleaded parliamentary immunity.

The calculated execution of Blum on 9 November showed the Austrians' disregard for the claims of the Frankfurt Parliament and indeed all the institutions of the revolution, including the government which their own Archduke Johann headed. One month later, the new Austrian chancellor, Prince Felix von Schwarzenberg (1800–52), the able brother-in-law of Windischgrätz, had the eighteen-year-old Francis Joseph I (1848–1916) supplant his epileptic uncle Ferdinand as emperor, thus cutting across the plans of the Regent to unite in his own person the regency of the German Confederation and the imperial crown of Austria.

The counter-revolution in Berlin

The Berlin counter-revolution was less violent and its agents less vindictive than in Austria. True, the radical Prussian National Assembly was transferred from the capital to Brandenburg, forty miles to the west; it was dissolved on 5 December. On the same day the king imposed a constitution on Prussia. "It is always a bad thing," mused Theodor Fontane with pertinent understatement, "when freedom and suchlike starts being imposed on people." An assembly based on the new constitution met in February 1849, but its considerable talents proved too much for the king and again he dissolved it in April. In May he substituted for manhood suffrage the much more restrictive three-class indirect franchise, designed to ensure the preponderance of rank and wealth in the state legislature. It remained in force in Prussia until the fall of the Hohenzollern dynasty in 1918. But at least Prussia had a constitution and a two-chamber parliament, which Austria did not. In Prussia as in Vienna, the army was used to restore order and prevent rioting. The caustic slogan coined by the Prussian civil servant and patron of Fontane, Wilhelm von Merckel, was frequently reiterated in the months and years to come: *Gegen Demokraten helfen nur Soldaten* (Only soldiers can deal with democrats). General Wrangel, veteran of the Schleswig-Holstein campaign and in his youth a friend of Kleist, entered Berlin at the head of his troops in December 1848. Known for his wit as "Papa" Wrangel, he managed to avoid bloodshed. In keeping with the paternalist traditions of the pre-March days, the populace were won over by his decision to allow the traditional Christmas market to be held in the city. Things were clearly getting back to normal.

The end of the revolution

The German revolutions did not end with the forcible suppression of the revolt in Austria and Prussia. The Frankfurt Parliament continued in session, debating the national constitution for Germany from October 1848 until it was at last ready for promulgation in April 1849. By then, however, the power to effect change had clearly been lost by the revolutionaries. May and June 1849 saw a struggle for the recognition of the new constitution, sparking major uprisings in Saxony, where Richard Wagner (1813–83) fought on the barricades of the capital city of Dresden, and in Baden. Gagern's decision to resign in May over the failure of the Regent to support the imperial constitution for Germany was a bitter blow to the moral authority of the Parliament and to the hopes that such a unified constitution could ever be realized. The decision of many German states to recall their deputies just one year after the opening of the Frankfurt assembly and the strategic decision of the remaining deputies to move on 30 May to safety in Stuttgart, signaled the effectual capitulation of the revolutionaries before the power of the princes. From the late autumn of 1848 the counter-revolution had demonstrated far greater solidarity than the revolutionaries, in line with the old adage that the badger thinks of only one thing, while the fox thinks of (too) many. In a final symbolic act, Prussian troops forcibly dispersed the rump parliament at Stuttgart on 18 June, the anniversary of the battle of Waterloo. Meanwhile, the economic and social consequences of the revolutionary year were beginning to make themselves felt.

Economic and social problems in 1848

Early in the revolution, the adverse economic effects of the unrest became a significant influence on the further course of events. The decline of business confidence was everywhere evident. By the early summer of 1848, trade lagged, credit tightened, and a run began on savings accounts. This in turn led to a hoarding of gold and silver, with dire consequences for employment, production, consumption, and trade, both domestic and foreign. Prominent Rhenish businessmen had been the natural leaders of liberalism in Prussia in the years before the revolution, and many, such as David Hansemann (1790–1864) and Ludolf Camphausen (1803–90), received ministerial posts in the new governments of March. Yet only weeks later, political organizations were being set up by members of the middle class with the aim of "ensuring freedom and order." By late June, after the Paris workers' rising had taken place and been brutally suppressed by General Cavaignac (1802–57), business circles in Germany were more frightened by the fear of anarchy than by authoritarian rule. By the autumn these fears communicated themselves to other social groups, many of whose members had originally been vigorous supporters of the revolution.

The most important social cause of the revolution in artisan and craftsman circles had been the fear of proletarianization. Once the initial excitement had worn off, the exacerbation of a difficult economic situation alienated support among those who had any property or status to lose. The feeling of "where is it all going to end?" was widespread by the late summer. The speedy and, as it proved, sustained economic recovery which followed the suppression of the revolution helped fuel confidence in the counter-revolutionary authorities. This was especially the case in heavy industry in the area of the Customs Union, where between 1848 and 1857 the production of iron ore increased by some 300 percent, and the number of works, and of those employed in them, increased by 40 percent. The activities of the Communist League, of Marx in Düsseldorf, of Engels in the textile town of Elberfeld, of Moses Hess (1812–75) in Cologne, had involved few workers, but the League's potential to do so aroused anxiety among employers, especially when faced with the strikes which erupted in the early 1850s. The Confederation won support in bourgeois circles by its energetic measures to suppress political organizations of working men and restrict associations to educational purposes. It was not just the factory owners who reacted in this way, but the master craftsmen, who had distanced themselves from liberal politics in the summer of 1848. This became evident in the summer of 1848 when, in an attempt to retain exclusive control of entry to their trade, the master craftsmen sought to exclude the journeymen and apprentices from the Craftsmen and Tradesmen's Congress at Frankfurt in July 1848. The response came in the form of the Democratic Workers Associations set up by the brilliant organizer and journeyman printer, Stephan Born, who had been the brains behind the first nationwide strike in the printing industry in April 1848. The General German Workers' Fraternity from Saxony, Prussia, and other parts of northern Germany was the creation of late August and early September and became a political force over the next months. Many radical craft apprentices continued to play a prominent role in the demonstrations, street fighting, and barricades of the autumn of 1848. In May 1849 they made common cause with the workers and intellectuals who were behind the rising in Dresden, or with the Jacobin element in Baden and the Palatinate. Many small businessmen and master craftsmen, on the other hand, began to rediscover their former loyalty to the traditional order, thus anticipating political attitudes among the propertied classes in the second half of the century.

The Revolution and its consequences

The political constellation of German politics in the second half of the century was largely determined by the experiences of 1848–9, and the harsh repressive measures which followed its failure. The representatives of big business and finance would, in time, enter into a political alliance with the traditional ruling classes, not least in order to block the advance of organized labor. This lay in the future, but memories of civil disturbance are long, and employers, as well as politically committed working-class men and their leaders, remembered that the origins of German socialism lay in 1848. The revolutionary year did indeed witness the beginning of a German labor movement, to which Born contributed more directly than did Marx or Engels. In their early years, working-class organizations had been mainly concerned with self-help. These groups were distinguished by an idealistic commitment to humanity in general, with the desire "to assist human society on to its feet," as a cabinetmaker's apprentice put it in a letter asking the Central Committee of Worker Fraternization at Leipzig for some teaching materials. But the revolutionary potential of the brotherhood of workers had been clearly demonstrated in the revolution. The hostility between the petty bourgeoisie and the organized labor movement belongs to the later history of the nineteenth century; at the time the distinctions between the two were less clear. Yet that hostility was also a heritage of 1848. The petty bourgeois leaders of the democratic movement in 1848-9 provided most of the victims of the counter-revolution, but they left behind them no organization to defend their former supporters or to provide them with political representation in the decades to come. Unlike their opposite numbers in Britain, they lacked the cultural focus of identity as well as the religious solace offered by the nonconformist churches. Despite the brief resurgence of popular democratic pressure groups in the 1860s, centered especially in smaller central German states or the free cities of Hamburg or Frankfurt, or the small capitals, such as Karlsruhe or Gotha, this most populous sector of German society failed to make an impact on domestic politics or to create organizations in the decades between 1850 and 1880 to look after their interests. Nor did any party comparable with the British Tory party emerge with which they could identify and which could command their natural loyalty. The politically energetic tended to move to the extremes of the political spectrum. Several joined the emerging socialist party in the 1870s—August Bebel, the longtime leader of the parliamentary party, was a former turner. The majority remained politically apathetic and gravitated in times of economic crisis to the right wing of the conservative parties. The paternalist state had long been the protector of these largely preindustrial social groups, and they identified with the nation-state after 1870. Gradually the ideals of nationalism and dynastic loyalty claimed their support, and by the last decades of the century their commitment to the status quo and their opposition to liberalism and, especially, to socialism, were often as adamant as that of the authoritarian state itself.

The revolution gave members of the public at all social levels a taste of political activity, and Germans showed in diverse ways that they were just as capable of effective political organization as their counterparts elsewhere in Europe. Even those who had not been active in the deliberations or the struggles were drawn into participation by the revolution of the media: by the broadsheets and posters published at so many centers right across Germany—at Frankfurt and Offenburg, at Karlsruhe and Magdeburg, and Leipzig, Düsseldorf, Cologne, Hamburg, Vienna, and Berlin. Some were grotesque, most were savagely witty in their persecution of favored targets. It was part of Heine's extraordinary talent to have captured in the imagery of his political poetry, in the mock heroic epics *Deutschland: Ein Wintermmärchen* and *Atta Troll* in 1844, and in satiric poems such as *Beruhigung* or the posthumously published *Die Ratten* the emblematic character of these handbills and caricatures in short-lived journals, political ephemera of *das tolle Jahr*. The age of mass politics was still a generation away, but the overall effect of the revolutionary year was to change people from being mere objects of government administration to potential agents of political action. The German ruling classes became sensitive to the potential of the masses from 1848-9 forward, and they showed themselves more modern in their approach to power politics, than, with notable exceptions, did the liberals and their supporters.

The degree to which 1848 enhanced the collective political education of a broad spectrum of the German populace is worth emphasizing. It prepared for the emergence of organized political associations at a later date. But the failure to harness these initiatives into a more broadly based political culture in Germany, as a result of the harsh repression by the authorities in the so-called *Nachmärz* or post-March, as the decade following the revolution is styled, brings home the real tragedy of the revolution's failure. Some of the associations did, however, outlast their defeat or resurfaced after persecution at a later date. The origins of the German women's movement go back to the revolution, and women became a particular focus of police harassment, among them the courageous journalist and novelist, Louise Otto, or the provocative and fearless barricade fighter and poet Louise Aston. Although rarely mentioned by historians, Catholic women took on what was undoubtedly a political role in the mass Catholic organizations which did survive the revolution. Most prominent among these were the mass annual Catholic rallies or *Katholikentage*, whose prototype, the *Piusvereine*, named after Pope Pius IX (1846-78), had been developed in 1848 and which began to meet in different parts of Germany from the early 1850s forward to this day.

The German Revolution of 1848-9

The achievements of the 1848 Revolution were not commensurate with the intelligence, energy, dedication, enthusiasm, and, in general, the restraint of its spokesmen. The most important were the emancipation of the peasantry from feudal burdens, the abolition of patrimonial jurisdiction (i.e., the lord being judge and jury in his own court), and the introduction of constitutional government to Prussia, though not to Austria. It was a bitter blow to the many Jews who had been prominent in the revolution as deputies of the Frankfurt Parliament and the Berlin and Vienna assemblies, and as agitators and commentators, that *Nachmärz* regimes chose to ignore or curtail the legal emancipation decreed by Article Five of the Basic Rights resolutions of the Frankfurt Parliament. In Prussia, Friedrich Wilhelm IV abrogated in the spring of 1849 the constitution he had imposed in December 1848, though in January 1850 a new constitution was promulgated. The Austrian authorities either disregarded or rescinded the constitutional achievements of the revolutionary year. In December 1851 the 1849 constitution was withdrawn and a neo-absolutist regime introduced by Schwarzenberg. The prime minister died prematurely in 1852, however, and his advisers acted on the somewhat cynical assumption that in Alexander Pope's dictum: "Of forms of government let fools contest, What e'er's administered best is best." Certainly, the reform of the Austrian administration, and notably of the finances, marked the beginning of an era of prosperity for Austria.

Of those who had supported the revolution, many were executed, imprisoned, or driven into exile. Emigration claimed a significant proportion of the population of the German Confederation as an indirect or direct consequence of the failed revolution. The unrest which had characterized the revolutionary year was not so easily assuaged. Some 80,000 Germans left Baden, the majority for economic rather than political reasons. Only a minority of those Germans remaining behind who had been active in the revolution continued to be active in pursuit of their political goals, not least because of the intensity and range of police repression. Resignation rather than protest became characteristic. Fontane, who for economic reasons joined the service of Prussia's reactionary government in 1850, tried to justify himself and his kind in a letter to Bernhard von Lepel on 17 January 1851:

> All one can do is to escape with one's mind into the past and one's heart into one's circle of family and friends ... I've tried the right, the left and the center; the madness of the extremes and the pusillanimity of the 'juste milieu' are equally repelling.

The economic liberalism of the Prussian administration in the years of political reaction following the suppression of the revolution proved an acceptable distraction to many professional people. Many educated Germans began to come around to the view in the course of the 1850s that living under a constitution, however deficient it might be, was at least a small step forward, but progress nonetheless, and thus a justification of their belief in the progressive character of their age. "A liberal, or indeed a conservative, unless of course he were a died-in-the-wool reactionary," wrote a high-ranking member of the Berlin National Assembly at the time of its dissolution by Prussian troops, "must surely feel a sense of relief at having been freed from the arbitrary tyranny of government and the bureaucracy of the pre-revolutionary years." For businessmen and financiers, traders, householders, and a substantial sector of the general public, a confident expectation began to manifest itself in the early 1850s, that a strong government would restore the economy.

Domestic consequences of 1848

In the sphere of domestic politics, the most important short-term consequence of 1848–9 was the changed relationship of Austria and Prussia within the Confederation, and the general public's growing awareness of the fact. Austro-Prussian dualism or rivalry had been a vital strand of German history now for a century, since Frederick II of Prussia first seized the strategically important province of Silesia (now Poland) from Austria in 1740. Austria's greater power in the first half of the nineteenth century had been reflected in her holding the presidency of the Confederation. This she continued to do until it was dissolved in 1867, following Bismarck's successful prosecution of the war of 1866. Austria's military success against her own revolutionaries strengthened her hand in Germany in the immediate aftermath of the revolution. Indeed, in May 1850 at Olmütz (Olomouc) in Bohemia, Austria publicly humiliated Prussia by outmaneuvering her attempts to pursue a Prussian-led policy of national unity. The Confederation was restored on Austria's terms under her forceful chancellor, Felix von Schwarzenberg.[2] Austria's hegemony in Germany was attributed to what had been the Danube monarchy's traditional role in German affairs for centuries, one which was broadly accepted by the European powers. Prussia and the rest of Germany fell into line, though individual Prussians, among them Bismarck, never forgot the humiliation suffered at Olmütz. However, the course of events in 1848–9 caused many Germans to ask some searching questions about the continued basis of Austria's authority in the Confederation, both on political and

---

[2] It is interesting to speculate what might have been the outcome of the struggle between Austria and Prussia for hegemony in Germany had Bismarck been faced with an Austrian opponent of the caliber of Schwarzenberg.

economic grounds. The Revolution had caused Austria to experience difficulty in reconciling her involvement with German affairs and the increasing complexity of administering her multinational empire. The Prague uprising of June 1848, which had been so swiftly crushed by the Austrian general Windischgrätz, had been led, not by German constitutionalists, but by Czech liberals and democrats. In neighboring Hungary the challenge to Austria by the revolutionary leader Lajós Kossuth (1802–94) had brought the issue of ethnic conflict into even sharper focus. During 1848–9 Austria's high-handed treatment of the Frankfurt Parliament and her lack of understanding of the burning issue for so many Germans of the Schleswig-Holstein affair, along with her alleged concessions to her Slav peoples at the expense of the hitherto culturally dominant Germans, suggested little sympathy both at the time and in the future, with the aims of German nationalists. Moreover, Austria's decision to call in Russian help to suppress revolution within her borders in Hungary, and the brutality shown toward the Viennese revolutionaries, was contrasted by observers with the relative absence of bloodshed during the counter-revolution in Prussia. However, in contrasting repression in Prussia and Austria, one should not underestimate counter-revolutionary victimization of the revolutionaries nor the systematic blackening of their memory in the years and decades to come. The Prussian army long remained intensely unpopular for its part in suppressing the uprisings in Saxony and Baden in the spring and summer of 1849, as well as for its forcible dissolution of the Prussian national assembly in Berlin in the winter of 1848 and of the rump of the Frankfurt Parliament in Stuttgart in the summer of 1849. Yet, because the desire for a unified state became more pressing as the country advanced economically in the 1850s, people both inside and outside of Prussia began increasingly to distinguish the current administration of Friedrich Wilhelm IV and his advisers, the so-called Camarilla, and the Prussia which his brother, Prince Wilhelm, would one day take over. One of the lessons learned from the failure of the Frankfurt Parliament in the Schleswig-Holstein affair, was the need for a military arm to implement national policy. While this knowledge did not assuage feelings of hostility to the troops of the crown, either in Prussia or in Germany as a whole, it was an important element in conditioning influential sections of the public to accept the Prussian army's role in the process of national unification in the wars of 1864, 1866, and 1870–1.

A further vital experience of 1848 for Germans was that it gave them a new perspective on the problems of nationality. Broadly speaking, nationalism now began to be seen not as a struggle against the privilege of the rulers but rather as a successful assertion of one's own nationality against the conflicting claims of other ethnic groups. As in all revolutions, the central problem of 1848 had been that of power, and for the revolutionaries, their failure to effect a transfer of real power. Observation of the political power struggle during the revolutionary year, whether it was of the failure of the Frankfurt Parliament to uphold the demands of the Germans in Schleswig against the Danish king, or of the struggle of the one-million-strong Poles in the Prussian provinces, led many Germans in the years which followed to consider the role of state power in achieving national goals. Would not perhaps the power of the Prussian state be the only effective means not only of unifying their country, but also of protecting German interests against those of less well-organized minorities within their borders? One who, as it were, observed the observers was Otto von Bismarck. He came to realize that national patriotism was eminently compatible with the monarchic order and could in fact be used, as Marx was equally quick to appreciate, to buttress an authoritarian state.

Chapter 6
The Development of the German National Movement

Germany seemed to change character in the decade 1840–50, a fact of which contemporaries were profoundly conscious, whatever their political loyalties were or whatever modifications these had undergone. The failure of the revolution to achieve national unity was to remain a source of bitterness for a generation to come, and even longer for those who remained faithful to their liberal beliefs. But the sense of German nationhood, which prior to the 1840s had been characteristic of particular social and regional groups only, was by the 1850s something to be taken for granted by all who were in the least politically minded. General Joseph Maria Radowitz (1797–1353), conservative confident of Friedrich Wilhelm IV of Prussia and briefly in 1850 his foreign minister, had described national sentiment on the eve of the revolution as "the most popular and powerful force animating our people." But the events of 1848–9 had changed Germans' perception of national sentiment. In the 1830s Germans

Detail from *Italia and Germania* by Friedrich Overbeck.

had broadly regarded the national movement, bound up as it was in the public imagination with the idea of emancipation of "the peoples," as a shared experience of European peoples. As the contradictions between the aspiration of Germans for national unity and the claims of their neighbors, especially the Poles, were made evident, the tendency to regard the quality and worth of nationalism as determined by its exclusively German character became an intrinsic feature of German society.

Origins

The vital force which gave birth to the national movement in late eighteenth-century Germany lay not in the field of politics but in the realm of ideas. Central to an understanding of the complex nature of German nationalism is that it formed part of the secularization process of thought and belief to which the Enlightenment had given such a powerful impulse. The movement was, initially at least, a product of Protestant northern and central Germany, where secularization in intellectual circles was so much more rapid than in the Catholic South. The writings of German poets and philosophers in the ages of the Enlightenment and of Romanticism helped to create a sense of national identity based on a shared awareness of Germany's cultural traditions. For all the German character of the work of her great classical writers, Johann Gottfried Herder (1744–1803), Kant, Humboldt, Goethe, and Schiller, the framework within which they wrote was a European one. The development of the human personality to its fullest creative potential, which was the ideal of late eighteenth-century German humanism, was the antithesis of that chauvinist exclusiveness which later came to be associated with German nationalists. The aim of Germany's humanist poets and thinkers was to release their fellow countrymen, East Prussians and Saxons, Rhinelanders and Thuringians, from the provincial obscurity to which political divisions and economic backwardness had condemned them for so long. Provincial Germans did indeed respond to such ideas. Discussion groups and literary circles sprang up in towns scattered across the country, especially in the northern half, to discuss and speculate upon aspects of nationhood. Their leaders were mainly educated burghers, and their discussions focused, in particular, on the future of the aristocracy in the modern world and the contribution people like themselves might make to their country's government and administration. The cosmopolitan character of early German nationalism owed much to the conviction that the political divisions of Germany, the traditional multiplicity of sovereignties, constituted the most effective obstacle to the liberation of the burgher from feudal bonds. The formulation of some of their ideas could be quaint, a mixture of ponderous sincerity and flights of fantasy—thus the members of the 1790's Oldenburg Literary Society in the northwest styled themselves "Members of the German Parnassus! Authors of Germany! High-minded citizens of the world!"

The effect of the American Revolution of 1776 on Germans was profound. So too was the impact of the French Revolution of 1789 and of the wars of the 1790s: the tremendous energy which events in France had seemed to release in the French people greatly impressed Germans. This deep impression was a characteristic response of men like the ethnographer and companion of Captain Cook, Georg Forster (1754–94), whose name is associated with Germany's first Republic of Mainz in 1793 (and who died in a French prison). Young intellectuals were in the forefront of the debate inspired by events in France, particularly members of the Romantic movement, who had been born in the late 1760s and in the early 1770s. Among them were Ludwig van Beethoven (1770–1827), the brothers August Wilhelm Schlegel and Friedrich Schlegel, Heinrich von Kleist, and Ludwig Tieck. Many Germans hoped the revolution would come to Germany to destroy the old feudal order, and unite the German people. The French nation, who scarcely a generation later was being seen as "Germany's hereditary enemy," seemed at this stage in German history not a danger to resist, but rather a model to imitate.

The Napoleonic era

Even after the French invaded Germany and occupied the left bank of the Rhine, even after Napoleon's conquests, his abolition of the ancient Holy Roman Empire in 1806 and his reduction of the majority of her princes to vassals, even after the defeat and dismemberment of Prussia, the German national movement lacked a political dimension. There was, as yet, no such thing as political nationalism. The French occupation of half of Prussia, the setting up of the kingdom of Westphalia under Napoleon's uncharismatic brother Jérome, even the levies by Napoleon of soldiers from the German states who were members of the Confederation of the Rhine, took some time to provoke active resistance. Comments at first took the form of exasperated or satiric depreciation of the German national character. Thus the political commentator and travel writer Johann Gottfried Seume (1763–1810) could observe in 1807 that the Germans had a favorite phrase: "I can't put up with that," but yet there was, in his view, simply nothing irrational, stupid and base which the Germans had not put up with in the last 500 years and more particularly in recent times, either from each other or from their neighbors.

It was the gradual accumulation of grievances over a period of years which created a political national movement in the years 1810–3. It is understandable that it should have erupted in Prussia, which by 1813 had endured for seven years the humiliations and attendant ills of occupation. Prussia provided the forum for the most tenacious of Napoleon's German opponents, though few were native Prussians. It was in Berlin, close to the French garrison, in the winter of 1807-8 that the Romantic idealist philosopher Johann Gottlieb Fichte held his notorious *Reden an das deutsche Volk*, whose powerful rhetoric excited his listeners. It was in Berlin that the dramatist Kleist introduced a new note of vituperation to intellectuals' efforts to foster a sense of nationhood in his *Catechism of the Germans* of 1809. And of course it was here that the Nassau nobleman, Karl Freiherr vom und zum Stein, had introduced the pioneering reform program for Prussia in 1807, which included emancipation of the peasantry and self-government for the municipalities. Stein's dismissal by Napoleon's order in 1808 made him into a figurehead. His own strong personality and vision, epitomized in the much-quoted phrase, first made in a letter of 1811—*Ich habe nur ein Vaterland und das ist Deutschland* (I have but one Fatherland, and that is Germany)—all contributed to helping Germans glimpse an alternative to the old ways in their country. A significant event of a different order was the founding of the new "royal" universities of Prussia, at Breslau in Silesia, at Bonn on the Rhine, and, above all, at Berlin in 1810. It was a fitting symbol of the moral regeneration of Prussia, which the king, Friedrich Wilhelm III, had promised in the hour of defeat. The men responsible for initiating this great project, Wilhelm von Humboldt, founder of Berlin University, Fichte, its first rector, its professors of the philosophy of religion and of law, Friedrich Schleiermacher and Friedrich Karl von Savigny (1779-1861), and many more aroused the keenest interest among their contemporaries. Close friendship or kinship bound them to zealous patriots; Schleiermacher, for example, was Ernst Moritz Arndt's brother-in-law. As usual in human affairs, it was really only when people became personally affected by the war and occupation that they became fully receptive to the ideas of the patriots. As the demands of the French grew, and more and more husbands and sons were drafted to fight for Napoleon, in the Peninsular war in Spain and especially in 1812 in Russia, a national movement committed to the expulsion of the French began to evolve.

Popular national feeling, both among those who fought and those who wrote, tended to be Christian and monarchist in sentiment, despite the fact that the ideas of leading exponents of nationalism in Germany during the Wars of Liberation in 1813-5 were strongly influenced by French Jacobinism. The very vocabulary of early German nationalism was in part derived from Pietism, a religious movement within the Protestant churches which stressed inwardness and the emotional experience of the Divine presence in the world. In Prussia the king appropriated the rhetoric of his own clergy to preach a kind of crusade against the "godless" French. It might seem surprising that the princes, who had shown varying degrees of servility in their accommodation to Napoleon's wishes, should have been evidently absorbed into the national movement. At the time, the leaders of the resistance to the French were well aware of the value of the monarch as a rallying point of popular nationalist sentiment. Thus Baron Stein and the generals Scharnhorst and Gneisenau, authors of the liberal reform of the Prussian army after 1806, and the bluff soldier Gebhart Leberecht Blücher (1742–1819) from Mecklenburg, together with Schleiermacher, directed their energies to persuading the recalcitrant Prussian king to put himself forward as the leader of the national resistance to Napoleon. The heady atmosphere of the wars of liberation was especially infectious to the young and idealistic. Evocative symbols of princely love of country and even royal martyrs for the cause were provided by the deaths in battle in 1806 of the dashing if unreliable royal Prussian prince (and composer) Louis Ferdinand and the Duke of Brunswick. The queen of Prussia herself provided a most potent royal myth: it was rumored that the death of Louise of Prussia in 1810, at the age of only thirty-four, was the result of privations she was forced to endure as a consequence of the French occupation. Those who had lived through these years and later recalled them in their memoirs, tended to speak of the "shame" their princes endured at Napoleon's hands, rather than of the rank opportunism which characterized the behavior of most of them. The princes in their turn, their numbers sharply reduced by Napoleon, but the territories of many, especially in southern Germany, much increased, found the national movement of only limited usefulness in their overriding aim in 1815, namely to restore "order" to Germany.

After the final defeat and exile of the French emperor, not only were the wishes of the patriots overruled, but individual monarchs showed themselves determined to repress or to doctor the legend that the war against the French was fought and won by German patriots. They preferred to see it as a traditional war of cabinet government. In this the princes were correct. The role of the nationalist movement in the defeat of the French was indeed a myth, and one which would be sedulously fostered by middle-class liberals, their novelists, and historians after mid-century. But many princes undoubtedly felt threatened by the implications of "a nation at arms," once peace approached and the issue of social control became paramount in their minds. Others, notably Ludwig I of Bavaria, were devotees of cultural nationalism, though Ludwig was determined to dictate the forms himself. His primary aim, mocked roundly by Heine in his *Germany: A Winter's Tale* (1844), was to make Munich the cultural capital of Germany, his predilection for neoclassical munificence earning it the sobriquet of "Athens on the (river) Isar." Alas, his many idiosyncrasies made him the subject more of parody than praise. These included a fondness for writing bad verse and his self-styled hall of fame, Valhalla on the Danube, built, as he put it, with the avowed aim that "*teutscher der Teutsche aus ihr trete, besser als er gekommen*" (the German may emerge more German and a better man than when he entered).[1] Certainly, few themes lent themselves more readily to Heine's satiric pen than the sentimental nationalist on the Bavarian throne. In a similar way to Ludwig, the new king of Prussia, Friedrich Wilhelm IV, who came to the throne in 1840, tried to direct his people's ambitions to the symbols of national unity and away from the realities of power. Such a symbol was the completion of Cologne's medieval cathedral by subscription. The publicist Joseph Görres (1776–1848) spoke of the cathedral as the *Allerdeutschenhaus,* the house of all Germans, and the young Swiss historian from Basle, Jakob Burckhardt, felt fired by a deep sense of his German heritage when he traveled to the Rhineland in 1841. But in the 1840s "cathedral-fund patriotism," in spite of the generous response by Prussian Protestant and Jewish subscribers as well as Catholics, only appealed to a narrow segment of society. It appeared as a mere palliative at a time of growing popular frustration with princely tutelage.

The Grimm brothers and the awakening of German nationalism

A unique contribution was made to the development of national self-consciousness of Germans in the first half of the nineteenth century by scholars, who collected, classified, wrote about, and discussed the achievements of past generations of their people. Among these, the brothers Jacob and Wilhelm Grimm deserve a particular place. The brothers dedicated their lives to making their fellow citizens aware and proud of their identity as Germans, primarily through the medium of research into their language. Their famous descriptive dictionary of the German language, the *Deutsche Wörterbuch,* was begun in 1838 (and finally completed in 1960). It was preceded by their scholarly "rediscovery" and publication of their collection of German fairy tales, the celebrated *Kinder und Hausmärchen* of 1812–22, of German sagas (1816–8), the collections of ancient German legal documents, *Deutsche Rechts-Alterthümer* (1828), alongside *Grammatik* (1819–37), *Deutsche Mythologie* (1837), and pioneering editions of German classical poetry. In 1848, the year in which he was elected a member

---

[1] Though Ludwig assembled a gallery of "beauties" and had their portraits painted, where they can today be seen at his Nymphenburg palace in Munich, he did not envisage German woman as having a similar capacity to be truly *teutsch*. In this he was no different from the majority of his contemporaries.

of the Frankfurt National Assembly, Jacob Grimm wrote with reference to his *History of the German Language*, "my book is political through and through." He could have said it of all his and most of Wilhelm's work. But perhaps the most political act of the brothers Grimm was their role as founding fathers of the academic study of the national language and its literature: *Germanistik*. The term was coined at the first meeting of German "*Germanisten*" in Frankfurt in 1846, two years before the outbreak of the Revolution.

The Restoration years

Once the Napoleonic wars were over, most people lost interest in politics. True, six days before the battle of Waterloo, students at Schiller's old university at Jena, where the Schlegels and Novalis had studied, founded on 12 June 1815 the movement known as the *Burschenschaften* or fraternities. Two years later, on 31 October 1817, the anniversary of Luther's alleged nailing the theses to the Wittenberg University church in defiance of Rome, large numbers of fraternity members assembled to celebrate the "national" victory of Germany over Pope and Catholic emperor. But the students soon became the particular objects of authoritarian attention by the political police; the *Burschenschaften* were proscribed after the murder in 1819 by an unbalanced student of the dramatist August von Kotzebue (b. 1761), as an alleged Russian spy, and the passing of the Karlsbad Decrees.

Partly because of the persecutions, partly as a response to the long years of war and upheaval, people lost interest in the cause of German unity. Ludwig Börne's caustic observation of 1819 that "the thinking part of the German people has returned to their studies, and they are already stretched out on their bellies," may have been broadly true. Those few dedicated nationalists who remained active showed themselves sympathetic to other national movements in Europe. Following the example of the English Romantic poet, Lord Byron, who actually died in the struggle for Greek independence, German poets and their readers identified with the cause of emancipation in the 1820s and 1830s, whether of the Greeks or the Poles, the Belgians or the Irish. Whereas the writers and commentators of the national movement in the early part of the century had been preoccupied with Germany's national destiny as part of what they styled "historical necessity," in the Restoration era, by contrast, their successors looked to natural law in support of their pleas for a unified constitutional state. The two, they believed, were simply part of the same process, and thus the aspirations of their neighbors were as justified as their own. Heinrich Laube called his three-volume novel of 1833–7 not *Young Germany* but *Young Europe* and sent his hero dashing off to succor the Poles in their struggle against the Tsar of Russia. In the 1840s the popular political poets Ferdinand Freiligrath and Georg Herwegh wrote rousing songs of Irish suffering and English oppression and sentimental ditties of the Irish emigrants bound for America. Germans shared with other Europeans a sense of outrage at being mere pawns in the hands of their rulers and their ministers. "Nothing," wrote a Rhinelander called Weitzel in the early 1840s, "has done so much to encourage the revolution which so many appear to dread, than the treaties, the peace negotiations, the territorial bartering of the last forty years." Accordingly, the aspirations of thinking men that their rulers should at least trust them figured ever more prominently in discussion. The national movement at this period of Germany's history encompassed diverse aims, most of which were common to liberal nationalist movements in other parts of Europe at some point in the century. While Germans were enthusiastic monarchists, they wanted the right to political institutions, such as a free press and elected assemblies, which could put a check on the arbitrary power of monarchic government as well as of central and local administration. Furthermore, the ambitions of the workingman for a degree of social justice was allied in their minds with the development of a nationalist consensus and movement. The journeymen, who were one of the few mobile elements in society and the principal victims of the economic crisis of the 1830s and 1840s, looked in vain to their local ruler or town council to right their wrongs. Because they moved about the country so much, and indeed abroad to France, Belgium, and even England, they proved to be particularly effective agents of disseminating nationalist, liberal, and even early socialist ideas through the Confederation.

Hambach

The revolution of 1830 engendered much excitement but little change in the political scene. The year 1832 saw one of the few mass public demonstrations of the popular will of the era, at Hambach in the Bavarian Palatinate, where police surveillance was less stringent than elsewhere. It was typical of the sociable character of the national movement in southern Germany in those years—an aspect one should not forget when trying to account for its mass appeal—that a large section of the 30,000 demonstrators consisted of families and friends supplied with provisions. Many had come along simply to enjoy the Maytime outing, to hear the speeches and gaze at the brightly colored banners. Academics played a prominent role at Hambach, but artisans were also well represented. On this occasion and for more than a decade, the authority of the professoriate was still accepted by those who would have liked to see more action, but who were impressed by the record of university teachers and their students as political martyrs of liberalism and nationalism. A third or so of professors and lecturers in German between 1830 and 1848 suffered setbacks in or even dismissal from their careers or fines and/or imprisonment for their political beliefs and activities. The opening speech at Hambach was given by the lawyer and publicist, Philipp Jakob Siebenpfeiffer (1789–1845), and was described in poetic language in the media as "the German May." The black, red, and gold of the banner of the volunteers against Napoleon, which the *Burschenschaften* at Jena had also adopted and which from now on was the symbol of German unity, flew alongside the red and white Polish flag. There were many Poles present, refugees from the Russian suppression of their revolution of 1831; a generous welcome was given them by the Germans. Siebenpfeiffer's rhetoric seems to have been wholly in keeping with his listeners' mood and their general sentiments, at least judging from memoirs and reports of the event. He ended his address with the following high-flown and, in the light of events to come, revealing appeal: "Long live a free united Germany! Long live the Poles, allies of the Germans! Long live the French,[2] brothers of the Germans, who respect our nationality and our independence."

The Rhine crisis and chauvinist nationalism

But less than a decade later, in 1840, the French created a war scare and were suspected by German nationalists, not without reason, of renewing their designs on the left bank of the Rhine. A wave of patriotic indignation was orchestrated by the authors of a new style of chauvinist rhetoric which directed rather than reflected public opinion in the future. Notorious here were the "Rhine songs," *Sie sollen ihn nicht haben, den freien deutschen Rhein* (They Shan't Have It, the Free German Rhine) by Nikolaus Becker (1809–45) and *Die Wacht am Rhein* (The Watch on the Rhine) by Max von Schneckenburg (1819–49). Set to music, in the first case in seventy different versions, including one by Robert Schumann (1810–56), and in the second by one Karl Wilhelm, who was given a pension of 900 talers in recognition in 1860, the *Rheinlieder* gained general currency both during and after the 1870–1 Franco-Prussian war (and were widely sung in the Third Reich). They represented an important stage in the evolution of nationalist image-making. One year after the Rhine crisis, a provincial professor of German by the name of Heinrich Hoffmann von Fallersleben, on holiday in Helgoland in 1841 wrote the most celebrated of

---

[2] He styled them "Franks," a term which denotes an ancient Germanic tribe which originally inhabited northern France and western Germany.

all such songs in Germany, the *Deutschlandlied*. In *Deutschland, Deutschland über alles*, he tried to express the love of country, the ideal of brotherly love based on common destiny. In his view, he was providing Germany with her equivalent of the French anthem, the *Marseillaise*, which, only a week before, he and his friends had been prohibited from singing. With his long blond curly hair and dandified dress, Hoffmann von Fallersleben was no bluff German chauvinist like Arndt, no coarse-grained vilifier of French ways in the mode of "*Turnvater*" Jahn or, in the 1830s, Wolfgang Menzel (1798–1873), the influential racist journalist whom Ludwig Börne styled *der Franzosenfresser* (guzzler of the French). He was one of the Young German writers and used the vehicle of (mild) satire in his popular *Unpolitische Lieder* of 1841–2 to try and persuade Germany's rulers to grant constitutional government and a national parliament—his songs actually costing him his teaching post at Breslau. The quality of German nationalism between Napoleon's fall and 1840 had been broadly inclusive and liberal. The nationalist songs of the early 1840s supplied a later, more aggressive generation with an instrument of vilification of their closest neighbors.

1848 and its consequences

Initially, the outbreak of the revolution in the capital cities of German states in the spring of 1848 was, in part at least, the expression by Germans of their solidarity with their brothers in Europe. Yet by early summer, a change of heart was becoming evident, both among the spokesmen of the revolution and in the general mood. The brutal suppression of the Czech revolutionaries in June 1848 by the Austrian military commander Windischgrätz evoked no reproof from the Frankfurt Parliament. Furthermore, during the debates in July on the national question, Prussian delegates showed themselves unwilling to concede the same rights for the Poles that they claimed for Germans living under foreign rule. The historian and writer Wilhelm Jordan (1819–1904) declared in a speech to the parliament on 4 July that "All who live on German soil are Germans, even if they are not German by birth or language. We decree that they are Germans, we accord the term 'German' a sublime meaning. From now on it will be a political concept."

However, the ineffectiveness of either parliament or the liberal ministries to assert the claims of the nation against the European powers in the Schleswig-Holstein affair, brought home to nationalists that fundamental changes in Germany's political states could only come with the support of the princes, not in opposition to them. But the question began to crystallize itself: With the support of which princes? Austria's forceful opposition in the 1850s to any

Portrait of Heinrich Hoffmann von Fallersleben by Carl Schumacher.

initiative in the direction of greater unity left little hope that support from that quarter could ever be forthcoming. People had lived so long with the fact of Austria's being the leading power in the Confederation, and of her being an integral part of Germany, that it was difficult even to imagine the idea of Germany without her. But in the course of the 1850s, businessmen, academics, and politicians began to accept the term *kleindeutsch* or Germany without Austria, as against *großdeutsch* Austria as part of Germany, terms first coined in the revolution. By the end of the decade *kleindeutsch* and *großdeutsch* parties were arguing the merits of their respective cases. A leading liberal politician from Baden named Friedrich Daniel Bassermann (1811-55) urged his friend, the Kiel historian Johann Gustav Droysen, who, like himself, was a former delegate to the Frankfurt Parliament, to write a history of Prussia. This history would demonstrate to "the nation" the stages by which Prussia gradually became the leader of the national movement. Droysen's celebrated liberal history, *Geschichte der preußischen Politik*, was indeed written and began to appear in 1855. However, before the last volume came out in 1886, its liberal tone had made it seem old-fashioned in the Germany which identified with the chauvinism of Heinrich von Treitschke's (1834-96) literary masterpiece, *Germany in the Nineteenth Century* (1878-94).

Increasingly in the 1850s individuals began to transcend the particularist loyalties of their homeland. The most dynamic agent of this process was the media (see chapter 8). In the south, this was particularly evident in the Protestant areas, in Württemberg, Franconia (since 1806 part of north Bavaria), and Hesse-Darmstadt. Ludwig Bamberger (1823-99), Jewish revolutionary, banker, and Reichstag deputy, Bismarck's adviser on free trade, and later a member of the Left Liberals, recalled in later years how he won his first electoral victory in Hesse-Darmstadt precisely by enlisting Protestant middle-class sentiment in favor of closer links with the north. Among the industrial and merchant classes in Saxony, similar rational options for greater collaboration with Prussia were voiced, despite Saxons' natural antipathy for the powerful state which had managed to win one-third of its territory in 1815.

For all the idealistic language in which much of the speculation and commentary about Germany's situation were couched, the years between the revolution and the wars of unification of the 1860s were characterized by an increasing preoccupation on the part of German businessmen with practical necessities. German commerce and manufacture could only benefit from a politically unified state—as indeed the partial economic coalescence of the Customs Union, from which Austria was excluded, continued to demonstrate. As Friedrich Engels was to put it provocatively but not inaccurately many years later in 1895, the preoccupation of mid-century German nationalists with unity was primarily about removing unnecessary obstacles at home which prevented the German businessman from entering the world market, obstacles which his competitors were spared. In other words Germans had come round to the view that German unity was no more and no less than an economic necessity. Prussia's impressive performance on the economic front, despite the extreme reactionary nature of her government in 1850-8, was of very considerable weight in any consideration of future political policy. Bismarck, when he came to power in 1862, showed himself thoroughly aware of the political muscle with which Prussia's economic achievements endowed her. The decision of a substantial section of liberal politicians and public figures to support Bismarck in the late 1860s should therefore be seen less in terms of "a betrayal of liberal principles" or even "rank opportunism" than as a calculated opting for the best solution in the circumstances. Not that it was a straightforward matter. There are many testimonies from the time which suggest that their authors felt apprehensive as to the outcome of their choice, or even felt pangs of conscience at having allowed Prussia's economic success, and in 1864, 1866, and 1870-1 her military success, to win their support for her leadership in Germany.

Economic and psychological aspects of nationalism

One must also keep in mind the contrast on the economic front between the quarter of the century preceding unification and that succeeding it when considering the changing temper of German nationalism in the second half of the century. The optimism engendered by the rapid expansion of the economy between 1849 and 1873 suffered a sharp shock at the stock exchange collapse of 1873, which affected small savers too. Moreover, the long years between 1873 and 1896, when the economy experienced sectional recession and periods of stagnation and relatively poor growth, coincided with an epoch in Germany's history when very considerable psychological adjustments were demanded of her people. The effect was to stimulate popular anxieties. These anxieties concerned Germany's future status among the nations. People feared the centrifugal forces within the state, particularly national and religious minorities. They also worried about the lack of homogeneity in Germany's regions, notably in the south, where federal traditions remained strong. Popular anxieties overemphasized the vulnerability of German society in times of economic crisis and the alleged need for security for their new state from what people believed, or were led to believe, were envious neighbors. These fears were not felt uniformly throughout society, but they were a general feature among the ruling classes and the middle ranks of society. Paradoxically, they could act as a kind of cement, fostering a feeling for the new Reich as embodying "the nation." The effect of the many international crises during the Bismarck period also operated in a similar way. These included the "war in sight crisis" of 1875 with France, which was largely a propaganda exercise by Bismarck, and the various crises of the 1880s and 1890s involving Austria and Russia. In a different way, the 1878 Congress of Berlin where Germany's great power status received international acknowledgment, helped promote a sense of national solidarity. Germany had by the 1880s become a dynamic society and economy, and this raised people's expectations, fostering public ingratitude at what was seen not to have been achieved, rather than stressing what had been. Furthermore, increasing awareness of the competitiveness of modern industry and the state's clear involvement in supporting and subsidizing both heavy industry and agriculture from 1879 onward made Germans see production and export in terms of national prestige. While such knowledge fostered a sense of solidarity, it also made for greater aggressiveness toward the outside world.

Nationalism and the Empire

Up to about the 1860s national feeling among the middle classes of north and central Germany, and to a lesser extent in the south, was predominantly antifeudal. Between the mid-1860s and the mid-1870s, this altered subtly, a process well documented in the widely read novels of Friedrich Spielhagen (1829–1911), such as *In Reih' und Glied* (1866), *Hammer und Amboß* (1869), or *Sturmflut* (1877), whose affirmative tone contrasted with his self-consciously bourgeois and critical *Problematische Naturen* of 1861. By the mid-1870s the ruling elite claimed to embody national virtues and were admired for so doing.

Proclamation of the Emperor in Versailles 18 January 1871. Painting by Anton von Werner. Note the absence of civilians; even Bismarck is wearing a military uniform.

A considerable propaganda effort went into such projection. It was fixed in the public mind by visual symbols—most famously perhaps by the painting by Anton von Werner (1843–1915) portraying, in the first (1877) of a series of such paintings, the proclamation of the German Emperor in the Hall of Mirrors at Versailles in 1871. Here the Emperor is surrounded by princes and generals, with Bismarck (in military uniform) as the sole civilian representative present. The Victory Column in Berlin (known today as *der goldene Engel*, the golden angel), which was completed in 1873 and was a genuinely national monument, is a revelation of how the national ideal had changed in the course of the previous sixty years. The figure of Borussia at the summit represented the Prussification of the German nation,[3] and the inscription read: "*das dankbare Volk dem siegreichen Helden*" (to a victorious hero from a grateful people). The attempts of successful bourgeois to win titles and patents of nobility, to buy their sons into good regiments, to marry their daughters into the nobility, was in part the desire to join the ranks of those held to be "the best of the nation," those who held "true national sentiments." Criticism of the *kleindeutsch* national state was made to seem a criticism of the nation itself; the process was reinforced by the creation of a whole series of "outsiders" or "enemies of the Reich" (*Reichsfeinde*). Among the latter were the Catholic clergy during the *Kulturkampf* between state and Catholic church, the socialists, the racial minorities, Poles, Alsatians, and Danes. Methods of discrimination included bypassing individuals for posts in the civil service, or, more particularly for chairs at university or senior legal jobs. Here Catholics, Jews, socialists, and, in Bismarck's later years, liberals, encountered considerable difficulties. The strongly democratic and constitutional element characteristic of the mid-century national movement, which survived in central Germany and in much of the south and west up to the mid-1860s, was thus tacitly consigned to oblivion in the 1870s. Popular literature played a role in promoting that provincial chauvinism which became the characteristic form of late nineteenth-century German nationalism. Inherited feelings of inferiority toward France were exploited after 1871 to vilify the defeated enemy. A crass, but characteristic example was to be found in *Ein Volksbuch für das Jahr 1872* by one von Horn, who wrote under the pseudonym of Pastor Oertels. Here the writer purports to show of the French "how horribly dirty their underclothes are beneath the external show of fine clothes," adding in an appeal to base instincts: "the reader knows what I mean." A veritable spate of popular songs

---

[3] Fontane subtly draws a parallel between this process and the subjugation of women in contemporary marriage by the narrator's allusion to the Victory Monument, glimpsed by his heroine from the railway carriage in the first chapter of his novel *Cécile*.

The unveiling of the Victory Column on the Königsplatz in Berlin in September 1873.

contrasted the simplicity and virtues of the Germans with the decadence and falsity of the French.

It was symptomatic of the artificiality of the new state that it had no national anthem. The Prussian anthem *Heil dir im Siegerkranz* was sung on occasions where the Kaiser or the military were present, but it was ironic that the nation which used music, especially the brass band, so lavishly in support of national occasions, could not agree on a musical symbol for the nation—or even a flag, though the Prussian colors, black and red, were combined with the Hanseatic (and the Hanoverian) red and white to form the black, white, and red imperial colors. This was a decision not popular among Prussian conservatives, as Dubslav Stechlin's old manservant articulates in the comic exchange on the topic in the opening chapter of *Der Stechlin*. In other ways, however, state promotion of national feeling was more successful, as with the Kaiser's birthday or with the national holiday, Sedan Day, on 2 September. This last commemorated the great victory by Helmut von Moltke over the French and the capture of Emperor Louis Napoleon in 1870, and was associated with family or business days out in the country, with song and beer to round it off. But even here a certain inappropriateness did not escape the critics. Indeed, the author of the victory, Moltke himself, asked once how it was that the anniversary of Germany's greatest victory over France should be celebrated on 2 September, since the battle had taken place the day before.[4]

Social imperialism

In the 1890s, the character of German nationalism underwent a further modification, corresponding to the transition from loyalty to the national state to national imperialism. Already in the 1880s the state under Bismarck's leadership had actively fomented chauvinistic nationalism by his policy of Germanization, well funded by the exchequer and directed against the Poles living in Prussia's eastern provinces. What is known as social imperialism, the galvanizing of national energies toward securing for Germany equal status with "imperial powers in Europe," had the advantage, at least from the perspective of the authorities, of directing attention away from the domestic political and social problems of the Reich. The Pan-German movement was founded in 1891; other organizations followed which expressly underlined the chauvinistic mood of the country. Germany was not of course unique in this, but the forms of its expression seem, by comparison, more extravagant, the yellow press more stridently racist. Spokesmen of chauvinistic organizations in Germany contributed regular columns to national newspapers, and these were read abroad as indicative of the general mood. In the age of mass democracy and ever-expanding mass media, people had access to the public sphere as never before and felt the need to communicate with the like-minded or convert the wavering. The navy became a particularly evocative symbol of national aspirations. But the navy-building program aroused much anxiety and anti-German feeling in Britain, while also provoking acute anti-British sentiment in Germany. A fairly typical example of the tone of public debate among supporters of new-style German imperialism is to be read in the September 9, 1912 edition of a local Erfurt paper, following the meeting of the Erfurt branch of the Pan-German Association. The President, Baron von Vietinghoff-Scheel, started by reminding his audience of what he styled the glorious historic monument of

---

[4] That this is not unique is seen in northern Ireland today, where July 12 is sacred to the memory of the Protestant king William III's victory over the Catholic Stuart king James II. The battle was actually fought on July 11th.

some forty-two years since, namely the foundation of the Reich, and went on to highlight the spectacular advance since that time in Germany's wealth, knowledge, and skills. However, in recent times, he declared, Germany's international status had been declining and discontent spreading through the nation. The remedy lay in dealing with Germany's restrictive frontiers. What the nation needed now, in his view, was to develop an appetite for territorial aggrandizement, for the conquest of new colonies. The alternative was the decay and disappearance of the German race. In a similar vein, one year later General Keim, founder and president of the so-called Defense League, whose very title pandered to the myth of Germany's "encirclement" by hostile powers, declared to the annual general meeting of his organization in 1913 that German youth, both boys and girls, must be told in no uncertain terms that they too had the right to hate the enemies of their country.

Critical assessment of such speeches was not lacking in the country, and the Peace Movement, for example, had redoubtable and influential leaders. But, as they said of themselves, they were officers without men and were frequently denounced as unpatriotic or even as traitors by the populace. In the years before 1914, the myth of Germany's encirclement gained currency among the nation as a whole, and was not subjected to critical examination by decision-makers. German economic and military power had failed to gain her authority in international affairs and had not won her friends. The growing sense of moral and psychological isolation in Europe felt by many Germans inclined many to the view that "there was no smoke without fire," and that no doubt the Pan-German League, the Navy League, the Association for the Promotion of Germanness in the East, and all other such groups had sources of information unknown to them. The social organization of the country had by 1914 two generations of Germans' experience of social togetherness, of national bonding, not, as in the 1840s, in the literary clubs, the gymnastic and singing associations, but in organizations like the war veterans, still going strong forty-two years after the event, and still recruiting new members. These and similar organizations devoted themselves, among other things, to collecting subscriptions for national monuments, as for example that to Hermann the Cherusker of 1913, brandishing his sword; the monument to the martial Germania on the banks of the Rhine near Rüdesheim, in the direction of France, or for those three hundred and more statues to "William the Founder," Kaiser Wilhelm I.

Everyone, or nearly everyone, one could say, was either for something or against it, but everyone was doing something, as Siemann notes in *Gesellschaft im Aufbruch* (1990, 264). A restless and self-conscious people is accessible to mass propaganda.

Chapter 7
The Growth of Prussian Hegemony in Germany 1850–71

From the perspective of German nationalists in 1900 or on the eve of the 1914 war, the decade and a half which intervened between the collapse of the revolution and the wars of unification of 1864–71 seemed lacking in consequence. Nationalist commentators used the patronizing phrase "liberalistic" of many of the public figures of the day, who sought, without much success, to pursue a unified, constitutional German state. Friedrich Nietzsche once referred contemptuously to the "fetid air" (*Sumpfluft*) of the 1850s, the lack of intellectual energy and provincialism, which was surely also a reaction to the failed revolution and to the vigorous repressiveness of the now ubiquitous political police. Yet the 1850s and early 1860s had an importance in determining the future course of Germany's history in a way that was only appreciated when historians began to give due weight to economic factors.

The economic background

"No aspect of nineteenth century German history is more important than the economic expansion that took place during the century's middle decades," wrote the American historian J. J. Sheehan in *German History 1770–1866* (1989, 731ff). "This economic growth touched every facet of life, from the conduct of war to the character of sexual relations, from the organization of the state to patterns of recreation, from what people believed to what they wore." The period between the reestablishment of the Confederation by the princes in 1850 and the founding of the Second Empire in 1871 coincides with the take-off into sustained industrial growth in Germany, predominantly in the northwest and in Saxony. For over a generation, Germans witnessed the rapid expansion of heavy industry in the Prussian-owned Rhine-Ruhr valleys, the Saarland in the west, Silesia in the east, and Germany's oldest manufacturing center, the kingdom of Saxony. They could note the steady rise, albeit from a fairly narrow base, in exports of German manufactured goods. The metal and machine tools industries took off in the 1850s. Germany now made her own machines instead of being dependent on mainly British imports, showing that Germany was coming of age industrially. In 1837 the young August Borsig (1804–54) came to Berlin and set up his own engineering works; the year after he died, the 500th steam locomotive produced in the Borsig works was completed. Germany was eager to learn from Britain in these years, and the British engineer was a popular figure in German industrial circles and in literature. At the same time, German scientific and technical education began to be seen as a model to follow in certain British circles, notably in the northern part of the country. Thus when Owens College, now the University of Manchester, was founded in 1854, the governing body made a point of recruiting Germans to chair appointments in science and technology. An exemplary document of the new spirit of partnership between the great British industrial nation, whose queen, Victoria, was married to a German prince, and the developing industrial economy of Germany, is the correspondence between Werner Siemens (1816-92) and a Scots engineer by the name of Lewis D. B. Gordon during the 1850s. Here they discuss as practical men the symbolically resonant issue of oceanic electrical cable-laying.[1] The massive increase in Germany's national wealth which occurred in the 1850s and 1860s did not benefit the whole population, as is eloquently verified in official reports of the day. But the terrible food crises of the 1830s and 1840s were relegated to history, for between 1850 and the mid-1870s German agriculture registered spectacular growth figures. The years immediately following the "Hungry Forties" began with a series of good summers and abundant harvests. Already by the end of the 1850s, and in sharp contrast with Britain, Germany went from being a net importer to a net exporter of food. She sustained that remarkable achievement, despite massive population increases in the period up to 1890, by which time the German Empire was one of the world's leading industrial economies.

The increase in Germany's national wealth had long-term implications for Germany's citizens and also for her political weight in Europe, though the latter would not become fully evident until the end of the period 1850-71. Meanwhile, the optimism that was engendered in the Confederation in business, commercial, and financial circles began in due course to react positively on public opinion generally. Prussia was a particular beneficiary of this process. Despite the unpopularity of her extremely reactionary government in the 1850s, despite the bitterness engendered against Wilhelm I (regent 1858-61, king 1861-88) and his military advisers during the clash between parliament and the army in the 1860s, the Prussian government found support

---

[1] Fontane's sense of the symbolic character of technological advance is one of the underlying themes of his entire oeuvre, from the time when he wrote about the London traffic and the tunnel beneath the river Thames in the 1840s and reaching down to the dinner-table conversation about the telegram and the dislocation in our sense of time in the opening chapters of *Der Stechlin*. It is perhaps nowhere better attested to than in his novel *Cécile* (1887), whose hero bears the name of—Robert Gordon.

among those whose business prospered, and among those whose living standards rose in consequence of Prussia's economic leadership. For Prussia's administration in this period was characterized by a unique mix of authoritarian politics and economic liberalism and a commitment to free trade as pragmatic as that of Britain. At the federal level, developments occurred which facilitated business and mobility of goods as well as people. A postal union was set up in 1850, and in 1857 a monetary convention sharply reduced the number of different currencies. Tariff negotiations between the Customs Union members and Austria promoted business, especially with the development of the Austrian railway links between Budapest, Vienna, and Munich in 1860, and with the building of the line linking Vienna to Linz and Salzburg and to Passau on the Bavarian frontier.

To simplify a complex process: the economic context of Germany's unification provides a key to understanding many of the problematical features of her history at that time. Austrian policy in the Confederation was often defensive in character after 1850, not least on account of a number of structural weaknesses in her economy. More and more members of the German business community in these years were benefiting from Prussia's economic policies, though many of these Germans might feel closer to Austria than to Prussia in political sentiment. The growing support among Germans for free trade began to be manifested in the 1850s and 1860s right across the northern part of the Confederation and in the more industrialized parts of the south also. In the lands lying east of the Elbe River, the grain-producing landowners who had built up a lucrative trade with England after the repeal of the (British) Corn Laws in 1846 began to invest in industry, in the railways as well as in agricultural machinery. Similarly, merchants and traders in the northern ports, in Hamburg on the mouth of the river Elbe, in Stettin on the mouth of the river Oder, in the East Prussian ports of Königsberg (Kaliningrad), Memel, and Danzig, as well as in growing urban centers of commerce and manufacture in the Rhineland, central Germany, and the south, saw free trade as a key factor in their prosperity. German businessmen supported the movement toward progressive liberalization of Germany's trade laws, which the Prussian administration was known to favor. A national movement in support of economic liberalization began to emerge, spawning in its wake a host of organizations at local, regional, and, by the late 1850s when police surveillance grew less onerous, at the national level also. Two such influential organizations were the 1858 commercial Congress of German Economists (CGE) and the political *Nationalverein*, founded in Coburg in central Germany one year later. The CGE was founded to promote free trade and encouraged local branches to set up in every larger German town. Both organizations attracted much interest in a key sector of modern Germany, the print media. In these branch associations, businessmen, civil servants, professional men and academics, bourgeois and noblemen, avidly discussed ways and means of liberalizing the economy and the administration, the two being seen as necessarily part of the same process. The totally divergent speed of change in the economic sector, by contrast with the political system, was made manifest in the repressive pedantry of the Dresden police. They assembled a systematic table on which was recorded in synoptic form the names of those who attended the meetings of these organizations, and how many times they had done so (Siemann 1990, 262). But both the logic of the situation, namely Prussian economic leadership in the Customs Union, and the presence of able and articulate Prussians at these meetings, gradually wore down the fears of members from other parts of Germany of Prussian political hegemony and its possible consequences for them.

But there were some who were less easy to convince. Among them were Bavaria and Württemberg in the south and Hanover and Saxony in north and central Germany. The last two knew that their geographical position made them vulnerable to Prussian expansionism—Saxony, after all, had had a taste of it in 1815, when she lost one third of her territory to Prussia. Hanover would, in fact, be swallowed up by Bismarck after the defeat of Austria and her Confederate allies in the 1866 war, along with Hesse-Kassel, Nassau, and the free city of Frankfurt. All of these states favored Austria's influence in the Confederation as a political counterweight to Prussia. Yet at the same time material advantage for them seemed more and more to lie with Prussia. As the current phrase had it: material factors can count more than people (*Die Dinge sind stärker als die Menschen*). Though the Austrian economy experienced boom years in the 1850s, her industries needed protection. She was unlikely to be in a position to join the Customs Union under the conditions prevailing in the 1850s, yet she had to be a member before she could conceivably offer an economic counterweight to Prussia. Even then, "the causes of Prussia's economic superiority had more to do with the location of coking coal than with tariff boundaries and political institutions" (Sheehan 1989, 747). Austria's financial problems were strikingly demonstrated in the early months of 1859, just after Prussia established a new, relatively liberal regime after the king's mental health forced him to allow his brother, Prince Wilhelm, to take over as regent in 1858. This became known to contemporaries as *die neue Ära* or new era. What in hindsight proved to be a key event in the unfolding drama of Austria's "German destiny," was her war with France over Italy. Austria was defeated by Louis Napoleon (1808–73) in June 1859. By late April of that year Austrian state bonds had already registered a fall from eighty-one on 1 January 1859 to thirty-six.

By contrast, the powerful political implications of Prussia's economic bargaining power became evident in the negotiations leading to the trade agreement of 1862 between Prussia and France, to which the member states of the Customs Union acceded. This agreement gave German member states direct access to the west European free trade area, including France, Britain, and Belgium. Prussia consulted the member states before proceeding to negotiate with the government of Louis Napoleon III but threatened to leave the Customs Union when they hesitated to join. Their decision in favor was a vital preliminary option for the *kleindeutsch* solution to German unification. Political union under Prussia was neither a direct nor an immediate consequence, but the trade agreement did provide a further barrier between the Customs Union territory and Austria, and one which was likely to increase rather than the reverse. At the time, the Austrian ambassador to Württemberg reviewed the developments in Prussian policy over the previous quarter of a century for his foreign minister, Johann Bernhard von Rechberg (1806–90), as quoted in Helmut Böhme *Probleme der Reichsgründungszeit 1848–1879* (1972, 210f). He wrote:

> Through the Customs Union the royal Prussian government increased its influence steadily up to the year 1848 with other German governments; by the (=1862) Trade Agreement this influence was cemented and the industrial class won for Prussia, while the German bureaucrats became the servants of Prussian interests. It was through the Customs Union that the Prussian government forged the unity of material interests and so promoted the desire for political unity in people's minds.

Yet to contemporaries, politics were more important than economics. Thus, when Austria did go to war with Prussia in 1866, most states of the Confederation, many of them members of the Customs Union, fought on the Austrian side.

The Constitutional Conflict

It was not only in the power struggle between Austria and Prussia that Prussia's economic liberalism won her major gains. It also helped determine the outcome of a critical domestic conflict which broke out in the early 1860s, known as the Constitutional Conflict. This was a trial of strength between the Crown and the Prussian officer corps, on the one hand, and on the other, the *Landtag*, the Prussian house of deputies or lower house of parliament. The issue at stake was budgetary control of the army and the role of the army in state and society. The conflict arose out of the question of how the army reform was to be financed. This was the brainchild of Albrecht von Roon (1803–79), Prussian minister of war, Bismarck's personal friend, and a former tutor of the crown prince, later emperor Friedrich III (1888). The *Landtag* accepted the need for the increase to take account of the massive population rise. However, its members were angered at the proposed abolition of the (bourgeois) militia as a separate entity—bound up as this was in the myth of the militia as a key instrument in the defeat of Napoleon in 1813-15. Equally, as men of affairs, they objected to the extension of military service from two to three years. King Wilhelm I, a professional soldier, refused to contemplate, let alone accept, parliamentary competence in matters relating to the army, apart from rubber-stamping the budget. Confrontation between king and parliament resulted. The king dissolved the *Landtag* in 1861, the year of his accession, but it was returned with a greatly increased liberal majority. He tried the same strategy in 1862, ordering the influencing of electors by landowners, employers, and pastors. The result was decimation of the conservative element and overwhelming victory for the liberals. Contemporaries mocked the conservative members of the *Landtag*: now they could all fit in a single carriage. The three-class franchise in Prussia, based on tax paid, had been imposed in 1849 with the objective of keeping the landowning interest in power. However, in the intervening years the economic situation of the bourgeoisie and the free trade politics of a number of aristocratic and bourgeois entrepreneurial landowners, especially in East Prussia, changed both the social composition and the political attitudes of the *Landtag* members. Both sides of the dispute appealed to principle. Roon declared sonorously that "the destruction of the army will mean the ruin of all orderly social relationships." For members of the parliamentary opposition, it was a matter both of constitutional government and of the political emancipation of the bourgeoisie. The optimistic mood engendered by the sustained growth in the economy convinced German business and professional men that the emancipation of their class was but a matter of time. History was on their side. A leading democratic liberal, the lawyer Karl Twesten (1820–70), had articulated the current feeling in the influential scholarly periodical, the Prussian Yearbooks (*Preußische Jahrbücher*) in 1859, when he wrote that "those classes which are the most important for society must inevitably become the political ruling classes too." The Constitutional Conflict was not a clash between the aristocracy as such and the middle classes, but, broadly speaking, between the spokesmen of modern citizenry, the representatives of trade, industrial and agrarian enterprises and the professions, opposed by a preindustrial elite, whose power and state derived from their traditional function in court and in the army. The *Preußische Jahrbücher* described it in 1862 at the height of the conflict as a "struggle between the bourgeoisie in the widest sense of the term against the Junkers backed by absolutist prejudices."

Bismarck

In the summer of 1862 an impasse was reached. The government resigned and the king considered abdication. At this point Roon intervened decisively. Roon, whom the Baden prime minister described a few years later as "a strict systematician, wholly identified with the machine which he had created," telegraphed Bismarck to come to Berlin from his post in Paris. The king proved reluctant to see him, recalling Bismarck's ultrareactionary stance in the 1848 Revolution, a "Junker stained with blood," as he termed him, and fearing the provocation which his appointment as prime minister would represent.

Bismarck in 1871 by A. Weger.

However, in a famous interview in the palace gardens, much dramatized by Bismarck in his mendacious memoirs, the future prime minister overcame the monarch's scruples by his diplomacy and sheer force of personality. Bismarck did not share his king's view on the need for a three-year military service, but he accepted it as the price he must pay, as the necessary qualification for high office and as a means necessary to preserve the traditional monarchic order in Prussia. Entering his new position in September 1862 with zest, he justified his policy by a specious reading of the Prussian constitution: since it failed to provide for the present situation, he alleged, he must govern without a budget, which he proceeded to do for the next four years. He drew on the buoyant customs and excise revenue and was supported by able advice and loans from banking interests, identified particularly with the man who became his own banker, Gerson Bleichröder (1822–93), the first unbaptized Jew to become a Prussian nobleman. The muted response from the *Landtag* deputies is easier to account for when we recall that Bismarck's highly unpopular administration continued to pursue policies in the economic field which corresponded to the wishes of the business community and to the progressive ideology of the bourgeoisie.

In their material interest, both liberal bourgeois and capitalistic noblemen were at one. In 1863, the Berlin stock exchange registered "confidence in the prime minister." There was a further reason why the prime minister's policies did not result in open warfare: so many of the liberal leaders, such as Karl Twesten or Benedikt Waldeck (1802–70), had had direct experience of 1848 and feared isolation between right and left should the conflict erupt in violence. Many liberals were aware that their political ideology, if one can term it thus, represented a class rather than a national interest. In the words of Leopold von Hoverbeck (1822–75), the East Prussian spokesman of the left liberals, the Progressive Party (see chapter 10), Prussian liberalism simply lacked "a firm social basis in the country." Many of Prussia's military ardently longed for a showdown with parliament. Plans for a coup d'état lay sealed in their Berlin headquarters for just such an emergency. Bismarck recognized the paramount importance of the economic factor in the struggle and instinctively appreciated that the interest of the propertied and educated classes in retaining a powerful, if authoritarian state was greater than they supposed. True, for a time, in 1863–4, he appeared to consider forming an alliance of sorts between the ruling classes and the new urban working class against the liberal bourgeoisie. This would have been an extension of traditional Prussian paternalism, but it did not materialize. It was the national issue which enabled Bismarck, a master of political timing, to resolve the conflict more or less on his own terms.

Otto von Bismarck held the position of Prussian prime minister for twenty-eight years from his appointment in 1862. In time he added the posts of Prussian foreign minister, minister of trade, and chancellor of Imperial Germany. To his contemporaries and for at least two generations after his death in 1898, Bismarck was the "arbiter of the national destiny," the "architect of the fatherland," *der Reichsgründer* (the founder of our empire), a nineteenth-century Siegfried hailed in countless rhymed tributes on state and private occasions. Today, we can still recapture something of the force of his personality in the massive statue of the Iron Chancellor in central Berlin, which still stands, flanked by the two generals, von Roon and von Moltke, a little back from the street built by Kaiser Wilhelm II as the *Siegesallee* (Victory boulevard, now dedicated to the workers' rising of 1953), and opposite the huge gilded *Siegesengel* monument. Appropriately, perhaps, the statue is now half-shrouded by trees. Bismarck has been the subject of more than 10,000 books. For many years, accounts of the struggle for German unity were written in terms of his biography. Modern historians, among them Hans-Ulrich Wehler, have made us much more aware of the importance of underlying political, social, and economic structures as determining both timing and form of German unification in 1871. Some historians, such as Helmut Böhme, have gone so far as to describe him as but "one force among many." But Bismarck was more than that. His unique stature as a historical personality lay in his awareness of these structures, based both on observation and rational calculation, and on intuitive response. It was not just his precise gauging of the temper of national feeling in Germany, it was also his extraordinarily dextrous exploitation of economic interests and pressures and of the international situation which helped him establish Prussian hegemony Germany and unify the country in the Second Empire.

The wars of unification: the Danish war of 1864

The unification of Germany was the result of three wars, fought by Prussia for or against the German Confederation between 1864–71. The first, the Danish war, broke out over the vexed question of the Schleswig-Holstein duchies. For various reasons, the European powers, who were guarantors of the status quo under the Treaty of London of 1852, did not intervene. On this occasion, in contrast with 1848, decisive victory was won by the Prussian and Austrian troops. The Austrians actually proved the better force on that occasion, which materially influenced Austria's fateful decision to go to war against Prussia in 1866. The war ended with the cession of the duchies by Denmark to the victors. In considering the psychological effect on Germans of the military victory over the Danes, one should remember what an emotional issue

Schleswig-Holstein had been in their youth. For those who now held positions of responsibility in their professions and in public life in 1864, Schleswig-Holstein had been a highly emotive issue. It had been a potent symbol of German nationalism and the federal defeat by Denmark in 1848, through the intervention of the great powers, had been seen as a source of "national shame and dishonor." Bismarck's handling of the Schleswig-Holstein issue and his political exploitation of the successful campaign, recorded by Theodor Fontane in *The Danish War*, the first of his three war journals, did not conciliate Bismarck's critics inside and outside of Prussia. By the Treaty of Gastein in 1865, Austria occupied Holstein, Prussia Schleswig. The solution angered German nationalists who saw it, rightly, as a continuation of traditional "cabinet" wars which brought German unity not a whit further. But the military victory over the Danes could not but be a source of satisfaction, not just to men of influence in the community, but also to the "little man," whose sense of his own consequence was enhanced by his participation.[2] Bismarck's utterly pragmatic handling of the whole issue did not conciliate his many critics inside and outside of Prussia, but it helped condition their subsequent attitudes. Meanwhile Austria's contribution to the war was played down in the media controlled by Bismarck. This management of public opinion over the next years was a significant feature of Bismarckian policy and part of his character as a modern politician. In 1866, he successfully made the issue of the joint administration of the duchies into a *casus belli* between Prussia and Austria in 1866.

The Austro-Prussian war

Following so closely on the Danish war and preceded by intense diplomatic activity by Bismarck, the war between Austria and Prussia of 1866 might seem a natural and obvious sequence to 1864 and a necessary preliminary to unification in 1871. But this is not how it seemed to contemporaries. Bismarck, on the other hand, had had no such set agenda. The war, which was not popular in the Confederation, was extremely short. It broke out in April and ended only a few weeks later, following the overwhelming defeat of Austria and the federal armies at Königgrätz (Sadowa) in Bohemia on 3 July 1866. As with the Danish war, and as in the Franco-Prussian war of 1870-1, Theodor Fontane provides us with an illuminating contemporary account by an eyewitness. Peace was signed at Prague in August 1866. Austria lost no territory, but Article IV of the treaty required her exclusion from Germany. From a long-

---

[2] This is the point Fontane is making with the figure of Kluckhuhn, the "hero" of the storming of the Düppler Schanzen in the Danish war of 1864, known as Rolf Krake, in *Der Stechlin*.

term point of view, the outcome of the 1866 war resolved the century-long Austrian-Prussian dualism in favor of Prussia. Furthermore, it led to the establishment of *Kleindeutschland*, that is, Germany without Austria, a situation once described by Prussia's previous king, Friedrich Wilhelm IV, as a face without a nose. The year 1866, as modern historians, such as Gordon A. Craig and Thomas Nipperdey, have signaled by its use in the title of their histories, was truly a historic date. The year was more far-reaching in its consequences than 1806, the year of the abolition of the Holy Roman Empire. Austria had been part of "Germany" for almost a millennium, and for half of that time its leading power. Now, and despite the political, cultural, and economic weight of her German population (some 13.7 millions in 1865) she was no longer "German." "Hitler[3] was Austria's revenge for Sadowa," declared a French historian and wit many years later, an observation which is true in the sense that it took until after 1945 before the issue of Austria's "German" identity was finally resolved. From 1866 on, the Austrian Empire was perforce directed south and southeastward, concerning herself primarily with the problems of her multinational empire. Prussia, who had led much of the German Confederation economically for half a generation, found herself fighting most of the federal states in 1866, notably the medium states of Bavaria, Hanover, the two Hesses, Saxony, and Württemberg, as Austria's allies in the 1866 war. Prussia emerged with major acquisitions, which consolidated her territory, notably the former kingdom of Hanover, along with Hesse-Kassel, Nassau, home of Baron Stein, and the city of Frankfurt, where for centuries the kings of the Romans had been crowned. She annexed both Schleswig and Holstein, causing a rift in the fragile friendship between the Prussian Fontane and the native of Husum in Holstein, Theodor Storm. The territorial aggrandizement of Prussia established her hegemony in Germany, but for the moment at least, unification was neither attempted nor desired. Bismarck formed the short-lived North German Confederation in 1867 (till 1871).

But the effect of the victory on the internal history of Prussia was no less significant. The response of Bismarck's liberal opponents to the extraordinary success of Prussia's reformed army revealed the dilemma in which it had placed them. Liberals in Germany had been long wedded to the cause of national unification, both for its own sake, and because they believed it would make the process of liberalizing government an easier one. The Prussian parliamentarian Karl Twesten, a representative of the left wing, spoke of it as the means of winning for the German people a position of power and influence in the world which corresponded to their intellectual and material development; national

---

[3] Adolf Hitler was of course Austrian by birth.

unity represented the nation's real interests and would provide the necessary security against outside intervention in Germany's internal affairs.

The establishment of the North German Confederation made it abundantly clear that Prussia had taken a mighty step forward toward realizing this aim. Accordingly, the ideological justification of the liberals' position was not long in coming. Prussia's victory began to be presented in terms of liberal Prussia's triumph over obscuranticist Catholic Austria (whose liberal government under Schmerling had been replaced by a conservative clerical administration in 1865). On 30 June 1866, three days before the battle of Königgrätz, a correspondent wrote in the *National Zeitung*:

> Even if we have not a democratic ministry at the helm, Prussia undoubtedly represents vis à vis Austria the rights of the people, in the same way as the orthodox Lutherans and Calvinists represented freedom of conscience at the time of the Thirty Years War.

This newspaper had been up to this time the organ of Prussian liberals; in subsequent years it would become a strongly pro-Bismarck paper.

Just before the *Landtag* election in early July, a speaker at an election rally declared that "North Germany is about to be saved from the Jesuits and economic ruin." The fact that Prussian voters went to the polls on 3 July is one of German history's many coincidences. News came through on the electric telegraph in the early afternoon from the battlefront at Königgrätz, and caused a swing away from the liberals and in favor of the Prussian conservative party. The realization of how tenuous their hold on the electorate actually was, helped in the following months to persuade a majority of Prussian liberals to modify their stance over the Constitutional Conflict. The Progressive party split, those in favor of Bismarck's solution styling themselves the National Liberals (see chapter 10).

Outcome of the Constitutional Conflict: the army

Almost immediately after the end of the war, a compromise was reached between the prime minister and a substantial number of his liberal opponents, now joined in the *Landtag* by those new members of the lower house of parliament who had been elected from the recently annexed states. The former prime minister of Hanover, Rudolf von Bennigsen (1824–1902), became leader of the newly formed National Liberal party, which decided to accept Bismarck's compromise plan. In the so-called Indemnity Bill, Bismarck accepted that his course of action had been wrong in law but that, politically, events had legitimized his stance. The change in public opinion was reflected in the *Landtag* vote: members voted by a large majority, 230 to 75, in favor of the Bill.

On the crux of the matter, budgetary control of the army, the compromise was clearly in favor of the government: the amount of money available for military spending was set at a fixed ratio in proportion to the population. Renewed in 1874 under the name of *Septennat*, it was automatically granted for seven years, later reduced to five (*Quinquinnat*). Parliament in fact lost its key function—annual budgetary control—and since Prussia's population continued to rise spectacularly, so too did the military budget. Neither the discussions nor the compromise solution dinted the certainty of Prussia's king and her senior officers that parliament had no rights in military matters. The military command, vested in the person of the king of Prussia and thereafter in the German emperor, who nominally led his army into battle, implied, in the view of the army's commander-in-chief, Wilhelm I, and the officer corps, a complete separation of the civil and military spheres. Though no champion of the military as such, Bismarck himself contributed to underpinning the army's claims by his defense of the crown's rights against those of an elected parliament. He strengthened those claims by the manner in which he institutionalized the special rights claimed by the Prussian king by virtue of his royal prerogative in the constitution for the North German Confederation, later adapted by Bismarck for the Empire. That theory and constitutional practice were not always in harmony in the Empire seems obvious enough to later generations. At the time, there was less resentment of the privileged status and political role of the army in Imperial Germany than might have been expected. But more important for public opinion at large was the association in the mind of nationalists of the special role of the army in bringing about the unification of Germany, or, as the emotive organic term had it, *die Nationwerdung*, the "becoming" of a nation. The brilliance of the Prussian army's performance in the 1866 and again in the 1870–1 campaigns was seen as a direct result of Roon's reforms, which had precipitated the Conflict. By contrast, Austria, whose military forces had been, and had been seen to have been, superior to Prussia's in the recent past, was now paying the price of its financial problems and the weakness of its military leadership. Moreover, Austria unlike Prussia in these key years, lacked continuity of government. For, following the fall of Schmerling's four-year liberal government in 1865, which had finally won the right of constitutional government in the Austrian monarchy, his successors abrogated his 1861 constitution. The septuagenarian Viennese dramatist, Franz Grillparzer, always an acute political commentator, addressed himself to Bismarck: you claim to have founded a Reich. What you have done, is to destroy a people.

The Franco-Prussian war

The Franco-Prussian war not only confirmed people's belief in the validity of the Prussian army reform; it also made people identify with "the nation," through the participation of so many Germans in what was made to seem a kind of crusade against a national enemy. The outbreak of war in 1870 took place against a very different background of events on the domestic front than in 1866. Now, in place of domestic conflict, there was evidence of growing prosperity and public optimism. Popular chauvinism was widespread, reflected in speeches and gatherings, in music and literature, and already by the first weeks expressed in hundreds of martial popular songs. The martial Rhine songs of the 1840s underwent a huge popular revival. Between 1866 and 1870, influential circles in Europe began to look on war between France and Prussia as well nigh inevitable. In Bonapartist circles in France, there were many advocates of a preventive war to check Prussian expansion. Among them was the Duc de Gramont (1819–90), appointed French foreign minister in May 1870. Following the news early in July of the acceptance of the Spanish throne by a member of the south German Catholic branch of the Hohenzollern family, Gramont declared that the French nation would vigorously oppose the candidature and would administer a severe diplomatic rebuke to Prussia for thus "interfering with the balance of power in Europe." But the French proved no match for Bismarck's diplomatic sophistication and he exploited the opportunity both for foreign and domestic political ends.

The mishandling of the situation by emperor Louis Napoleon's government enabled Bismarck to cast Prussia in the role of champion of "German liberties" in the face of French aggression. Even after the prince renounced his claim to the Spanish throne under pressure from France, it seemed as if Louis Napoleon was determined to win compensation in the form of German territory and that only united resistance on the German part could stop him. A tremendous surge of patriotic fervor in favor of war with France swept across Germany, including the southern states, most of whom had formerly been extremely suspicious of Prussia. Even Fontane, who on 19 July 1870 referred to the mood of the country as *unendlich viel Blech* (so much bombast), confessed himself moved, as so many were, by the dignified appeal of the seventy-three-year-old king Wilhelm I to all Germans to make common cause against the ancient foe. On a superficial level, it seemed that what Karl Marx like to term contemptuously "south German beer patriotism" lay behind the response of Bavaria, Baden, Württemberg, and Hesse-Darmstadt[4] the image of

---

[4] That is, the part of Hesse-Darmstadt territory south of the river Main which had joined the North German Confederation in 1867.

The Growth of Prussian Hegemony in Germany 1850–71

the Fatherland in danger. To resist the inevitable would be politically impossible, wrote the Bavarian king, Ludwig II (1864–86), to his brother in 1870, since both the army and the people would strenuously oppose such a decision. By 1870, the southern states had already been sitting for two years in a national German Customs Parliament based in Berlin, legislating on commercial concerns common to north and south. Two years earlier, they had signed a secret military agreement with the North German Confederation in 1868 which provided for their defense by Prussia in case of attack; in such a case the south Germans would put their army contingents under Prussian command. The reason why states such as Baden and Württemberg in the southwest were ready to do this, derived from their genuine fear of French designs on the Rhineland. Furthermore, it was widely known that Louis Napoleon had become more restless for foreign prestige as his health deteriorated and his policies at home faltered.

Accordingly, when the French declared war on 19 July, some 260,000 Frenchmen found themselves facing an army of 450,000 men led by a tried and able commander, von Moltke. By early August the Germans were on French territory, in a region which Prussian officers, disguised as amateur painters,

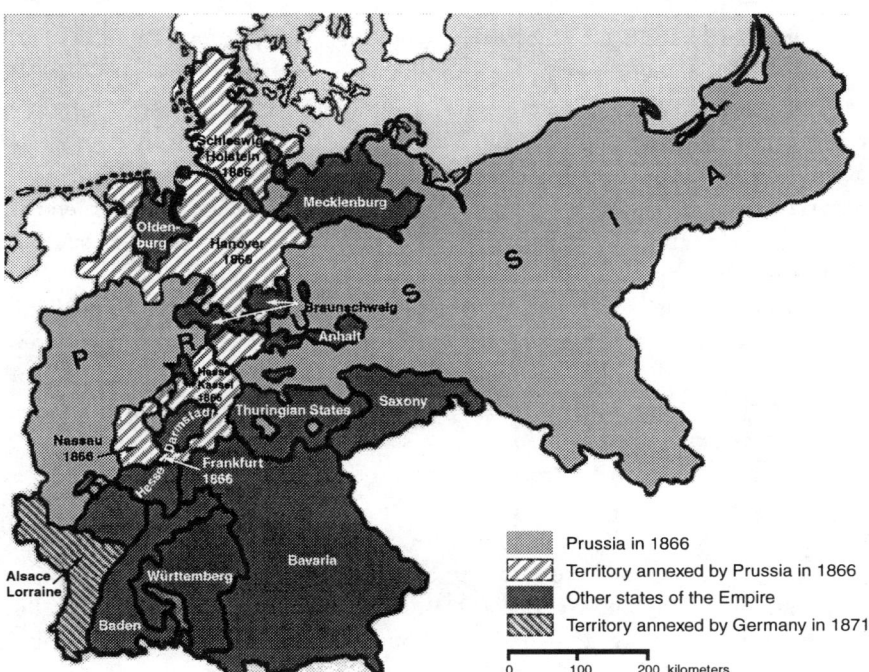

The evolution of Bismarck's Germany.

had studied with just such a conflict in mind. The equipment of the Prussian-led army and their exploitation of the railway system ("the nomadic invasion by train," as Fontane called it in a letter of 5 August 1870), made a formidable war machine. Within a little more than a month after bitter fighting in Alsace-Lorraine, described by Émile Zola (1840–1902) in his novel *Le Débâcle* (1892), Louis Napoleon was defeated at the battle of Sedan on 1 September 1870 and taken prisoner, capitulating on the following day. The Second (French) Empire collapsed, but the war went on under what was now the third French Republic, largely on account of Prussia's insistence that Alsace-Lorraine must be ceded. Some four months later, on 18 January 1871, Wilhelm I was proclaimed German Emperor in the Hall of Mirrors at Versailles. He was flanked by the assembled German princes, as recorded in Werner's painting (see page 110). That is, apart from Ludwig II (1864–86) of Bavaria, who by his absence laid his claim to special status in the new Germany. He remained in his capital in Munich where also on 18 January, in tandem with events in Versailles, the Bavarian *Landtag* proclaimed the second Empire. Ten days later an armistice was signed, followed by the peace of Frankfurt in May 1871.

The south German states

Protracted and difficult negotiations had been going on since September 1870 between Prussia's representative, Rudolf (later: von) Delbrück (1817–1903), and the southern states. Baden, ruled by Wilhelm I's cousin and son-in-law, was the first to accede, followed by Württemberg, whose relatively democratic traditions earned it the name of "crowned Switzerland," and Hesse-Darmstadt. Bavaria proved difficult, but was won by a well-tried Bismarckian blend of enticement (paying the king's debts on his flamboyant palaces, such as Neuschwanstein) and threat (expulsion from the Customs Union).

Low taxes, little industry and a reasonably liberal administration, made life in southern Germany generally an agreeable affair. Many southerners were apprehensive at the idea of Prussian domination, but policymakers and opinionmakers were broadly committed to a united Germany, and the visible success of German arms proved to be a subtle persuader. However, the subordination of the south to Prussia was an intrinsic feature of the new state, as became clear, especially to Bavarians, in the years to follow. Although much less mobile than their brothers and sisters north of the Main, south Germans would in years to come become accessible to the often chauvinistic patriotism of the Empire. Hans Thoma (1839–1924), the popular Bavarian painter, recalled its southern flavor with dry—and wry—humor in his memoirs. He described the inhabitants of the small south Bavarian town of Prien flocking to the station on hearing that Bismarck would be passing through by train to catch a glimpse of the great man, while at the same time insisting on their disdain and dislike of Prussia. Yet in other ways, south Germans preserved a certain critical detachment from the main sources of tension in the first two decades of the new Reich, such as militarism, the neofeudal character of society, and the hysterical fear of social democracy.

Unification

The Franco-Prussian war played the supremely important role in the domestic political history of Germany of translating into reality the *kleindeutsch* blueprint for unification The international consequences were even more considerable. The defeat of France, which brought Germany Alsace and parts of Lorraine along with a war indemnity of five milliards of gold francs, changed the balance of power in Europe. For centuries, France's rulers, one of whom, Louis XIV, had seized Alsace-Lorraine from Germany when the Holy Roman Emperor was involved in war with the Turks in the 1680s, had been committed to keeping Germany disunited. The power vacuum at the heart of central Europe, which had been the source of endemic conflict for some three centuries, was filled in 1871 by the unification of Germany. Over 40 million Germans, whose economy was booming, a young country in every sense, whose population was rising annually, and who were united in a sense of common achievement and destiny, now formed one of the great powers alongside Britain with its 32 millions. The current political witticism, coined by a member of the British House of Commons that with 1871 Europe had lost a mistress (France) and gained a master (Prussia), suggests that contemporaries were well aware of the significance of the events they were witnessing.

It is hard for us today to have the kind of sympathetic insight into 1871, not least because of the links between the Second Empire and the origins of the Third Reich, postulated by the research of twentieth-century historians, some of whom, or whose parents and grandparents, were victims of Hitler's regime and Hitler's war. However, in the opinion of most European governments and of most nations at the time, including the United States but with the exception of France, the "solution of the German question" offered by the founding of the Second Empire seemed one of the more positive achievements of the nineteenth century, a genuine contribution to the overall stability of Europe. In international relations Bismarck would do his best in the years that followed to reassure them that this was indeed the case.

Chapter 8
The German Writer and the Literary Market

German writers had played a vital role in the rise and development of the nationalist movement which eventually led to the exclusion of Austria from 'Germany' and to the creation of a second Empire of German-speaking peoples in central Europe. Yet neither German literature nor the literary market after 1871 institutionalized those political divisions, except, paradoxically, in Switzerland. Austrian writers continued to read literature written and published in the Second Empire as they would their own. Some, such as Karl Emil Franzos (1848–1904), author of popular tales and essays on Jewish life in far-off Czernowitz and Galicia (modern Rumania and Poland), even looked to Berlin rather than Vienna as their cultural home. Austrian writers continued to publish in Germany, just as writers living and working in the Second German Empire also published in Austria. German writers regarded the extraordinarily rich literature of post-1866 Austria as an intrinsic part of German literature, as we do today. By contrast, German Swiss writers felt estranged by Bismarck's Germany. Prior to the breakup of the Confederation in 1867 and the founding of the German Empire, though not members of the Confederation, they had felt culturally part of Germany. Now they no longer felt this way. The process of such cultural withdrawal is subtly documented in the correspondence of Jakob Burckhardt and of Gottfried Keller.

The German book trade and the "reading revolution"

The nineteenth century made Germans into a nation of readers, a people with the highest literacy rates in the world. In the century in which Germany finally became a unified state, her literature held a special place in the imagination of her people as a key constituent of their identity. Structural changes in the eighteenth-century German literary market had prepared for those revolutionary changes in the communication of the written word, which is the hallmark of her nineteenth-century history. In seventeenth-century Germany, over half of what was published had been written in Latin. By 1800 this share was reduced to less than 4 percent. Similarly, religious books, which had traditionally dominated the market, had by 1800 long since given way to books and journals of secular interest. Intellectuals in 1800 were more interested in philosophy and anthropology than theology. Imaginative literature, which in 1740 had accounted for less than 6 percent of the annual publications displayed at the Leipzig book fair, by 1800 constituted over 20 percent. The number of books published in German rose sharply in the same period. So too did the numbers of readers and the manner in which they read. Literary and social historians acknowledge the so-called "reading revolution" of the late eighteenth century as a major phenomenon of the era. Women began to represent a significant proportion of the reading public in Germany. They, like men, began to read differently than in times past. Instead of reading the same few books, such as the Bible, devotional books, and popular almanacs offering practical advice, Germans began to read extensively, constantly looking for novelty in the literary market. Leipzig, the commercial and financial capital of Protestant Saxony and an important university town, had long since replaced Frankfurt as the center of the leading book fair, and also of the book trade. It was the merchants of eighteenth-century Leipzig who introduced modern commercial practices into the publication, distribution, and sale of books. Books were no longer sold by a system of barter but by cash transaction.

On the eve of the nineteenth century, a split became evident in the literary map, with the Protestant north and center of Germany representing the modernizers, and the Catholic south, notably Austria, resisting these developments. One particularly contentious issue was that of piracy, that is, the illicit printing and selling of books already published by another publisher. The pirates, of course, paid no royalties to authors and had no marketing costs. Austria actually protected pirates in her territory in the interests of providing (and controlling) new publications, at a fraction of the original cost. The institutions which promoted the reading revolution, the elitist reading circles and the more popular reading societies, were concentrated in Protestant Germany. It was in central and northern Germany that one found most of the new book shops, which were a feature of the literary landscape between 1815 and 1848. Shopowners invited customers to browse, even if they did not buy, and gave them facilities to discuss the latest books and magazines. When Friedrich Perthes (1772–1843), a leading Hamburg publisher and perceptive observer, traveled through Germany in the second decade of the nineteenth century, he noticed a marked contrast between the two halves of Germany. Apart from Augsburg, there were scarcely any book shops in the southeast; indeed, between Regensburg on the Danube and Vienna, some two hundred miles downriver, he could not find a single one. A few years earlier, Heinrich von Kleist, on a visit to Würzburg on the river Main, had noted the dearth of reading societies by comparison with the north. When in 1825 German publishers and booksellers decided to create a national organization (the *Börsenverein*), the initiative came from Saxony in northern Germany.

Leipzig remained the center of the book trade well into the second half of the century, only ceding its primacy, though not its significance, to Berlin as the capital city of the new Reich after 1871.

Control of the printed word: the legal situation

It was not, however, until well into the nineteenth century that Germany's writers, their publishers, and their readers saw an end to the severe legal difficulties and disadvantages under which the German book trade labored. The main causes of these were the different laws of its thirty-nine component states and the authorities' justified fear of the democratic influence of the printed word. Censorship in Germany was both onerous and arbitrary, yet it was several decades before either author or publisher could enjoy some measure of protection of their rights, which they might expect from a paternalist state. The Prussian civil code of 1794 was the first German legal code to recognize intellectual property rights. Few legal problems at that time attracted such discussion and so much published opinion by lawyers and nonlawyers than the issue of intellectual property and piracy. Both Fichte (1793) and Kant (1798) wrote on the subject of piracy. As early as 1765 the publisher Philipp Erasmus Reich (1717–87) had attempted to set up a professional organization of booksellers to provide some defense against piracy, but public opposition by authors and readers who feared higher prices prevented it. The Austrian Johann Thomas von Trattner (1717–98), who had been one of the tutors of the emperor Joseph II, was a vigorous defender of piracy, and made a great deal of money from it. Austria, which published relatively little by comparison with Saxony or other Protestant German states, got many of its books, as it were, on the cheap. Under French occupation, west Germany enjoyed the short-lived benefit of French law, and when the Congress of Vienna convened, German booksellers delegated two of their most prominent members, Friedrich Cotta and Friedrich Justus Bertuch of Weimar (1747–1822), to seek legal protection for authors and publishers. However, the Congress failed to address the issue, leaving it instead to the sovereign states of the new Confederation. Differences between the states were profound, and it was really only when Prussia took the initiative and negotiated agreements with thirty-three other states (but not with Austria) to outlaw piracy, that the Federal Assembly finally agreed in 1832 to support a system of copyright valid for the Confederation. This was only achieved in 1835—at the same time as the Assembly banned the works of a number of Germany's most discussed writers, among them Heinrich Heine. It was Prussia's 1837 copyright law, imposing a period of thirty years after the death of an author, which provided the model to be followed. Accordingly, in 1867, when the copyright on the first protected works lapsed, cheap editions of Goethe, Schiller, and others came on the market, immensely enhancing the capacity of students and less well-off readers to start buying their own books.

At the Congress of Vienna, Article 18 (d) of the Federal Act had promised freedom of the press and protection against piracy. Instead German writers got the Karlsbad Decrees which imposed police surveillance on intellectuals and especially on writers. The Vienna conference of ministers following the 1830 Revolution imposed even harsher measures. In 1839 and 1840 lists of "culpable persons" who were thought to be politically active or critics of the regime contained the names of over 2,000 so-called political suspects. But the decades following the 1848 Revolution proved far worse in terms of censorship. Prior to 1848, the censor was usually, though not always, a man of letters. In the 1850s, the ministries of the interior, effectively the police, were charged with the task. The person, rather than his work, became the object of their often arbitrary attention. The 1874 Reich press law did not end censorship, but it unified the law and it transferred the issue of freedom of the press to the jurisdiction of the courts. However, the arbitrary persecution of Catholic journalists during the *Kulturkampf*, and the systematic hounding of the socialist press after the passing of Bismarck's antisocialist legislation (1878–90) showed the limits of the law's protection.

By 1886 Germany had become a signatory of the Bern Convention, which stabilized prices and established copyright on an international basis. By the end of the century, the German book market was one of the most vigorous and productive, but also the most highly commercialized in the world. This is nicely illustrated by the letter written by the Viennese author Friedrich Schlögl (1821–92), author of celebrated sketches, to his friend Peter Rosegger in his capacity as editor of the journal *Heimgarten*: "Dear Editor, You thank me for my contribution. I am not interested in thanks. I want to be paid. The children need food and their father needs beer. Yours etc." Culture was becoming a commodity and people its prisoner, as the sociologist Georg Simmel (1858–1918) was to note in his *Die Philosophie des Geldes* (1900) and other seminal writings. For the individual writer, however, the economic and legal situation in 1900 was incomparably better than in 1800. Writing had truly become professionalized, and its rewards were real. Whether the status of the writer had improved was a matter of dispute. At all events, the issue of German writers' place in society provided a rich source of inspiration for the generation which came to adulthood in the 1890s.

The reading public

The identification of literacy rates in the past is notoriously difficult and its results disputed. In 1700 10 percent of Germans are thought to have been able to read and write. A century later some 25 percent of Germany's 23 million inhabitants are estimated as having been functionally literate. The percentage had doubled by mid-century. In 1900 some 90 percent of Germans were literate. In the first half of the century, the principal reasons for this extraordinarily rapid increase appear to have been the impact of the educational reforms of the Enlightenment and the greater access to the printed word through the reading societies of the late eighteenth and early nineteenth centuries. In the second half of the century, the lending libraries also played a key role. Two representatives from different generations of socially disadvantaged Viennese can exemplify the benefit of the school reforms introduced under Empress Maria Theresia and her immediate successors. One was the tragicomic actor and playwright of the Viennese popular theater, Ferdinand Raimund (1790–1836). Raimund was the son of poor immigrants to the city and was forced to leave school at fourteen to support himself. Yet he wrote eight comedies, three of which still form part of the repertory of the Viennese theater, among them the brilliant anticipation of Freudian therapy, *Der Alpenkönig und der Menschenfeind* (The King of the Alps and the Misanthrope) (1828). The second such representative to benefit from the Austrian school reforms was Schögl, already mentioned, and one of fourteen children of a hatmaker. Schlögl recalled how in his childhood his father read Schiller's and Bürger's (1747–94) ballads after their dinner of soup and potato cake. Undoubtedly, the upheavals of the Napoleonic wars gave a further impulse to literacy through the mobility they generated. Regional and social mobility was accelerated by the introduction in a number of German states of freedom from restraint of trade. The German education system in the Metternich era proved notably accessible to the very large strata of society broadly termed lower middle class. The years between the revolutions of 1830 and 1848 gave a powerful impulse to Germans' interest in the printed text, to take the term in its broadest sense. This impulse made itself increasingly felt across regional and class divisions. Texts included not just pamphlets, but also songs, speeches, manifestos, and especially broadsheets, with cartoons and accompanying texts.

Literacy rates were consistently higher in the Protestant areas of Germany (including Württemberg in the south), because Protestants were trained from childhood to read the Bible. Saxony and Austria pioneered primary education for all subjects of the realm, but Prussia was the first state to introduce compulsory schooling. However, enforcement only became effective in the second half of the century. Yet even as early as the 1820s, the Catholic church showed itself very aware of the dangers to their flock of the modern media, and set about providing, with ever greater sophistication in the second half of the century, a highly diverse alternative program of reading material which would socialize both traditional and new Catholic readers in their faith. The history of literacy in this period shows continual evidence of new strata of readers emerging. Among the numerically most significant of these were women. Schiller was known to encourage women writers, not least because, as an editor of periodicals, he knew the importance of the female reading public. His own scholarly *History of the Thirty Years War* (1788) was actually published in a women's magazine, the *Calendar für Damen*.

Even in that era, rural literacy rates are thought nowadays to have been higher than once believed, though the actual reading material might be relatively untaxing. On the eve of the nineteenth century, the printers of the small Swabian town of Reutlingen, for example, supplied a legion of distributors with popular reading material. These were the *colporteurs*, or peddlers, who penetrated remote regions to supply their customers with works of popular entertainment, such as the old chapbook tales of Faust or fair Melusine, and early versions of horror stories, alongside works of popular enlightenment. On the eve of the new century, the reorganized German book trade scored its first modern commercial successes with works of popular enlightenment. Most notable of these were the paper for children, *Der Kinderfreund*, edited by the librettist Christian Felix Weiße (1726–1804), which proved a resounding commercial success, and the *Noth- und Hülfsbüchlein für Bauersleute* (Little Book to Aid and Help Farming Folk) by Rudolf Zacharias Becker (1752–1822). The latter was a particularly interesting phenomenon, because it was launched with what we might call today a modern mass advertising campaign. Subscriptions were invited and some 28,000 received before the work was published in 1788. It could thus be sold at low cost. By 1800, the publishers—who included Goethe's sometime publisher Georg Joachim Göschen (1750–1828)—had disposed of the extraordinary figure of 400,000 copies, many of them distributed by the authorities as school readers. Pirates and translators helped to ensure that for a brief period Becker's *Noth- und Hülfsbüchlein* became one of the best-known books in the German language.

The lending libraries

In the nineteenth century, books about popular enlightenment began to lose their appeal in favor of fiction and works of topical interest. Formerly one had read and reread a few books. This was called intensive reading. Now, by contrast, people wanted novelty. The new manner of reading, declared one concerned author in 1795, makes people "physically and psychologically ill."

Reading societies were denounced as "moral bordellos," and the *colporteurs* attracted the particular vigilance of the police. Lending libraries, a key agent in the communication revolution of the early and mid-nineteenth century, aroused even greater anxiety. Yet it was through them that Germany first achieved, on a mass basis, a degree of national cultural assimilation, and it was through the agency of the lending libraries that Germans were linked to the national literatures of other European nations and America, either in the original or in translation (Martino 1990, 661). Books remained expensive until after unification and the number of books published per year did not rise significantly until the 1870s. Early and mid-nineteenth-century German readers borrowed rather than bought books. Indeed, as late as the 1850s, publishers decided the size of an edition in terms of the number of lending libraries likely to purchase copies. When calculations did not turn out as envisaged, and a novel did not sell, the author had a problem in persuading his publisher to take future work. Gottfried Keller found this out to his cost when *Der grüne Heinrich* (1854–5), his great novel of childhood and education, one of the classics of the century, only sold a fraction of the estimated number. In fact, it was only when the national economy had created a class of readers with some disposable income that book ownership became a status symbol and the commercial lending libraries began to decline.

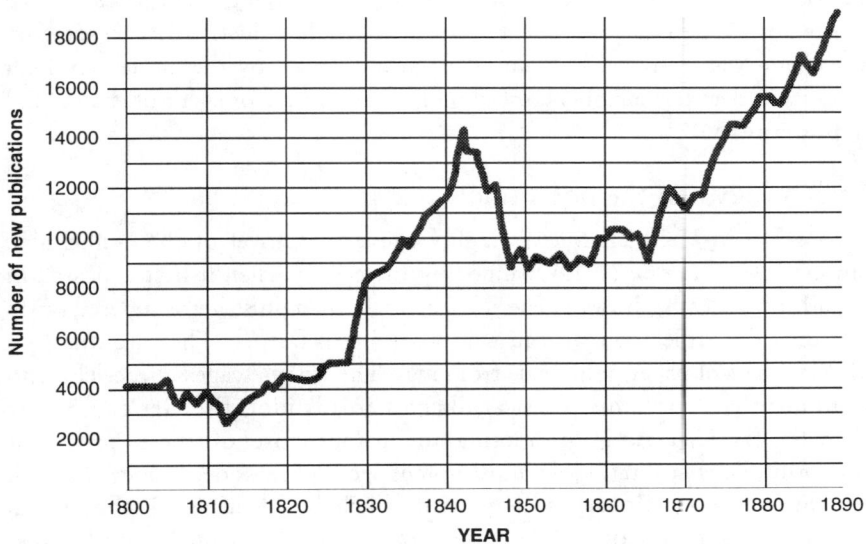

The number of books published in nineteenth-century Germany.

In the Metternich era, the substantial number of educated but un- or underemployed men, who sought a livelihood by writing, became the particular target of Germany's censorship laws. German state governments were concerned at the proliferation of readers, fearing, quite rightly, that literacy ultimately promoted criticism of the established order. It was more difficult to censor readers, easier to punish those who provided the reading material. Following the imposition of the Karlsbad Decrees in 1819, mass arrests were made of so-called demagogues in the universities. In the period 1830–48, government agents targeted the new phenomenon of the editor-journalist, such as Karl Gutzkow and the Young Germans, or the Young Hegelians, while continuing their persecution of politically active students and their associates. One typical victim was a former student and later publisher by the name of Robert Binder (1808–70), who was an associate of the young Fontane in Dresden in the 1840s. He spent over three years in Prussian and Saxon jails in the 1830s for publishing allegedly seditious material, and fell victim to the persecutions of the counter-revolution in 1849, when he was condemned to and served ten years in prison from 1849 to 1859 for the same crime, as well as for having collected and channeled monies to assist political refugees. In the 1850s and 1860s, when industrialization demanded functional literacy, the authorities were presented with an acute dilemma: how to keep the economy on course and yet keep the masses quiescent by denying them access to the printed word. As if to prove the authorities' fear justified, the socialist movement was characterized, almost from the outset, by the immensely high value its leaders and members placed on literacy as a major agent of change and empowerment.

Technology and the book trade

A scene in Heinrich Mann's highly subversive novel of the Wilhelmine Empire, *Der Untertan* (1918), banned by the censor when it first appeared in serial form in 1914, shows Diederich, the male chauvinist hero, superciliously regarding the proletarian women who work in his factory. They are stirring a stinking mass of paper pulp made from rags. The irony escapes Diederich, who sedulously cultivates his physical likeness to his idol, the German Kaiser Wilhelm II. That is, in promoting the manufacture of cheap paper for newsprint, he is facilitating the most potent agent of mass democracy that will overthrow the reactionary society with which he identifies. Technological advance in the production, distribution, and sale of the printed word fostered change in attitudes and in the ways people behaved.

The principal advances came in the first half of the century: 1806 saw the development of a process enabling the gluing of books to be done mechanically. In 1810–4 Heinrich König (1774–1833) developed his mechanical steam printing press and had the good fortune to sell his invention to the London *Times*. By 1824 Cotta was publishing the *Allgemeine Zeitung* on a König press. Brockhaus and the Stuttgart publishing house of Metzler followed suit two years later. The new process could publish multiple copies in a fraction of the time formerly taken and thus made possible both an increase in market products and a substantial lowering of costs. In 1844 paper began to be manufactured from wood pulp and paper costs dropped.

At the end of the decade the 2,500-mile railway network was ready to be exploited to distribute the printed word. In the 1850s, popular magazines began to use illustrations, modeled on French methods of lithographic reproduction, to attract what proved to be the beginning of a mass reading market. In 1872, the first rotary printing presses were installed. Subsequent decades saw a massive increase in the number of newspapers and their readers, at national and at local level, as well as new regional centers for the production of books, journals, and other publications for niche marketing.

Zurich in Switzerland had provided the location for the opposition press in the *Vormärz* and again during Bismarck's persecution of the socialists (1878–90), when their publications were proscribed. In Germany the vibrant socialist press was concentrated in Leipzig and Berlin. The Protestant churches traditionally had important publishing centers in different parts of Germany, among them Berlin, Halle in central Germany, Hamburg in the northwest, and Cannstadt near Stuttgart in the south. The Catholic book trade was largely a nineteenth-century creation. The center of the large and ever-growing Catholic communications industry under the Empire was in the Rhineland, at Mönchen-Gladbach, not far from Cologne. Catholics proved at least as versatile as their secular counterparts in niche marketing, if not more so. Thus in the small Bavarian town of Donauwörth, an enterprising editor named Ludwig Auer (1839–1914) built up a mass communications industry for a new section of readers: the young. Uncle Ludwig, as he was known to his readers, produced weekly magazines for adolescent boys and for adolescent girls, and he also supplied young children, servant girls, and apprentices each with "their" magazine. Copiously illustrated to encourage reading, Auer employed all the tricks learned from Christoph Martin Wieland (1733–1813) and from the older popular works of the Enlightenment to give his readers a sense that they were personally known to him, and, what is more, that he understood and sympathized with the small tragedies of their private lives. By the last years of the century, his distribution network extended to include German-speaking Catholic parishes of the United States.

In the second half of the century, increasingly sophisticated technology brought down the price of books in Germany. By contrast with the 1850s and 1860s, when the price of books was high and wages low, real wage rates rose in the last third of the century. This meant that the possession of books, something which increasingly had status, became possible for many who could not have afforded to buy them a few years previously. By 1899 paper costs had fallen to 33 percent of what they had been in 1871.

The market and its agents

The significance of the figure of the publisher for established and for aspiring German authors has already been touched on (see chapter 4, beginning on page 43). A feature of the German literary market between the mid-eighteenth and mid-nineteenth centuries was the key role played by entrepreneurial publishers and editors in creating new market demands. Thus, following the example of Brockhaus, Otto Wigand (1795–1870) began his career by publishing a Hungarian popular encyclopedia which provided the capital base from which he later established one of Germany's leading publishing houses. Publishers had not enjoyed a high reputation in the Enlightenment, with notable exceptions such as Reich, the Leipzig reformer, and Friedrich Nicolai (1733–1811), friend of Lessing and Moses Mendelssohn. Kant went so far as to compare publishers in 1798 to factory owners. Indeed, Tieck found employment as a very young man with a Berlin publisher, as part of a team producing novels to order. The great names in the early nineteenth-century publishing world, Perthes and Göschen, the Cottas, father and son, or the Campes, uncle and nephew, were men of vision and cultivation. The elder Cotta had studied law and mathematics at Tübingen, before finishing his education and making useful contacts in Paris, which stood him in good stead during the years of the Napoleonic administration. Cotta was both generous and shrewd. Schiller's family was cared for after the poet's early death in 1805 on the basis of contracts with Cotta, but the firm made a great deal of money over the years from Schiller's works, as it did from Goethe's later works. Cotta used some of the profits to finance little-known authors and to publish in fields other than literature. It was he who launched Alexander von Humboldt's *Cosmos*, a compendium of contemporary scientific knowledge (1845–62), which proved to be an impressive intellectual and commercial initiative. In time the firm of Cotta merged with Göschen's Leipzig publishing house (Göschen's descendants became prominent in British business and politics). In the later nineteenth century, the house was bought by Adolf von Kröner (1836–1911) of Stuttgart, whose popular editions of the classics had few rivals in Germany, at least before the advent of the twentieth-century paperback.[1]

At the end of the nineteenth century, many of the most powerful and influential names in publishing came from cultivated Jewish families, among them Mosse and Ullstein, who dominated the newspaper industry. Kaiser Wilhelm II continually referred with disparaging crudeness to "the Jewish press." Certainly, as in the earlier period, individual publishers could have a major impact on the development of the purely literary market. Thus, just as every aspiring lyric poet in the age of Metternich hoped to get published by Cotta, so too in the 1890s novelists aspired to get on to Samuel Fischer's list. The shrewdest of businessmen and a generous patron of the arts and artists, Fischer had been born in Hungary in 1853, had trained as a bookseller in Vienna, and opened his own firm in Berlin in 1886. Thomas Mann made his name as a Fischer author, following the publication of his first novel *Buddenbrooks* in 1901. Many women novelists also owed their literary success to Fischer. One of them was Gabriele Reuter (1859–1941), whose novel of frustrated bourgeois girl- and womanhood, *Aus guter Familie*, was published by him in 1895; another was Helene Böhlau (1859–1940), author of angry naturalist novels and daughter of the publisher of one of the standard editions of Goethe's works; a third was Clara Viebig (1860–1952). His list included German translations of Dostoyevsky, Tolstoy, Zola, and Shaw, and he became known as "the Cotta of naturalism." Among his authors were many major names of their generation, such as Gerhart Hauptmann (1862–1946) and Hermann Hesse (1877–1962), as well as Austrians such as Hugo von Hofmannsthal (1874–1929), Arthur Schnitzler (1862–1931), and Peter Altenberg (1859–1919). Altenberg offered an ironic view of his colleagues' opinions on the great man when he declared: "Samuel Fischer is publishing me—therefore I am!"[2]

Initially, books and journals were published and sold by the same person or firm. Around 1800, this process tended to become separate. Bookshops increased threefold in the last four decades of the eighteenth century and this trend accelerated over the following decades, notably in Prussia. But book production, which had expanded rapidly over the previous decades, was severely hit by the Napoleonic wars and took nearly a generation to recover. By 1843 it had more than trebled its production of 1820, to some 14,000 new titles per annum, a peak not exceeded until 1880. Of these, 8 percent or some 1,200 titles, fell into the category of polite literature. The chief centers of literary production and

---

[1] Kröner is still, in the field of literary publishing, notable for its literary handbooks (for example, Goethe, Thomas Mann, Theodor Fontane, etc.).

[2] The reference is to the French philosopher Descartes' famous refutation of doubt: "I think, therefore I am."

distribution varied relatively little over the century as a whole, with the significant exception of Berlin. After 1871, Leipzig inevitably ceded pride of place in sheer numbers of publications to the new imperial capital at Berlin. However, its book fair retained its dominant role, and it was in Leipzig that the main publishers' stocks were held (and hence so many were lost when Leipzig was firebombed in the Second World War). Alongside commercial cities, like Hamburg, the university towns, such as Tübingen, Jena, or Göttingen, remained important centers of publishing, as they still are today. Other regional centers developed more specialist publishing in the latter decades of the century, as business, along with the reading population, and the demands of an ever-more sophisticated knowledge market, continued to expand.

Print media: journals

Given the disadvantageous relationship among the middle and lower ranks of society between salaries and wages and the cost of books, and given, moreover, the relative lack of wealth-producing classes in Germany before the age of industrialization, it is not surprising that periodical literature, rather than books, was a very significant means of access to imaginative literature for Germans in the period around 1770–1870. Journals had been the principal repository of the German Enlightenment, whether we are speaking of the older moral weeklies, which aimed to develop the aesthetic taste of its upper- and middle-class readers, or the influential periodicals which fostered intellectual debate. Two leading examples of the latter were, firstly, the *Berlinische Monatsschrift* (founded in 1783), for which Kant and Fichte, Benjamin Franklin (1706–90), and Thomas Jefferson (1743–1826) wrote, and, secondly, Nicolai's review journal, the *Allgemeine deutsche Bibliothek*. Between 1765 and 1806 this journal managed to review some 80,000 publications. Over 2,000 new journals appeared in German in the years 1765–90, 1,225 alone in the 1780s. Germany reacted to the epoch of French Revolution with an explosion of journals of political opinion, but before the end of the century, only in part as a consequence of harsh censorship laws, educated debate had turned rather to philosophical and literary topics. The turn of the century saw the appearance of short-lived journals which pioneered some of the most important debates of modern aesthetics, notably in journals such as Friedrich Schlegel's *Athenäum* (1798–1800), which cost Cotta money, but which he supported nonetheless. In common with most of the romantics' journals, those of German classicism, such as Goethe and Schiller's *Thalia* 1875–91 or Schiller's *Die Horen* 1795–7, were generally short-lived and not commercially successful. It was characteristic of the regionally vigorous German literary landscape in these years that their centers were so diverse. They included Leipzig, Hamburg, Berlin, Göttingen, Frankfurt am Main, Halle, Kiel, Jena, Nuremberg, and Stuttgart (all of them Protestant cities and towns, and all but two in north and central Germany). Women writers, notably Sophie von la Roche (1730–1807), boldly entered the periodicals market in the 1780s and, perhaps more importantly, acted as role model for others.

In the period 1815–40 a type of journal known as the almanac or pocketbook became the key means of access to imaginative literature for both readers and writers. Many readers were encouraged to try their hand at verse or short prose by their contacts with the almanacs, which favored 'feminine' titles such as *Flora*, *Iris*, *Aglaia*, or *Penelope*. Because of their form—they were very small, so as to fit into a man's pocket or lady's reticule—and often of few pages, they influenced the preference for the shorter literary forms characteristic of these decades, the lyric poem, short story, sketch, travel reminiscence. But because foreign authors in translation could make no claims for payments, publishers of almanacs favored translations over German works. Thus the medium became an important channel for German readers to the popular English-language and French authors of the day, or at least until the lending libraries established their monopoly in this regard. In the absence of a recognized public sphere, literature in the Metternich age became a form of public utterance, with the local almanac offering an unknown local author the chance of a (local) audience and, if successful, the entrée to a wider national public.

There were a number of remarkable long-lived journals which published many major and minor poets in the first half of the century and employed others as editors. The most notable were the *Zeitung für die elegante Welt* (1801–59), published in Leipzig, which the Young German Heinrich Laube edited for a time, and the *Morgenblatt für gebildete Stände* (1806–49), which was published by Cotta. Cotta enabled Gutzkow to show his remarkable energy and flair as a journalist at a time when his works were banned by the Federal Assembly (in 1835), when he appointed him editor of *Telegraph für Deutschland* (1838–48). Its very name linked the printed word with the engineering revolution just beginning. So too did the periodicals which Friedrich List published, such as *Eisen-Journal*, with the aim of promoting railway travel, providing entertainment "on board," and, not least, helping to create a 'nation' of liberal, openminded people. List's periodicals also featured imaginative literature. Much more short-lived on account of police persecution were the influential political journals of the day, of which Arnold Ruge's *Hallische Jahrbücher* (1838–43) was the most important.

Among the consequences of the failed revolution of 1848-9 was that Germany's periodical press took a new direction. Reflecting a greater material culture and the commercial demands of the publishing houses, the market of the 1850s and 1860s was dominated by liberal journals, such as the *Preußische Jahrbücher* and by the new mass phenomenon of the *Familienzeitschriften*. Of these the so-called "Garden Bower" (*Die Gartenlaube*), edited by a former political prisoner-turned-marketing man, Ernst Keil (1816-78), was soon in a class of its own. Auerbach, whose own books started to sell extremely well in these years, noted in a letter to his cousin that Keil's marketing genius put the *Gartenlaube* into the hands of an impressively wide readership. Keil himself identified two particularly important target groups, "the ordinary craftsmen and (especially) women." By the late 1870s, nearly 400,000 copies were sold annually, each copy undoubtedly being read, at the very least, by one further reader. Some of Germany's major authors of realist narrative fiction, such as Fontane, published from time to time in the *Gartenlaube*, because it paid well. Others, such as Raabe, favored the so-called "novel-newspaper" or *Roman-Zeitung*, published by a leading supplier to the lending libraries by the name of Otto Janke. Raabe published eleven of his novels here. But to win recognition from the critics, and from one's peers, it was important to be published in serialized form in the leading literary journals, the *Deutsche Rundschau*, based in Berlin, and the older established *Westermanns Monatshefte*, founded in Stuttgart in 1856. The *Deutsche Rundschau*, founded in 1874 by the Berlin Jewish writer and entrepreneur, Julius Rodenberg (1848-1904) and edited by him until his death, exercised a major influence on German prose fiction in the late 1870s and the 1880s. Among Rodenberg's authors were Marie von Ebner-Eschenbach, Fontane, Louise von François (1817-93), Keller, C. F. Meyer (1835-98), Raabe, and Storm. By the end of the century, the *Deutsche Rundschau*, now conservative in its opinions, lost ground to the *Neue Rundschau* (founded in 1894 as the *Neue Deutsche Rundschau*, 1904-44: *Neue Rundschau*), which attracted the younger authors. In Munich, Michael Georg Conrad (1846-1927) made his journal, *Die Gesellschaft* (Society), founded in 1885, the periodical of the early naturalists. In 1896 the satirical illustrated paper *Simplicissimus* in the same city attracted some of the most gifted graphic artists inside and outside of Germany (see illustrations on pp. 218, 230, 253, 262, and 276). Particularly feared were the two brilliant satiric talents, who edited and wrote their own journals, in Berlin Maximilian Harden (1861-1927): *Die Zukunft* (Future) and in Vienna Karl Kraus (1874-1936): *Die Fackel* (The Torch). Kraus accepted contributions for his journal in its first years (1899-1911) but thereafter and until his death in 1936 produced that brilliant satiric corpus entirely on his own.

One of Karl Kraus's pet targets were the authors of what became an influential subgenre of literary journalism in its own right in the cultural life of later nineteenth-century Germany and Austria. This was the feuilleton. Its immediate origins lay in the political journalism of the *Vormärz*, with metropolitan authors such as Heine, Börne, or Glassbrenner. In the hands of its most skilled practitioners, mainly Austrians, such as Ferdinand Kürnberger (1821–79), Daniel Spitzer (1835–93) and Schögl, it provided personalized comment on literary and cultural events, personalities, and institutions, especially the theater. In the way he (it is almost invariably "he") writes about and addresses his readers, the feuilletonist is an ethnographer, but an ethnographer of the city. Indeed, the popularity of the genre provides evidence of the increasing urbanization of German language culture in the last decades of the century.

Print media: newspaper press

In 1785 a spokesman for the German Enlightenment declared that "the invention of the newspaper is indisputably one of the great boons conferred on humanity by the European nations." Metternich would most certainly have begged to differ. The press helped create, define, and maintain communities within the state and in due course to create a national community. The old established newspapers, such as the Berlin *Vossische Zeitung*, for which Fontane worked as theater critic from 1871–89, went back to the eighteenth century; others, such as Cotta's *Allgemeine Zeitung*, managed in difficult times to establish and maintain something approaching a national newspaper in the age of Metternich. In the 1840s, the newspaper press played an immensely stimulating role in preparing for and promoting the revolution. Probably the best-known example is the *Neue Rheinische Zeitung*, which Marx edited for a brief period in the 1840s. The Christian press began to develop as a vigorous special-interest press in the era following the revolution, known as the *Nachmärz*.

By 1871 there were 126 Catholic papers. A decade later, despite or perhaps because of active persecution by the state in the *Kulturkampf*, there were 221 and more than twice that number in 1912. All ideological camps, Protestant, Catholic, and liberal, favored a popular paper known as the *(Volks-)Kalender*. The *Kalender* was a type of almanac written in a folksy style and sold for a few cents, but commanding print runs of up to hundreds of thousands. By contrast, the socialist newspaper press, with its leading organ, *Vorwärts*, was much more serious in tone and more demanding in content. Newspapers sprang up in the second half of the century to represent different party political positions. Alongside the socialist *Vorwärts*, the *National-Zeitung* represented the National Liberals, the *Voßische* broadly based liberal opinion, while the *Kreuz-*

Zeitung was the organ of the conservative Junker interest.[3] Toward the end of the century, an astonishing array of regional newspapers reflected the resurgent energy of conservative organizations, as described in James N. Retallack's *Notables of the Right* (1998, 235ff).

In the last decades of the century, newspapers offered a successful challenge to the market position of the family magazines by providing serialized novels, poetry, literary criticism, and light literary entertainment in their supplements (*Beilagen*). Illustrations, and above all topical photographs, proved highly attractive to the mass reading public. As the century drew to its close, the new vogue for advertising helped newspaper proprietors to drop the price of their product significantly and to publish more frequently and in greater quantities. In 1850 Germany had had some 1,500 newspapers; twenty years later the number was some 2,400; in 1885 over 3,000. The real difference lay in the numbers of copies sold: what used to be an elite had been transformed in half a century into a mass readership. The Berlin *Morgenpost* sold half a million copies daily in 1898. In 1900, newspapers began to be sold on the streets, rather than at newsagents only. By 1914 the *Berliner Illustrirte Zeitung* was selling one million. German newspapers, like those in other industrial countries, were served by international news agencies, Wolff's *Telegraphenbüro* for Germany, but cooperating with Reuters in London and Havas in Paris. The Germans, like the British, had once been known as readers and listeners with an impressively long attention span, who could listen to a sermon or a speech of more than one or two hours in length. By 1914 the majority had been socialized, or perhaps manipulated, by their own commercial press to demand news and features which could be absorbed in minutes.

The evolution of genre

One of the less-noted results of the developing literary market in nineteenth-century Germany was the way in which some genres became popular, others went out of fashion. The evolution of genre in German literature over the years between 1800 and 1900 is fascinating and complex. Hegel established a notional hierarchy of genre with tragedy at its zenith, and effectively excluded novels from the literary canon. This inevitably influenced what aspiring authors wrote, but in time market forces intervened to challenge literary ambition. As the century passed, the increasing preference of publishers

---

[3] Fontane drew broadly on his daily reading of the last two organs for his novels, as will be evident to scholars investigating the sources of his last novel, *Der Stechlin*, where the references to the Paris Commune, the rats, and revolution are foreshadowed by a four-part report in the *Kreuz-Zeitung* on the twenty-fifth anniversary of the Paris Commune.

and editors for prose fiction and journalistic feuilleton, rather than the older established forms of epic and lyric poetry, idyll, and even drama, had its impact on literary production. Karl Gutzkow is a good example in point. A born journalist, though not, like Heine, a natural stylist, he responded instinctively to what the market liked. After his pedagogical tales of the early 1830s, he made his name with an allegedly salacious novel, *Wally die Zweiflerin* (1835), which led to the proscription of his work and that of other political writers. He wrote a novella on a famous martyr to religious tolerance and then rewrote it several years later as a tragedy (*Uriel Acosta*, 1846), when he had access to the stage as theater director in Dresden. He correctly gauged public taste for comedy in the mid-1840s and 1850s, both on the stage and in the form of prose tales. The 1850s saw him produce the multivolume novels of contemporary life, *Die Ritter vom Geist* (The Knights of the Spirit, 1850–1), which would bring such handsome profits to his contemporary, Gustav Freytag, and to Gutzkow's less ambitious but commercially cannier imitators, such as Friedrich Spielhagen, Felix Dahn (1834–1912), Georg Ebers (1837–98) in the 1870s and 1880s. By the beginning of the next decade, daily newspapers and the innumerable journals in the mass market needed constant copy. With the steep rise in circulation figures at the end of the century, editors' appetites for serialized novels and for novellas seemed clearly insatiable.

But other factors were also significant, not least for women. Numerous writers, among them the Austrian contemporaries, Marie von Ebner-Eschenbach and Ferdinand von Saar, spent years attempting to establish their reputation by writing dramas, only to realize belatedly that their forte lay elsewhere. Fontane tried his hand unsuccessfully on the ever-popular subject of the English martyr-king, Charles Stuart. Market demand made him turn to ballads, which met the new fashion for patriotic verse. He was nearly sixty before his first novel was published and he could risk the attempt to earn his living exclusively by his pen. Ebner's self-confidence as a writer was cruelly undermined by her failure as a dramatist. Not simply because of family disapproval, but because she had publicly exposed herself by competing so blatantly in a man's world. Women were constantly given to understand that their métier as writers was the realm of feeling, not of action. This was made particularly evident in the lyric poetry of the mid- and late-nineteenth-century anthologies. In the age of nationalism, German lyric poetry written by women had the function of preparing people psychologically to come to terms with economic and technical progress which might otherwise have unsettled them (Becker 1994, 123). Gender stereotyping approved "female" genres such as the novel, lyric poetry, and the short story, but denied women the capacity for, and by implication the right to, the stage or the epic. Charlotte Birch-Pfeiffer (1800–68), one of the century's most successful stage writers after Kotzebue, was the object of constant malicious criticism by her male colleagues. Droste wrote a self-ironic play (*Perdu*) with herself cast as the blue stocking. Germany's finest woman dramatist of the century, Elsa Bernstein (1866–1949), wrote under the male pseudonym, Ernst Rosmer, which she chose as a tribute to the author of *A Doll's House* and *Rosmersholme*, Henrik Ibsen (1828–1906). Even Schiller (Schieth 1987), for all his open encouragement of women writers, was not prepared to accept them as anything but writers of lyric poetry and novels, not tragedy or epic. Clemens Brentano opposed the literary ambitions of his wife Sophie Mereau after they were married, despite her previous success as a writer. Women writers were encouraged to concentrate on "what they knew best," to record their feelings and emotions within the narrow confines of the autobiographical genre: not "memoirs," since these belonged to the public sphere and therefore to the male, but rather the diary or the letter. By 1900, however, the commercialization of the literary market in Germany offered women writers the opportunity to challenge the stereotyping to which they had been subjected throughout the century that had just ended.

Chapter 9
German Women and Their History in the Nineteenth Century

Is there not something a little old-fashioned about a history of Germany in the nineteenth century which, as it were, separates women for special treatment in a chapter of their own? Is it not rather time to write a gendered history of nineteenth-century German political and social history, as Peter Skrine and I have done for German literature from the invention of printing to the age of the internet in *A Companion to German Literature* (1997)? It is of course rather easier to integrate women in a meaningful way into the history of German literature than into her political and economic history. In the first case, woman's absence from, as well as her presence in a particular literary genre or epoch conveys much information about the constitution of the literary market at that time. In the second case, it is difficult to include women systematically in a short survey without distorting the account, since so much of nineteenth-century Germany's political, economic, and social history was demonstrably made by men. But the principal reason for devoting a separate chapter to women in the present volume is a pragmatic one. The reader of a textbook addressed primarily to the student of literature wanting some background knowledge of Germany's development in this complex century requires easy access to a body of information on a variety of aspects of nineteenth-century women's lives. The present chapter begins by discussing the ideological context in which men were wont to perceive women, as a result of their Enlightenment heritage. It begins with an outline of the demography of women and a brief account of some of the ways in which women's lives were changed by changes in technology and fashion, followed by a survey of their education (or lack of it), the world of work, politics, the emancipation debate and of the literary market as it affected women. There follows a short consideration of the world of German family life, and the chapter ends with a review of some of the myths which had such a potent impact on German perceptions of women, and hence on the way they were treated.

Women's *Bestimmung*: the debate on women's function in society

In 1869, the English political thinker John Stuart Mill (1806–73), published one of the seminal essays of the century on women's place (or lack of place) in contemporary civil society. He described it in his *Autobiography* as being inspired by his (step-)daughter and he gave his work the provocative title: *On the Subjection of Women*. Just four years earlier, in the same year (1865) the first German national women's association was founded, Rudolf Virchow (1821–1902), a distinguished German medical professor and cellular pathologist, later a leading member of the German liberal party, had published his contribution to the debate. Virchow entitled his work: *Über die Erziehung des Weibes für seinen Beruf* (The Education of Woman for Her Vocation). A British or American reader might wonder why Virchow could be classed as a liberal. His views on women, on their education and role in society, differed in no significant way from those on the conservative right. In expressing them, Virchow was writing within a

Frau Wilhelmine Begas. Painting by the elder Karl Begas.

paradigm which had originated in the late Enlightenment and one which was not systematically challenged during the century that followed by any spokesman or group representing the public sphere in Germany. The notion of a specifically female *Bestimmung* or destiny, determined not by the needs of society but by women's 'nature' and her physiology, had been elaborated in the anthropological debates of the last years of the eighteenth and the early years of the nineteenth century. Subsequently, such notions were popularized in the media, notably in those compendia of popular learning for the middle-class reader, the encyclopedia, such as the *Conversationslexikon*, published by the influential house of Brockhaus and imitated by many others. These encyclopedia were widely bought by middle-class households and went through successive editions throughout the whole of the century. To read these articles on women, as published in successive editions over the nineteenth century as a whole, is an illuminating, but sobering experience. Woman was here primarily defined by and in her relationship to man. Her claims to education were to be defined, not by her personal need or wish for self-development but by the requirements of husband, household, and children. This was tantamount to saying that the *Bildungsideal* of German classical humanism was and must remain an exclusively male affair. In defining women as "the fair sex," in emphasizing their superior grace and taste, the anthropologists of the late Enlightenment and Romanticism, and their later popularizers, believed they were paying an acceptable tribute to womankind. In fact, they were effectively excluding them as functioning members of the public sphere. The widely consulted popular encyclopedias invariably contained long articles on women under the headings of *Frau* (woman) and *Ehe* (marriage) which identified female physiology and biology as determining woman's social role. Thus the author of the closely written six-page entry on women in the 1876 edition of Brockhaus' *Conversationslexikon* declares:

> All branches of knowledge, the arts or public affairs, which require systematic thought, the capacity for abstraction, deduction, the kind of imagination and feeling which are subordinate to the guidance of mind and reason are almost exclusively the domain of man. We attribute to women the kind of knowledge, art and activity which requires quick comprehension, good powers of observation, awareness of one's immediate surroundings, the gift of doing the right thing, memory for images, concern for detail, and the kind of rich, brilliant, abundant imagination which has more to do with the senses than with the metaphysical domain.

The issue of women's education is presented in the same article (not for the first or last time) in terms of a false antithesis: "No education is better for women than the kind of education which gives them false ideas." Apart from a new, self-congratulatory note at the more chivalrous manner in which Germans treat their womenfolk than do other nations, later editions of Brockhaus suggest no diminution of misogynist prejudice. A typical entry from 1876 reads:

> Man's achievements lie in the field of action, communication and creativity, woman's special quality are patience, receptiveness, care for others ... Man's thinking is consistent and logical, woman does not think, she perceives, instinctively, intuitively.

Men and women, it seems, were part of a "binary system," preordained by nature and impervious to cultural or social influence. Of course, modern readers need to remind themselves constantly that the notion of equality, whether of peoples, races, or the sexes, was a novel one when first articulated in the early Enlightenment. Invariably, it was going to meet incomprehension or arouse atavistic opposition. The father of the Enlightenment, Christian Thomasius (1755–1728), had written boldly in 1692: "Women are just as capable of learning as men." The admired Leipzig writer and professor of aesthetics, C. F. Gellert (1715–69), and the dramatist and critic Gotthold Ephraim Lessing acknowledged women's wit and natural powers of reasoning, by making their women characters at least as moral and even linguistically more dextrous than their menfolk. This is nowhere more wittily presented than in the mistress-servant pair, Minna and Franziska, in Lessing's great comedy of 1767, *Minna von Barnhelm*. But scarcely a generation had elapsed before the views of Lessing and other like-minded men and women were challenged by poets, philosophers, educationists, and anthropologists. Here the role of gender stereotyping, as elaborated in the late Enlightenment, and its marriage with the national mythmaking of Romanticism, would prove more enduring than the logic of Thomasius or Lessing. Furthermore, the secularization of Christian mythology about the relations between the sexes, a characteristic development of the new century, would prove a vigorous weapon in the armory of those opposed to the emancipation of women.

Demography

Accurate and differentiated statistics which would permit us to generalize about female demography in Germany in the period under discussion are not available until the last decades of the nineteenth century. But sources do exist which allow us to appreciate the revolutionary differences the century wrought in women's lives. By 1900, for example, women were living far longer than their grandparents. Between 1870 and 1900, life expectancy for women had increased by more than a quarter. Diet had improved, including even the diet of the urban poor. The "killer diseases," such as typhus, had slowly begun to yield to improvement in water supplies and better distribution and preservation of milk. Infant mortality, always high in past times, began to decline rapidly at the turn of the century. Couples began to regulate their families. This had a demonstrable effect on women's health, though class, regional, and religious differences remained very marked in this, as in other aspects of Germans' social behavior. Thus Catholics were much slower than Protestants and (more affluent) Jews to limit their family size. However, despite the rapid and sustained rise in Germany's population throughout the nineteenth century and up to the eve of the war, a change in the birth-rate was on its way. This was the cause of deep and often hysterically voiced concern to those observers of society influenced by the biological or Social Darwinist thinking of the Wilhelmine era. The number of births per union in Germany was in fact declining dramatically; the 1914–8 war would exacerbate the inherent trend, until by 1933 the number of children born per union was less than a third of the average rate of more than four in the last decades of the previous century.

On average, women did not marry as early as traditional views have often suggested. The later decades of the nineteenth century show 25 or 26 as the average age for first marriage, with the men being two or three years older. But of course here as elsewhere, 'average' is a deceptive word. Those without substance or hope of improvement of their lot tended to marry early; the better-off could provide their daughters with the necessary dowry and marry them off at an early age—the best known literary example is, no doubt, Fontane's *Effi Briest* (1895). But the age of marriage for men in the middle and upper ranks of German society tended to be much older. Thus Effi marries a man twice her age, because Innstetten, her future husband, like so many Prussian nobles, was a former officer and subsequently a career civil servant without private means. He had been in love with Effi's mother Luise, but had not been in a position eighteen years earlier to marry her. Instead Luise settled for marriage to the prosaic Briest, also several years her senior. For Prussian army officers and civil servants were relatively poorly paid and often had to save for years, even decades, in order to set up a home which would reflect their status in society. The future field marshal and victor of Germany's wars of unification, Moltke, had to postpone marriage until his mid-forties and even then found it difficult to afford the furniture needed. The idea of marrying before one had the necessary possessions was simply not acceptable. So, too, men and women at lower levels of society, but for whom status in the community was a major issue, had to earn and save before they could marry. This included the subaltern officials, small traders, artisans and white-collar workers, and of course small- and medium-sized farmers. Some German governments in the early decades of the century had imposed marriage prohibitions on those who did not have the wherewithal to nurture a family. The result was a massive increase in illegitimate births. The possession of savings in the case of lower-class girls or a dowry among bourgeois or aristocrats made a woman attractive to suitors, or unattractive, as the case of Mete Fontane (1864–1916), the clever daughter of Theodor and Emilie, exemplified. Fontane's inability to provide the required dowry for his daughter adversely affected her chances in the marriage market, and was the source of tension in the family and of psychosomatic illness for her, as the family correspondence attests. Only in the year of Theodor Fontane's death, when Mete was thirty-eight, did she marry, to be the third wife of a wealthy septuagenarian who could afford to do without the dowry. The need for women from more modest backgrounds to contribute in a material way to the new household was one of the reasons why domestic service, both on the land and in the town, was favored, not just by working-class women, but also by the daughters of middle- and lower middle-class girls, particularly in the first half of the century. They got bed and board as part of the job and could save most of their earnings. In the 1830s and 1840s, some of the more civic-minded authorities began to set up savings accounts precisely to help such women maximize their wages. Domestic service also taught skills very necessary for married life, where running a household meant hard, physical, time-consuming work and the need to make small budgets stretch to the utmost.

The sheer amount of physical work to be done by women in a household, before the age of consumer durables, is hard for us to imagine today. Before the age of running water and bathrooms, every bucket of water for washing and cleaning had to be carried by hand, from the local pump or well, and, later, in the urban housing blocks, from the communal cellar. Before the advent of domestic gas lighting and electricity, candles were the only source of light (apart from the open fire). Along with countless other household necessities, candles were produced at home, being prepared from fat discarded from the kitchen. The German household continued to be a unit of production long into the nineteenth century. In the summer women made preserves from fruit, drying mushrooms, preparing the barrel of sauerkraut in the autumn, and salting meat or fish to last the winter. The washday, a good deal less frequent than today, was nothing short of a marathon. Bettine von Arnim, wife of the poet (and herself a writer), described getting up at four in the morning with her daughters and the servants and spending the whole day in hard physical labor until the wash was done. Demographers believe that the physical demands made on women in their child-bearing years increased in the early and middle decades of the century, rather than the reverse, and that these were responsible for the higher-than-average mortality figures for younger women at the time. So much of that physical burden went unrecorded, though we catch a glimpse into the reality of family illness from correspondence. In Annette von Droste-Hülshoff's letters, for example, we read of the wearying and enervating task of sitting up over many nights with the sick, which of course exposed oneself to infection. And yet Droste, being unmarried, was not subject to the additional burden of many pregnancies. It was as much the need for a housekeeper than any other reason, that made men remarry quickly following the death, often in childbirth, of a wife. Fritz Reuter's portrait of the maidservant, Dürten Holz, in his comic novel, *Serenissimus Dörchläuchting* (1866), provides a splendid insight into a real social situation. Dürten, a fine, strong woman, is sitting in her little room, reflecting on her future; she is now "gone thirty," heading toward spinsterhood, a state which implied a lifetime of subordinate status. But she has her comforts in her present job—and she has her savings. A local man has lost his wife and is left with three children; another is also looking for a wife to help look after his aged parents. Should she opt to be a respectable married woman and a household drudge? Would it really be worth it? She is, she decides, a very good catch for either man in question. Too good, in fact. Neither gets her. But not everyone had Dürten's advantages—a "good place" and a little put by against the rainy day—or, indeed, her choice. Life, war, desertion, multiple births, loss of earnings, were the reality for many women in the past whose history we shall never know. However, there is considerable historical evidence available for Germany in the late nineteenth century to suggest that the lives of women above the poverty line were, by and large, better than those of their grandmothers and great-grandmothers.

Women's lives, more than those of men, were affected by changes in fashion, based on developments in manufacture and technology. While lower-class women and women in farming life had traditionally wore serviceable clogs, whose thick wooden soles and raised toes protected the foot from wet and muddy surfaces, in the late eighteenth century upper- and middle-class women's lives were revolutionized with the advent of leather shoes in place of those made of fabric. Such women could now take outdoor exercise, and even engage to a degree in outdoor pursuits. By the end of the nineteenth century, the better-off women were riding bicycles, despite their cumbersome skirts—for the sight of a woman's leg was still regarded as "shocking." Women's dress, perhaps even more than that of men, is a reliable indicator of social mores. The soft lines of Biedermeier dress emphasized femininity but did not restrict movement. By contrast, the mid-century crinoline, with the skirt or skirts resting on a vast cagelike wire structure, obstructed movement. Seduction must, at least in the initial stages, have been not a little difficult, reminiscent of the conquest of a fortress so beloved of writers of military memoirs. The whaleboned corsets of the Empire, which emphasized women's waists and bosoms, were, to a later generation a powerful symbol of the inhuman restriction imposed by society on their womenfolk. At the end of the century popular discussion focused on the damage they inflicted on their internal organs; magazines supplied lurid but 'scientific' illustrations contrasting healthy livers with the deformed organs of 'fashionable' women. The so-called *Reformkleidung* movement of the *fin de siècle*, which excited intense and emotional debate, was much more than a challenge to received notions about women's dress: in its advocacy of practical, comfortable garments and, in particular, clothes hanging from the shoulder, it questioned the received notion of women as defined exclusively by their relationship to men. It influenced the lives of children, or, rather, children of a section of the middle ranks of society, in seeking forms of dress more relevant to the actuality of young lives. For the *Reformkleidung* debate and the naturist movement, limited as both were to a small and better-off or better-educated section of society, were of course a calculated provocation of contemporary society, not an affirmation of it. However the debate is of interest because it anticipated the arguments and, in some ways, the actual lifestyle of significant sectors of the late twentieth-century alternative movement in the modern Federal Republic of Germany.

Women in the labor force

Debates in nineteenth-century Germany on the issue of women in the work force were often conducted in a manner that was quite unreal. Discussion, especially in the later decades of the century, liked to focus on the negative effect on society of female employment outside the home because of its alleged damage to the family, the resultant neglect of the children and, not least, of the husband. But, of course, some women always had to work, if their husbands earned too little, or died, fell ill, or deserted them. If such women had not worked, their children would have gone hungry. Moreover, large sections of the economy could not have functioned without women's work, notably on the land. This had been the case from time immemorial and continued to be so, long into the twentieth century. In 1907, 4,650,000 women worked in agriculture. As Germany became an industrialized country, women were needed in ever-increasing numbers in industry and the small but growing service sector. However, the pattern of women's work was different from that of men.

With the exceptions of agriculture and domestic manufacture, full-time work by women was, broadly speaking, pre- or postmarriage. Statistics for the German Empire in 1907 estimate that only one-quarter of married women were in employment, that 40 percent of widows worked. The bulk of the female work force was single. In 1907, 70 percent of their cohort were registered as working (just under 80 percent in Berlin). Very few professions, including medicine, law, teaching at grammar school and third level, and the senior civil service, were open to women before the twentieth century: women were not admitted to study at university. They could and did train as elementary teachers and as teachers in private schools. Some types of female work required women to resign on marriage. Teaching was one such occupation, yet it was a profession which became increasingly attractive to middle and lower middle-class women toward the end of the century, as the state took over greater responsibility for and invested substantially in public schooling. At the same time, teaching at primary and nongrammar school secondary level began to be less attractive to men, not least, because, in their view, it lacked status. Women teachers, who comprised about 20 percent of the cohort around 1900, tended to come from a higher social stratum than their male colleagues, a situation which was an obvious source of tension. Yet, by contrast with other types of work available to them, such as being a governess, a companion or even an office worker, teaching did carry a certain social status for women, as exemplified in the figure of Mathilde Möhring, in the last chapters of Fontane's eponymous novel, as she, complete with pince-nez and her dead husband's title, embarks on her new career.

The actual number of women in paid employment rose steadily during the Empire and sharply during the 1890s, during the very period when public debate about women's place, situation, and rights was most acute. Statistics reflect this clearly. Against a background of a rapidly rising population, the years 1882–95 saw the number of working women increase by 0.6 percent; in the following twelve years, 1895–1907, the increase was as much as 4 percent. There were, in fact, almost one million more women in Germany in 1895 than men. The overall number of women in the labor force almost doubled in the twenty-five years from 1882 to 1907, from an estimated 5,540,000 to 9,490,000. Within these statistics, considerable variations existed with regard to employment sector. It is not surprising that women were poorly represented in the civil service and the professions, as the following table shows. However, new openings for women were created by the increasing bureaucratization of life characteristic of late nineteenth-century German industrial society and by the expansion of the retail trade, leading to a proliferation of shops. By the second decade of the new century, about half a million women were employed as office workers and shop assistants.

It was in some ways more difficult for middle-class women to find work than for the wives and daughters of manual workers. It was generally frowned upon for such women to seek employment, because it reflected badly on the husband or father as provider. Broadly speaking, it ought to have been less necessary for them to do so.

Table 1: Employment of women in the Second Empire (in 1,000s)

Economic sector	Year	Total no. of employed	Total no. of women	Women in percent
Agriculture	1882	8,236	2,535	30.8
	1895	8,293	2,753	33.2
	1907	9,883	4,599*	46.5
Industry	1882	6,396	1,127	17.6
	1895	8,281	1,521	18.4
	1907	11,256	2,104	18.7
Commerce and Transport	1882	1,570	298	19.0
	1895	2,339	580	24.8
	1907	3,478	931	26.8
Domestic service	1882	1,723	1,466	85.1
	1895	1,772	1,548	87.4
	1907	1,736	1,570	90.4
Administration, Military and the Professions	1882	1,031	115	11.2
	1895	1,426	177	12.4
	1907	1,739	288	16.6
Together	1882*	18,957	5,542	29.2
	1895	22,110	6,578	29.8
	1907	28,092	9,493	33.8

Source: Hohorst, Kocka, Ritter, *Sozialgeschichtliches Arbeitsbuch,* Munich 1975, p. 66.

However, social studies and records from individual sectors of manufacture and industry suggest that, from the late eighteenth century onward, considerable numbers of women and children from the middle ranks of society were trying to support themselves or to provide a vital supplement to the family budget. While the mid-century invention of the sewing machine was a boon to middle- and lower-income women seeking work, it also, like the typewriter at the end of the century, laid them open to exploitation by middlemen, as in the clothing industry.

Rural labor

Traditionally farming had employed and depended upon female labor. Biedermeier literature, most notably the novels and stories of the Swiss Jeremias Gotthelf, offers rich insights into the hierarchy of agrarian labor relations, both male and female. Other writers of the time, such as Berthold Auerbach in his story of the rural Cinderella, *Barfüssele* (Little Barefoot, 1856), sentimentalized and implicitly denied the sharp division between farmer's son and day laborer's daughter. Barfüssele marries the farmer's son and lives happily ever after, something that was extremely unlikely to happen in the real-life rigid rural world of hierarchical relationships, based on property. The Jewish peddler's son, Auerbach, achieved astonishing sales with this utopian tale, his story being reprinted continuously till the time of the Nazis and published widely in English translation in England and the United States. The numbers of women agricultural laborers increased in parallel to their male counterparts, but the scarcity of rural labor, as a consequence of the mass migration during the later decades of the German Empire to the towns and cities, invariably helped improve the unenviable lot of rural wage laborers, both female and male. Women and children also formed a substantial percentage of the most exploited sector of the working population in 1900—workers in domestic manufacture. Social historians believe the numbers were rather higher than official statistics suggest, though the remuneration was often pitiful, and such workers had no form of social welfare, a situation only regulated in 1911.

Factory work

Factories were not a main employer of women in nineteenth-century Germany. However, this began to change in the last decades of the century. Between 1882 and 1907 the numbers of employed women rose from approximately half to one and a half million. Men and women belonged to different shop-floor cultures. Women were more likely to be found in the textile, readymade clothing, and food industries. One of the most graphic accounts of early factory life by a woman is the autobiography of Adelheid Popp (1869–1939), the Austrian political activist. Her memoir was published in 1909 under the auspices of August Bebel, leader of the German Social Democratic party and himself the author of a seminal work *Die Frau und der Sozialismus* (1879), reached its fiftieth edition in 1910. Popp's memoir documents the common experience of women factory workers, namely, poor pay (for the most part), lack of security and, on the workers' part, a high rate of mobility from job to job. Although Popp casts her account in a slightly comic mode, sexual harassment appears to have been a serious hazard of factory life for women, and also a reason for moving on.

Domestic service

Far more women sought work in domestic service than in factories, and this remained true, despite the relative and, subsequently, the absolute decline in numbers recorded in the table on page 160. As the nineteenth-century German economy repositioned itself (see chapter 12, beginning on page 233), domestic service ceased to be a more or less equal option, as it had been in the past, for men and women, and became almost exclusively a female preserve. But bourgeois (and aristocratic) lifestyles depended on the availability of domestic service, a life which usually put extreme physical pressure on those so employed and rewarded them meagerly. Nineteenth-century German literature abounds in portraits of women servants, but German realist literature was in general no different from its counterparts in England, France, and the United States in retaining the notion that literary servants belonged *de facto* to the comic genre. An important exception was Gutzkow in his arresting portrait of the household slave, her calculating mistress, and the police in his novel: *Der Zauberer von Rom* (The Sorcerer of Rome, 1858–61). Even Raabe and Fontane, whose novels contain a great deal of information on the lives of female servants, usually convey that information through humorous minor characters (such as Hedwig in *Der Stechlin*).

Education

If eighteenth-century Vienna had been, through Maria Theresia's educational reforms, a pioneering influence on the development of education for the common people in German-speaking countries, it was nineteenth-century Berlin which became a center of educational reform and change for women. Progress, however, as in the case of men's education, was crablike rather than linear, full of false starts and stops. As early as 1830, a teacher's training college for women had been founded in Berlin (as it had been for Jews). However, scarcely half a generation later, the king of Prussia, Friedrich Wilhelm IV, was berating the heads of teacher training colleges with having been responsible for the outbreak of revolution. "All the misery that has visited Prussia in the last year is your fault and yours alone," he fulminated in 1849, following the collapse of the revolution. Not for the last time in the history of education, male and female, teachers were being blamed for government policy failure.

The failed revolution had a serious and long-lasting impact on initiatives to the education system. A mixture of pious religiosity and (Prussian) nationalism was prescribed as the appropriate diet for young Prussian citizens of both sexes. It was not until 1908 that Prussia finally addressed the issue of women's secondary and tertiary education and gave women access to university education, although other German states, such as Baden, had marked the new century by doing so in 1900. The first women students in Germany accordingly matriculated at the Baden state universities of Heidelberg and Freiburg. But from the late 1880s onward, largely through the initiatives of Helene Lange (1848–1930), Berlin women could prepare for the *Abitur* in private colleges, and a number studied in Zurich and took their doctorates there, among them the novelist Ricarda Huch (1864–1947) and the revolutionary Rosa Luxemburg (1877–1919). Helped by Berlin professors who gave tuition in mathematics, science, and Latin, Lange's first pupils—six in all—had taken the *Abitur* in 1896. By the first decade of the twentieth century the pioneering figure of Helene Lange had largely achieved what she wanted. Education, rather than political emancipation, dominated the agenda of the early history of the women's movement in Germany, and it continued to play a central role in the bourgeois women's movement until well into the new century.

Politics: *Die Frauenfrage*

The history of the political emancipation of women in Germany does not begin, as in France, in the revolutionary era of 1789. Unlike England, there was no Mary Wollstonecraft (1759–97)[1] to demand the rights of German women or to provide at least a symbolic birthday at the beginning of the century which would create *die Frauenfrage*. On the other hand, the proliferation of women writers in late eighteenth- and early nineteenth-century Germany, a number of whom also attempted to provide journals devoted specifically to the concerns of their own sex, is a testimony to the growing consciousness of German women of themselves and their position in society. The late Enlightenment was, after all, the time when the renowned German philosopher Kant could assert in his *Anthropologie* that no woman, whatever her age, could be a citizen in the eyes of the law and when his somewhat younger colleague, Fichte, could deny that woman had any sexual instinct: women simply felt love.

The politicization of German women, the founding of their first political organizations, the emergence of female political writers and journalists, and their direct participation in the public life of the nation all date from the 1848 Revolution. An important stimulus to this process was undoubtedly provided by religious and educational initiatives of the late 1830s and 1840s. The most important of these were the popular movement in Saxony and central Germany for Protestant church reform, known as the Friends of Light; in northern Germany the radical Protestant Free Communities movement, which was the attempt to found a German (as against a Roman) Catholic church and which is associated with the name of the revolutionary democrat

---

[1] Wollstonecraft's *Vindication of the Rights of Women* was published in 1792.

Robert Blum; and the Fröbel movement at primary school. The Friends of Light movement attracted the particular opprobrium of the authorities for allowing women to take part in demonstrations. The founder of the Kindergarten movement, Friedrich Fröbel (1782–1852), challenged received assumptions about the role of schooling in the education of the citizen; he relied in his work on the active participation of women, one of whom, Malwida von Meysenburg (1816–1903), left a graphic account of the movement in her much-read *Memoirs of an Idealist* (French edition 1869, German 1875). That these initiatives were actually attempts to create an alternative public sphere in the repressive climate of pre-March Germany was made evident by the authorities' response. For example, Fröbel's movement, which was primarily about reassessing the way children learn, was banned as "atheistic and demagogic" in 1851 by Prussia, following the collapse of the revolution, and he and his associates were persecuted.

Women participated in the 1848 Revolution in a whole series of roles, ranging from the traditional ones of tending the wounded and supplying the revolutionaries with food and clothes, to stitching revolutionary banners, forming women's political clubs, building barricades, casting bullets, acting as messengers and distributors of seditious material, organizing the escape of prisoners, hiding fugitives, and assisting them to elude their pursuers and flee the country to exile. One of the most rational and patient of the early leaders of the women's movement in Germany was Louise Otto,[2] who was born a year after Karl Marx, in 1819, the daughter of a lawyer, but, orphaned as a teenager, turned to writing to support herself. Following a visit in the early 1840s to her married sister in the coalmining region of Silesia, she witnessed the reality of proletarian life; she saw for herself the conditions under which the Silesian weavers, once a prosperous artisan class, were now forced to work to keep body and soul together. Besides writing a novel on factory life (*Schloss und Fabrik*: Castle and Factory, 1846), which got her into trouble with the censor, she made her own modest contribution to the genre of proletarian lyrics which Heine had immortalized in 1844 in his *Song of the Silesian Weavers*. In 1849, Otto became the founding editor of a journal, *Frauen-Zeitung*, explicitly devoted to women's political education and concerns. The journal managed, through her ingenuity, to survive the initial year of counter-revolutionary repression, until finally a law, subsequently known in Saxony as the Lex Otto (=the law against Otto), was introduced to forbid women from owning and editing a journal. Otto was a consequential woman: in 1850 she closed down her journal.

---

[2] American feminist literary critics, notably Ellen Boetcher-Joeres, were among the first to draw international attention to the figure of Otto.

The German woman lecturer of the future (1848).

In common with her more radical sisters and fellow writers, Louise Aston and Louise Dittmar, Louise Otto was no doubt named after the former queen of Prussia. In the course of the nineteenth century, Louise of Prussia was made into an icon of German womanhood. Or perhaps rather of the incarnation of what German men wanted their women to be—fair, tender, wholly consumed by their role of wife and mother. The new Louises of the revolutionary era offered another reading of the old stereotype: they showed that there was quite another dimension to modern German womanhood. Besides Louise Otto, Louise Aston, who donned men's clothes and fought on the barricades, offered a courageous and even aggressive response to the political police who arrested and interrogated her, while Louise Dittmar, who denounced contemporary marriage in *Das Wesen der Ehe* (The Essence of Marriage), castigated the pusillanimity of Germany's male revolutionaries. Many contemporary cartoonists made fun of the very notion that women might wish to attend university. The authorities, for their part, showed that they were quite aware of the charges. The *Prussian Law on Associations* of 1850 explicitly banned women from attending public meetings, a measure that was replicated in many other German states. German women were never granted right of assembly in the nineteenth

Queen Louise of Prussia.
Painting by G. Grassi (1802).

century. Only three generations later were they permitted, by the *Reich Law on Associations* of 1908, to meet in public. The year 1848 is an important date in the history of German women's awakening political consciousness generally.

Attempts by liberal and democratic women in the 1848 Revolution to create a women's movement, like the movement for democratic reform itself, fell victim to the persecution of the so-called post-March or *Nachmärz* era. Almost a generation had passed before any new development occurred. In 1865, Louise Otto-Peters, who had been widowed the previous year after a brief marriage to a writer, former revolutionary, and political prisoner, became the cofounder of the first national German women's organization, the *Allgemeiner Deutscher Frauenverein*. Its aims were not explicitly political. Even apart from the problem of police surveillance, the climate of opinion in middle-class circles had changed in Germany: national and economic issues dominated public discussion. Moreover, the bulk of women's writing in the 1860s and 1870s suggested that they had internalized German society's conservative values. In 1865, Otto founded an association for women's education and an institute of further education for girls. With Auguste Schmidt (1833–1902), she edited *Neue Bahnen* (New Paths), the journal of the German Women's Association, and continued to do so until her death in 1895. The *Frauenverein* never achieved mass membership; even when the energetic teacher Helene Lange led it in the 1880s, it never achieved more than 14,000 members. From the outset, it focused on women's right to education. German society in the second half of the century was faced with the growing problem of middle-class women needing to find work in order to support themselves, yet being prevented from doing so for lack of skills, and on account of the prejudices of paternalist society. The year 1866 saw what seemed a pragmatic response to the problem in the form of the *Letteverein*, an association of organizations promoting women's training and employment, named after its (male) founder, Lette. It supported the provision of the kind of skills necessary for finding employment or supplementing the household income. (Readers of Fontane's *Frau Jenny Treibel* will recall that the heroine Corinna determines to persuade the English Mr. Nelson that German girls are not just intelligent and charming, but they are also incredibly accomplished. She, for example, can do invisible mending to perfection, having learned it at the *Letteverein*.)

One further generation had been born before the German women's movement began to reflect in a more appropriate manner the process of modernization which was radically altering Germany. In 1894 the League of German Women's Associations, the *Bund Deutscher Frauenvereine* (BDF), was founded in Berlin and became affiliated to the international organization. Women's professional organizations emerged in the early years of the 1890s, a decade in which *die Frauenfrage* became a major public issue. Under Helene Lange, the German Women Teachers Association was founded in 1890 and a decade later had 16,000 members. As such, it was the largest organization of professional women in Germany. Meanwhile, Minna Cauer (1841-1922), soon to emerge as one of the movement's radical elements, had helped pioneer the association of female employees in business and commerce (*Kaufmännischer Verband für weibliche Angestellte*). This was the beginning of the age of the office worker, the shorthand typist in high-collared white blouse and long black skirts, on whom the English humorist, G. K. Chesterton (1874-1936), exercised his patronizing wit in the much-quoted phrase: women rose up and declared: "We will not be dictated to—and became stenographers."

The issues animating the women's movement in this seminal period, coinciding with the reign of Wilhelm II (1888-1918), were determined as much by class as anything else. The movement divided sharply between the bourgeois and socialist feminists. In 1891, at the Erfurt Party congress, the Social Democratic party gave women's rights equal status in official party policy with those of men; they, that is, proletarian women, were part of "the struggle of humanity" for emancipation. In practice, women activists tended not to come from the ranks of women on the production line, but rather from the wives or family members of male activists. The party began to record impressive increases in the numbers of its women party members, but only after 1900. Between 1908 and 1914, the figure rose from 30,000 to 175,000. Before 1908, the party protected its women from state harassment, to which they laid themselves open as political activists, by setting up liaison mechanisms. Prussian police still rigorously enforced the 1850 law on associations. Bourgeois feminists, themselves separated into moderates and radicals, focused on the highly emotive issue of prostitution, on the reform of family law, the right to divorce, contraception, and abortion, while also challenging the patriarchal state prohibition on married teachers. (Fontane's Mathilde Möhring, we recall, was a "respectable widow" when she entered the profession.)

Many women who identified with the conservative values of Wilhelmine society and were not interested in, or even actively critical of, the emancipation movement, nevertheless became politicized in consequence of it. One group sought to create a public role for women, not in competition with men,

Picture of the future Munich (1847). The German woman student of the future. Note the Jewish star, implying the Jewish associations with women's emancipation.

but in a sphere different from that inhabited by men and one which was, in their view, equal in value. Such women sought at an ideological level to win recognition for the female qualities which modern industrial society threatened and yet clearly needed. In a manner much criticized by later feminists, they identified women's public contribution to the national life as being the caring professions. At a practical level, they demanded recognition for the double burden carried by working women, especially working-class women; they helped to set up training in childcare and household management, and they agitated for the provision of childcare facilities for women obliged to work outside the home. The other, much larger, group was the Christian women's movement— or rather movements, for they were strictly divided along sectional lines. The *Protestantische Frauenhilfe* or Protestant Women's Aid, had the inestimable attraction of having been founded by Empress Auguste Viktoria in 1899. By the end of the decade it had some 200,000 members, and by the end of the 1914–8 war had become the largest women's organization in Germany, though still subordinate to the male-dominated parent body. The *Deutsch-Evangelische Frauenbund*, or Protestant Women's League, had been founded shortly after as a (Christian) rival to the BDF, but it remained a relatively small body, reaching 10,000 members in 1910. There were also small but active Jewish women's organizations with their roots in the Jewish tradition of philanthropy and self-betterment by education. What was remarkable about the German Catholic Women's League, or *Katholischer Frauenbund*, founded in the Rhenish city of Cologne at the turn of the century, was its refusal to submit, as the Protestant women's groups did, to male direction. The German Catholic bishops responded by refusing to give official recognition to the League in the first decade and a half of its existence. They would not permit it to be affiliated to the central organization of Catholics, the *Katholikentag*, until 1921, despite its explicit charitable and pastoral purpose, because the League was not prepared to have its president subordinate to clerical control. Moreover, unlike the bourgeois and socialist women's movements, class was not really an issue in the German Catholic Women's League, which aimed to be, and broadly speaking was, a mass movement defined by its commitment to conservative Catholic values.

One of the most striking points of difference between the German women's movement and those of English or American women was the relative insignificance of voting rights for women as a specific issue. In fact it proved a divisive issue for women themselves, even as late as the immediate pre-1914 war years. As always in German circles advocating change of any kind, journals played an influential role. In 1893, following the example of the Social Democrats, Helene Lange founded *Die Frau: Monatschrift für das gesamte*

Frauenleben unserer Zeit (Monthly Review for the Entire Life of Women in Our Time), whose title reflected its inclusive ambitions. The radical bourgeois women's movement had as their organ, *Die Frauenbewegung* (The Women's Movement), which had a monthly supplement on legal issues of interest to women, edited by the lawyer, Dr. Anita Augspurg, under the title of *Journal for the Enfranchisement of Women*. The most impressive of these publications, however, was the work of one intellectually dominant woman, the socialist Clara Zetkin (1857–1933), a former teacher and vigorous party activist, who edited the extraordinarily successful organ, *Die Gleichheit* (Equality, 1891–1919). Its circulation rose from 10,000 in 1903 to 125,000 in 1914, which, given the reading practices of the time, suggests a readership of nearer half a million. Zetkin was provocatively described, along with her Polish-born fellow activist, Rosa Luxemburg, a cofounder of the Communist party, as "the only two men in the Social Democratic party." In time, Zetkin became too forthright for her own male colleagues and was sidelined. However, her considerable achievements were given prominent recognition by the German Democratic Republic (1949–1990), when schools, institutes, and city streets were named after her. It is to be hoped that 'political correctness,' with its penchant for indiscriminate changing of street names, will not allow modern Germany to forget this doughty advocate of the rights of the oppressed.

The rather meager achievements of the German women's movement in the half century between 1848 and the late 1890s were not proportionate to the efforts of those involved. In particular, the new Civil Code (*Bürgerliches Gesetzbuch*) hardly reflected the aspirations of progressively minded women. Following years of debate in parliament, in which the Social Democratic spokesman, Karl Liebknecht (1871–1919), son of one of the party's founders, had vigorously and systematically attacked individual measures on behalf of women, the code was finally drawn up in 1896 and promulgated in the symbolical year 1900. As the lawyer (and wife of Max Weber), Marianne Weber (1870–1954), pointed out in her analysis of 1907: *Ehefrau und Mutter in der Rechtsentwicklung* (The Married Woman and the Mother in Legal History, reprint 1971), the new code was actually less favorable to women than the old Prussian code of 1794, notably in the realm of family law. However, a decade later, a significant change had taken place: the issue of women's rights was now firmly on the political agenda. Between 1900 and the outbreak of war in 1914, a quantitative change took place in the German women's movement. Thus some 70,000 women were represented in the BDF in 1901; by 1914, it had 500,000 affiliated members. The quantitative increase in the membership of women's organizations of all kinds had effected a qualitative change. Women were now politicized, and the (male) politicians realized it. Moreover, the fact that the exigencies of war brought women of very different ideological outlook together to work in a common cause had a material impact on the movement to secure the enfranchisement of women. Almost immediately after the collapse of the Wilhelmine Empire, following Germany's defeat in late 1918, German women got the vote—and they exercised it.

Women and the literary market

In a later much-quoted observation from her compendium of German women authors published in 1898, *Lexikon deutscher Frauen der Feder*, Sophie Pataky estimated that at the time of writing there were some 5,000 women writers in Germany. This represented a putative tenfold increase over the period some seventy years earlier, when in 1823–5 the influential publishing house of Brockhaus in Leipzig had brought out Carl Schindler's dainty three-volume lexicon with the names of some 500 women writers: *Die deutschen Schriftstellerinnen des neunzehnten Jahrhunderts*. In the interim years, writing had provided German women with a vital source of livelihood, particularly those from middle-class backgrounds who had found themselves in economic difficulties. They owed this less to a putative increase in society's tolerance of the female voice, than to the increasing sophistication of the capitalist German literary market. In particular, they owed it to the growth of a national distribution network for the printed text, and, toward the end of the century, to the emergence of the mass media. Women, it seems, were on the whole more likely to embark on a writing career after their children had grown up, or after divorce, desertion, or simply the death of the male provider. When they did so, it was often to write in the genre "favored by women," namely the novel, the short tale or novella, or the lyric poem. Feminist literary criticism has traditionally seen this in terms of women writers' continued subordination to the dictates of patriarchy. The somewhat patronizing relationship, for example, of Friedrich Schiller, to the women who asked for his advice or sought to publish in one of his journals, is a good example of this. Women continued to use male pseudonyms well into the nineteenth century, particularly early in their career, or they published their work anonymously. The highly intelligent Therese Huber (1764–1829) actually allowed her husband to publish her work in his name and only used her own after his death. The voluminous correspondence of this remarkable woman, writer, literary editor, sometime literary agent, and director of an unofficial employment exchange for her wide circle of female acquaintances and their daughters, is at present being prepared under the sponsorship of the German Research Society (DFG) by Magdalene Heuser. The first of the nine volumes already provides a new understanding of the functioning of the early and mid-century literary market, as it affected women.

But what critics are inclined to forget, is that probably most women writers were first and foremost interested in getting published. With some and very notable exceptions, their literary ambitions or their ideological principles either came second to their financial needs, or else they believed that only once their reputation was established, could they influence the views of readers.

The institutions of the nineteenth-century capitalist book market certainly favored women writers concerned to earn money. The proliferation of the commercial lending libraries in the early and middle decades of the century stimulated growth in the numbers of women readers. Equally they created an ever-growing demand for the fiction and poetry the majority wanted to read. Women were in demand as translators in the same period, especially from French and English, not least because publishers paid no foreign royalties. Women wrote for the regional and national almanacs and pocket books so popular up to mid-century. In the second half of the century they supplied the massive demand for books on etiquette, deportment, cooking, and household management. Many women catered to the large reading public for devotional and edifying literature, including literature for children, as the successful career of the Swabian writer, Ottilie Wildermuth (1817–77), would show. By the 1870s and 1880s, the family magazines were vying for copy, notably for the now-popular serialized stories and novels. The most successful authors, notably Eugenie Marlitt (1825–87), Wilhelmine Heimburg (1850–1912), and Hedwig Courths-Mahler (1867–1950), became wealthy women. Women were active as editors, though usually in a subordinate capacity, such as Therese Huber from 1816–23 in the *Morgenblatt* or Luise Köppen (1855–1923) in the Protestant family magazine, *Daheim*, for which she also wrote, as well as editing the weekly magazine *Die deutsche Frau*. The fact that such activities could provide a reasonable income for someone like Köppen, a former teacher and daughter of a high-ranking clergyman, showed how significant the capitalist press had become for women. It has been estimated that some 25 percent of literature produced in the Wilhelmine Empire was written by women. They demonstrated a particular facility for writing what their (female) reading public wanted, principally short tales and novels for serialization in the newspapers.

It was much less easier for women to compete in the 'serious' literary market, as the careers of notable women writers showed, among them Annette von Droste-Hülshoff, Louise von François, or the Austrian Marie von Ebner-Eschenbach. Here the *Bestimmung* debate and family pressures placed real obstacles in women's paths. The most serious obstacle was, perhaps, psychological: fear of failure, lack of self-confidence. Some women, such as Ebner and her circle, operated a kind of "pre-public" (as described by Konstanze Fliedl in Brinker-Gabler's *Deutsche Literatur von Frauen* (1988)) in which women tried out their work on their friends before approaching a publisher. Ebner herself acted as a mediator between a number of lesser-known writers and Julius Rodenberg, publication in whose journal, the *Deutsche Rundschau*, was a guarantee of success. It was Rodenberg who commissioned Bettine von Arnim's son-in-law, Hermann Grimm (1828–1901), Wilhelm's son, art and literary critic, to write an assessment of contemporary German women's writing in the *Rundschau* in 1893. By the turn of the century, a number of influential male critics or historians had published major studies on past and recent women's writing and women's periodicals, and they had written biographies or edited the letters of women writers and literary personalities, such as Caroline Schlegel-Schelling (1763–1809) or Therese Huber. Such serious discussion of women's writing around 1900 had a positive effect on contemporary women writers. Thus, to take but one example, Hedwig Dohm (1833–1919), who had scarcely published for years, suddenly emerged again on the literary market with a trilogy about three generations of representatives of a family, published between 1896 and 1902; the last, *Christa Ruland*, identified its twenty-year-old heroine as a typical representative of an age of transition, a kind of "woman-without-qualities" (Brinker-Gabler). During the war the intrepid Dohm was forthright in her advocacy of the unpopular cause of pacifism. One likes to imagine the kind of conversation Thomas Mann must have on occasion found himself forced into, when he visited the home of his parents-in-law in Munich and met his wife's clever grandmother. Did Hedwig Dohm feel that Thomas's wife, Katja, her granddaughter, was prevented by her husband's demands on her from developing her own potential as a member of that transitional generation? One wonders, whether, like some of the outspoken old ladies of Victorian fiction, such as Lady Cumnor in Elizabeth Gaskell's *Wives and Daughters* (1866), Dohm did not on occasion penetrate the comfortable male egotism of the young writer with her sharp eye and acid wit.

Childhood

An important chapter of social life in nineteenth-century Germany remains to be briefly mentioned. It is Germany's contribution in this period to the imaginative life of the child. It has particular reference to women's lives in that so much of the stimuli of Germans' early childhood experience was gained in the presence of mothers, grandmothers, aunts, and sisters, and under their tutelage, especially in families where there was enough income for children to be able to stay at home until adolescence. The discovery, investigation, and exploration of childhood as something fundamentally different from adulthood was mainly the work of men, who were little concerned with the gender-stereotyping tendencies of the majority of their late eighteenth- and early nineteenth-century contemporaries. But that discovery helped to create a new kind of relationship between mothers and their children. It was a German author, Karl Philipp Moritz (1756–93), who produced one of the first acute, and devastating, portraits of the effect of an unhappy childhood on the later adult. This was the psychological novel *Anton Reiser* (1785–90), by the editor of the earliest journal of empirical psychology, *Magazin zur Erfahrungsseelenkunde* (1783–93). It was the Swiss educationist Johann Heinrich Pestalozzi (1746–1827), and the already-mentioned Friedrich Fröbel, who pioneered child-centered learning in the late eighteenth and mid-nineteenth century. The period in which Fröbel developed his prototype of the German *Kindergarten*, in the 1830s, was also the time when German parents, and subsequently German manufacturers, began to develop toys, games, and festivals for children which had children's imagination rather than adults' prescriptiveness at their heart. The imaginative celebration of Christmas and birthdays, celebrations particularly dear to children worldwide, originated mainly in Biedermeier Germany and Austria, though it might well be argued that the Jewish festival of light provided at least one model for the Christian Christmas celebration. The rituals of Advent, with the wreath made by the older children and adults, and the four candles lit in turn on each Advent Sunday, the baking and sending of Christmas biscuits to relatives and friends, the *Christkindlmarkt* or Christmas market at Nuremberg and elsewhere, all go back to the early and middle decades of the nineteenth century in Germany. The Christmas tree, decorated with candles, sweetmeats, and decorations produced at home, was the invention of the Biedermeier period, but soon spread via England to North America.

The celebration of the child's birthday, with the birthday table arranged with presents from the immediate and extended family, gave a child a sense of his or her own importance, especially since it seems to have been the practice to include something a child would like which was not simply utilitarian. Home entertainment, as in other European countries of the time, was common in families free from poverty. Thus Bettine von Arnim and her daughters wrote fairy tales together to entertain themselves and the rest of the family, just as the royal families enjoyed a game of charades and dressed up to perform tableaux. Much of literature for children written in the nineteenth century was indeed didactic. But it was less overtly so than had been the case when Christian Felix Weiße had pioneered his first journal for children with its philanthropic title, *Der Kinderfreund* (The Children's Friend, in twenty-four volumes 1775–84), and when J. H. Campe (1746–1818) had written his influential version of *Robinson Crusoe*, the younger Robinson: *Robinson der Jüngere* (1779).

German Women and Their History in the Nineteenth Century

Take the immensely popular tales of the Bavarian Catholic priest, Christoph Schmid (1768–1854), which sold an estimated million copies over the century, and were translated numerous times into English, by Presbyterian, Anglican, and Episcopalian ministers in Scotland, England, and North America, as they were by fellow Catholics. Schmid's best-known tales, *The Easter Eggs* (1816), and his many other sentimental stories of how virtuous little girls and little boys were rewarded, even in this life, had the great merit that they were written from the child's perspective. Childhood was a particularly popular subject for painters in

At the window Painting by Ferdinand Waldmüller (1840).

the early and middle years of the century, among them Ferdinand Waldmüller (1793–1865). Allowing for a degree of sentimentalization, which was a feature of representations of family life in the Biedermeier, there was a great deal of authenticity in such painting: Waldmüller's little boys really fight and his babies resemble babies and not miniature adults.

Many of the country's best-known writers of early and mid-century wrote sympathetically and imaginatively about children. This included much work by the Grimm brothers, especially Wilhelm (though, as we now realize, some of their stories were much more brutal than a superficial reading might suggest). Jean Paul (1763–1825), the Austrians Adalbert Stifter, Marie von Ebner-Eschenbach, Peter Rosegger, and Theodor Storm allow the reader to see the world through the eyes of the child. The account, for example, of Storm's ten-year-old Nesi waiting at the top of the stairs for the first sight of her new stepmother in the story *Via Tricolor*, is a good example of the originality of German literature in this regard. The awkward positioning of the child's body behind the banisters expressed the contradictory feelings Nesi could neither understand nor articulate. Storm, like Friedrich Rückert, also wrote much lyric poetry of married love. Rückert, today chiefly remembered as the author of the texts of Mahler's *Kindertotenlieder* and some of Robert Schumann's songs, was one of the most popular authors of his day, chiefly because of his poetry of domestic life. He wrote with deep feeling of the death of his children, and expressed in one of his best-known poems his remorse at having played the disciplinarian father toward his small daughter. Rückert was far more popular in mid-nineteenth-century anthologies than either Goethe or Schiller, suggesting perhaps that poems about love of spouse and children had a wide and receptive public. Painters as well as writers took children as their models, particularly in the earlier half of the century. And though the framework was one of discipline and love, the children depicted by these artists were real children, doing the things that children want to do, including running about and fighting, and not just what their elders felt children ought to want to do. This is well illustrated in Gärtner's (1801–77) painting *Panorama of the Werdersche Church* of 1837 (see page 178).

Child-centered family life and art depicting children belong to those strata of society who were middle-class or had at least a modest provenance. (Aristocratic education tended, by and large, to be more frugal, less indulgent toward the young.) The best-known toys, and to small children the most delightful, simply because they were small, were the little painted wooden villages, farm animals, and figures associated with the Erzgebirge region. For boys, the famous Nuremberg *Holzschächtelchen*, wooden boxes filled with cheap painted tin soldiers including famous regiments of the German army and of many foreign armies. The soldiers could be had in all sorts of positions, attack, fire, drilling, wading through water, lying, kneeling down, falling, dying, and so on, and allowed children to fight the campaigns of the Napoleonic wars and later the wars of unification. However, many of the toys with which parents could give pleasure to their children, simply because they were cheap, were in fact the work of other, much less fortunate children, who worked inhuman hours, often from ages as young as four or five, in the sweatshop cottage industry of Germany's poorest regions.

In later decades, the increasing wealth of bourgeois circles in Germany was reflected in the massive expansion of the toy industry and in the successful promotion of what were virtually luxury toys, from the miniature prototypes of German high-tech achievements, such as locomotives, dolls' sewing machines, guns of various kinds, three-dimensional lead soldiers, lifelike dolls, prams, dolls' houses complete with furniture and lights that worked. Where once mothers and female relatives made toys for the Christmas tree, now at Christmas time the shops in German cities were filled with goods thought appropriate to the solid citizenry of the Empire. Both in the stress laid on material goods as due reward for industrious and patriotic little citizens and in the inevitable barriers raised between those who could and those who could not afford such things, the characteristic tensions of Wilhelmine society were reflected. It was particularly because the authorities and their spokesmen promoted a view of society in which all righteous burghers had their share and because the celebration of family festivals was now so rooted in German family life at all levels that the disappointment of expectations strikes us as so cruel. Proletarian childhood memoirs contain many reminiscences of parents' efforts to defy circumstance and produce something special for the occasion. Of these perhaps the most bitter is the passage in which the Austrian socialist Adelheid Popp recalls the Christmas of her fifth year in her memoirs, *Jugend einer Arbeiterin* (1978, 26):

> One Christmas when I was not quite five still remains vivid in my memory. On this one occasion I nearly got a Christmas tree. My mother wanted me, who was her youngest child, to see just for once what Christmas *could* be like. For weeks she had striven to save a few coppers to buy me a toy kitchen set. The Christmas tree was decorated with colored paper chains, with gold-painted nuts and with the little toys. We waited for the lighting of the candles until Father came home. ... Six o'clock came, then seven, then eight. Still Father hadn't come... . I had to go to bed without seeing the candles alight on the tree... . At last Father arrived... drunk. He got a poor reception and a quarrel started... . The noise made me peep out from where I slept to look at my parents, and then I saw. Father with an axe chopping the tree and everything on it to pieces. I didn't dare scream, I just cried.

Details from *Panorama from the Werdersche Church* by Edward Gärtner. Note how realistically the children, especially the older one, are portrayed, and how ready the parents are to enter the spirit of the thing, while at the same time pointing a moral.

The sentimentalization of German Christmas and its exploitation by chauvinist writers as evidence of the superiority of German culture was a phenomenon of the last years of the nineteenth century. Christmas was presented in the popular media as a microcosm of German society, with father as the omnipotent provider, mother as the busy executor of his wishes, and the children happy and grateful. Inevitably the trend in bourgeois circles to make the Christmas festivities the occasion of ostentatious present-giving attracted the attention of the satirists. Journalists, graphic artists, and literary figures mocked the self-indulgence masquerading as *Kultur*. A light-hearted instance is a certain Max Müller's poem *Die Kolonien*. The author shows father asking the family what they would like for Christmas. Grandfather wants a cane with an ivory handle, mother a fur coat, daughter a sewing machine, and son a bicycle. "Our colonies will provide all," father declares, and so they did. The satisfaction of all their wishes is hailed as a triumph of German foreign policy in the age of imperialism. But perhaps the most famous account of Christmas is to be found in Thomas Mann's novel *Buddenbrooks*, written at the end of the old century and published at the beginning of the new, in 1901. In its ironic account of bourgeois ritual it belongs to the body of imaginative literature associated with the names of the Mann brothers, Franz Wedekind (1864–1912), the dramatist Carl Sternheim (1878–1942), Hermann Hesse, and others, who collectively began the process of critical evaluation of bourgeois society under the German Empire, more than half a century before historians began to submit the period to critical scrutiny.

Myths

A cultivated and observant traveler to Germany on the eve of the twentieth century could not but conclude that the public face of Wilhelmine Germany and the images employed to convey that value system were uncompromisingly male. The evident ubiquity of the military uniform in public places was replicated in public monuments, commemorating battles won and fallen or triumphant heroes. The emperor and the highest public servant, the Reich chancellor, wore uniforms in everyday life and in the numerous public monuments to them, set in city squares and main thoroughfares or set just at that point in the rural landscape, where families went for picnics and excursions. In the case of public monuments and parades, it was not just women, it was also the citizens who were being excluded, as the novelist, Fanny Lewald, had caustically and aptly pointed out in mid-century in her comments on the equestrian statue raised in 1851 to king Frederick II ("the Great") of Prussia (1740–86) on Berlin's main thoroughfare, *Unter den Linden*, where it is still to be seen today. The king is flanked on all sides but one by uniformed Prussian officers. The only representatives of civic life, of culture and the arts, noted Lewald, are positioned beneath the raised tail of the royal horse. Not only did the Empire sedulously and ostentatiously proclaim military values in its symbols, but when a female allegory of the nation was erected, one year before the outbreak of the 1914 war, the result was a caricature: on the banks of the Rhine, facing France, Germania, her broad bosom clad in armor, brandished a sword so vast that only a (male) giant could conceivably lift, let alone wield it. What a contrast with the female images of the French Republic, Marianne or *la République*, valiant, defiant, and feminine! Of course, there was Queen Louise of Prussia, whose cult was revived at the turn of the century and the centenary of whose death in 1910 stimulated a whole series of commemorative efforts, including a trilogy by the early German cinema industry. But, as has already been said, Louise simply affirmed the image of the passive dutiful woman, and was in many ways a deliberate provocation to the efforts of the women's movement.

In a variety of other ways, female values were diminished in public discourse. The "heroic" German race, it was so often alleged, was the epitome of the male virtues. The enemies of the Reich, the French, or indeed the Latin peoples, like the Slavs, were the "womanish races," degenerate, untrustworthy, incapable of honor. Probably more insidious was the way in which the secularization of Christian myth in literature and the arts perpetuated the notion of male superiority and female inferiority. The ancient Christian *topos* of Christ as the head, his church (ecclesia, *die Kirche*) as the body, was secularized in such a manner as to attribute to man, the authority figure, a kind of divinity, with woman representing mere humanity.

Many of late nineteenth-century Germany's leading writers challenged these received assumptions in their work. They included Fontane, born in the second decade of the century, but reaching his peak as a writer in the 1880s and 1890s. Part of Fontane's failure to win a popular audience for his work in his lifetime derived from the fact that he tried to challenge the approved national stereotyping of Germany and her neighbors, France and Poland. Thus in his first novel, *Vor dem Sturm* (1878), set in the time of the French invasion of Germany under Napoleon, he displayed the Poles and French as at least the equal of the Prussians in terms of their courage, and as often superior in human understanding. In his prison journal, *Kriegsgefangen: Erlebtes 1870* (1871), written largely while in a French prison awaiting possible execution as an alleged spy, he subverts both gender and national stereotypes, in his portrayal of the French men and women whom he encountered. In his remarkable novel *Cécile* (1886), which purports to be a kind of case study of a nervous, even hysterical woman, but which is equally about the pathology of its two (male) protagonists, he challenges their value system by permitting the reader a glimpse of the social cost for men as well as for women of contemporary misogyny. This last issue is an understated but important subtheme of his best-known novel, *Effi Briest* (1895). At key points in the narrative Effi's husband, Innstetten, who had banished his adulterous wife because he felt society forced him to do so, is seen as much as a victim as a perpetrator of the Wilhelmine value system. In their different ways, the contributions made by the dramatists Gerhart Hauptmann and Franz Wedekind and others to the debate of the 1890s and early 1900s about the nature and sexuality of women, about their situation and aspirations, form an integral part of the history of German women. But the German publishing industry recognized that a substantial proportion of the nation's readers preferred traditional ways. In the first year of the new century, not only did the neurologist Paul Möbius find a publisher for his *Über den physiologischen Schwachsinn der Weiber* (On the Physiological Idiocy of Women) but it reached its eighth edition in less than seven years, while Arthur Schopenhauer's deeply misogynist text *Über die Weiber* was reissued in attractive binding and format in 1902.

The nineteenth century in Germany is thus characterized by very conflicting views on women. However, taking the century as a whole, the body of received opinion on their social (and intellectual) inferiority was reinforced rather than undermined in the second half of the century. The formative influence of German national mythology on the nation's view of women at the beginning of the twentieth century had been shaped by the political events of the decades, whose history is traced in the next two chapters.

Chapter 10
The Army, the Parties, and the State after 1871

The unification of Germany in 1871 did not bring with it the automatic centralization of government and administration in Berlin. German unification was in fact a compromise with German particularism, especially with those princes who, unlike the deposed king of Hanover and the grandduke of Hesse-Kassel, had survived Bismarck's wars. The new German Empire actually consisted of twenty-five states. These were made up of four kingdoms, Prussia, Bavaria, Saxony, and Württemberg; six grand duchies; five duchies; seven minuscule principalities, the largest of which, Lippe, had an area of merely 469 square miles and just over 110,000 inhabitants; the three free cities of Hamburg, Bremen, and Lübeck (the ancient city of Frankfurt having fallen victim to Bismarck's annexation in 1866); and the so-called Imperial Territory of Alsace-Lorraine. Emperor Wilhelm I bore the title of German Emperor. In the view of other princes, notably Bavaria, he was most decidedly not Emperor of the

The entry of victorious troops into Berlin in June 1871 (one of the first photographs of such a public event).

Germans. The Bavarian king, Ludwig II, had in fact been most reluctant to accept the Prussian monarch as head of state. After tenacious negotiations, he accepted Wilhelm I as *primus inter pares*, the first of equals in a confederation of territorial sovereigns. In return, Ludwig retained certain rights over the Bavarian army in peacetime and, in common with Württemberg, control of its own state postal system.

Table 2: Germany's population

States of the Empire	Area (English sq. miles)	1871	1875	1900	1905	Density per square mile (1905)
Kingdoms						
Prussia	134,616	24,691,433	25,742,404	34,472,509	37,293,324	277.3
Bavaria	29,292	4,863,450	5,022,390	6,176,057	6,524,372	222.7
Saxony	5,789	2,556,244	2,760,586	4,202,216	4,508,601	778.8
Württemberg	7,534	1,818,539	1,881,505	2,169,480	2,302,179	305.5
Grand-Duchies						
Baden	5,823	1,461,662	1,507,179	1,867,944	2,010,728	345.3
Hesse	2,966	852,894	884,218	1,119,893	1,209,175	407.6
Mecklenburg-Schwerin	5,068	557,897	553,785	607,770	625,045	123.3
Saxe-Weimar	1,397	286,183	292,933	362,873	388,095	277.8
Mecklenburg-Strelitz	1,131	96,982	95,673	102,602	103,451	91.5
Oldenburg	2,482	34,459	319,314	399,180	438,856	176.8
Duchies						
Brunswick	1,418	311,764	327,493	464,333	485,958	342.5
Saxe-Meiningen	953	187,957	194,494	250,731	268,916	282.2
Saxe-Altenburg	511	142,122	145,844	194,914	206,508	404.1
Saxe-Coburg-Gotha	764	174,339	182,599	229,550	242,432	317.3
Anhalt	888	203,437	213,565	316,085	328,029	369.4
Principalities						
Schwarzburg-Sondershausen	333	75,523	76,676	80,898	85,152	255.7
Schwarzburg-Rudolfstadt	363	67,191	67,480	93,059	96,835	266.7
Waldeck	433	56,224	54,743	57,918	59,127	136.5
Reuss-Greiz	122	45,094	46,985	68,396	70,603	578.7
Reuss-Schleiz	319	89,032	92,375	139,210	144,584	453.2
Schaumburg-Lippe	131	32,059	33,133	43,132	44,992	343.4
Lippe	469	111,135	112,452	138,952	45,577	90.4
Free Cities						
Lübeck	115	52,158	56,912	96,775	105,857	920.5
Bremen	99	122,402	142,200	224,882	263,440	2661.0
Hamburg	160	338,974	388,618	768,349	874,878	5467.9
Imperial Territory						
Alsace-Lorraine	5,604	1,549,738	1,631,804	1,719,470	1,814,564	323.8
German Empire	208,780	41,058,792	42,727,360	56,367,178	60,641,278	290.4

The army and the state

Although concessions were made to Bavaria in this regard, and, to a lesser degree to some other southern states, the special position enjoyed by the military in Prussian society was not diminished but rather enhanced under the Empire. The emperor Wilhelm I was profoundly convinced of his exclusive royal prerogative in military matters, a view which even Bismarck found impossible to counter. True, army matters were debated, often vigorously, in the imperial parliament or Reichstag, but no army bill was ever defeated in parliament between 1871 and 1914. Though Germans in the south and in the west might be more critical of the military, there was widespread acceptance and indeed appreciation of the key role played by the army in the foundation of the state. While conscription was felt by many to be onerous and in some sections of the populace resented vigorously, such was the national cachet of the service, that on the eve of the 1914 war, after almost forty-three years of peace, nearly 3,000,000 Germans were members of ex-servicemen's associations.

The constitution laid down the peacetime strength of the Germany army as a fixed proportion of the population, namely 1 percent. As the population grew, the peacetime strength rose, from 400,000 in 1871 to 600,000 in 1900 and, thanks to new measures designed to assist Germany's "war-preparedness," to 800,000 in 1913. The army budget was regulated according to the terms of Bismarck's resolution of the Constitutional Conflict by the so-called Iron Budget. This allocated a notional 225 marks for every soldier. In 1874 this was replaced by the so-called Septennat, or seven-year fixed budget, later replaced by the Quinquennat (for five years). That the Iron Budget made nonsense of the budgetary rights of the legislature is evident when we consider that even in peacetime almost all the revenue of the North German Confederation, under which this agreement had been introduced, was spent on defense. In 1868 some 88.8 percent had gone to the army and 10.7 percent to the navy. Yet Wilhelm I, both as Prussian king and German emperor, had utterly opposed conceding even this modicum of parliamentary influence over the army. It was, he believed, an unwarranted infringement of his royal prerogative as supreme commander of the armed forces. In fact, the semiabsolute powers claimed by the Hohenzollerns in military matters were even greater under the empire than they had been in Prussia prior to 1867. Wilhelm's powers as commander-in-chief of the armed forces were derived not from the fact that he was German emperor, but were exercised by him as king of Prussia. Yet the constitution extended all Prussian military laws, ordinances, and instructions to apply to the contingents of the other member states in 1871, despite the concessions to the kings of Bavaria and Württemberg over their armies in peacetime.

There was no imperial minister of war, only a Prussian minister of war. As time passed, even his powers were curtailed, not by the Reichstag, but by the existence of the military cabinet of king and emperor. The military cabinet operated virtually outside the system in the sense that its members had rights of access to the sovereign not available to the minister and certainly not to parliamentary spokesmen on military affairs. The personality of the head of this inner cabinet could thus exercise a crucial influence on policy, a situation potentially much more dangerous under the intemperate and emotional Wilhelm II than under his cautious grandfather, Wilhelm I. The emperor's supreme authority over the imperial army operated with regard to key elements, such as armaments, command structure, organization, and training. Moreover, in the last years of the century, the German general staff, which in the Empire's first years had been headed by the circumspect Helmut von Moltke, hero of the wars of unification, gradually emancipated itself from control by the Prussian war ministry and hence from potential control by the civil authority.

The special position of the army in the state was accepted, if reluctantly, by parliamentarians after 1871, because of the patriotic aura attached to it. The Progressives or left-wing liberals had voted solidly in the debates of 1866–7 against the military clauses of the North German Confederation, on which the Reich constitution would be based. But their strength declined after the heady days of the Constitutional Conflict and members of other liberal groups hesitated to be seen as antinational by criticizing the armed forces. In the 1880s and 1890s, respectable parties of the center and the right did not want to be associated with the hostility of the Social Democrats to the special status of the army—a hostility exacerbated by the heavy-handedness of the army when used to break strikes and impose public order.

But certainly the army enjoyed great popularity in the years following unification. Family magazine stories and popular novels presented a stereotyped brave, handsome, and noble officer for the delectation of the reading public. (Was it so very

Portrait of an officer.

different in imperial Britain?) Military parades continued to play a role in the social life of people of all ranks of society long after the much photographed victory parades of 1871 had passed into history. The delights of the military band, as in Victorian England, were widely appreciated by the populace. What was fundamentally different from western democracies, however, was the superior regard enjoyed by the military uniform over civilian dress which became part of the lifestyle of the empire. What would have been inconceivable for the President of the United States or the British Prime Minister was taken for granted in imperial Germany: the wearing of military uniform in parliament. As chancellor, Bismarck wore the black and gold uniform of a Prussian general of the cuirassiers in parliament (Fontane makes much play of this, both in his letters and in *Der Stechlin*, where the cuirassiers' gold epaulettes are likened to the sulfur which was the traditional mark of Satan himself.) When the then chancellor Theobald Bethmann-Hollweg (1856–1921), no militarist, was appointed to his post in 1909, he held the rank of major and was forced to sit below generals and colonels at court banquets. When the news of his promotion to general reached him, he showed himself both delighted and moved.

Military service consisted of three years for every man fit to serve, other than those who had left school with a formal exam qualification; they could then serve as volunteers for one year. Fontane, for example, made use of this, as did his fellow member of the Kaiser-Franz regiment, Friedrich Engels. Military service was presented, and was generally regarded, as being a necessary part of training for citizenship. Much play was made of the Prussian virtues of order, discipline, and subordination to authority in the hierarchical world of the German workplace, school, and even the family. True, the sentiments of a contemporary military manual did not pass without criticism in bourgeois as well as Social Democratic circles that military service was designed to as a school to inculcate blind obedience to those in authority and to foster monarchic sentiments in the citizen. Yet the experience of army service, harsh and even brutal as it often was, and leading inevitably for some to suicide, was viewed positively by many, especially in retrospect. The framed photograph of 'our Hans' in his uniform, the pictures of regimental companions on the wall of the home, told their own story in a society where orderliness was a supreme virtue and which respected the professional way in which things seemed to be done in the army. Theodor Fontane was among the most subtle critics of the social militarism (and dual standards) of the empire, especially during the reign of Wilhelm II. In his novel *Effi Briest* (1895), he tells how Effi was ostracized by society for the rest of her life for her adultery as an nineteen-year-old with

Crampas, an army major of forty-five. Her husband, Innstetten, himself a former officer, challenges Crampas to a duel and kills him. Six weeks later, the emperor allows him to appear back again in society, sufficient time having been deemed to have elapsed to have "expiated" the killing of a former comrade and married man. Yet Fontane was proud of his two sons, who were regular officers in the army.

The attitude of the officer corps toward society changed in the course of the nineteenth century. The 1848 Revolution played a crucial role here. Troops were widely used to quell disturbances and subsequently to disband popular assemblies in 1849. The revolution served to make the Prussian army politically aware in a way than it had not been prior to the 1840s. The clash between crown and parliament also influenced the officer corps and of noncommissioned officers, to see their primary role as guardians of the peace against internal hostile elements, rather than as defenders of the realm. In Bismarck's last years, the army was frequently called in to impose order, often with scant regard for civil rights. In the not uncommon siege mentality of the late nineteenth-century German ruling classes in their response to the growing power of organized labor, the idea of the army's capacity to strike a preventive blow against the "revolutionary proletarian hordes" began to seem a positive, socially reassuring feature of their state.

Table 3: Strength of the German Army 1880–1914

Year	Total strength	Officers	Ranks	Of these NCOs	Total strength as a percentage of population
1880	422,589	17,227	401,659	48,531	,937
1881	449,257	18,128	427,274	51,586	,989
1887	491,825	19,262	468,409	55,447	1,035
1891	511,657	20,400	486,983	58,448	1,028
1894	584,548	22,534	557,112	77,883	1,138
1900	600,516	23,850	571,692	80,556	1,065
1905	609,758	24,522	580,158	82,582	1,006
1910	622,483	25,718	589,672	85,226	,959
1914	800,646	30,739	76,438	105,856	1,181

One of the effects of the growth in the size of the army under Wilhelm II—a common characteristic of European states at the turn of the century—was to improve the career opportunities for bourgeois officers. Fontane's second son, Theo, for example, who was born in 1856, reached the rank of lieutenant colonel. Professional men of middle-class background had good career opportunities in the service, as engineers, for example. But noblemen, whether of ancient or modern lineage, continued to dominate the higher ranks and the better regiments. The army was socially divisive in other ways—for example, in its discrimination against men who spoke their minds. One such was Werner Siemens, who left the Prussian army precisely for this reason and embarked on his meteoric career in the private sector. Even more so did the army discriminate against those not favored by the All-Highest (Wilhelm II): Catholics and Jews. There was not a single professional officer of Jewish faith in the imperial army between 1878 and 1910. Many Jews, however, sought and gained admission to the position of officer of the Reserve, a distinction which carried social cachet and was shared by some 120,000 Germans by 1914.

Criticism of the overweening power of the military in the decades before the 1914 war was most cogent in the satirical papers, especially in the graphically striking and sophisticated cartoons in the columns of the Munich *Simplicissimus*. But the special position of the army in the German state and in imperial society was not seriously challenged by any state government, political party, or pressure group between 1871 and 1913, apart from the efforts of the Social Democrat deputies in the Reichstag and the state assemblies. When, however, the so-called Zabern affair occurred, and public opinion right across the country was scandalized, critics were soon forced to acknowledge their impotence to challenge that political and social supremacy. A young Prussian lieutenant of twenty submitted the townspeople in the Alsace garrison town of Zabern in 1913 to insulting and humiliating language, and the military authorities responded by proclaiming a state of siege and arresting many of its citizens. The emperor intervened personally on the side of the military, choosing to see the whole affair as part of his royal prerogative and actually refusing an audience to the civil governor of Alsace. At a subsequent military court, the officers involved were acquitted and the findings of the inquiry kept secret. The failure of the Reichstag, where stormy scenes broke out over the debate, to gain justice for the people of Zabern and the clear case in law against the arrogant officers made the scandal of the Zabern Affair an exemplary illustration of the constitutional defects of the Empire and apparently impregnable position of the army in the state.

Parliament and parliaments in the Second Empire

The failure of the German parliamentary system to assert its authority over the armed forces during the Second Empire earned it harsh criticism from a vocal minority. The socialist deputy, August Bebel, famously and provocatively described the German Reichstag or lower house of the imperial parliament as "the fig-leaf of absolutism." Karl Marx was no less savage in his comments. Of course the Empire itself was formed in 1871 without direct reference to the parliamentary parties. Yet to Germans living at the time of the *Reichsgründung* or foundation of the German state, the existence of a national parliament elected on the basis of universal manhood suffrage represented a major advance on what had existed before. Moreover, the fact that the Empire had been founded after a lengthy system of horse-trading with the sovereign princes, made the emergence of an effective parliament, on the English or North American lines, highly unlikely. In twenty-two of the twenty-five states of the Empire in 1871 there existed representative assemblies. These continued to function and to legislate for the areas which were not the responsibility of the Reichstag, such as education. The states which did not possess parliaments of their own were the recently conquered Alsace-Lorraine, which had its own governor and administration and was in effect treated as a kind of colony, and the constitutionally backward Mecklenburg duchies of Mecklenburg-Schwerin and Mecklenburg-Strelitz.

However, the composition and influence of German state parliaments could vary widely. In south Germany with its more democratic traditions, virtually all citizens who paid direct taxes were represented in these assemblies. Prussia's restrictive three-class franchise, dating from 1849, remained unmodified until 1918, and in Saxony a similar franchise was introduced in 1896 in place of the former more liberal one in a vain attempt to check the progress of social democracy in that state. The Prussian three-class system determined representation in the lower house of the Prussian parliament, the *Landtag*, on the basis of amounts of tax paid. In the 1860s the *Landtag* had had a liberal majority. After 1871, and more particularly as the flight from the eastern rural provinces into the cities began to gather momentum, the failure of the state to adjust electoral boundaries to reflect population density, ensured that a minority group, namely the Prussian conservatives or their nominees, had undue weight in the *Landtag*. The Mecklenburg duchies were even less accessible to pressure for modernization and constitutional reform. Nowhere were the peasants more oppressed. Up to the end of the Empire the local landed nobility, the *Ritterschaften*, sedulously and effectively repressed efforts both by liberal spokesmen and by the dukes themselves to widen the social basis of the state assembly, composed of delegates of the nobility and of the few towns in the region. Under the Empire, state governments and assemblies retained their power over such matters as direct taxation, education, and transport.

The Reichstag

The Reichstag's parliamentary parties did not, as in western constitutional states, make and unmake governments. Up to the end of the Empire in 1918, Reich governments were formed and dismissed independently of the political parties, by the Kaiser. The parties' relationship with the government was determined by whether or not they supported it, as the conservatives and the National Liberals generally did throughout Bismarck's time, and as the Progressive or left-liberals sometimes did. The most prominent and numerically powerful opponents of the government in the Bismarck era were the Catholic Center party in the 1870s and early 1880s. Thereafter the Social Democratic party represented the most vigorous opposition, but their spectacular rise in numbers of deputies belongs to the period after Bismarck's fall. The opposition also included the Polish and Danish nationalists, and the so-called particularist parties, representatives of Alsace-Lorraine, taken from France in 1871, or the territories annexed by Bismarck in 1866. The actual government of the Empire lay in the hands of the emperor, assisted by the fifty-eight members of the *Bundesrat* or Federal Council. The *Bundesrat* represented the state governments (but not necessarily the people) of the twenty-five constituent states of the Empire. Bismarck had, as it were, tailor-made the position of Reich chancellor for himself, and he held it for nineteen years, from 1871 to 1890. He had six successors between 1890 and 1918, who served for periods ranging from nine years (Bernard von Bülow, 1900–9) to five weeks between 30 September and 9 November 1918 (Max von Baden, 1867–1929). The emperor exercised legislative power, together with the *Bundesrat*, the upper house of parliament, and the Reichstag or Imperial Diet, the lower house. In 1871 the Reichstag had 397 members elected for a five-year term and, by contrast with the franchise to the state assemblies, on the basis of universal suffrage of males over twenty-five years of age. Ostensibly a concession to democratic opinion, universal suffrage was in practice severely curtailed. Payment of members had been expressly precluded by Bismarck's constitution, to ensure the election of men of substance and, ideally, conservative opinion. Payment was only conceded in 1906. Bismarck also hoped that the election of landowners, industrialists, and men of affairs, who had their living to make, would ensure short sessions and prevent the emergence of professional politicians. Secret ballots were also successfully opposed in order to maintain the traditional authority of landowners and employers over their dependents. However, the capacity of Bismarck's contemporaries on occasion to undermine his carefully designed plans is well exemplified by the Catholic Center party's exploitation of universal suffrage and public ballots to influence the voting behavior of German Catholics.

The effective powers of the Reichstag were restricted according to the Bismarckian constitution in such a manner as to deny the German Empire the title of a genuine constitutional state. Legislation could not be initiated by the lower house, but only by the *Bundesrat* or upper house. No political party could aspire to form or bring down the government of the Empire, nor could parliament appoint or dismiss the chancellor. Contemporaries used the word *Reichsleitung* (Reich leadership) rather than the normal German word for government, *Regierung*, as if to emphasize the anomalous character of their political system. The chancellor was not responsible to parliament and there were no imperial ministers to be responsible to. Instead government departments were headed by permanent secretaries of state (*Staatssekretäre*), that is, by civil servants. True, there were Prussian ministers of war, of foreign affairs, and so on, testifying to the predominance of Prussia in the Empire. But either their powers were curtailed and their authority bypassed by the crown's special powers in military matters, as in the first case, or, as in the second, the office was combined by Bismarck with that of Reich chancellor and Prussian prime minister, and also minister of trade and commerce (*Handelsminister*).

The constitution of the Second Empire was an adapted version of that of the North German Confederation (1867–71). It was clearly an *ad hoc* arrangement, designed by Bismarck, despite certain economic liberal features, to perpetuate the traditional rights of the crown and the special powers and privileges of army and bureaucracy. Only a few years after the founding of the Empire, Bismarck determined to curtail the growth of liberal institutions in the state. Senior civil servants of liberal conviction were eased out of office and liberally minded junior civil servants were passed over for promotion. Thus in 1876 Rudolf Delbrück, responsible for Prussia's successful economic policies in the 1850s and 1860s and a key negotiator in the preliminaries to unification, felt forced to resign. A series of policy initiatives marked the end of what, in the early 1870s, had still seemed to many observers the corollary of Prussia's military leadership, the gradual and pragmatic liberalization of the German political system. The new direction was marked by the so-called civil service reform under the new and reactionary Prussian minister of the interior of 1878, Robert von Puttkamer (1828–1900) the notorious Anti-Socialist legislation introduced in the same year, Bismarck's breach with his former National Liberal partners in the Reichstag, and his policy of protective tariffs of 1879. These last aimed to bolster the position of the landowners in the eastern provinces, who now found difficulty in competing with cheap imported grain. Even in 1890, the year of his fall, Bismarck was engaged in a scheme designed to abolish universal suffrage. It had demonstrably failed to perform its prime function as envisaged by the Iron Chancellor, namely, to return a conservative establishment to the Reichstag. He and others even envisaged using repressive measures to provoke civil disturbances, to be countered by a *coup d'état*. The reorientation of domestic policy in 1878–9, the subsequent concentration of real power in the hands of individuals and elitist groups, is referred to as the second or "inner" foundation of the Reich. This shift in policy was a significant influence on domestic politics of German governments between 1871 and 1918.

Yet at the same time, and in spite of the severe limitations on its functioning as a modern parliament, the Reichstag, its parties, and its elections did indeed operate as the motor of popular political participation. The practice of attending the debates by members of the public increased in the later years of the century. One such member of the public was Theodor Fontane, who attended the house regularly, commenting on speeches in his letters to his wife and daughter. In a state where party politicians could not vote the chancellor out of office, it was paradoxical, but nonetheless a fact, that electoral participation was high and rose steadily throughout the Empire. In the 1887 or "Cartel" elections, voter participation reached nearly 80 percent and, with the exception of the 1890 elections (69 percent), never dropped below 70 percent for the rest of the Empire (Sperber 1997, 201). Particularly in the 1890s and early 1900s the political parties displayed well-focused energy and virtually all of them developed a vigorous party organization in that period.

Parliament and the parties

The Reichstag was not the hub of political life as was the House of Representatives in the United States or the House of Commons in Victorian Britain, yet its activities attracted ever-increasing interest and comment in the national newspapers and in the vigorous satirical periodical press. It was, after all, a place where leading figures in public life met and bonded. At the same time the rising number of Germans who went to the polls at election times, particularly after 1890, demonstrated that the Reichstag, for all the limits on its public influence, was seen to have a role in the political life of the nation. Parliamentary politics attracted some gifted individuals, though they tended to be more numerous among the parties opposed to or critical of the government than among the government's supporters. The Hanoverian Rudolf von Bennigsen, leader of the National Liberals in the 1870s, when the party came close to being Bismarck's governmental party, was found wanting in the kind of skills or vision which might have enabled Bennigsen and his party to counter Bismarck's realignment toward the conservatives in the period of the "second foundation of the Reich." By contrast, no one could contest the brilliant parlia-

The chancellor Bismarck at the laying of the foundation stone for the new Reichstag, 1884. Contemporary engraving. Note Bismarck's dress.

mentary and political skills of Bismarck's most dogged adversary: Ludwig Windthorst (1812–91) also came from the central German state of Hanover, which Bismarck had annexed to Prussia in 1866/7. He was half Bismarck's size and almost wholly blind, yet led the Catholic Center party for over twenty years until his death in the year following Bismarck's dismissal. Cartoonists loved to portray the two men, whose marvelous rhetoric could fill the House and the gallery, though Windthorst, on account of his sight, had to learn his one- or two-hour speeches by heart. Another famed speaker was Eugen Richter (1838–1906), leader of the Progressive liberals. Innstetten in Fontane's *Effi Briest*, who is portrayed in the novel as enjoying Bismarck's special favor, expresses the irritation of his master in his disparaging reference to Richter. He was indeed a constant thorn in Bismarck's side, not least because of his unrivaled expertise on military matters and his capacity to ask the chancellor awkward questions. Over the period of the Empire as a whole, perhaps the most memorable party leader was the long-serving socialist August Bebel. Yet Bebel had to contend with immense practical and psychological difficulties during his long parliamentary career. The nature of these and indeed the character of political culture in the Second Empire, are well exemplified in an anecdote he told at the end of his life. After an absence of some six weeks through illness, he returned to the Reichstag and was addressed by the then chancellor, Bethmann-Hollweg, who inquired about his health. It was the first time in forty years that a member of the German government had spoken in the House to the leader of the Social Democrat party, yet that party was now (since the 1912 elections) the largest party in parliament.

In the parties other than the Socialist party, the composition of party leadership changed during the Empire from being primarily local notables, who only became active at election time, to being the spokesmen of well-organized political and economic pressure groups. Indicative of the evolution of political attitudes among the bourgeoisie were the changing fortunes of the liberals. Their amoeba-like behavior, fragmenting, coalescing under a new name, splitting yet again, was a seemingly inexorable accompaniment of the process. Yet after 1900 liberalism showed surprising vigor in attracting sizable numbers of new voters at election time, more particularly where specific issues were concerned. The conservative parties witnessed a decline in electoral support from the 1880s onward, although the electoral system ensured them a percentage of seats both in the Reichstag and in the Prussian *Landtag* in excess of their percentage of the vote. Splinter parties, such as the anti-Semites, benefited from this situation, winning Reichstag seats in 1893 and again in 1907. After the end of the *Kulturkampf* or conflict between the Bismarckian state and the Catholic church, and more particularly after Bismarck's fall in 1890, economic and nationalist issues, rather than church-state relations, became dominant even in Catholic voters' minds. Now even the tactically so skilled Center party found itself losing votes to other parties.[1]

A small percentage of votes and seats were held by the ethnic and other minority groups in the Empire. Among the ethnic groups, the Poles were numerically the most significant; initially they voted for the Center party, but the Polish Nationalist party made significant gains in response both to the increasing integration of the Center into mainstream imperial politics and to the systematic Germanization program of the Prussian Polish provinces, under Bismarck in the 1880s and notably under Bülow after 1900. Other ethnic groups included the Danes of North Schleswig and the Alsace-Lothringians, whose share of the vote declined from about 4 percent in 1874 to approximately 2 percent in the three elections between 1903 and 1912, suggesting a degree of

---

[1] As a prescient chronicler and commentator on the German political life of his day, Theodor Fontane features the decline of ideology as an issue for German Catholics in their relation to the state, in the conversational exchange about the papacy between Dubslav Stechlin and his old friend, the Bavarian Catholic Baron Berchtesgaden, in chapter 14 of *Der Stechlin*.

integration of their voters into mainstream politics. The so-called particularists were the Hanoverians, representing a more liberal tradition of politics than in Prussia, as well as the rights of their king, deposed and exiled by Bismarck when he annexed their territory, and the Hesse-Kassel voters, who had less to lament in the passing of their unpleasant ruler. After 1890 the particularists gradually ceased to be a factor of much consequence in party politics, while the prominence of economic and social issues led to formation of new small parties, of which the Peasants League (*Bauernbund*), largely based in Bavaria, was the most significant. The chief beneficiary of changes in voting habits during the history of the Empire was the Socialist party, now, since its Erfurt party congress of 1891, the Social Democratic party. Yet the ruling classes convinced themselves that the party should continue to be treated as disloyal citizens, and might never aspire to government. When Friedrich Ebert (1871–1925), later first prime minister and first president of the Weimar Republic, took over as secretary of the Social Democratic party in 1905, he felt unable to install a typewriter at party headquarters, for fear of police raids and confiscation of party files.

Origins of political parties

When Germany's political parties were formed, they grew up alongside a bureaucratic and military establishment, whose origins lay in the former absolutist states of the seventeenth and eighteenth centuries. In south Germany, which had some form of constitutionalist government since the early nineteenth century, political groups roughly analogous to the major part of the later party divisions already existed in the pre-March era. In the north, political parties were not constituted until the 1860s, although the 1848 Revolution had seen the growth of liberal, democratic, Catholic, labor, and conservative groups in the Frankfurt Parliament and other assemblies. Such groups inevitably disintegrated after the suppression of the revolution. The reactionary climate of the 1850s did not favor their revival. By contrast, the climate of the early 1860s was buoyant, the political situation at home and abroad fluid. To contemporaries, the age seemed to be rich in potential. Opportunities seemed to be at hand for men of public spirit to have the chance to steer German politics in a new direction. The optimism engendered by a dynamic economy and the fluidity of the international situation, particularly in countries contiguous to Germany, seemed to point in the direction of a new Germany. In 1858, the marriage was celebrated between Friedrich (1888), son of Wilhelm I, and Victoria (1840–1901), the eldest daughter of Queen Victoria. Given the known liberal sympathies of the young couple, many saw this symbolical union between Prussia and Britain as a portent of Prussia's own movement toward constitutional government. Contemporaries speculated that the unified Germany of the future, in whatever form that unity came, would be a European constitutional state, rather than the semiabsolutist one she had so long been.

All over Germany in the late 1850s and in the 1860s, organizations were formed with the specific aim of fostering and winning the support of public opinion, of increasing political participation, to be directed toward the goals of national unification, constitutional government, and liberal economic policies. Some of these organizations, such as the liberal *Nationalverein*, founded in 1859 under the patronage of Prince Albert's elder brother, Ernst II, duke of Saxe-Coburg-Gotha and including among its members the historian Theodor Mommsen (1817–1903) and the engineer Werner Siemens, were forerunners of national political parties. Its conservative and Prussian equivalent, the *Volksverein*, was founded in 1861. The early 1860s also saw the meteor-like career of the Silesian lawyer, Ferdinand Lassalle (1825–64), champion of working men and founder of the first German labor party in 1863. Its basis lay in Berlin, Frankfurt, and the Rhenish cities, though the actual numbers involved were small. The Constitutional Conflict in Prussia had aroused a vigorous response in bourgeois circles in Germany generally. It also gave a major boost to the emergence of liberal parties, both in Prussia and in other German states. Meanwhile petty bourgeois democratic organizations, centered principally on Hamburg in the northwest, Karlsruhe, Baden's capital in the southwest, and Frankfurt and Coburg in central Germany, sought to involve small-town tradesmen, professional men, and also farmers in political decision-making. Mass public meetings in the south and center of the Confederation were called in 1866 to protest against Prussia's aggressive policy over Schleswig-Holstein, drawing for the time astonishingly large crowds, many of whom now experienced railway travel for the first time. The vigor with which political issues were discussed in public and in the journals during this decade of more relaxed censorship suggested that the traditional character of politics was changing. In fact, the numbers of the politically active or even the politically conscious were not very high, certainly by comparison with the mass organizations of the 1900s. The *Nationalverein*, the largest such group, never exceeded 25,000 members; Lassalle's working-class movement had some 4,600 members in 1864. Even journals and newspapers with a reputation for genuine popularity, rarely had a circulation of more than 5,000, although we have to remember that there were probably rather more readers and listeners[2] to a single copy than would be the case today.

---

[2] The culture of reading aloud in the age before gas and electrical lighting should not be forgotten, when studying this period. It is particularly relevant to the study of literary genre.

The liberal parties

The first modern political party in Germany was the *Fortschrittspartei* or Progressive party, which formed a distinctive group among the liberal deputies of the Prussian *Landtag* or lower house during the Constitutional Conflict and which led the opposition to Bismarck's policies. In September 1866, precisely two months after the victory of Prussian arms over Austria and her allies, Bismarck offered his domestic opponents a compromise solution, the so-called Indemnity Bill, which brought a split in the party. A new party, known as the National Liberals, was formed from the Prussian liberals who accepted Bismarck's compromise, as well as from representatives from the new territories of Prussia, such as Hanover and electoral Hesse (Hesse-Kassel), who had not been involved in the dispute. For the next decade, the National Liberals, under their leader and former Hanoverian prime minister, von Bennigsen, came close to being a government party in its collaboration with the chancellor Bismarck on an impressive body of liberal legislation. In terms of historical importance, perhaps the most significant was the emancipation of the Jews in 1871, which followed similar measures in the Danube monarchy (1866–8), and which Switzerland would emulate in 1874. Germans in the 1870s felt proud of having standardized the currency, weights, and measures which anchored German unity institutionally and made the conduct of business so much easier. The new currency was appropriately called the Reichsmark. It existed alongside the Prussian taler, but gradually replaced it, remaining Germany's currency until the introduction of the *Deutschmark* into the future territory of the Federal Republic in 1948. However, the National Liberals were not successful in gaining the all-important concessions of ministerial responsibility to parliament nor budgetary control of military expenditure. The leaders of the Progressives, notably Eugen Richter and Eduard Lasker (1829–84), recognized very clearly the implication of Bismarck's refusal and his essential contempt for the parliamentary process, but which he knew he required to govern.

Despite the diverging roles played by the two parties in the Reichstag, both the National Liberals and the Progressives regarded themselves as part of the "liberal party." The same was true of the later splinter groups of liberals, formed after the splits in 1881, 1884, and 1893. The different groups frequently campaigned for each other's candidates at elections. The National Liberals ran many more candidates in the 1870s; in the 1880s the reverse was true. A party apparatus was not developed by the liberals until the 1890s. In the 1870s and

---

Thus in the nineteenth-century novel, the interplay between author, narrator, and reader becomes much more evident on listening to someone read aloud or to a recording, than it is to the silent reader in her or his room.

1880s the party, apart from their parliamentary representatives, tended to disappear between elections. The process of selecting candidates or checking their views could be haphazard. It was a characteristic of the liberal parties that the local member largely determined the political line taken, in contrast with the opposition parties, the Catholic Center, and the Socialist parties. Toward the end of the Bismarck era, the dynamics of a modern industrial society began to have its impact on the political parties, which developed in the 1890s from being collections of notables to pressure groups representing sectional interests. The dividing line between the right and left wings of the liberal movement became ever more pronounced. For all intents and purposes, the National Liberals were by the 1890s a conservative political party, drawing their support from north German businessmen and large farmers of central Germany.

The conservatives

At no time between 1871 and 1914 did the conservative parties of the empire enjoy support of the Reichstag electorate comparable to that given to the liberals. Yet the conservatives continued to wield considerable power and influence throughout the political system. This is less an indication of liberal failure than of the limits to the effectiveness of the political parties in the Reichstag as a force in public life, relative to other, less democratic institutions. Thus, many of the crucial issues of domestic policy continued after 1871 to lie within the competence of state governments and, to a lesser extent, state assemblies, and many of these were not liberal. The Prussian *Landtag*, which in the 1860s had been the focus of the Constitutional Conflict and dominated by the liberals, came from the 1870s onward increasingly under the control of the conservative interest. Prussia, after all, comprised some three-fifths of the population of the Empire. In the Reichstag there were initially three conservative parties. One, a short-lived nationalist conservative party, disappeared in 1874. The *Deutsche Reichspartei*, generally known as the Free Conservatives in Prussia, who represented the left-wing of the conservative party, were led by Wilhelm von Kardorff (1828–1907), founder of the German Industrialists Association in 1876. It drew electoral support from Lower Silesia, Berlin, and the Rhineland and was the party of heavy industry.

The old Conservative party, earlier known as the *Kreuz-Zeitung* party from the title of its newspaper, which carried a Prussian cross on its title page, represented the landowning interest in the eastern provinces of Prussia and in Mecklenburg. In 1876 the Prussian conservatives reinvented themselves in a significant move. They now styled themselves the German Conservative party, thus emphasizing their new, national character. In a sense, it was analogous to the marriage between Prussia and Germany as represented in the new Reich, though electorally the German Conservatives only attracted single figure percentages of the vote at Reichstag elections. When Wilhelm II came to power, the influence of special interest groups, notably the Agrarian League, on the Conservative party grew marked, so much so that the phrase about the Agrarian League's wagging the tail of the Conservative party dog is apt indeed, as noted in David Blackbourn's *The Long Nineteenth Century* 1770–1918 (1997, 337). The conservatives relied even less than the liberals on a party apparatus. Instead the local nobility and Protestant clergy brought pressure to bear, where necessary, on tenant farmers and workers to vote as their masters wished. They assigned a role in the conduct of elections to subaltern officials and teachers, who, quite by contrast with Republican France, identified with and promoted the conservative interest.[3] Broadly speaking, constitutions, elections, and parliament were seen by the majority of the landowners and magnates as a necessary evil of modern society. They therefore regarded it as their duty to future generations to ensure the preservation of their culture and hence to see that their dependents voted conservative. The preservation of what they liked to regard as the Prussian tradition of habits of mind and a way of life which was that of a preindustrial society was more or less absolute and presented in moral terms. Deviation from the pattern was regarded as an affront. Hence the outrage when a member of one's family or circle voted for one of the liberal parties or, worse still, gave their support to the Socialists. The decision by a local teacher whose appointment was dependent on local patronage to vote for a candidate other than the recommended one was tantamount to inviting dismissal from employment, and probably also from one's home. There was considerable voter movement between the conservatives and (the National) liberals throughout the empire, but when rural dwellers, traditionally conservative voters, moved to the cities, they tended to be lost to the conservative interest, as noted in Jonathan Sperber's *The Kaiser's Voters* (1997, 129).

The Center party

The third major party in German parliamentary life was something of an anomaly among European parliamentary institutions. This was the purely religious Catholic Center party, destined to play a prominent role in parliamentary politics throughout the Empire, never more so than in the years of conflict between state and Catholic church in the 1870s and 1880s fomented by

---

[3] Chapters 17 to 20 of Fontane's *Der Stechlin* provide a whimsical portrait of this local notable system still in operation in rural Brandenburg in the 1890s. Fontane was a lifelong, if critical, reader of the *Kreuz-Zeitung*, for which he had worked in the 1860s. The principal irony of his fictitious election lies in the fact that the local landowner loses out to the Social Democrat. Fontane's attribution of electoral success to the Social Democrat candidate (like Bebel, a turner by trade), is of course prescient.

Bismarck and known as the *Kulturkampf*. The movement which led to the founding of the party in 1870 began with a group of upper-class Catholics in the Rhineland and Silesia. It drew its socially and regionally disparate electoral support from the propertied and professional classes, from smallholders in the west and south of Germany, and also from the urban working classes of the western regions. The Center party played a supremely important role in developing political awareness and promoting political participation among German Catholics in a period of their country's history which was largely unfavorable to them as a community. Prussia's defeat of Austria lost them the natural protector of Catholic interests since the days of the Holy Roman Empire, while Austria's expulsion from the German Confederation and the subsequent formation of the *kleindeutsche* Empire changed Catholics from being the majority of the German population to a minority. During the early years of the Second Empire, when the German nation was presented as a compound of Prussian military achievements, Protestant fervor, and liberal philosophy, Catholics felt threatened and grew defensive. The *Kulturkampf*, a church-state conflict which had parallels in most of Germany's Catholic neighbors, notably in France and Italy, as well as in Austria itself, and in former member states of the Confederation, such as Baden, was particularly acute in Prussia. It encouraged a siege mentality among the country's Catholics, but it also greatly increased the homogeneity of the German Catholic community, for all the differences in its members' social and regional backgrounds. Despite the hierarchical organization of the *Zentrum* (from 1911 the *Deutsche Zentrumspartei*) under its traditional leaders, despite the losses among its urban working-class voters after 1900 to the Social Democrats, the party showed remarkable resilience and managed to retain the support of a substantial percentage of German Catholics throughout the Empire. As for other German voters, economic and social issues replaced ideology after the death of its leader Windthorst in 1891.

In common with the conservatives and liberals, the Center was slow to develop a party apparatus, but in a sense it needed to do so less than they did. In the Catholic regional and national press, in the annual *Katholikentag* or assembly of German Catholics, and in the various Catholic associations formed for charitable or social purposes, it possessed effective agencies for promoting Catholic awareness among constituents and directing their support to the party. Most Center party candidates were expected to have prior experience in these associations before presenting themselves for selection. The most prominent of such associations was the already mentioned *Volksverein für das katholische Deutschland*, founded in 1890. It played a key role in helping the party, by and large, to retain the loyalty of the urban vote, at a time when the leadership of the party favored the agrarian interest over that of industrial workers. In the loyalty of its supporters to the party and its policies, in the sense of community within the wider parameters of state and nation, and in its defensive mentality, which was to some extent thrust upon it by the Second Empire, the Center party bore some resemblance to the German Social Democrats, but, unlike them, it was fairly well integrated into mainstream politics by the late 1880s.

The Social Democrats

The German Socialist Workers Party, from 1891 the Social Democrats, came from small beginnings to being by 1912 the largest and best organized labor party in Europe. The movement's beginnings lay in the 1840s. The 1848 Revolution did not witness the emergence of a labor movement as such, but a milestone in the history of Socialism was the realization among workers' leaders, in the second wave of revolution in the autumn of 1848, that their interests were at variance, or indeed in fundamental opposition to those of bourgeois liberals. That year brought the labor movement its first martyrs, in the arrest and trial of German "Communists" in the revolution's aftermath. Under orders from the Federal Diet to proscribe workers' associations, German state governments initiated repressive policies in the 1850s which destroyed all but educational initiatives. These more often than not were under the direction of liberals. The first German Socialist party, the *Allgemeiner Arbeiterverein* or General Workers' Association, was founded not in Prussia but at Leipzig in Saxony in the presence of the delegates from eleven German towns. The date was May 1863 and the delegates came from Dresden, from the free cities of Hamburg and Frankfurt, from Hanover and Bad Homburg near Frankfurt, and from five Rhenish towns, among them Cologne and Düsseldorf. The *Arbeiterverein* was the first explicitly national German workers party and the first to disassociate itself from bourgeois liberalism. Its founder was Ferdinand Lassalle, a Jewish businessman's son and a lawyer from Breslau, Silesia's capital. He believed that the state should and could take over the role of protecting its workers against the egoism of the bourgeoisie. This was a view that made sense to the skilled or semiskilled craftsmen who would provide the backbone of the movement for decades to come, many of whom had been the victims of newstyle industrial capitalism. As industrialization gathered momentum in these years of take-off into sustained industrial growth, the interests of left-wing liberals and the workers' associations, which in the early months of the 1848 Revolution had seemed at one, began to diverge. The use in Progressive party circles in the 1860s of the offensive term "*die unzeitgemäße Arbeiterbewegung*" (the ill-timed labor movement) suggested to labor leaders that liberals' promotion of working men's associations might be more concerned with the liberals' political advantage, than with self-improvement of the workers.

However, Lassalle's party, for all the publicity it attracted, was anything but a mass organization. Moreover, in 1863, a rival workers' organization had been founded by the journalist and veteran of 1848, William Liebknecht (1825–90), together with August Bebel, a master turner and son of a Prussian NCO, both of whom had been deputies in the parliament of the North German Confederation and were elected to the Reichstag. The amalgamation of the two groups was delayed in part as a result of the courageous opposition of Liebknecht and Bebel to the Franco-Prussian war in the former assembly and to the annexation of Alsace-Lorraine in the latter; this lost the young party electoral support and also earned the two leaders prison sentences of nearly two years. At Gotha in 1875, after extended consultation and confrontation with Karl Marx in exile, unity was achieved under the name of the Socialist Workers Party of Germany, a revolutionary Marxist party, committed, in theory at least, to the overthrow of the state and the monarchic order. In the early years of the party, there were many constituencies with Socialist candidates. Where the party fielded candidates, they received on average some 10 percent of the vote. Not least among the factors contributing to its success was the violent suppression of strikes by the police and the impact of the stagnation of the economy in the mid-1870s on industrial workers. After Bismarck's fall and the end of the Anti-Socialist legislation, the percentage of votes gained by the Social Democrats rose at every election. In 1903 the party won an impressive 24 percent of the vote, and in the last prewar elections of 1912, a hitherto unique achievement for a political party in the Wilhelmine Empire: 29 percent.

The growth of the Socialist vote and hence the implication of universal suffrage for its future progress, as well as Bismarck's own need for a national scapegoat in the new reactionary orientation of his domestic policy, had led the chancellor in 1878 to move over to the attack. Exploiting the coincidence of two assassination attempts on emperor Wilhelm I's life in 1878 as allegedly the work of Socialists, he introduced the Anti-Socialist Bill into the Reichstag. The measure was eventually passed by the support of the conservatives and the majority of the National Liberals, opposed by the two unlikely bedfellows of Progressives and the Center under Ludwig Windthorst (who clearly appreciated the danger such utterly illiberal measures could hold for the Catholics). All working-class associations were proscribed, and all but two of the fifty-one party papers. This last measure not only seriously hampered party activity, but it also constituted a serious threat to the many who earned their living as journalists; equally it hit at a vital source of party funds. Since members of the Reichstag were not paid, Socialist deputies, though not affected directly by the ban, since they were elected as individuals rather than as party members, were particularly dependent on such funds. The authorities' demand for vigilance against known or suspected Socialists was met by the police, particularly in northern Germany, with alacrity. In the twelve years between 1878 and the nonrenewal of the legislation in 1890, some 900 labor leaders were expelled from their place of domicile, and some 1,500 served prison sentences. The party showed impressive energy and ingenuity in dealing with the emergency. The leading Socialist paper, *Der Sozialdemokrat*, was printed in Zurich, which was now and had been for almost half a century, the refuge of illicit German protestors. It was smuggled into Germany and distributed nationally. Families of imprisoned or expelled party members were helped, and successful party congresses held abroad in Switzerland and Denmark, despite the authorities' efforts to prevent their transit. Certainly, the *Kampfzeit* or period of struggle, as it came to be called in Socialist mythology, fostered a sense of solidarity and awakened the political and proletarian consciousness of working men, and also of women. The party extended its support basis beyond Saxony and Berlin into the Rhineland and south Germany in these years. But the years of persecution also inevitably isolated the party from the state and aggravated relations generally between working men and the police, the military, and the ranks of officialdom. Elections played a particularly important part in the self-advertisement of the Socialists, who displayed a marked degree of effective interaction between agit-prop and policymaking (Sperber, 1997). Not that this was without dangers: particularly, though not only, in Bismarck's last years, Socialists were the victim of repressive measures by the authorities which could even include arrest of candidates and electoral committees. However, the independence of the judiciary in the Second Empire frequently led to defeat of the authorities, which goes some way to explain the peculiar split allegiance of militant Berlin workers, exemplified in the phrase of the day that they were loyal to both 'Willems'—to the Kaiser, and to the co-founder of their party, Wilhelm Liebknecht.

In the 1880s Bismarck had embarked on a palliative to Germany's urban working classes in the form of a program of social welfare legislation. It did not succeed in its designer's aim, to "wean workers away from Socialism," but it represents a pioneering effort in the context of the time, when few European governments felt called upon to show responsibility for the physical well-being of the nation's workers. In 1883 sickness insurance was introduced, the cost being shared by employers and insured, for Bismarck, as he put it in a speech to the Reichstag on 18 May 1889, wished that "the common man might learn to regard the empire as a benevolent institution." In 1884 accident insurance had been brought in; old age insurance and invalid benefit followed in 1889. The scheme was extended in subsequent years to cover rural laborers and other categories, and by 1900 some five and a half million Germans were insured, five billion marks having been paid out in benefit to them; that sum would double by 1910. Although Bismarck failed to win workers away from their allegiance to the Socialist movement, his policy did bring about a split between the former supporters of Lassalle, on the one hand, and the Marxists on the other, a split which Bebel managed to heal in 1887, and thus restore the ideological unity of the party on a Marxist basis.

The era following Bismarck's fall and the nonrenewal of the Anti-Socialist law, seemed to augur well for the relations between state and the urban working classes. But not for long. The self-styled "People's Kaiser"(*Volkskaiser*) held rather different views on how the proletariat should behave from those of organized labor. The Socialist party's steady gains at the polls were hardly designed to allay the emperor's deeply emotive suspicions of the movement, nor indeed by the fact that the party advanced steadily in every national election between 1890 and 1912, apart from the so-called "Hottentot elections" of 1907, fought by Chancellor von Bülow on an extreme chauvinist imperial platform. The Social Democrats had benefited, as the Center party had done to a lesser extent, by their imaginative wooing of new voters and of those who up to that had tended to abstain at the polls. Conservatives had proved much less adept at tapping this important source. By 1913 the Social Democratic Party had almost 1,000,000 paid-up members and employed fifty regional and one hundred district secretaries. It owned more than ninety daily papers and sixty-two printing presses. The cohesion and unity of the party, sustained through many decades and many vicissitudes, owed a great deal to the character and ability of its leaders. Rapid industrialization and mass movements of population to the urban centers, along with the response of the authorities and society to the emergence of a dynamic Socialist movement, helped to create a sense of proletarian consciousness among workers of widely differing skills and trades.

It is true that many regions of Germany and a number of areas of working-class life remained apparently immune to the appeal of social democracy. The largest potential area of support was the rural labor force, which in 1871 embraced some 60 percent of the workforce and by 1913 about 30 percent. For a variety of reasons, the party made few converts here, particularly in eastern Germany. The most palpable reasons were the difficulty of access for party activists to the still feudal social structure of many agrarian regions. Part of the reason was the lack of interest shown by doctrinaire Marxist Socialists in what Karl Marx had chosen to regard as a dying race, although the Erfurt Party conference of 1891 had explicitly mentioned the rural laborer as an object of concern. However, on any reckoning, especially given the obstacles it faced, and the massive changes in the size, distribution, and occupation of the German working classes during the Empire, the achievements of the German Social Democratic party were remarkable. Moreover it succeeded, as few other parties apart from the Center did, in becoming a truly national party.

Chapter 11
Politics, Government, and the Masses 1890–1914

Bismarck's heritage

Bismarck resigned his office at the request of the emperor on 18 March 1890. The English satirical magazine, *Punch*, created the cartoon that became famous under the heading "Dropping the pilot," in which Bismarck walked slowly down from the ship of state. For the next two decades and more, Germans became involuntarily aware of the degree to which Bismarck, for all his achievements, had stifled the growth and functioning of political institutions in their country. Bismarck had held the reins of power in his hands for well over a generation in Prussia (1862–90) and almost a generation in the Empire. In these years he had used the immense resources of men and material at his disposal to try to perpetuate the power structures which he had created. Fontane, originally an admirer, became ever more eloquent in his criticism in the 1890s. As he confessed to the journalist Maximilian Harden in a letter of 4 March 1894, he, Fontane, had written virtually nothing since 1870 without the unspoken presence of "this devil." Nearly seventeen years of Bismarck's nineteen-year term of office as Reich chancellor, from 1873 to 1890, had coincided with an initial crisis of confidence, over the stock market collapse in 1873, followed by a protracted period of industrial stagnation. From 1876 onward, a severe structural crisis in agriculture put an end to almost half a century of boom years. Contemporaries may have exaggerated the degree to which the industrial sector was actually in recession, but undoubtedly the unfavorable economic climate accounts in large measure for the pessimism which characterized these years in Germany. Such pessimism encouraged a sense of unease or even anxiety about the future in the new nation, whose exploitation the American historian Fritz Stern described in the title of his study of the social psychology of Wilhelmine Germany as "the politics of cultural despair." The focus on problems rather than opportunities in post 1871–Germany had a negative effect on popular attitudes to the outside world, and encouraged a cast of mind in many Germans which looked for scapegoats, abroad and at home. They found them, in the early and mid-seventies in the Catholic church and the Jesuits, later in the Jews and the Social Democrats. The immense vogue for cult books, which promised the answer to life's and the nation's problems, were another facet of people's unease in the ostensibly so secure and well-regulated nation they inhabited. Bismarck's own natural misanthropy affected those around him, and was well illustrated by the negative assumptions on which he based his electoral politics of the 1880s. As the years went by, he was visited by visions of catastrophe. He even saw Germany in his dreams, he said, as a leprous body, from which the parts dropped off, a graphic image of his fear for the future of his life's work.

Although the Bismarck cult was still vigorous in the late 1880s and would be artificially nurtured after his fall on his birthday and on national holidays, through demonstrations and loyal addresses designed, not least, to annoy Kaiser Wilhelm II, there was a widespread feeling by 1890 that the seventy-five-year-old chancellor had become something of a dead hand, and that his departure offered the chance of new and vigorous policies. Many Germans hoped for more harmonious relations between classes and economic groups in the future. Bismarck was seen to bear the main responsibility for social tensions consequent on the Anti-Socialist legislation he had introduced in 1878 and renewed regularly throughout the 1880s. His determination to extend it in a more stringent form had been an important cause of his dismissal, and the legislation was repealed in 1890. This did not, however, prevent official and unofficial harassment of Socialists and of working class organizations in Germany thereafter, a policy which found tacit approval among the propertied classes. But Germans in the 1890s were now becoming more concerned, as they saw it, by their country's vigorous pursuit of Germany's global role. Bismarck, it was commonly felt, was too much bound by age, origin, and political experience to mere European horizons. Germany's opportunities and Germany's security at the end of the century, it was believed, lay most certainly overseas. Imperial expansion, which was what was envisaged, was described at this time by the influential liberal thinker, Friedrich Naumann (1860–1919) to be but the natural "urge of the German people to extend its influence across the globe." Modern historians of Germany properly stress the dangerous absurdity of much of Wilhelm II's imperial ambition, and students of German literature recognize the aptness of the witheringly satirical verses on the Kaiser's foreign travel which got their author, the playwright Franz Wedekind, into such trouble. But at the time many Germans identified with, and saw an enhancement of themselves in the visions of world power status promised by their emperor. They also felt an enhancement of self in the growing importance of their country, in much the same way as respectable working class and petit bourgeois Victorians gave their neat, identical red-brick houses exotic names drawn from Britain's overseas empire, such as Kilimanjaro or Shangri-La.

When Germans in the 1890s distinguished between the old-fashioned Europe-centered policies of Bismarck, with his carefully balanced alliance system, and the modern world-political outlook of the new generation of policy-makers, they were guilty of a misconception. Bismarck was not the reluctant exponent of colonialism, as his celebrated aphorism might seem to suggest: "I do not," he once observed in the Reichstag, "wish to resemble the Polish nobility, whose fur coats conceal the fact that they cannot afford a shirt." He appeared suspicious of colonial ventures in the early 1880s, but he came to appreciate their value as a distraction from the increasing tensions and problems of domestic politics. There was, however, indisputably a marked change in the style of German politics after Bismarck's fall in 1890. This was particularly apparent in two ways: in Germany's relations with her neighbors and in the dominance of socioeconomic issues in electoral politics, both at local and at national levels. However, the central aims of Germany's rulers remained fundamentally unchanged, namely to preserve intact the power structures of imperial Germany, and, by satisfying the nation's need for material and social security and for prestige, thereby assure the general acquiescence of the governed in the status quo. This is not to deny the existence and the vocal character of opposition, not least from Germany's writers. However, the force and originality of Germany's (and, even more, Austria's) cultural critics in the late nineteenth century are probably more evident to us today than they were to their contemporaries. A further difference in style of Germany's politics after 1890 was the ever-increasing role played by political and economic interest groups. In time, style would become substance. Some of these interest groups in due course began to participate in national political decision-making, as they pressured or even bypassed constitutional institutions such as the Reichstag or even the imperial chancellor himself. In other cases, their role was more social, a substitute for lack of participation in direct decision-making, absorbing and distracting those concerned by giving them importance in their community and region.

Wilhelm II and his chancellors

Although the term "Wilhelmine" applies to the Second German Empire as a whole, there is a tendency to speak of the reign of Wilhelm I, emperor of the Germans from 1871–88, as the Bismarck era, and of those of his grandson, Wilhelm II (1888–1918) as Wilhelmine Germany. In June 1888, the *Dreikaiserjahr* or year of the three Emperors, Wilhelm II, aged twenty-nine, succeeded his father Friedrich III, who died of cancer after only ninety-nine days in power. Less than two years later, the young emperor requested Bismarck's resignation. The real object of his decision was, in the Kaiser's own words, that he should "rule as well as reign," and his strategy, if one can call it this, was to appoint those who would be accessible to his ideas. Like his granduncle, Friedrich Wilhelm IV, whose emotional temperament, artistic gifts, nervousness, and lack of balance he had inherited, Wilhelm II lacked self-reflective capacity. This made him susceptible to manipulation by those more astute than he. His first chancellor, Leo von Caprivi (1831–99), was soon a target and ultimately the victim of vested interests. Caprivi, a professional soldier and recent chief of the Admiralty, was a reluctant successor to Bismarck. He showed more initiative than his royal master wished, for he was perhaps the only one of Wilhelm's chancellors who faced the realities of Germany's transformation from an agrarian to a modern industrial state and who tried to legislate for the consequences. The greatest political problem of these decades for Germany was mastering and mediating the modernization process. Modernization was occurring piecemeal, transforming whole areas of the economy, of people's lives and stretches of the landscape, and yet leaving others scarcely touched. Both the ruling classes and the people feared modernization, even while benefiting from its many achievements.

Caprivi made genuine efforts to think strategically, and he was bound to encounter opposition from vested interests, quite apart from those occasioned by his own upright, inflexible character and his lack of political experience. His efforts to reform tariff policy in the interests of the German manufacturing industry and urban consumers, and his hopes of conciliating Germany's minorities, aroused immediate resentment. Most notable among the vested interests challenged were the landowners of East Elbia, who angrily dubbed their fellow aristocrat "the Knight without ear of corn or blade of grass," for Caprivi had no private means and owned no hereditary estate. The fact that a brief upswing in trade in the year following the young Kaiser's accession (1889–90) was followed by a downturn in the economy which lasted until 1895–6, made the task of Caprivi's government the more difficult. He succeeded in lowering agrarian tariffs, which both helped the consumer, notably the lower orders for whom brown bread was a staple in their diet, and opened the Russian frontier to the German export trade, which had come to a virtual standstill over earlier German tariffs on Russian grain. But his success stimulated the most vociferous interest group in Germany, the East Elbian landowners, to organize resistance. In 1893, the so-called *Bund der Landwirte*[1] or Agrarian League was founded and became a major political force in subsequent years.

---

[1] The German word *Landwirt* suggests a substantial or "strong" farmer, but the League won support also from small peasant proprietors who found themselves the victim of adverse economic developments, inherited debt, as prices for their products fell, failure to mechanize because of lack of access to capital, lack of access to markets, and so on.

The Agrarian League was dominated by the East Elbian landowners, but it drew support right across Germany, although in the south, the Bavarian Peasant League and other Christian peasant associations were more representative of local interests. The East Elbian landowners, in which ennobled bourgeois played an important part, were in a position to exercise influence on political decision-making at the highest level through their families' access to key posts in government departments and ministries, particularly in Prussia. The failure to readjust electoral district boundaries to reflect the massive migration of population from the land into the cities, together with the three-class voting system, gave the League's supporters undue influence in the Prussian *Landtag*.[2] The implications of Caprivi's limited attempts at conciliating dissident opinion in post-Bismarckian Germany were clearly evident to the ruling elite. This elite, which consisted of the landowners, the military, the upper echelons of the bureaucracy (all three could of course overlap) and now also the captains of heavy industry, such as Fritz von Krupp (1854–1902) or Karl von Stumm-Halberg (1836–1901), determined to offer collective resistance to the Caprivi government. He was forced to resign in 1894 and under his seventy-five-year-old successor, Chlodwig von Hohenlohe-Schillingsfürst (1819–1901), these forces attempted, with the support of the emperor, to bypass state institutions and to create corporate bodies which would wield real power in Germany.

A mediatized prince, that is, one of the many hundreds of once-sovereign princely families who had lost their sovereignty in 1803, Hohenlohe was a former Bavarian prime minister and governor of Alsace-Lorraine and held the office of chancellor from 1894 to 1900. His first three years in office saw a series of minor crises, associated with the successful attempts by the Kaiser and his close associates to replace independent-minded ministers and state secretaries with more pliant ones. This process was complete by 1897. Nominees of the emperor now held the key ministries in the Prussian government, that is, in three-fifths of the empire, and in the key posts in the imperial administration.

The new setup seemed in every way a victory for Wilhelm II's personal rule, and the emperor certainly saw it in this light. But although his personal power was immense, his political substance was too slight for him to rule in any genuine sense. This situation created a power vacuum in domestic politics, which was a prime source of instability for Germany in the next decade and a half. The powers behind the throne, the strategic alliance, or "the cartel based on fear," as it was described by Hans Ulrich Wehler, in his book *The German*

---

[2] Their declining capacity to manipulate elections to the Reichstag in a similar manner is cleverly encapsulated in the already mentioned "election" chapters 17 to 20 of Fontane's last novel, *Der Stechlin*.

Empire 1871-1918 (1985, 97) wielded effective power, determining the oligarchic character of government in the almost two decades up to the outbreak of war in 1914. Initially the most influential figures were: Johannes Miquel (1828-1901), a former mayor of Osnabrück and of Frankfurt, now secretary to the Reich Treasury and Prussian minister of finance[3]: Bernard von Bülow as secretary of state for foreign affairs and from 1900-09 chancellor; Philipp von Eulenburg (1847-1921), Wilhelm's confidant until the scandal of 1906; and the secretary of state for the interior, Arthur von Posadowsky-Wehner (1845-1942). A new face in imperial governance was the man whom Wilhelm appointed in 1897 secretary of state for the navy, later Admiral, Alfred von Tirpitz (1849-1930). The navy was the area, one could say, that was closest to the Kaiser's heart.

Sammlungspolitik

The policy of successive governments in the years between 1897 and 1914 was not to deny the profound changes in German society but to try, by a mixture of manipulation and repression, to transform the masses into active supporters of the status quo. Miquel gave his name to what became a contemporary slogan, *Sammlungspolitik* (colloquially translated as "a policy of togetherness"). It aimed to conciliate the conservatives by tariff concessions and by authoritarian domestic policies, while the bourgeois parties were to be won over by imperialist policies overseas and domestic peace. Bismarck's provocative division of Germans into *reichsfreundliche* or *staatserhaltende* elements (those friendly to, or supportive of, the state) and *reichsfeindliche* (its opponents) was no longer the coinage of contemporary political life under his successors. But old habits die hard, and in crisis times, the emperor's intemperate language and deep-seated prejudices contributed again and again to the polarization of society. The military and some of Wilhelm's advisers were well aware of the plans for a coup d'état as an eventual option against radical or allegedly radical forces in German society. Sometimes they showed their hand or their minds too openly, and even the seventy-five-year-old Fontane was one of those who in 1894 boldly signed a protest against the proposed suspension of the constitution. In fact, most such initiatives from the Kaiser and his entourage proved abortive. However, in general *Sammlungspolitik* struck a chord, at least in the minds of property-owning classes. They believed, as they had not always done under Bismarck, that the government's intention was to adhere to the constitution. They noted with satisfaction that all around them were signs of the numerous

---

[3] An instance of Fontane's perceptiveness as a political chronicler and critic of Wilhelmine Germany is the way he weaves into the subtext of his novel *Cécile* (1887) a (critical) commentary on Miquel's career.

tangible benefits, in terms of schooling, transport, public health, and culture, of being a German on the eve of the new century.

The fact that wage laborers were organized by the Social Democratic party and the trade unions, and that the *Volksverein für das katholische Deutschland* came increasingly to be regarded as the spokesman of German Catholics since its foundation in 1890, made the establishment see these two very substantial minority groups as beyond the reach of, or at least less accessible than, others to organized consensus policies. Attitudes on the part of the authorities to political Catholicism were modified by the 1890s, not least because of the Catholic Center party's support for conservative politics. However, the engrained anti-Catholic prejudice of the emperor, occasionally strident in expression, and the equally fervently held but more muted prejudice of his consort, Empress Auguste Viktoria (1858–1921), affected both the public position and the self-confidence of some 40 percent of Germans. Prejudice was made evident in active if covert discrimination against Catholics. Against Jews and those of left liberal or Socialist views it was generally more blatant. The new activist consensus politics of the later Wilhelmine era was directed therefore toward winning support from the so-called *mittelständisch* groups of Protestant background, notably middle-ranking and lower officials, white-collar workers, craftsmen, small businessmen and traders, and farmers. These people tended to combine a pride in Germany's achievements with complex and deep-seated fears for their own position and status in society, and for the future of their own particular livelihood, which found expression in a collective consciousness of being under threat. But one would not want to overlook the growing readiness of many Catholic small businessmen and farmers, from the late 1890s onward, to associate themselves with certain aspects of this mindset, especially as directed against "Jewish" capital.[4]

The Navy

An apt illustration of the character of domestic politics in Germany during the years 1890 to 1914 was the Navy League, founded by Admiral Tirpitz in 1897, the year of his appointment as secretary of state for the Navy. The issue of the navy is perhaps the supreme example of the interaction of domestic politics on Germany's relations with her neighbors. Tirpitz, bewitched by his own eloquence and the success of his organization, pursued the specious "risk

---

[4] It is revealing to trace the evolution of changing Catholic attitudes to the institutions of the Second Empire, especially from the late 1890s up to the 1914–8 war through the pages of the highly successful magazine for servants, *Notburga*, published between 1878 and 1939 at Donauwörth in Bavaria and sold through Catholic bookshops and parishes throughout Germany and abroad and increasingly subscribed to by middle-class Catholics.

theory" of equipping Germany with a massive battle fleet, in order to make war the less likely for the simple reason that it was too dangerous. Kaiser Wilhelm gave backing to what was to him the prestigious symbol of his empire. The German ruling elite was at least as concerned with its palliative influence on the internal situation, as with the significance of the naval program for the country's security and expansion. "Without sea power," wrote Tirpitz in his very revealing memoirs, "Germany's influence in the world will be like that of a mollusk without a shell."

Table 4: Strength of the German Navy 1880–1910 in terms of manpower

Year	Total strength
1880	11,116
1881	11,352
1887	15,244
1891	17,083
1894	20,498
1900	28,326
1905	40,862
1910	57,374

To adapt a quotation from another context, Tirpitz "played like a virtuoso on the well-tempered pianoforte of middle-class German ambitions." Part of his popularity among the bourgeoisie derived from the fact that, unlike the army, the highest naval officer ranks were open to middle-class aspirants. How well Tirpitz articulated contemporary neuroses when he spoke on public occasions of *unser geschichtliches Zuspätkommen* (the historic fact that we became a nation too late) while stressing the unique capacity of a great navy to set this "unfair" situation to rights. In a letter to a former head of the Prussian Admiralty, Albrecht von Stosch (1816–96), he wrote evocatively: "In my view Germany will sink rapidly in the next century from her great power status, unless our naval interests are pursued systematically and energetically, without further delay." Such a policy would, he added, provide valuable "immunization against both the educated and the uneducated Social Democrats." The alternative to a fleet program and an aggressive imperial policy, he averred, was simply a return to earlier policies of emigration to the United States and overseas, "leaving the world to the Anglo-Saxons and the sons of Jehova." The sentiments and resentments which Tirpitz evoked were characteristic features of the climate of the late 1890s—xenophobia, especially against the British, anti-Semitism, anti-Socialism, fear of modernization, illusions of grandeur, antagonism to the different kinds and forms of emancipation, or aspiration to emancipation which were also characteristic of the age.[5]

Tirpitz encountered initial opposition among the ruling oligarchy and particularly from the Reichstag to his ideas, but by the early 1900s the naval program was well underway. However, developments on the international front gave a lie to his and to the Kaiser's confident assertions about Germany's growing influence in the world. To be sure, after 1896, her economy began to boom; production and sales figures rose rapidly. Her population was increasing all the time, from 49.5 million in 1890 to 60 million in 1910. On the eve of the war, Germany was a very young country. But the very success of her industrial production made the problem of markets and supplies more acute, especially to a generation whose scientific thought was dominated by biological metaphor, and which was deeply persuaded by the Social Darwinistic arguments that the supply of both raw materials and outlets to market products was finite. As the process of global industrialization brought ever more competition to the scene, Germany, they argued, would fail to win the race against the established industrial giant, Great Britain, and her young partner, the United States of America, unless her economy were backed by a powerful naval force.

International relations

On the international front, Germany's policy from the 1880s onward had been characterized by a persistent restlessness. Bismarck had been constantly aware of Germany's exposed geographical position in Europe and attempted to offset it by his multiple alliance system. This was based on the Dual Alliance of 1879 with Austria, his recent foe, the (secret) League of the Three Emperors (German, Austrian, and Russian) of 1881, the (secret) Triple Alliance of Germany, Austria, and Italy (1882), and on the controversial Re-Insurance Treaty of 1887 with Russia. His broad strategy was to make it difficult for the major powers to form coalitions hostile to Germany, who would therefore become the indispensable arbiter of continental European affairs. But Bismarck, and even more so his successors at the helm of German government after 1890, placed too much trust in power and too little emphasis on the need to foster goodwill in international relations. He was wedded to a policy of containing Russia, though he in no way shared the anti-Russian sentiments of his younger contemporaries. He was aware of Russia's structural weaknesses and of the dangers, to her as well as to her neighbors, of Pan-Slav imperialism. Bismarck's

---

[5] Significantly, Fontane's visionary Pastor Lorenzen in *Der Stechlin*, expresses vigorous anti-British sentiments.

support of colonial politics in the mid-1880s was prompted, among other things, by his desire to reduce German investment and trade with Russia and divert it to other parts of the world.

His successors did not renew the Re-Insurance Treaty, which lapsed in 1890, partly because a secret protocol of the Treaty actually ran counter to Germany's obligations to Austria under the Dual Alliance. But relations with Russia had sharply worsened even before Bismarck's fall, and by 1893 Russia and France, were for all practical purposes in alliance with each other. Germany had for some years been pursuing a policy of trade agreements with politically weak states, such as Serbia and Rumania, whom she believed she could dominate. The notion of *Mitteleuropa*, a central European trade area, providing both a market for Germany's industrial goods and a source of raw materials, began to exercise a brief fascination for Germans in the 1890s. Initially, representatives of the export industry, and liberals more generally, hoped thereby to provide a counterweight to the reactionary agrarian party at home and a safer colonial policy than the overseas challenge to the established colonial powers of Great Britain and France might offer. However the concerted power of the agrarians and their allies in heavy industry (the so-called "Iron and Corn League") proved stronger, and *Mitteleuropa* did not materialize. Instead the new higher tariffs on Russian grain, a sop to the East Elbian landowners imposed in 1902, antagonized Russia still further. By this date, however, increasing numbers of middle-class Germans had in fact transferred their interest to the alternative imperial dream, which the fleet was to help realize.

Both Bismarck and his successors, as has been said, placed too little reliance on forging international relations based on mutual trust. Bismarck, to be sure, had confidently asserted that he observed much greater courtesy in international than in domestic political relations, but that his courtesy was based on nothing more than what he styled healthy self-interest. German chancellors and Prussia's foreign ministers after Bismarck were far less skilled in the art of diplomacy than he. They were influenced by his devious practices and the egoistic principles on which his policies were based. What is often referred to as the Byzantinism of Wilhelm II's court, which in time affected those who lived and worked in its ambience, prevented German leaders from taking a fresh approach to their country's international situation. Few had contacts with cultures other than their own; not many could speak foreign languages.

How often in fact had Bismarck been abroad since his ambassadorial days in the 1850s and early 1860s? How many of Germany's policymakers, such as Johann (von) Miquel or the *eminence grise* of the foreign office, Friedrich von Holstein (1837–1909), or indeed the chancellors Hohenlohe, von Bülow, or

Bethmann-Hollweg, had genuine links with other countries based on bonds of friendship? True, Hohenlohe had a Russian wife and Bülow was married to an Italian, but in each case personal shortcomings prevented this fact from redressing the imbalance in their governments. Of course it is equally true that the British had little understanding for foreigners (and that many felt a smug contempt for them, based on ignorance). But the British in a sense could afford to think and behave in this way, in the security of their island kingdom and their possession of a vast empire. Germans were instinctively aware of the potential weakness of their geopolitical situation but lacked the confidence and patience to pursue the kind of informal colonialism in which they could have done so well. Informal penetration by German banking and industrial investment overseas might have provided a relief to domestic tensions as well as satisfying what were felt to be Germany's vital economic and psychologic needs.

Domestic implications of foreign policy

The special and urgent role reserved for a demonstrably successful foreign policy to act as a palliative on the domestic front made the emperor and his cabinets prefer the short-term gain to the less spectacular long-term understanding. Bülow, then secretary of state for foreign affairs, speaking as his master's voice, declared roundly in 1897 that "only a successful foreign policy can succor, conciliate, soothe and reconcile." Yet little progress was made in terms of territorial expansion for Germany or her greater international security. The determination of the emperor to have Germany set the international agenda, to have other nations dependent on her goodwill, injected an unsettling element into interstate relations and, more seriously, progressively isolated Germany in Europe. Bismarck's devious Russian policy in the last years of his administration was not without responsibility for the Russian-French rapprochement, which had for decades seemed so unlikely, given the fundamentally different nature of their regimes, authoritarian Christian Tsardom and secular Republic. By 1904 another permanent factor in Bismarck's political arithmetic had gone wrong. England and France settled their colonial differences and came together in the so-called *Entente Cordiale*. Of course the Entente was not in itself a guarantee of friendship between the powers involved, except as continued evidence to both sides that they in fact had common interests. Germany's behavior, personified in the Kaiser's personal aggressiveness and diplomatic ineptness, provided such evidence in a negative way. Germany's isolation was exemplified at the conference at Algeciras in 1906, when she tried and failed to drive France and Britain apart. In 1907 Russia's joining what was now known as the Triple Entente demonstrated the failure of Reich diplomacy.

Das alte Märchen

Der Hase und der Swinegel wollten miteinander um die Wette laufen,

und da legte der Hase los.

Aber wie er nach Paris kam, war der Swinegel schon da,

und da lief der Hase, was er nur konnte.

Aber wie er nach Rom kam, da war der Swinegel schon da,

und da lief der Hase furchtbar.

Aber wie er nach Petersburg kam, da war der Swinegel schon da.

Und da saß der Hase erschöpft auf dem Feld und war glanzend isoliert.

Skit on Wilhelm II's love of travel and his ineffective efforts to outdo his uncle (Edward VII) in popularity among the European nations. Drawings by O. Gulbransson from *Simplicissimus*.

However, the German authorities and their mythmakers chose instead to give credence to the thesis that Germany was a victim, not of her own ineptness, but of an international conspiracy, of a planned encirclement to rob her of her rightful place.

Over the next crucial years, the notion of a preventive war as the solution to Germany's problems, real and imagined, began to gain ground in the national imagination as well as the councils of policymakers. As early as 1907, the year of the Triple Entente, the German generals took the decision that Belgian neutrality would have to be violated in order to win the quick victory which Germany would need to concentrate her forces against Russia. Since Britain was a guarantor of Belgian neutrality according to the 1839 Treaty, the risk of war with Britain was envisaged at this time, if perhaps not with due seriousness. Such an option was, however, implicit in attitudes articulated at the highest level since the 1890s. Friedrich von Holstein, a man with some thirty-six years of service in the department of foreign affairs, had observed on 30 April 1897 to a later state secretary for foreign affairs, Alfred von Kiderlen-Wächter (1852–1912), that "success can only be expected as the result of a European war," or by "the acquisition of territory outside Europe." He was quite aware that such options were a gamble, describing them somewhat portentously as "a world historical game of chance." German historians have tended in the past to discuss the "will to war" in the years leading up to 1914 and the enthusiastic response to the decision in 1914 as something particularly and perniciously German. This was perhaps a natural response to the debate on the revelations in the 1960s by the Hamburg historian, Fritz Fischer, who showed the degree to which the German nation as well as its rulers knew what they were doing, rather than stumbling into war, as it were by default. For many years Fischer was the object of the bitter opprobrium of his colleagues and was even branded as a kind of intellectual traitor to the good name of Germany, but his essential thesis, refined and developed by international historians, was not gainsaid. As cultural historians have shown, the deep pessimism characteristic of Germany's ruling classes in the years immediately preceding 1914, was a powerful influence, as was the specter of revolution at home, exacerbated, it seemed, by the sharp downswing in the economy in 1913.

The notion of a nation at arms had undoubtedly visionary appeal as a counterfoil to domestic divisions. As one contemporary writer put it fulsomely, the declaration of war was "a great and unforgettable moment, the ringing opening chord of an immortal song of sacrifice, loyalty, and heroism." It should not be forgotten that most other European countries, like Germany, had not known a European war for two generations. In the age of imperialism, war appeared to offer excitement, especially to the young, and, in marked contrast to the outbreak of war in 1939, the call to battle in 1914 was greeted with enthusiasm in Britain as it was in Germany.

However, a consideration of the course of domestic politics in Germany during the regime of Wilhelm II suggests that, while the July crisis of 1914 and the resultant declaration of war brought a sense of release to many governments and nations in Europe, in Germany there was a different dimension to the situation. Here, war had the nature of a deliberate gamble, embarked on with the specious reasoning that it would ward off even greater evils. What these evils were remained nebulous.

Internal problems of the empire

Germany's most pressing problem was that its political structures were being preserved, fossilized one might even say, at a time when the enormous industrial and democratic changes taking place demanded a highly flexible system. Bismarck's state had many merits but, politically speaking, it was not a modern state. It had originated as a kind of imperial federation of twenty-five kingdoms, principalities, and cities, although dominated by the largest state, Prussia. In order to guarantee the traditional privileges of the princes and the preponderance of Prussia within the empire, Bismarck had set important limits to the evolution of a central government. This created complex problems for the Reich's chancellors after Bismarck, particularly in fiscal matters. The imperial budget was set at a certain sum under the constitution, and revenue from whatever source that exceeded this, was paid back to the constituent states of the empire on the basis of their share of the total population. The strains on the budget became evident once the state began to take over responsibility for more and more areas of daily life, including also the social welfare of its citizens. A whole host of vested interests vigorously opposed any modification of the financing of the Reich, and deficit budgeting was therefore chronic in the prewar period. At a time of great social dislocation alongside growing national wealth, the agrarians, the military, the captains of industry, and the senior civil servants adhered to the received wisdom that revenue needs should be funded from indirect, not from direct, taxation. However, every increase in indirect taxation almost invariably led to a rise in the socialist vote, and, to a lesser extent, to support for the left liberals, who constantly exposed the injustice of the system. The fleet, for example, was financed in its early years by indirect taxation, which fell heaviest on the less well-off. At the same time both the imperial and the Prussian governments were paying substantial sums by way of subsidies to the East Elbian landowners in the form of tariffs, export premiums, cheap transport for their goods, and subsidies on industries based in the estates, such as sugar or distilling. By the end of the first decade of the twentieth century, it was clear that the fleet could not continue to be financed by dearer bread for the urban poor, while the agrarians used their considerable political clout to oppose reform. Mass redundancies in the ship-building industry suddenly seemed imminent, with all their expected social and political consequences. In 1911 the cost of living rose sharply, after a period of relative price stability through a prolonged period of rising real wages.

The 1912 elections exacerbated the anxiety of government and the establishment. In a political culture, such as that of the empire, in which voter turnout to elections had been so high, it caused a major shock to the system that now the Social Democratic party attracted nearly one-third of all the votes cast and became the largest political party in the Reichstag. There seemed no reason to suppose that their vote would not increase progressively. True, the effectiveness of forceful opposition to the imperial government in the Reichstag was limited, as long as the three-class franchise in Prussia and in Saxony excluded the vast majority of the population in these states from influence over their internal affairs. Hopes of a reformed franchise diminished rather than increased in the prewar years, simply because the power of conservative interests rested in their domination of the *Landtage* or state parliaments, and in their power to influence senior official appointments. To surrender or modify these privileges would effectively destroy their power base.

German political parties in Wilhelm II's reign proved to be deeply affected by the prevailing national ideology, even where, as in the case of the Socialists and the Polish Nationalists, they might define themselves as its critics and opponents. The fact that Germany's parties had an ideological rather than a tactical base, and that they did not produce the kind of catch-all party which made British Toryism such a buoyant political phenomenon, made it difficult for leaders and voters to accommodate policies to a such rapidly changing social and economic situation. Yet in terms of European history between 1871 and 1914, indeed until 1928, the German party political system proved remarkably stable. It has been argued by Rainer Lepsius ("Parteisystem und Sozialstruktur. Zum Problem der Demokratisierung der Deutschen Gesellschaft" in Gerhard Albert Ritter (ed.) *Die Deutschen Parteien vor 1918* (1973, 56–80) that the system articulated structural conflicts which preexisted the Empire, and that these became ritualized in politically mobilized ideological groups. Yet there is evidence of considerable voter movement between the parties in the two decades preceding the 1914 war, according to Jonathan Sperber's *The Kaiser's Voters* (1997, 282ff). Germans were, in fact, anything but quiescent subjects of

His Imperial Majesty, Kaiser Wilhelm II, but they were accessible to propaganda. Economic and social issues dominated voters' minds in the 1890s and early 1900s; after 1910 it was questions of national prestige, expressed often in chauvinistic forms. Of course it should not be forgotten that these had their equivalent in most other European countries, not least in Britain.

Special interest groups

A characteristic development under the Empire were the so-called special interest groups, which increased significantly in numbers and influence between 1893 and 1914. The existence, activities, numbers, and percentage of the population involved in these organizations, directly in the case of men, and usually, indirectly, in the case of women, is striking. Their function and manner of operation varied considerably and modified or constrained the development of the more regular channels of communication between the government and the governed. Thus the Free Trade Unions, or *Freie Gewerkschaften*, came toward the end of the century to be regarded as the spokesmen of the workers, yet the workers party remained effectively excluded, up to the last weeks of the Second Empire, from participation in government. Large and powerful pressure groups, such as the Navy League or *Flottenverein* or the *Hansabund* (the Hanse League) agitated successfully in favor of imperialist policies without being held in any way responsible for the consequences. Moreover, the two most powerful sectional interests, heavy industry and the agrarian party, managed to win a powerful influence on legislation and administrative practice through the activities of their pressure groups, the elitist *Central-Verband deutscher Industrieller* (CDI), the industrialists, and the Agrarian League of 1893 which originated in the so-called Popular League for Economic and Tax Reform, also of 1876; between the 1890s and 1911, its membership grew from 200,000 to 328,000. The impact of these organizations grew in pre-1914 Germany, their weight being reflected in the variety and astonishing numbers of those who joined them. The stereotype of German love of association, which is still vigorous today, no doubt traces its origin back to the variety of nineteenth-century practices, and the network of political, socioeconomic, and citizen associations which, quite literally, spanned the German nation at the turn of the century. Space precludes inquiry into the abundance of Germany's national, regional, and local associations, each with its meetings as important events in the individual's or group's social calendar, with the outings and gala nights, not least of whose attractions were their role in assisting one's sons and daughters to "meet their own kind." In a socio-political context, the varied special interest groups have much to tell us about the functioning of the state in the age of mass democracy. Some, such as the CDI, had few members. Their weight, like those of their modern equivalents, derived from the standing, connections, and wealth of their members. The Free Trade Unions, by contrast, rose from 77,000 members in 1877 to over one million on the eve of the war, attracting by the latter date growing numbers of Catholic workers who for decades had been staunch supporters of Catholic or Christian trade unions.

Some groups pursued an ideological and religious agenda, others were concerned with economic interests, yet other groups with social bonding. The *Volksverein für das katholische Deutschland* represented all of these. It had 500,000 members in 1906 and 800,000 in 1914, over half of these in the Rhineland and Westphalia alone. (It should be remembered that a prime impulse to the growth of political Catholicism was the resistance of Rhenish Catholics in the 1830s to what they saw as discrimination by their new, post-1815 Protestant Prussian masters.) The *Volksverein* became the largest organization in Germany after the Social Democratic party, and, like the latter, had a variety of associated organizations, such as the Catholic Workers Association, the Christian Peasants League, and, in south Germany, Catholic servant-girls' organizations, an interesting feature of which is the role played by the servants themselves in the organization, unlike that of their male counterparts. One ideologically driven and influential group which was indeed conservative but not representative of the propertied classes was the Hamburg-based *Deutsche Handlungsgehilfenverband* or German National League of Commercial Employees. Through its press organs, it exercised a powerful influence on the awakening political awareness of mainly lower middle class groups; membership was specifically confined to "Germans not of the Israelite faith"—which meant that they defined themselves as the opponents (or, in their language, victims) of modern financial capital and the new retail department stores.

The conservative special interest groups did not see themselves as agents of the government. Rather they treated the state authorities as if they were a fortress to be attacked, conquered, and cleansed of hostile elements. Nor were some averse to criticizing or even defaming government ministers or secretaries of state in public, when policies did not accord with their own sectional interests. The Agrarian League helped to bring about the fall of three successive chancellors and their ministries, that of Caprivi in 1894, Hohenlohe in 1900, and Bülow in 1909, and also the resignation of Miquel. The age of mass democracy created a new style of vilificatory rhetoric, on the platform and in the media. It was almost inevitable that such groups identified their own vested interests with the national good, coining or adapting emotional slogans which anticipated Nazi practices. Typical examples were "protection of national labor" (which in practice meant discrimination against foreign workers, although landowners in the eastern provinces did not hesitate to bring in cheap casual labor from Poland to harvest their grain); or "securing the staple diet of the nation"—in effect protective tariffs and subsidies for grain producers, thus greatly increasing the cost of the nation's food; or "guaranteeing Germany's defense," or rather special protection for German heavy industry (at a cost to the rest of the manufacturing and to the consumer industries). The more powerful special interest groups financed candidates for parliament, and succeeded in securing the election of 118 such candidates to the 1898 Reichstag (out of a total of 397). In the 1912 Reichstag election the CDI paid the election expenses of some 120 deputies.

The trade unions

The relationship between the trade unions and their parties was different again. The Christian Trade Unions were based mainly in the Rhineland and Westphalia, and although their members, like the members of the Free Trade Unions in the Socialist party, voted solidly for their own party, they were by no means uncritical of their leadership. The Liberal or Hirsch-Duncker Unions had affiliations with the left liberals, but represented only a fraction of the union movement. Up to 1890, the Socialist trade unionists had relatively little political influence on the party. The massive increase in union membership from the mid-1890s onward gave weight to their councils in organized working-class circles, so much so that a growing number of labor leaders, at least in Prussia, began to find their own party doctrinaire and inclined in their view to be divorced from political and economic realities. In the less ideologically charged atmosphere of southern Germany, partly thanks to the popular touch of the long-time Social Democratic leader, Georg von Vollmar (1850–1922), this was not the case.

Table 5: The German trade unions

Year	Free Trade Unions	Percent of total	Christian T. U.	Percent of total	Hirsch-Duncker*	Percent of total
1869	47, 192	—	30,000	—	—	—
1889	174, 608	—	62,688	—	—	—
1890	294, 551	—	62,643	—	—	—
1894	245, 723	—	67,078	—	—	—
1899	580, 473	80.2	56,391	7.8	86,777	12.0
1900	680, 427	80.2	76,744	9.0	91,661	10.8
1909	1,832,667	82.1	280,061	12.6	108,028	4.9
1913	2,548,763	85.0	341,735	11.4	106,618	3.4

*founded 1894

The origins of the German trade union go back to the 1860s, predating the employers' organizations by a decade, and the agrarian interest group by more than a generation. Originally, many early factory workers came from a skilled background, which helps to account for their capacity to organize. However, most trade unions inevitably fell victim to the Anti-Socialist legislation in the period 1878–1890. They reemerged thereafter as a centralized, yet flexible and even pragmatic organization under the leadership of Carl Legien (1861–1920), earning the 1890s the name of the decade of the unions. Over the next decade and a half, two-thirds of all organized workers were brought into a single Socialist movement. Steady improvements, albeit from a low baseline, in terms of employment and earnings between 1890 and 1913 gave union leaders increasing authority in the working-class movement, even vis à vis the Social Democratic party itself. A sense of collective destiny had drawn workers together in the years of persecution and aggressive discrimination by institutions of state, and it remained an authentic experience after 1890. It was kept alive by the tacit assumption of many upper- and middle-class Germans that the working man was a potential enemy of the state. This attitude was especially associated with drill sergeants, convinced that the working-class conscripts coming to do their military service had to have Socialist sympathies drilled out of them by the army, the "school of the nation." Strikes and lockouts, such as the Ruhr miners' strike of 1889, which involved some 90,000 workers and their families and constituted the largest trade union action of the century in Germany, or the 1890 lockout of 3,000 workers in an attempt to break the union, became part of the common memory of the working man.

Although the failure of strike action in several cases in the early 1890s caused many members to leave, the leaders learned from the experience to use the strike weapon more sparingly but with greater strategic impact. The energy and militancy of the employers' organizations in the 1890s stimulated the formation of a more sophisticated organization. The experiences of the early 1890s influenced union thinking in the direction of organization by industry rather than by trade, although some branches and concerns remained resistant to the idea. Older trades, such as the construction trade, proved volatile in their support for unionization, the numbers swelling in good and declining in bad years. Some unions, such as that of the tobacco workers, the second oldest and, at the time of the Anti-Socialist legislation the largest of them all, were thoroughly militant. Unlike in the great foundries, their workplace had little or no background noise and workers could discuss and instruct each other as they worked. Other employees, such as the textile workers, were difficult to organize; they had large numbers of women, and often a high turnover of workers.

Others again, such as the metalworkers, proved adaptable and very efficient at bringing together the skilled and the unskilled. By the eve of the war, the metalworkers possessed an organization of considerable power and militancy and were critical of party leadership and the moderate stance of the rest of the union movement.

In the late 1870s the printers, tobacco workers, and other skilled workers with strong craft tradition in medium and small concerns had been the center of the movement. By 1913, 60 percent of the entire trade union movement were recruited from the metal, wood, transport, construction, factory, and textile workers. The skilled workers, generally younger men, were dominant in the leadership. Increasing mechanization, as well as the attitudes of state and society, tended to make the sense of a common group-consciousness of greater importance than in the older skilled traditions. The geographical strength of the trade union movement in late nineteenth-century Germany depended naturally on the degree of industrialization of the region, its principal centers being Hamburg and Bremen, Hanover, and the Thuringian states. Surprisingly, it was less strong in Saxony, the oldest industrial landscape in Germany (and the birthplace of Socialism), both on account of the severity of the authorities there toward organized labor and because domestic manufacture was still the predominant form of enterprise. The Christian Trade Unions had their base in the Rhine and Ruhr valleys; in the years 1900–14, their numbers, together with those of the Liberal unions, accounted for some 10–12 percent of the whole.

In the prewar years the pragmatic influence of trade union leaders was an important influence in modifying relations between the urban working classes and the state, especially outside Prussia and Saxony. Tangible benefits came in the form of rising real wages, particularly in the first decade of the new century; in less militant areas of Germany; for example, in Württemberg, the eight- or nine-hour working day was conceded. However, the attitude of employers is well illustrated by the way Robert Bosch (1861–1942), founder of the electrical firm which bears his name, was bitterly criticized by his fellow industrialists for his "overly liberal" attitude to labor relations. Dubbed "the red Bosch," he was one of the first to introduce the eight-hour day to his Stuttgart factory. His many concessions, based as much on his concern for efficiency as on altruism, spared his rapidly expanding firm the kind of labor disputes common elsewhere in prewar Germany.

The social role played by the unions should not be forgotten. Carl Legien played a key role in fostering group consciousness, which defamatory propaganda of many state institutions made the more necessary. Trade union clubs were meeting places, and they also provided social occasions which included wives

Adolph von Menzel's famous painting, *The Iron Foundry* (1875).

and families, and offered educational opportunities. They offered the kind of service parallel to what the Social Democratic party provided, as in a previous generation the churches had done. Though the primary function of the trade union movement was that of a special interest or pressure group, for its members it was far more than that.

Other political interest groups

A late arrival, as it were, among the special interest groups in the Second Empire was the *Hansabund*, founded in 1909. It was formed and supported by medium and small entrepreneurs, with strong representation from the north German Hanse towns (such as Hamburg, Bremen, and Lübeck). It had political as well as economic dimension in that its leaders aimed to break what they saw as Prussian conservatives' stranglehold on political power. It was one of a number of initiatives in the five years preceding the outbreak of war by politicians and industrialists, and to a lesser extent by journalists, church leaders (as in the Peace Movement), and academics to bring about a new orientation on the domestic front. Economic and fiscal issues, such as the tariff question or tax reform, began to lose primacy in public debates and attention began to focus on issues such as the limited franchise of Prussia and Saxony, which provided conservatives with their power base. The *Hansabund* was less successful than its promoters hoped, but it was symptomatic of a general trend in this era for pressure groups to provide a kind of parallel political system to the parliamentary parties.

The latter years of the prewar German Empire also saw the growth of numerous and increasingly vocal organizations agitating in favor of "national solidarity." Their appeal can be judged by their numerical success. Thus the Navy League, founded with the assistance of the industrialist Krupp in 1898, had a million members and associates by 1913, a Navy League in Britain at that time had 15,000. The German Social Democratic party now had 385,000 paid-up members. Admiral Tirpitz proved to be a genius in the field of public relations. How well he understood his compatriots' fondness for social occasions with a higher purpose! Tirpitz organized lectures, social evenings, visits on board ship for regional associations from all over Germany, paying particular attention to the provinces. The element of popular nationalism in the Navy League and in the notorious Pan-German League (*Alldeutscher Verband*), founded in 1891, had marked success. It was absent from the so-called HKT elitist association, founded in 1894 with Bismarck's expressed blessing by three millionaires, by the names of Hansenau, Kennmann, and Tiedemann. Their aim was nothing less than the Germanization of the Prussian Polish provinces, even where, as in East and West Prussia, Silesia, and Posen (Poznan), many districts had a Polish majority. It throws an interesting light on official attitudes to learn that the Prussian minister of the interior actually encouraged the local government administrator, the *Landrat* (who was almost invariably, like Innstetten in Fontane's *Effi Briest*, a nobleman), to join the HKT. If the membership of the HKT suggested that the government was prepared to sponsor active discrimination against its own Polish (and Russian) subjects, another organization under the name of Reich Organization against Social Democracy, found favor with the highest powers in the land. Its patrons among the ruling classes were convinced of the patriotic and even altruistic character of their agitation. Although their activities were suspended in keeping with the national peace or reconciliation, known as the *Burgfrieden*, following the outbreak of war, it says much about official attitudes that someone as near to the person of Kaiser Wilhelm II as his own aide-de-camp, one Caprivi (no relation of the chancellor), could declare in 1914 that the death of a Social Democrat volunteer in battle was really a propaganda trick to force concessions out of the government to the Social Democratic party.

Germany on the eve of the First World War

It has been said of late nineteenth-century Germany that every second male belonged to some kind of organization. The popularity of associations such as the Colonial League (1882), the Defense League or *Wehrverein* (1897), and the nationwide network of war veterans' associations, still going strong forty years after the Franco-Prussian war of 1870–1, showed the appeal of protomilitary forms of socializing. They also served to divert political awareness from more fundamental problems of their own state. The most significant of these were the imbalance between the power of the preindustrial or neofeudal leadership of the German Empire, and the modern industrialized economy and its increasingly urban forms of living. Friedrich Naumann, the liberal political and social reformer, who served in part as model for Pastor Lorenzen in Fontane's novel *Der Stechlin*, likened Germany at the beginning of the twentieth century to a great and ever-expanding factory, built in an old barn, its steel girders gradually breaking through the mud-and-wattle walls. The tensions between different social and economic interests, the widespread fear among middle and lower middle circles of the organized labor movement, despite the latter's general quiescence in the last years of the Empire, were part of this discontent, as was the resentment felt in many regions at the predominance of Prussia and Prussian ways in the Reich. If political and to some extent religious reasons dominated the hostility felt by the less industrialized, socially and politically more cohesive southern part of Germany toward the north, more

Bismarck and Bebel from *Simplicissimus*.
'At last, Bebel, we've got to know each other properly!'
(Reference to the 'Burgfrieden' between the authorities and the labor movement on the declaration of war in 1914.)

fundamental differences in economic and social structure and in income divided east and west. The notion of the unity of the nation as its greatest asset was something that most Germans accepted and believed in. But the gap between myth and reality in this, as in many other respects, was in itself a prime source of tension in prewar Germany.

Alles ist sehr alt geworden, everything seems to have grown so old, wrote an acute observer of the German establishment, the secretary to the chancellor, Bethmann-Hollweg, Kurt von Riezler, then aged thirty-four, on the eve of the outbreak of the First World War. Whether one supports or rejects the emotional thesis of Germany's war guilt in 1914, there seems little doubt that the decision to go to war in August was taken with fatalism and in many quarters with manifest relief, as a kind of "last option" for Germany. Even the normally provocative *Simplicissimus* marked the announcement of a social peace pact or *Burgfrieden* between the authorities and the labor movement on the declaration of war in 1914 in utopian terms. It was accompanied by a dubiously sentimental cartoon, depicting the "meeting of minds" in heaven between the old adversaries, Otto von Bismarck and August Bebel.

Chapter 12
Developments in the German Economy 1850–1914

The decision to go to war in 1914 was taken by the German authorities against the background of an unprecedented economic boom which had lasted for almost a generation, from the mid-1890s to 1913. This boom or "second industrial revolution" had transformed Germany into a wealthy country and underlined the changes that had taken place in the European balance of power over the last half century and within the Empire itself.

Demography and migration

The most obvious change concerned Germany's population. To a people schooled in the late nineteenth-century age of imperialism to think in comparative, and indeed competitive, biological terms, it was a source of satisfaction that Germany's population, not much more than half of that of France in 1800, and roughly equal in 1870, should by 1900 be 50 percent greater and still rising. At the beginning of the century, the population of Germany (which until 1866 still included Austria), was something over 23,000,000. By 1871 Germany without Austria was nearly 41,000,000, and by 1914 a little short of 68,000,000. Life expectancy rose between 1871 and the early 1900s from an average of thirty-six for men and thirty-eight for women, to forty-five and forty-eight, respectively. Moreover, the age cohort on which the German armed forces could draw to fight the war was uniquely large. In 1914, 80 percent of Germany's population was under the age of forty-five. Furthermore, where there are a lot of young people about, as in Germany at the beginning of the twentieth century, society cannot but be dynamic. The contrast with half a century earlier was something of which Germans could certainly be proud, since for so long she, like Ireland, had been forced to send so many of her sons and daughters elsewhere to seek a new and better life.

The peak years for emigration in the middle of the century had been 1847, when the worst effects of the Hungry Forties were felt, and the early 1850s, especially in the southwest, where emigration was actively encouraged by the authorities seeking to export their most pressing social problems. Graphic literary portrayals of emigrants bound for the New World are to be found for the early period in Heine's polemical essay, *Ludwig Börne* (1840), and for the immediate postrevolutionary period in Wilhelm Raabe's first and most successful novel of small-town German life, *Die Chronik der Sperlinggasse* (1856).

Berthold Auerbach's sentimental story, *Der Tolpatsch*, 1842, about the village idiot who makes good in Ohio, was widely read. Certainly the most favored target of emigrants was the United States. Germans settled in a variety of locations and, like so many immigrants to the New World, in a variety of different types of work. German Mennonites favored Pennsylvania, where they managed to retain their way of life and their native dialect, confusingly dubbed "Pennsylvanian Dutch." Missouri developed a vigorous German publishing industry which catered, among others, to the Catholic servant girls who liked to read their own magazine, the weekly *Notburga: Zeitschrift für Dienstboten*. But by then most Catholic publishing houses had an office in Chicago, New York, or Missouri, whether it was Herder from Freiburg, Pustet of Regensburg, or Manz of Regensburg and Vienna. German literary portrayal of the world to which the emigrants came was usually, though not always favorable. In his only novel set in a non-European country, Fontane's *Quitt* portrayed a midwestern Mennonite community offering Lehnert, driven by poverty and a burning sense of injustice, to commit homicide, the vision of a new order of justice and equality; the young man responds by voluntarily expiating his crime. In the last decades of the century very substantial numbers of Germans were still leaving their native country, notably between 1864–73, when a million left, and 1880–93, with almost a million emigrating in the first half of the 1880s alone. After 1893, emigration fell off sharply, not least because of the massive upturn in the economy at home.

At least as profound in its social, economic, and political consequences was internal migration which took place on a massive scale in the century's second half. The main movement was east-west, with the poorer rural eastern lands of Pomerania, Posen, East Prussia, and West Prussia losing almost their entire natural increase between 1870 and 1914 to the urban centers, to the factories of Berlin, Saxony, and the Rhineland, and the mines in the Ruhr and the Saarland. Women moved in large numbers, sometimes to the nearest town but often considerable distances in search of work in the domestic labor market. Fontane and Clara Viebig have given us typical examples of such women in the person of Roswitha in *Effi Briest* and the servant protagonist in *Das tägliche Leben* (1900). Effi's nursemaid Roswitha, we are told, came from the barren area of the Eichsfeld in Hanover; very many came from the poor lands of Mecklenburg and Silesia. Many women from the rural proletariat might become pregnant by a local man and migrate to the city in search of anonymity. Like 'lütt Agnes' (little Agnes) in *Der Stechlin*, the child might be sent home to be brought up by its grandmother. The alternative, keeping it in the city or sending it to a foundling's home, was grim, for the child even more than for the mother.

Statistics on infant mortality show a hugely disproportionate percentage among the illegitimate. Much migration was local, such as the miners whom Blackbourn describes in eloquent detail in his remarkable study, *Marpingen*. We also have graphic accounts of boys and girls as young as eight traveling on their own from the Alpine regions to the hiring markets in Swabia and Bavaria as late as 1900 to sell their services to the highest bidder. In the Ruhr mining towns, a large colony of Polish workers established themselves and their own culture over the second half of the century, retaining their own language and distinctive religious practices and even, in the late nineteenth century, exchanging their traditional support for the Catholic Center party for their own Polish Nationalist party. The broad mix of the population's origin in the textile town of Barmen in the later nineteenth century was vividly recorded in more than half a dozen different types of bread baked for and bought by the various immigrant groups.

The change in the regional distribution of Germany's population was a further striking feature of the century as a whole, but one that was immensely accelerated after 1870. The capital city of the Austrian monarchy, Vienna, and of the German Empire, Berlin, which were the largest cities at the beginning and the end of the century, recorded massive population increases, from about one quarter of a million in 1800 to two million in 1910 in Vienna, and from 170,000 to over two million in the early twentieth century in Berlin and its suburbs. Yet perhaps the changing face of Germany in the post-1870 years is most graphically recorded in the growth of smaller and medium-sized towns. In the sixty years between 1850 and 1910 the Rhenish city of Düsseldorf grew from 9,000 inhabitants to 229,000, while the population of Dortmund rose from 11,000 to 214,000. The number of towns with over 10,000 inhabitants rose from 271 in 1875 to some 576,000 in 1910. Nor was it simply a matter of the lure of the city, but of an immensely increased restlessness in society expressing itself in movement from one's place of birth to a series of different locations. In the year 1907, for example, 2,326,700 of those born in eastern Germany, that is, in the provinces of East and West Prussia, Pomerania, Silesia, and Posen, had moved to other regions, while the provinces gained a mere 358,000 by immigration. Over one million inhabitants of Berlin's province Brandenburg in 1907 had not been born there. Westphalia and the Rhineland had by that time succeeded in attracting nearly one and a half million residents, although half a million would move on elsewhere. The distribution of wealth varied considerably across Germany. Average wages for late nineteenth-century East Prussia and for Pomerania were approximately two-thirds and three-quarters, respectively, of the national average. The figure for the largely industrialized

Westphalia, 117.4 percent, gives some guidance as to the reasons for such mobility. Many more people moved in and out of towns than settled there permanently. Yet, as the educational historian and Berlin professor, Friedrich Paulsen (1846–1908), recalled in his memoirs, in mid-century rural Germany the majority of people, and more particularly women, had lived and died within a radius of two to three miles of where they had been born.

Looking at the different sectors of the economy from the vantage point of the early twentieth century, we find that nineteenth-century Germany had experienced at least three revolutions in its economy: in agriculture, industry, and, inseparable from the latter, communications.

Agriculture

The commercialization of German agriculture, or the so-called agrarian revolution, spans the middle decades of the century, from the mid-1820s to the mid-1870s. Up to the 1860s, the amount of land under cultivation had risen significantly, especially in the East. The real source of that change, which in scale and impact merits the term "revolutionary," was the new interaction between farming, technology, and communications. Mid- and late-nineteenth-century farmers produced increasingly for the market, rather than just for themselves or their immediate community. In the improved methods of grain and of root vegetable production, which, with bread, formed the staple diet of Germans, German university research and its application played a significant part. The same was true of stock breeding, which subsequently helped boost meat production and consumption. True, agriculture's boom years came to an abrupt halt in the 1870s as the cost of intercontinental rail and shipping fell and American and Russian grain began to undercut German markets. Later refrigeration added American meat to the list of food commodities which undercut German production prices. To other global factors, such as intensive, specialized cultivation of land in huge units in the New World, was added the problem of farm debt at home. Debt was greatest among the large estate owners. As such, it represented a major political as well as an economic problem, given the political clout of the Junker landowners, who were linked by birth and marriage with the political and military establishment. But debt was a major factor as well for smaller farmers in much of Germany and Austria. The experience of the Austrian socialist Karl Renner (1870–1950), later the first chancellor of Austria's first Republic (1918–38) and first president of its second (1945–), illustrates what this could mean to the individual farmer and his community. Renner describes graphically in his memoirs the change-over from modest prosperity to misery in the case of his own family, winegrowers in southern Moravia. His eldest brother, twenty years older than himself, had started his farming career during the boom years for agriculture in the 1860s. With the help of accessible credit and thanks to rising farm prices, his brother rapidly established himself as a man of substance. Karl, the youngest of eighteen children, was born in 1870. As a child and adolescent, he witnessed his parents' struggle against accumulated debt, until they finally lost their family farm to speculators. Karl joined his sister as a poor emigrant to Vienna, where he was soon introduced to the socialist movement.

In Germany, the East Elbian landowners were among the prime losers in the structural transformation of economy occasioned by the agrarian crisis of the 1870s. As the region lost its entire natural increase to the cities in an accelerated flight from the land after 1870, landowners began to have recourse to migrant labor from nearby Russian or Austrian Poland. At the same time the Junkers successfully lobbied governments for support, winning a fivefold increase in tariffs on imported food from the government between 1879 and 1887. However, the very success of their "begging bowl mentality" was itself a factor in preventing the modernization of East Elbian farming. Yet, although now dependent on grain imports (and therefore vulnerable to global factors in wartime, as became evident in 1916–8), overall Germany had moved in the thirty years between 1860 and 1890 from being a food importing to a food exporting nation. This was an extraordinary achievement, given the fact that this was also the age of her industrial revolution. By 1910, for example, Germany was producing one-third of the world's potatoes, 40 million tons a year. The production of pork and beef grew on a similar scale. The fact that Germans' meat consumption rose from under 20 kg per annum in the 1850s to over 43 kg in 1910 contributed in its own way to pride in their nation.

Farmers in the northwest and the southeast were less affected by the fall in land values and the structural problems of farming in the rest of the country, because medium to large family farms proved successful in niche production and marketing. But, in general, the second half of the century saw a systematic decline in the once-dominant agricultural sector relative to other sectors in the economy. In the early 1860s agriculture had produced just under 45 percent of the gross domestic product; fifty years later the figure was just under 23 percent. In 1882, some 42 percent of Germany's rising population earned their living from agriculture, a generation later, in 1907, the figure was 35 percent. The 1882 figures for industry and the service sectors are 36 percent and 9 percent, and in 1907 they were 40 percent and 13 percent, respectively. Yet Germany's agricultural sector, to which her peasant farmers in the south and west made a signal contribution, remained a very significant part of her economy well into the twentieth century. For a variety of reasons, some of which go back to the

German Romantic movement and its cultivation of nature, German farming and its rural classes on the eve of the new century found their image immensely enhanced in the minds and hearts of Germans, in literature as well as in the propaganda of political demagogues.

Manufacturing industry

The history of the German industrial revolution, or, as it is more usually referred to today, German industrialization, has often been rewritten, but there is general agreement on at least two aspects. The first is the extraordinarily rapid transformation of Germany between about the middle and the end of the century from a predominantly agrarian, premodern economy to a highly capitalized industrial economy with a significant agricultural sector and a small but dynamic tertiary sector. The second aspect is the regional and temporal diversity of that record of growth and transformation.

Speaking very broadly, we can recognize a different economic flavor in each of the five decades constituting the century's second half. While Nietzsche might lament the general depressiveness of the 1850s or *Nachmärz* among the politically reflective, this was the decade in which business began to set the political agenda. Stimulated by Californian gold and an increase in the money supply, the availability of cheaper credit and good harvests engendered confidence, which led in turn to investment in enterprises rather than, as traditionally, government securities. Joint stock companies attracted the savings of ordinary people, gave them a share in the profits of industry and a sense of a stake in the economy. Germans imported English technology, and their well-educated entrepreneurs applied and developed it. An eloquent example is the already-mentioned Werner Siemens. In 1847 he had cofounded the firm of Siemens and Halske to manufacture telegraph systems. Within a few years, he was directing cable-laying in Russia, southeast Europe, and across the Atlantic. By the early twentieth century, Siemens employed a quarter of a million workers worldwide.

The 1860s saw a much greater degree of synchronization in German industrial development. Most, although not all, of Germany's regions were now integrated into the domestic market. Above all, the 1860s were the decade of the railway: in 1867, 74,000 worked on the railway, where a generation earlier there had been 7,000. Railway construction accelerated the demand for coal, iron, and steel, and stimulated a huge boom in building construction. The railways played a key role in the conduct of Germany's wars of unification, especially in the Franco-Prussian war of 1870–1, where the rapid transport of German troops to the battlefront in France had a material impact on the outcome. While German engineers' adaptation of the French *chassepot* to provide their soldiers with the needle gun had a material impact on the outcome of the wars of unification, two industrial inventions of the 1860s had a major impact on people's lives and also on the capacity of small firms to remain competitive in the industrial age. These were the dynamo, Werner Siemens's invention of 1866, and for women, the sewing machine: by 1890 half a million sewing machines had been produced, by 1907 the figure had risen to over a million. Pfaff sewing machines was now a household name abroad as well as at home. Some are still in service, antiquated and even collectors' items, a tangible tribute to German engineering skills. The sewing machine helped women to earn an independent living, to supplement their income at home, but it also contributed to the growth of piecework manufacture in the sweatshops of the ready-made clothing industry in Berlin and Breslau, in which the cheap labor of female immigrants to the city was easily exploitable.

In the 1870s, Germany got a new commercial code as part of post-unification's legislation program. Berlin grew to being a major financial center. The years from 1850 to 1873 are known in German literature, the arts, and history as the *Gründerzeit* or Promoters' Boom. The *Gründerzeit* favored the monumental style, as recorded in some extravagant public buildings in the new Reich capital, such as the massive Post Office, which was restored to its former magnificence following the fall of the Berlin Wall in 1989. The Promoters left their mark on the new railway station buildings, which became a new focal point in the urban landscape, and in massive factory buildings whose external appearance resembled mansions rather than sweatshops. This was also the age of the speculative building boom in cheap housing which transformed the new imperial capital. Furthermore, the later nineteenth century's taste for public monuments began to have an impact on the rural ambience of Germany's towns. Bismarck towers and monuments to the Emperor adorned the peak of many a low hill where in medieval times a chapel or religious image might have stood. Painters favored the monumental style as well, as can be seen in the case of the female model of one of the era's most popular painters, Anselm Feuerbach (1829–80), variously portrayed as Medea, Iphigenie, and others. But also we should not forget that the *Gründerzeit* was responsible for founding a substantial number of small and medium-sized enterprises which would prosper and continue to serve their local community for generations. Thus the grandfather and three granduncles of a Leutkirch brewer, Hugo Härle, who died in 1974 at the age of eighty-nine, all founded family breweries in towns and villages of their native Swabia between the 1860s and the 1880s. The four brothers came from a family of twelve children and their breweries have survived to this day.

The year 1873 was something of a landmark in the economic and social history of the Empire, more particularly because of the psychological effects of the sudden check it administered to over a generation of virtually sustained growth. The 1873 stock exchange crash, in which many small investors lost their savings, was caused by overspeculation, particularly in high dividend-yielding railway bonds, but also by the sudden injection of five billion gold marks in war reparations, which the French repaid much sooner than expected. The crisis materially affected the temper of the age. It checked economic growth over the next couple of decades, although certain sectors of the economy and particular regions were more affected than others. Yet the 1870s was also the decade that saw the growing structural links between, and to the mutual advantage of, banking and industry. This would prove to be a key component of future German industrial success. Over the next two decades, the production of capital goods grew more rapidly than consumer goods. By the 1880s, German industrialists were beginning to rationalize their production and marketing costs by reaching agreement with firms in the same area. Cartels helped to minimize competition, maintain prices, and, by maximizing profit, to direct capital toward financing innovation. Phenomenal growth rates were recorded from the mid-1890s onward, as the German economy entered a boom period which was sustained until the eve of the war.

In the mid-1890s Germany's so-called second industrial revolution took off. It was in the 1890s that German heavy industry, coal, iron, and steel began its systematic and successful challenge to British industrial supremacy. In 1880 Germany had produced half as much steel as Britain. Scarcely more than a generation later, the position was reversed: German steel production was twice that of Britain. The quality was as good and production costs lower. By 1913 Germany produced one-quarter of the world's coal, the bulk of it in the rich seams of the Rhineland and Westphalia. The numbers engaged in mining had quadrupled in the same period. Perhaps even more significant for the future of Germany as an economic power was the performance of her new industries, which were essentially knowledge-based: optics, chemicals, including dyes, pharmaceuticals, and electrics. By 1900 Germany was producing 90 percent of the world's synthetic dyes. She was a world leader in the production of industrial chemicals, sulfuric acid, caustic soda, and chlorine. The significance of this development is treated symbolically in the Globsow chapter of *Der Stechlin*, in which Dubslav brings his Berlin guests to see the factory workers, who pay their respects to the old estate owner—but vote Social Democrat. The guests remark on the huge containers of sulfuric acid, massed at the factory gate. Their contents, one of them alleges, will inevitably corrode the old feudal order: it is only a matter of time.

The astonishing pace of change brought about by Germany's industrial revolutions in the second half of the century widened the gap between the industrial centers and the rest of the country. The presence or absence of access to the railway network was a key factor in this development. The map of Germany's industrial landscape shows a clear dominance of west over east—apart from Berlin, Breslau, the Silesian capital, and the state of Saxony. Hamburg in the northwest continued throughout the second half of the century to develop as Germany's leading port, although Bremen's growing rivalry at the century's end is still evident today in the size and number of its remarkably fine *art nouveau* buildings. In Germany mineral riches were concentrated, apart from the Silesian coalfields in the east, near the western border of the Empire, in the coalfields of the Rhineland and Westphalia, and the Saar, and in the iron ore of eastern Lorraine, seized back from France in 1871. In central Germany, Saxony, the oldest manufacturing center of Germany, possessed rich lignite and bauxite deposits; it produced consumer goods and developed a high reputation as a center of the optics (Zeiss near Leipzig) and chemical industries. South Germany was much less industrialized. Apart from the engineering city of Nuremberg in Franconia (northern Bavaria) and Augsburg in western Bavaria, only Stuttgart had a significant industrial profile by 1900. Today the capital of Mercedes and Daimler-Benz, in the late nineteenth century, Württemberg's capital Stuttgart specialized in the production of high-grade machine tools. Before 1914, Munich was a provincial town with hardly any major industry until Krupp came to found armaments factories in the 1914–18 war. But it was a general feature of the less dynamic but relatively prosperous and socially stable south of Germany in the period 1870–1914 that its economic profile was created by small and medium-sized family firms which made their own significant contribution to the economy.

Many of the products of the second industrial revolution were the result of the links forged in the previous decades between university research and industry. By the end of the century industrial firms had their own research laboratories producing epoch-making discoveries, which in the new century would include high-marketable goods such as synthetic fibers and aluminum. The latter was the product of remarkable collaboration between the electro-chemist and later Nobel prize-winner, Fritz Haber, a scientist at the Technical University of Karlsruhe in the southern state of Baden, and the Baden Aniline and Soda Factory (BASF). Wilhelm II was genuinely interested in science policy. It was at his insistence that the right of the technical universities to confer doctorates was introduced in 1900. As a tribute to the monarch, and thanks to the enlightened collaboration between industry, the state and private or corporate donors, the Kaiser Wilhelm Society was founded in 1911. The new initiative incorporated a substantial and growing group of research institutions in the natural sciences, as well as the humanities and social sciences. The *Kaiser Wilhelm Gesellschaft* patented the so-called Harnack principle, named after Adolf von Harnack (1851–1930), theologian and friend of the Kaiser, that the director of each scientific institute should have complete freedom to set the research goals of his institute and recruit his collaborators. The Society showed the pragmatic side of German life in the Second Empire, in its willingness to promote basic or 'blue skies' research in so many of its institutes, side by side with others devoted to the resolution of important industrial problems, such as coal technology. In its modern reincarnation, the Max Planck Society (founded in 1948) perpetuates and enhances Germany's established scientific reputation to this day.

The spectacular advances in the German economy in the half century between 1850 and 1900 were underpinned by the German state's growing intervention in key areas of its citizens' lives. Two particularly significant ones were education and health.

Education

Traditionally, or at least since early modern times, education in Germany had been the concern of its rulers. In the sixteenth-century Protestant Reformation, Martin Luther (1483–1546) had entrusted the princes rather than his church with the charge of promoting grammar school and university education. In Catholic regions, the church retained its primacy in education, but as a rule worked with the secular authorities. Individual rulers, such as the dukes of Saxony or the Empress Maria Theresia of Austria and her son Joseph II, had also shown a benevolent interest in primary education, with resulting benefits to the economy. Social and literary historians of late nineteenth-century Germany have understandably tended to see state intervention in education in terms of control, of evidence of the increasing bureaucratization of life in the Second Empire. In this they are supported by the evidence of imaginative literature. The Wilhelmine school and its authoritarian culture became a target for the generation of writers growing to adulthood in the 1890s. They include major figures, such as Franz Wedekind, Heinrich and Thomas Mann, Hermann Hesse, and many more.

Yet it is equally true to say that late nineteenth-century German education enjoyed an international reputation which in many respects was deserved, and in some aspects richly so. For one thing, the Germans were the most literate people in the world. Apart from Bismarck's clash with the Catholic church in the *Kulturkampf* of the 1870s, Germany generally avoided the bitter ideological conflicts between state and church over schools which were characteristic of France, Italy, and Spain in the latter half of the nineteenth century. By contrast with British practice, the schools in which the German elite was trained were not exclusive private schools, such as Winchester or Eton, but were public schools, open to all who could afford the (relatively) modest cost. Most German grammar schools were maintained by the state, but several were municipal schools in which the community took pride. However, the fact that the much-praised *Gymnasium* cost money was enough to restrict its numbers to a minority, about 5 percent of the population. Of that percentage, about 70 percent were Protestant, 10 percent Jews (although the Jews represented but 1 percent of the population) with the Catholics significantly underrepresented, partly through their own choice. But the *Realgymnasien*, that is, grammar schools with a greater emphasis on practical subjects, experienced a massive increase in the second half of the century. From a low baseline of just over 50 in 1853, the number grew to over 500 at the beginning of the new century. The state made a major and sustained investment in education in the post-1871 period. Thus the primary school sector alone grew by a factor of thirteen between 1864 and 1911, reflecting the changeover from schools with predominantly one class to modern, multiclass schools.

Much justified criticism has been leveled at the authoritarian character of the state-controlled German university system in the Second Empire, at the "mandarin" nature (Ringer, 1969) of its professors, and at the barriers to appointment and promotion experienced by those who criticized abuses in the system, or abuses in society at large. But in terms of the quality of their education and scientific reputation, the German universities were indeed, as a contemporary American scientist phrased it, "a jewel in the imperial crown." Nineteen in number in 1871, three more were added (or refounded) in subsequent years, including the university of Strasbourg in conquered Alsace. The state made a major investment in university education and university research, and its investment paid off. German science and German medicine deservedly enjoyed a world reputation. Foreign students, often the elite of their home countries, came in significant numbers to study in Germany in these years. The university played a central role in the education of the intellectual elite. The numbers attending university increased fourfold between 1869 and 1914. The confessional disparities reflected the situation in the grammar schools, with Protestants overrepresented, Catholics underrepresented, and the Jewish student representation almost ten times the average of the age cohort. However, the later years of the Empire saw some adjustment in these ratios as the Catholics integrated into modern German society. A vital feature of the university landscape in terms of their contribution to scientific know-how and to the economy were the technical universities. They evolved from the old technical colleges, beginning with Karlsruhe in Baden, founded in 1865 as a technical university some six years before the unification of Germany. Initially, they met with strong resistance from vested interests within the universities, not least for their wish to be permitted to award doctorates. By 1911 there were eleven such institutions, and their record in world-level applied scientific research was enviable. Among other important educational innovations, the Cologne *Handelsschule* or School of Commerce, deserves mention, but the German Empire also invested substantially in a wide variety of specialist colleges, such as mining, agriculture, and forestry. Here, too, the characteristic feature of the German system prevailed in the sense that professional training was constantly improved and the skills of the students updated through the active research interests of the teaching staff.

Health

A somewhat similar pattern is evident in health. Although these gains were more modest than in the area of education, focus by twentieth-century historians on the problems has tended to obscure the real achievements of the state.

Many late nineteenth-century texts of varied provenance record the appallingly deprived lives of the urban poor. Examples include Gerhart Hauptmann's slum tenement drama *Die Ratten* (1911), accounts of the experience of slum doctors, such as those by the artist and wife of one, Käthe Kollwitz (1867–1945), portrayed in her haunting woodcuts, or the provocative vulgarity of the cartoons of Heinrich Zille (1858–1929), featuring procreation, birth, hunger, and death in the Berlin proletariat. Yet the public health record of Germany on the eve of the 1914 war could be compared favorably with that of almost any industrialized country in the world. True, it was really only from the 1890s that we can speak of a public health policy in any meaningful way, as municipalities and the German state began, in the wake of the Hamburg cholera epidemic, to engage in the provision of proper sanitation and be concerned with the health of the ordinary citizen. (Not least of their motivation, it must be said, was to improve the quality of army recruits.) The most obvious advance over earlier times was infant mortality, which had remained obstinately high until almost the century's end. Bald statistics of death in infancy hide the human suffering which the individual case brings home: eight children each were born to the novelist Fontane and the leader of the Catholic Center party Windthorst and their wives. Only four of Fontane's survived infancy; only one of Windthorst's lived beyond their mid-thirties. It was not until the 1880s that Germany's high infant and child mortality rates began to be modified, partly through advances in hygiene (notably among medical staff attending the newborn infant and its mother), partly through better public health and sanitation. But by the beginning of the twentieth century, the positive effects on people's lives were beginning to be evident. Advances in bacteriology in the last decades of the century also helped to combat infectious diseases, such as typhus and diphtheria, the great killers of children. Tuberculosis remained a scourge, especially of the poor, who were susceptible to the disease on account of their excessive working hours, poor diet, and the close proximity and substandard accommodations in which so many were forced to live. But considerable advances were made in combating the disease. The battle against tuberculosis received a major impulse from developments in instrumentation, notably the stethoscope. Criticism of Fontane's alleged anti-Jewishness, as exemplified in the figure of the awkward Berlin doctor Moscheles in *Der Stechlin*, has allowed readers to overlook a salient point about him: the old country doctor Sponholz draws Dublav's attention to the younger man's modern qualifications, especially his expertise with the stethoscope and diagnostic skill. Improvement in the national diet was the product of collaboration between the state (investment in research) and private enterprise. Thus by the 1890s, advances in food technology were beginning to produce some relatively cheap, nonperishable foods. Liebig's *Fleischextrakt* became a household word, as did Dr. Oetker's mass-produced and relatively cheap baking ingredients. Stollwerck's chocolate factories, meanwhile, brought within reach of the less well-off, at least on special days, what in the eighteenth century had been the preserve of the very rich.

The fruitful partnership between German research and German industry became evident in pharmaceutics in this period too. So much history must necessarily remain undocumented, and exactly how many sufferers from headaches, influenza, and menstrual pain benefited from the invention of patent medicines, such as aspirin (in 1893), we shall never know. But that they were made readily available, thanks to advances in marketing, and that they were cheap, must have represented a significant improvement in the quality of life for many Germans. Both medicine and nursing became increasingly professionalized in the period between mid-century and the outbreak of the 1914 war. Nursing became no longer the preserve of the religious orders, who had hitherto predominated in the care of the sick, along with the Protestant deaconesses, of whom more than 13,000 worked in social care by the end of the century. It is noteworthy that the actual numbers of doctors, dentists, and nurses increased far more rapidly than the population in the Wilhelmine period.

To a great extent this upward trend in the number of medical workers, teachers, and indeed state and municipal employees, was all part of the state's assuming ever-increasing control over the citizens' lives. As Max Weber, the father of sociology, noted in a series of subtle analyses of processes at work in Wilhelmine politics, administration, the economy, and in society at large, the most characteristic development of the late nineteenth- and early twentieth-century Germany was the bureaucratization of life. This was both positive and negative, and was perceived as such: positive in its efficiency and, in general, fairness; negative in the restrictions it imposed on human behavior and the imagination. But bureaucratization did not dispense with inherited social divisions. On the contrary, it hardened them.

Chapter 13
German Society in the Later Nineteenth Century

A cartoon in the Berlin satirical paper *Kladderadatsch* (meaning "disaster") depicts German society in the summer of 1885 as seen from the inside of a railway train—exclusive in the first class, prosperous and comfortable in the second, crowded but with seating in the third, standing room only in the hopelessly overcrowded fourth class. In Imperial Germany, despite her dynamic economy, social barriers were no less real than they had been earlier in the century, although in some ways they were of a different order. In 1848, many German revolutionaries had aspired to abolish the nobility altogether. They had not succeeded. But how had the German aristocracy responded to the massive economic changes of the subsequent half century, and how far were they still able to defend their political and social primacy in the age of urbanization?

The aristocracy

At the beginning of the twentieth century, the leader of the German Conservative party, a Prussian landowner named von Heydebrand, remarked to a Left Liberal member of parliament that, for them, the future was bleak, that the masses were set to rob the aristocracy of its influence. Even a strong statesman could only delay the inevitable. However, they, the aristocracy, had no intention of surrendering their position voluntarily. It was a cool appraisal of the German nobility's remarkable capacity to preserve and even consolidate their privileged position in the century of liberalism, nationalism, industrialization, and socialism. In most of the Empire's states, and above all in the largest of them, Prussia, the nobility retained throughout the nineteenth century its traditional monopoly of senior positions in the army and the bureaucracy, the two most powerful elites in the country. They continued to dominate the higher echelons of the army, even after the rise in the population brought a rapid increase in the army's size and, inevitably, a large influx of middle-class officers. The better regiments, such as the Guards and the cavalry, were the domain of the nobleman, artillery and infantry being regarded by them as appropriate to the middle class. In the later years of Bismarck's administration and under Wilhelm II, a determined effort was made to appoint noblemen to key posts at both state (i.e., Prussian) and Reich level in the government and administration. At a lower but influential administrative level, the practice in Prussia of appointing a nobleman to the position of *Landrat* or central government representative at local level, was a further endorsement by the state of inherited privilege.

German society as seen by its railway passengers in *Kladderadatsch* 9 August 1885.

The nobility could claim little justification for their continued privileges apart from tradition. This was one of the reasons why the notion of the court of honor and the obligation to obtain satisfaction through dueling was so important to the nobility. It was predicated on the idea that its proponents were more honorable than the rest of society, when in fact they were in conflict with the law. It was not as if the nobility as a caste had rendered special service to the community, either as a group or as individuals, apart from their association in the public mind as commanding officers in the victorious wars of 1864, 1866, and 1870/71. Through Prussian and Mecklenburg landlords' control of appointments to church and school on their estates, their influence over the local gendarmerie, in the German Conservative party, and in pressure groups, such as the Agrarian League in the 1890s, the German nobility, particularly in the north and east, presented itself as the spokesman and self-styled protector of the rural classes. As the great nineteenth-century historian Otto Hintze wrote: "the nimbus of local lordship" disappeared very slowly. Which is not to say that East Elbian landowners did not show genuine concern for their tenants: there was, or could be, a very powerful bond between the landowner and the families who had served him and his forebears for generations. Such loyalty was amply demonstrated in the manner in which estate owners like the Dohnas of East Prussia, fleeing before the Soviet armies in the horrendous winter of 1945, took charge of caravans of several hundred men, women, and children and personally led them hundreds of miles to safety in western Germany.

In the south, the nobility was generally less exclusively privileged than in the north. Württemberg, for example, had early on in its history curtailed the political privileges of its hereditary noblemen, denying them the right to be members of the estates of the realm. Personal nobility was another matter, being granted to every staff officer, government minister, and establishment figures such as the rector (president) of the University of Tübingen. In southern Germany as a whole, where many families had their estates, the nobility tended to form an exclusive social caste, marrying and moving within their own ranks. The Prussian tradition of state service was uncommon, and although the prime ministers of Bavaria and Hesse-Darmstadt were usually noblemen, and sometimes the prime minister of Baden, the middle ranks of society provided the state and local government with administrators, giving them access to the court in a way that was rare in the north.

A serious challenge to the status and functions of the East Elbian aristocracy emerged in the 1870s as a consequence of economic, demographic, and political change. Competition from cheap American and Russian grain threatened to undercut the financial basis of a whole political class. It was then, with the dextrous support of Bismarck, that the landowning classes in Prussia and Mecklenburg demonstrated what Max Weber, borrowing Nietzsche's phrase in *The Anti-Christ* (1888), aptly termed their "will to power." Appointing themselves spokesmen of the claims of the aristocracy, and the agrarian sector generally, to special treatment in the modern state, they organized themselves into powerful and noisy pressure groups. Their leaders demonstrated over the last years of the century that they had indeed a thorough grasp of modern methods of propaganda and public persuasion. As the historian Rudolf Stadelmann once observed, under Friedrich Wilhelm IV, Prussian conservatism was an ideology, under Bismarck it still retained some sense of moral tradition, but under Caprivi in the 1890s, it was no more than an economic interest group. In common with the representatives of heavy industry, with whom they had formed the tactical alliance known as "Corn & Iron," the Prussian conservatives laid claim to a monopoly of paternalist, preindustrial values, which also appealed to others of very different background from their own. However, it is important to understand that the term nobility covered an extremely diverse social stratum and also included considerable numbers of well-to-do and recently ennobled bourgeois, who invested in landed estates to which they brought new expertise and a capitalist approach to agriculture. By the early 1880s more than 60 percent of estates in the eastern provinces of Prussia were owned by bourgeois (caricatured by Fontane in *Der Stechlin* in the figure of Gundermann auf Siebenmühlen). However, some members of the nobility, such as the Silesian magnates, adapted energetically to the modern world about them: the Donnersmarcks grew wealthy through developing their interests in the upper Silesian coalfields and later became well-known producers of *Sekt* (German sparkling wine).

Middle-class attitudes toward the first estate (the aristocracy) underwent a considerable change in the second half of the century. Ute Frevert has shown in her fascinating study of dueling, how for example the (Protestant) German middle classes, who in mid-century had bitterly attacked the practice, came to accept and even to some extent identify with the aristocratic notion of defending one's honor.[1] One of the principal instruments of this change was the officership of the reserve, to which the bourgeoisie could gain entrance

---

[1] The Catholic church forbade dueling and even threatened with excommunication those who practiced it. In 1864 a young Catholic nobleman serving as a second lieutenant in the Prussian army refused to duel because his conscience and his church forbade it. King Wilhelm I, the later emperor, not only dismissed him and his two brothers from the army, ignoring the indignant protests of fifty-five Catholic noblemen from the young man's native province of Rhineland-Westphalia, but added insult to injury by refusing to give reasons for his action, saying that the brothers clearly lacked the necessary sense of honor to serve in "his" army.

after serving for a year as (unpaid) volunteers, financed by their families. To hold a commission was a highly useful entry ticket to professional and social advancement, not least because of the attraction of a smart uniform in a society where civilian dress came a very poor second to uniform.

The middle classes

Every social historian of nineteenth-century Germany writing in English tends to be apologetic about her or his capacity to deal adequately with this sector of society in what European historians rightly style the century of the bourgeoisie. A good part of the problem rests in terminology, both in German and in English translation.[2] The century of the bourgeoisie is commonly rendered in German as *das bürgerliche Jahrhundert*. But of course *bürgerlich* means both "belonging to the middle class" as well as being the German term for "civil" in the sense of "civil society" (*die bürgerliche Gesellschaft*) or civil rights (*Bürgerrechte*) or the Civil Code (*das Bürgerliche Gesetzbuch*). A further difficulty resides in the fact that the term *Bürger* changed in the course of the century. Its original meaning referred to citizenship of a town (one was a *Stadtbürger* or burger of one's town and one had rights of citizenship here or *Bürgerrecht*). The problem is compounded by the fact that English has dropped the very useful but now archaic word *burgher* as a term in common use. Furthermore, in the second half of the century the term bourgeoisie (as Marx also used it) tended to refer more to the upper strata of middle-class German society, especially those who had made money in commerce and industry. The term *Mittelstand* also changed its meaning in the course of the century. Traditionally, it denoted the middle strata of society, but by the last quarter of the century it meant "lower middle class." Broadly speaking—and accepting the fact that it is virtually impossible to generalize, not least in view of the immense regional variation—the middle ranks of German society were more preoccupied in the period between the Restoration in 1815 and until after the Revolution of 1848 with their disadvantaged position by contrast with the privileged nobility. In the following decades they tended to define themselves more by the world of work, by what they did and how this affected their position in society. In the last decades of the century, many spokesmen for the middle ranks of society in Prussia became increasingly resentful at the evident monopoly exercised by the nobility over membership of the government, administrative, and military elite. The last decade or so has seen the appearance of a great deal of important work on the nineteenth-century German middle

---

[2] Sheehan's *German History 1770–1856* (1989) has a useful discussion of terminology on pp. 132f. and 522f. *See also* Sagarra, *A Social History of Germany 1648–1914* (1977), pp. 253f.

classes, both in general and with regard to particular groups within them, such as Jürgen Kocka's edited volumes, entitled *Bürger und Bürgerlichkeit im 19. Jahrhundert* (1988), which forms part of the Bielefeld project. The student of German literature in this period will find it a stimulating framework in which to contextualize her or his reading of those writers who made contemporary middle-class society the topic of their work, most notably Theodor Fontane and Wilhelm Raabe, Karl Gutzkow, Gustav Freytag, Friedrich Spielhagen, and also, if sometimes more obliquely, Louise von François or Theodor Storm.

Civil servants

In the Germany of Goethe's youth, state service offered limited opportunities for employment to educated youths of middle-class origin who did not wish to follow their father's footsteps. The extraordinarily turbulent decades between 1789 and 1815 initiated a process of change in most German states. In 1807, just a year after the overthrow of the old Prussian order on the battlefields of Jena and Auerstädt, Napoleon wrote to his brother Jérome, recently made king of Westphalia. The effect of the *Code Napoléon* would, Napoleon said, be much more persuasive in winning the loyalty of Germans than all his victories. What the German people wanted more than anything else, in his view, was that those who were not of noble birth should have equal rights, on the basis of their ability, to posts and to marks of distinction. Recognizing the significance of Napoleon's legislative changes in those western territories occupied by the French, liberal-minded officials in Prussia and a number of other states were inspired to introduce wide-ranging reforms. Put at their most idealistic, these had a twofold aim. Firstly, a special category of persons, the civil servants, were to be brought into a direct relationship with the state, while the subjects of the ruler were to be transformed into free and self-reliant citizens. Secondly, encouragement was to be given to what we might call private enterprise, in order to increase state revenue. Undoubtedly, the rise of a capitalist economy in parts of Germany was, broadly speaking, facilitated by the subsequent introduction of freedom of trade in Prussia (but not in Austria or Saxony) and by the abolition of obligations traditionally associated with owning property, such as looking after one's peasants in time of dearth. The consolidation of the civil service into a kind of semi-independent class, which happened at different times in different states, did much to help Germans of middle-class origins identify with the abstract notion of the state. The state service was made open to competition in Prussia in 1834 and in a number of other states in the Restoration era. This meant that noble aspirants

German Society in the Later Nineteenth Century

Der – Die – Das –
Der Pöbel (the rabble), *Die Menge* (the masses), *Das Volk* (the people), from *Simplicissimus*

had to invest in higher education. Practice was different in the diplomatic service, as it was in other European countries, for the practical reason that the highborn diplomat had entry to the "best" society of the country to which he was accredited, in a way a rich bourgeois would not. Moreover, state officials were not so well paid as to be able to afford the lifestyle of a diplomat. (Even Bismarck, extravagant and self-indulgent, had some justification in complaining of being unable to meet the representational costs of his various government posts, that is, until he became intimate in the 1860s with the banker Bleichröder.)

The personal oath taken by the state official to the sovereign, the need to conform to a certain code of behavior, along with the existence of disciplinary procedures and the provision of economic security in the case of illness and retirement, helped to give government officials a sense of corporate identity. It is true, as Mack Walker noted in his study of Restoration Germany, *German Home Towns* (1972), that ordinary people, and in particular those such as small-town councilors and guild members whose older corporate privileges were being eroded by the legislative measures of reforming states, regarded rational-minded bureaucrats as a kind of corporate conspiracy against their way of life. In the second half of the century, not least under the impact of the Revolution in which very many middle-ranking and junior state officials had participated, the claims of the nobility to preferment in the upper ranks of the state service were reasserted. In the Empire, bourgeois officials found themselves discriminated against for the more senior positions, both at national and local government levels and in the army. Initially, the judiciary was much more liberal in recruitment and promotion, but increasingly from the late 1870s onward, the climate changed in favor of the upper class and supporters of the conservative interest.

The academics

One group of civil servants remained almost solidly middle class, regarding themselves as the repository of specifically middle-class values in the nineteenth century. These were the university professors and grammar school teachers. In the *Vormärz* or years preceding the 1848 Revolution, they had articulated liberal and national values, and very many had suffered for their principles both then and immediately after the crushing of the revolution. The political sympathies of most German academics changed in the second half of the century. They might not vote Conservative (though Fontane's headmaster Thormeyer in *Der Stechlin* or Thomas Mann's Wulicke, Hanno Buddenbrooks' headmaster in *Buddenbrooks*, surely did!), but they became conservative in their political sympathies and public behavior. Some, like the holder of the prestigious chair of history, Heinrich von Treitschke, were glad to forget their liberal pronouncements of the 1850s, to accept a patent of nobility, and actively promote chauvinist values. A few, like Treitschke's most effective opponent in the so-called 1879/80 Anti-Semitic Conflict, the historian Theodor Mommsen (1817–1903), grandfather and great-grandfather of historians, remained liberal in name as well as in mind. Certainly the professors were a highly status-conscious group, esteeming their membership of the *Bildungsbürgertum*, the educated classes, almost more than their income. As the sociologist Theodor Geiger (1891–1952) put it, their earnings were less crucial to this stratum of society than where they sat in the local inn. By the last quarter of a century those of liberal sympathies or Roman Catholics found it difficult to be appointed to permanent posts at university; for supporters of the Social Democratic party, it was virtually impossible. Increasing conservatism and support for nationalist and indeed imperialist values among the educated as a class toward the end of the century was motivated in part by their wish to defend the elitist position which they now enjoyed by comparison with most other middle-class groups. Nationalist pressure groups, such as the Navy League, enjoyed wide support among academics and members of the liberal professions, such as doctors, lawyers, and newspaper editors, but then the navy, unlike the army, opened the upper ranks of its officer class to the bourgeoisie. The militant Pan-German League proved particularly attractive to the socially prestigious educated bourgeoisie, namely university and grammar school teachers, higher civil servants, and established artists, who constituted some 50 percent of its membership. They, like the commercial classes, now tended to socialize and to marry within their own ranks. A similar professional training, six years of classical education at grammar school, followed by at least five or six years at university, fostered a homogenous mentality among their menfolk. This was developed further by membership of institutions such as student fraternities, with their active old-boy network, and, for some, the possession of a commission as an officer of the Reserve. This made them more accessible to the militaristic values of the court and the Prussian aristocracy, as Fontane shows in the scene in chapter 20 of *Der Stechlin* with headmaster Thormeyer, where the junior teacher rushes to play the Prussian "national anthem": *Heil dir im Siegerkranz*.

The commercial classes

Alongside the *Bildungsbürgertum* another successful middle-class stratum established itself, the plutocracy or *Besitzbürgertum* (*Besitz*=property). In fact it was in the quarter of a century between the end of the 1848 Revolution and the aftermath of the unification of Germany that a bourgeoisie in the modern sense of the term first emerged in Germany. The two groups had relatively little contact with each other until the latter years of the century, apart from the Rhineland and the smaller towns of southern Germany. The social origins of the early propertied middle classes lay in banking circles, in commerce and the retail trade, and later among the factory and mill owners. Social mobility was not a feature of the early industrialists. Few were self-made men, although some of the most famous names were the sons of craftsmen and traders. The locomotive manufacturer August Borsig was an exception, as was Carl Zeiss (1816–1888), who made his name in precision optical instruments. Of Borsig it was said that he might not have been much of a mathematician but that he had an unerring capacity to spot talent among his machinists. Bismarck's banker, Gerson Bleichröder, who used to play with Emilie Fontane when they were children, came from a family who had been market traders in the early nineteenth century, a process which Fontane reflects in some of his Jewish figures, notably those of his novels, *L'Adultera*, *Mathilde Möhring*, and *Der Stechlin*. Upward social mobility, where it did take place, usually spanned two generations. Most early German entrepreneurs differed in lifestyle and religion from the wider community. In the Catholic Ruhr and Wupper valleys, for example, the factory owners were Protestants, many of them Calvinists. The Aachen and Cologne merchants were Lutheran in the Catholic Rhineland, while in mid-century Berlin 50 percent of successful businessmen were Jewish. The close business links which grew up in the third quarter of the century between industry and banking were cemented by marriage. Their patriarchal lifestyle was not unlike that of the older commercial communities of the Hanseatic cities of Hamburg, Bremen, Lübeck, and Rostock, frugal in everyday life, munificent when it was a matter of representing the firm or the family. The *Besitzbürgertum* had little time or inclination for politics before the last decades of the century. First of all business, then politics, was the rule of the electro technician Werner Siemens, son of a Hanoverian tenant farmer.

The prodigious expansion of business and the accumulation of wealth in the *Gründerzeit* or Promoters' Boom in the 1860s and early 1870s, and again in the so-called second industrial revolution of the late 1890s, when the German economy became the most dynamic in Europe, inevitably brought about change in habits and values. Ostentatious villas sprang up in the larger towns and businessmen moved away from their place of work to more desirable residential quarters, far from the barrack-like blocks of flats and rooms in which working men and women had to live. Thus the ideological and material gap between masters and men was reinforced by the physical distance separating them in the towns and cities where each lived. Siemens even spoke of his own organization as an "industrial dukedom." The more successful entrepreneurs began to patronize art and music, to support the cultural development of the local municipality. A number now sent their sons to university, which had not been the practice a generation earlier. However, despite the increasing wealth and conspicuous consumption, the *Besitzbürgertum* did not see themselves as an independent voice in German politics—or indeed a liberalizing influence, such as one found in second- and third-generation British industrialists. They coveted awards, such as "commercial councilor," followed, with luck, by the exclusive "privy councilor" (*Geheimrat*). We recall the frustration of the ambitious parvenu Frau Jenny Treibel, in Fontane's eponymous novel of 1892, at her long-suffering husband's being so long 'stuck' at *Kommerzienrat*. Werner Siemens himself had rejected it as inappropriate for a technologist, but he accepted the title of *Geheimrat* with alacrity as acknowledging the scientific achievement of his life's work. The *Besitzbürger* of Wilhelmine Germany then, like the *Bildungsbürger*, broadly shared what Sheehan calls the "articulated norms and codes of behavior" which the young Second Empire had elaborated. By the last decades of the century the propertied classes could identify with a regime which, while it might be authoritarian and biased in favor of birth over talent, provided in their view a well-functioning governmental and administrative machine, a solid infrastructure of communications and good public order; in other words, an environment conducive to doing business.

The *Kleinbürger* or petty bourgeois

In nineteenth-century Germany—and in the minds of foreign observers for quite a while thereafter—the *Kleinbürger* represented the backbone of the nation. Not least, of course, to themselves. Artisans and traders, shopkeepers, publicans, subaltern officials in the state service or in transport, and the small farmers made up the bulk of this stratum of society. They were particularly well represented in the small communities of south, central, and northwest Germany. Up to the second half of the century, poor communications perpetuated the tendency to live in small, self-contained communities, with their accompanying value systems. This is the world so widely represented in the novellas of Tieck, Droste, Storm, and Ludwig or the Swiss and Austrian writers, Keller, Stifter, and Ebner-Eschenbach. Raabe's novels contain dozens of such *Kleinbürger*. The German petty bourgeois was traditionally thrifty and diligent, status-conscious, and, unless roused, politically passive. Several factors came together in the course of the century to affect his position, usually adversely.

Freedom of trade, the result of reform policies in many post-Napoleonic German states, cheap English-factory-produced goods, and the arrival of competition, once restrictions imposed by the guilds had been removed by "the officials," all conspired to make life difficult for the artisan class, for the masters, and more particularly for those who aspired to that status. The population explosion of the prerevolutionary years had a devastating effect on this class. The problems of pauperization of the lower ranks of the old middle class attracted the attention of governments, municipal councils, and social commentators by midcentury. They were right, since the revolution was not least the work of members of the disaffected and threatened artisan class and of subaltern officials on poor salaries, denied promotion. In the *Communist Manifesto,* Karl Marx observed emotively and accurately: "Those who were up to now members of the lower middle classes, such as the small industrialists, merchants and rentiers, artisans and farmers, are effectively sinking in the proletariat." Nowhere is the regional diversity of Germany more evident than in the history of her craftsmen. In general, the determined adherence to economic liberal principles by the Prussian state brought former artisans in the 1850s and 1860s to factories and workshops as suppliers to shops and middlemen. Borsig's locomotive factory in Berlin included numerous former artisans from the metalworkers' guild. In many regions of south Germany, despite rivalry from manufacturing enterprises, craftsmen continued to enjoy, and some even to regain, the kind of state protection they relied upon, and thus could regard themselves once more as men of consequence, if not necessarily of substance in their community. The fate of artisans and tradesmen in the industrial revolution depended both on the individual and the craft. Some trades, such as hat- and wig-making, suffered virtual obliteration. Others prospered, notably the metalworkers and, in the later decades of the century, workers in the food industry. In the last decades of the century craftsmen found their services in demand to repair or service products (including machinery). Many also provided specially commissioned articles at a higher price, such as leather and fashion goods. In general, then, after the severe dislocation of the middle years of the century, artisans broadly adapted to the changed economic situation and continued to exist alongside manufacturing industry. Whole groups had disappeared, one-man concerns became fewer and often poorer, but the role of the artisan was still useful. In industry, former artisans tended to regard themselves as an elite among workers. By the 1870s, however, many were beginning to identify themselves with the wage earners and be drawn to the socialist movement. The artisan tradition of mutual and self-help survived to find new outlets both in the party and, especially after 1890, in the trade union movement.

In later nineteenth-century Germany, the self-employed craftsmen and small traders felt a sense of solidarity with other social groups, such as the subaltern officials. It was not uncommon for a reasonably prosperous craftsman to keep one of his sons at school, and to have him sit an examination qualifying for entry to the lower ranks of the state service as a clerk or even as a primary school teacher. They were attracted by the status and economic security of the official position, although the salary might be low. Honorary office in the community, which might be denied a craftsman on educational grounds, was accessible to the holder of minor civil service or municipal office. After 1871, the state began to take on more and more of the tasks hitherto performed by individuals or the local community, thus increasing "status jobs." The state takeover of the railway lines in Prussia and the postal system brought thousands of new job opportunities, which involved the wearing of a uniform, and thus distinguished its wearer from the "common mass." The state's assumption of responsibility for the maintenance of roads, lighting, waterways, drainage, and the emerging social services are part of the same process. Municipal transport companies provided employment, and the smart uniform, including white hats for cab drivers, emphasized the notion of status in the mind of both employer and employee. However, many minor officials on low salaries, expected to keep up appearances in dress and in the manner they socialized, felt resentful at the conspicuous consumption they witnessed by those whom they felt were their social inferiors, many of them recent immigrants. In the south, social tensions were less in evidence, partly because of the more settled, but also less dynamic social structure, and because the state continued to give its employees perquisites of office; thus in Württemberg, officials of the law could keep a proportion of the fines imposed.

The last years of the century witnessed growing political awareness in the ranks of the so-called older *Mittelstand*, that is, the subaltern officials, the artisans, the small traders/shopkeepers. The reasons for this were, firstly, the growing solidarity of the wage-laborers in their various political and economic organizations, represented as they were by a dynamic political party, and, on the other, by the growth of a new social group, the white collar workers in industry and commerce or "new" *Mittelstand*. A common bond between both lower middle-class groups was their sense that their civic virtues of discipline, hard work, and obedience to their superiors put the authorities under a special obligation to protect their interests. Various governments in the Wilhelmine years did indeed make frequent reference to their concern for this section of society under the emotive term *Mittelstandspolitik*, but without putting a great deal of substance into any plans to interfere with the market in their favor. Instead they sought to reassure these potentially disaffected social groups by their use of such phrases of *staatserhaltende Kräfte* (forces which support and sustain the state), in sharp contrast to Kaiser Wilhelm II's intemperate use of the term "enemies of the state" (*Reichsfeinde*), applied to Social Democrats and (still occasionally) to Roman Catholics. The emperor, the court, and the upper echelons of the administration and army tended to indulge the *Mittelstand*, at least verbally, attributing to them special moral and national virtues.

Mittelständische and also rural values were sentimentalized by the upper classes and members of these strata themselves. Both were catered to by the purveyors of nostalgic literature, known as *Heimatliteratur*, whose authors made a fortune in royalties. The old *Mittelstand* order and the 'unspoiled' rural landscape of yore represented for many the traditional order whose passing they lamented. The rejection of industrialization and modernization was widespread in late nineteenth-century Germany, and often precisely by those who enjoyed the many resultant benefits. Both old and new *Mittelstand* proved enthusiastic supporters of nationalist organizations, for which political or social envy was a powerful recruiting agent, such as the Pan-German League, the Reich League against Social Democracy, or the Navy League. In the German Shop Assistants Association, which excluded Jews, one sector of this social stratum formed its own pressure group.

Wage laborers

The social origin of the manual labor force in early and mid-nineteenth-century Germany was very diverse. The majority of males worked in domestic craft and manufacture, but in some branches of textile production the labor force was even then predominantly female. The women workers were generally single, widowed, deserted, or the wives of ill-paid or invalid workers, or of former soldiers. Factory workers in the early years of industrialization were usually former artisans who had not been successful in establishing themselves as masters or whose trade had been destroyed by foreign or native factory competition. A number came from the landless rural laborers who had proved to be the victims of land reform. There were considerable differences of status between wage laborers, deriving from skills and traditions, conditions of work between one enterprise and another, or even within the same factory or workshop. In mid-century the word *Arbeiter* (=worker) generally meant someone with a skill, while the term *Proletarier* referred to the unskilled. Alfred Krupp (1812–87), founder of the firm which became a major manufacturer of armaments, declared in the 1830s that he took his workmen wherever he could get them, from the hearthside, from the ploughshare, from unemployed craftsmen. In the Berlin machine tools industry a decade or two later, most workers were skilled craftsmen. Paper and textile manufacture and the readymade clothing industry, which by the 1850s had its center in Berlin, tended to attract principally surplus rural population and a large number of women. In line with their diverging social and professional origins was the variety of educational backgrounds among Germany's labor force. A number did acquire skills on the job, but these tended to be the exception. Most found it extremely difficult to better themselves. Many had left school too early to possess or to acquire elementary skills. Educational facilities for children working in the factory were introduced by law in mid-century, but inspection was deficient. It was, said one contemporary critic, no more than the fig leaf designed to conceal the employers' disregard of educational requirements. Some altruistic entrepreneurs founded their own school for the factory children. One such was the father of Philipp Nathusius (1842-1900), cofounder of the German Conservative party in 1876, whose mother, Marie (1817-57), helped to run the school. (She was also a much-read author of pious tales for girls and of songs for children, such as *Alle Vöglein sind schon da*.)

The regional diversity of Germany, and especially the differences in the pace of industrialization between north and south, west and east (with the exception of parts of Silesia, now Poland) make it difficult to generalize about earnings and living standards. Real wages had been relatively stable in the 1820s and 1830s, but they plummeted in the 1840s at the same time as the price of basic foodstuffs soared. Wages recovered in 1849, dropped again in the next decade, then recovered steadily throughout the 1860s and early 1870s. Some branches of industry, notably mining and heavy industry, suffered more than the consumer industries in the years following the 1873 stock exchange crash, which administered a severe shock to business confidence. Hardship and exploitation found expression in strikes in the 1850s and again in the late 1880s and 1890s. In fact, up to the outbreak of war in 1914, the German labor force showed that it was much more defiant than Germans' long-held reputation for political quiescence would seem to suggest.

Initially the mass of uneducated workers were slow to develop group consciousness, aware perhaps of the fact that, as the mid-century sociologist, Wilhelm Heinrich Riehl (1823-1897), observed, their job could be filled tomorrow by a child and the following day by a new handle or screw. However, the hostile attitudes of the authorities, and then of bourgeois society to the urban wage laborer, which developed following the rapid expansion of the industrial workforce from the 1860s onward, helped to bring together the disparate elements of the workforce. Attempts by workmen or their spokesmen to develop political organizations were met with the 1869 law prohibiting combinations (*Koalitionsverbot*). Even as late as the prewar years, severe penalties were imposed for infringement of this measure. In the first volume of their famous dictionary or *Deutsches Wörterbuch*, the brothers Grimm had described the term *Arbeiterbewegung* (workers' movement) as *Aufruhr der Arbeiter, Arbeitskrawall*, that is, workers' revolt or rioting. How far this volume, which was bought by bourgeois householders and regarded as authoritative, actually influenced attitudes to the industrial workers, is impossible to say. But there is no doubt that hostile public attitudes to working men's organizations, which, after

Strikers at their employer's by O. Gulbransson from *Simplicissimus*. 'What does the rabble want?' 'We only want to learn from you, sir, what one does all day when one doesn't work.'

all, were primarily designed to improve their bleak lot, fostered a sense of social isolation among working people. This helps explain both the success and the militancy of the socialist movement as it grew and developed in the last quarter of the century.

The appeal of an organized labor movement was all the greater since immigrant workers from Protestant regions had all but lost contact with their churches. There were too few urban clergymen working in the areas in which wage-laborers lived, and moreover, the Protestant churches were closely identified with the establishment, since the ruler—in the case of Prussia, the king—was simultaneously head of the church. By contrast, Roman Catholic workers in the Rhineland, including the large immigrant Polish community, usually had their own priests and in due course their own Christian trade union. The church had taken the initiative early in confronting the problems for the institutional church and for the faithful that were being created by the industrial revolution. This initiative owed much to the energetic figure of Wilhelm von Ketteler (1811–77), a former Prussian civil servant and later bishop of Mainz, whose seminal work on the working classes and their relation with the Catholic church (*Die Arbeiterfrage und das Christentum*), published toward the end of his life in 1864, was to exercise a powerful influence on international Catholic social teaching in the decades to follow. The so-called *Kolpingvereine* had been founded in the 1840s by the journeyman, Adolf Kolping (1813–65), to provide lodging for indigent Catholic apprentices. The movement spread rapidly, and *Kolping* houses, albeit with other functions, are still to be found in many German towns today. Catholic urban wage laborers voted solidly for the Catholic Center party in the first generation of its existence; only around 1900 did they begin to switch allegiance in any significant way to the Social Democrats. One of the early Center party deputies elected to the Reichstag was actually a worker priest.

Socialism, as the political movement that would translate Communist thought into practice, went much further. From the first it was a movement focused on the victims of industrialization, the wage laborers, alienated, as Marx famously said, from their labor, from the product of their hands. Socialism's great attraction for working men was that it provided a political program, and, equally, that it gave them an ideology for its members which was oriented toward a better future in this life. Heine teased both Christian churches when he described their clergy in his mock heroic epic, *Germany: A Winter's Tale*, as fobbing off the poor with dreams of the next world: Communism, on the other hand, promised and would deliver the good life for everyone in this world, epitomized by sugar peas.

An intelligent and ambitious working man who joined the Social Democratic party in the late nineteenth century had every chance of becoming a person of consequence in his locality. After 1890, when the number of paid officials in the movement rose rapidly, he could reasonably hope for a career at national level also. While school and military service, the latter styled the "'school of the nation," were designed to imbue patriotic attitudes into the urban and the rural working class, this often had the opposite effect among the politicized urban workers. Their experiences, particularly in the army, frequently transformed workers into militants. In general, it would seem that most politically minded workers felt a dual, but not necessarily conflicting, loyalty to the emperor and to their party. But however genuine their patriotism might be, urban wage laborers were undoubtedly prone to be treated as second-class citizens. After 1890, workers became aware of their own powers. Spectacular electoral successes and huge increases in trade union membership were recorded in the same period, and a more pragmatic approach began to be characteristic of spokesmen of German labor and of some authorities. In south Germany, socialism was less militant than in Prussia or Saxony, for in the south a socialist was not some bogeyman, known only from reports, speeches, or caricatures in the middle-class press. Rather he was someone you might find yourself sitting beside in the *Landtag* or state parliament, in the town council or school board, even at the next table to your own in the local inn.

Rural workers and domestic servants: (i) Household servants

The vast mass of rural laborers in Wilhelmine Germany remained without contact with the socialist movement and lacked organizations of their own. The same was true of domestic servants, who in this bourgeois age remained a substantial numerical group. The most striking development to affect indoor household servants in nineteenth-century Germany was that they became a predominantly female group in the labor force. This process was also associated with greater differentiation within the profession and a drop in the status of the majority. Looking at the names and origins of domestic servants in records dating from the early decades of the century, one notices a large proportion of petty bourgeois among them. For many servant girls, service was a stage in their formation before marriage to a man of their class. By the end of the century, however, the servant in a bourgeois household was more likely to be of proletarian origin, the daughter of a poor rural laborer who came to the city in search of work. Manservants in the later nineteenth century tended to enjoy status, to be liveried servants with training as coachman, groom, personal valet, not to speak of *Haushofmeister* or butler. These, like the housekeeper or

The employment agency for domestic servants. Engraving (1889).

the cook in upper class and wealthy households, were as far removed, in their own eyes as well in those of their employers, from the "skivvy" in the kitchen, who slept in the notorious hammocks or cupboards above the stove in the kitchen, and whom we encounter in the novels of Gutzkow and Fontane.

Servants did not feel the same kind of class solidarity which factory workers did. They also moved about much less than industrial workers. Exploitation of domestic servants was a widespread phenomenon in Europe generally, and little of it was recorded in memoirs. Such texts as did advertise themselves around 1900 as such prove, on closer examination, not to be authentic. Such exploitation did not lead to rebelliousness. A much-commented exception was the street demonstration by Berlin housemaids in the summer of 1899 against their dismissal from their posts by their employers in order to save money when these employers were out of town. Most servants in bourgeois households were socially isolated, had little free time, and their legal position was especially disadvantageous. They were subject to servant ordinances, or *Gesindeordnungen*, a survival from the old corporate society.

These ordinances were reenacted throughout the century, in "free" Hamburg as late as the end of the century. They denied rural and household servants direct access to the law, subordinating them instead to the police. The provisions of Bismarck's social insurance legislation did not apply to them. Moreover the poor educational background of the majority of household servants acted as a barrier to awakening self-awareness, a trend encouraged by the types of literature marketed to them, pious Christian literature and sentimental novels of escapism. On the other hand there were some who saw the advantages of their position; many believed that service enhanced their chance of marriage. Toward the end of the century and in the early years of the new century, various agencies, including the churches and the Social Democratic party at their Erfurt party conference, belatedly agitated for the extension of worker protection to outdoor and indoor servants. In the case of the former, the work done by Max Weber and his colleagues on the situation of the rural laborers in East Elbia provided a powerful stimulus to debate. A peculiarity of the female servants' organizations, which were set up with the assistance of the local clergy in Bavaria and Baden after 1900, was the role of the women themselves in the administration and management of their associations. By the eve of the war, and although the *Gesindeordnungen* or servants ordinances were not repealed until the Revolution of 1918 (in Austria only in 1926), the term *Hausgesinde* (household servants) or *Dienstbote* was gradually giving way to the more euphemous *Hausgehilfe* (household assistant). Here too, although belatedly, we find a trend toward the professionalization of work, which was evident elsewhere in late nineteenth-century Germany.

Rural workers and domestic servants: (ii) Rural laborers

The largest social group in German society until the 1890s was that of the rural laborers and smallholders, numerically greatest in the northeast and also in the southwest, where farmland was divided among all the heirs. The agrarian legislation of the late eighteenth and nineteenth century, some of the most incisive and far-reaching laws of modern German history, had had a profound effect on the inhabitants of rural areas. Many of those at the bottom of the social scale lost their traditional rights of grazing an animal or gathering fuel—in other words, a vital source of food and heat. However, the changeover from a natural to a money economy, especially in the manorial lands of eastern Germany, created a demand for their services as day laborers, and this to some extent catered to their needs. In northwest Germany, a long tradition existed of smallholders renting a plot of land from the local farmer and working for him. The same was true of agricultural laborers in Westphalia, who might also ply a trade at home, such as weaving. The agricultural "revolution" began a process of mobilization on the land which led to mass movement of labor from the land, either to the cities or as emigrants to the New World. In the last decades of the century, the flight from the land gathered even greater momentum. The seasonal workers hired by the East Elbian estate owners were prepared to work for minimal wages and to live in conditions not acceptable to Germans. The increase in the number of bourgeois capitalists, who bought up estates of the nobility over the century, had also changed the relationship between landowner and tenant. Capitalist farming did not foster the kind of sense of responsibility for the physical welfare of the rural laborer on which East Elbian noble landowners had traditionally prided themselves. Thus, although there were very great local and regional variations, there was a trend for the so-called agrarian revolution of mid-century to bring about a similar situation as that obtaining between urban capitalists and their employees.

In the last years of the century, which were unfavorable to arable farming, many smallholders and medium farmers found themselves with debts they could not meet. This gave further impetus to the movement from the land and fostered a sense of resentment, frustration, and even conspiracy theory in the farming community, which made its members accessible to political agitators. However, for the peasantry living in regions near growing towns, the second half of the century could provide prosperity through improved markets for their produce. Here innovation and improved productivity were impressive. Regional variations across a country of such geographical variety as Germany were considerable. In Bavaria, for example, primogeniture ensured the survival of a sturdy peasantry, though farm debt was a factor for those living in the less fertile regions, such as the Upper Palatinate. In other states, such as Baden, division of land between all the sons brought impoverishment both to the land and the population. Socially, however, the rural community remained cohesive, where the continued survival of common land helped to offset the difference in status between peasant proprietor and wage laborer in the same village. In the country as a whole, the growth of credit and insurance schemes for farmers and of rural savings banks, as well as the creation of farmers' co-operatives, improved the economic situation of the peasantry in later nineteenth-century Germany. However, it was usually the medium farmers, and not the small-holders, who were in a position to take full advantage of these developments.

The political attitudes of farming communities, however diverse in economic and social character these might be across Germany, tended by and large to approximate those of the conservative ruling classes. Most laborers, especially in the east, had little political awareness, receiving their opinions from the "master" and identifying their interests with his own. In many cases, their parents and grandparents before them had worked on the same estate. The legislation governing the employment of rural workers, as of household servants, the *Gesindeordnungen*, was heavily weighted in favor of the employer. The peasantry and the larger landowners saw the growth of industry and the increasing economic power of new pressure groups in society in terms of a conspiracy against themselves and their way of life. Like the *Kleinbürger*, they felt that their contribution to society and the state in terms of loyalty and work entitled them to special consideration. Here, too, the authorities, whether in terms of fostering good relations with the spokesmen of agriculture or advocating an effective *Mittelstandspolitik*, addressed their concerns in speeches in parliamentary assemblies and on commemorative occasions. In terms of policy, much was simply for public consumption only.

The Jews

It is difficult within the narrow compass of the present work to do justice to Germany's economically and socially diversified Jewish community. Their contribution to German civilization was so immense and many-faceted; moreover, the research done on this roughly one percent of Germany's population is so rich as almost to defy synthesis. But perhaps the key feature of this sector of society in the nineteenth century was the way in which Jews interacted with their Gentile environment. Although, apart from some eastern provinces of Germany and the Austro-Hungarian monarchy, the Jews living in Germany in the second half of the century no longer formed a physically separate and hence easily identifiable group within society; as had been the case for centuries, they retained a distinctive sense of identity.

Father's birthday. Photograph (1880).

The social origin of the Jewish community in Germany was generally of one of three kinds. There were the older established and wealthy families settled in cities, such as Vienna, Frankfurt, Hamburg, and Cologne, connected by marriage with similarly situated Jewish families in Amsterdam, Paris, and Bordeaux. These represented only a small proportion of the community. They were generally Orthodox in the practice of their religion, as was the second group, those poor Jews, tailors, craftsmen, and small traders scattered across the country along with peddlers who purveyed small luxuries to rural communities in the sparsely populated regions of the East. A third group comprised those who, having migrated to Germany from Russia, including Russian Poland, in the later eighteenth and in the nineteenth centuries, had established themselves as merchants, manufacturers, and bankers. They were to be found in substantial numbers in cities and towns such as Berlin, in East Prussia's Königsberg, in Silesia's capital Breslau (Wrocław), in Nuremberg in Franconia, and in Bavaria's Augsburg. Liberal rather than Orthodox, many sent their sons via grammar school and university into the professions. Most of the many German Jews who made a name for themselves in politics or public life generally, as in law, medicine, business, and the arts, were sons and daughters of this group. Thus the lawyer Heinrich Simon (1805–60), who played a prominent role in the 1848 Revolution, and his first cousin, the best-selling novelist Fanny Lewald, were children of merchants in Breslau and Königsberg. The socialist leader Ferdinand Lassalle was a businessman's son from Breslau. The composer Giacomo Meyerbeer (1791–1864), brother of the banker Michael Beer, came from a similar background. The father of Bismarck's banker, Gerson Bleichröder, had worked for the Rothschilds. Bleichröder was one of the few such Jews prominent in public life and the business world not to submit to Christian baptism. Those who did, did so not for reasons of conviction, but to enter certain professions or get around the punitively restrictive legislation which, prior to 1848, limited the number of marriages that a Jewish community, such as those of Frankfurt or Königsberg, might celebrate in any year. How many experienced a crisis of conscience over this decision is hard to ascertain. Certainly Heinrich Heine seemed to trivialize his own baptism into the Protestant church when he called Christian baptism "the entry ticket to European culture." But much of his work and especially his later poetry suggests otherwise. It is clear that the decision to "convert" was less about religion and more about identity, and that it was an issue which the progressive integration of Jews into the rest of German society in the course of the century did not resolve.

The story of the emancipation of the Jews in Germany (including the Austro-Hungarian monarchy) is complex, but well researched. Representatives of the Jewish communities in the city states of Hamburg, Frankfurt, and

Bremen tried and failed at the Congress of Vienna in 1815 to win a general measure regulating the rights and obligations of their people in the new Confederation (1815-67). The real problem was that the Confederation was defined by its creators, who linked it with the restoration of the monarchy, as a "Christian" state. This was explicitly stated in a key paragraph of the founding document, the Viennese *Bundesakte* of 1815. Where did this leave the Jews? The member states of the Confederation took differing views of their obligations—that is if they thought about them at all. Theory and practice also diverged. One minuscule state in Hesse, in central Germany, did not bother to repeal an ancient law classing Jews as outlaws (and therefore to be killed with impunity); the idea that this could actually be acted upon would probably have struck the authorities as absurd. A further serious problem for the future was that the federal states legislated piecemeal to remove disabilities, or even, in a changed political climate, revoked liberal measures in response to public pressure. Civil rights for the Jewish community in Germany were a natural right in this "bourgeois century" for what was in the main an educated, serious, law-abiding social group. Yet the authorities converted that right into "the Jewish problem," *die Judenfrage*. In this it offered certain parallels with the emancipation process of two other, much larger sectors of society, the proletariat and women.

Napoleon had emancipated the Jews in the territories under his rule, but his measures were revoked after his defeat. The Jews in that part of Prussia not occupied by the French, that is to say, in the old provinces in the east, had benefited from Wilhelm von Humboldt's 1812 Edict of Tolerance. When Prussia recovered her western possessions and received a massive addition of territory in Westphalia and the Rhineland, the government failed to apply the Edict's provisions to the substantial Jewish community living here. A generation and a half later, Jews participated prominently in the 1848 Revolution, as members of parliamentary assemblies and as spokesmen of liberal and democratic causes. After the revolution had been defeated, reactionary ministries proved especially vindictive toward Jews, while self-styled spokesmen of progress, such as the journalist and writer, Gustav Freytag, in his influential essay *The Jews of Breslau* (1849), identified Jews with the forces of public disorder. It was only in 1874, as part of a body of liberal legislation accompanying German unification, that outstanding civic and legal disabilities were removed. Liberal Jews, who took a rational, optimistic approach to social and political problems, as befitted their Enlightenment origins, tended to regard the process of emancipation, assimilation, and integration as a matter of time. Many were awakened to the bitter reality of anti-Jewish prejudice at some time in their career. Popular anti-Jewish feeling was a gut reaction, common in time of social and economic dislocation, but bias could be fostered by the authorities, as was a common practice in Tsarist Russia. There was a vicious outbreak of anti-Jewish feeling in parts of southern Germany, notably Bavaria, in the aftermath of the Napoleonic wars. As had so often happened in the past, what became known as the *Hep! Hep!*[3] movement operated as a conditioned reflex to hunger, famine, epidemic, and cattle disease between 1816 and 1819. In the east of Germany and the Austro-Hungarian monarchy, the influence of pogroms unleashed sporadically and often with great violence against the Jewish community in nearby Russia was an ever-present specter. In these regions, the Jewish population was disproportionately high compared with the rest of German-speaking territories: in the towns of mid-century West Prussia, Posen, and in Austrian Galicia it could be as high as 50 percent of the total population. However, this changed radically in the second half of the century, as Jews migrated to the larger cities, and especially to Berlin and Vienna. Many of the poor Jews who had once earned their living as itinerant peddlers settled in the city to work for the burgeoning readymade clothing trade.

The opportunities offered by the German educational system for personal advancement and as a means to gain entry to positions of status in the government service had a special appeal to liberal Jews. Heinrich (Simon) probably chose a career in the civil service, because here it was easiest to hide one's racial origins, wrote a close friend in later life. Such reasoning was fairly typical of first-generation Jews who opted for Christian baptism. Increasing numbers of better-off Jews took advantage of grammar school and university education. Although most encountered endemic prejudice from their Christian environment, they identified themselves more and more with the values of the society in which they lived. Middle-class Jewish homes cultivated classical German literature, patronizing German art and music. Franz Rosenzweig (1886–1929) of Kassel, later a distinguished liberal rabbi, described his home as one where Goethe and Beethoven played a central role, Judaism none at all. In the last decades of the Second Empire, most German Jews identified with nationalist values. The highest legal offices might still be closed to them, despite emancipation, and anti-Semitic prejudice in military circles hidebound (in this, as the Dreyfus case would show so luridly, no different from France). Yet Jews preferred the legal career almost to any other, and many aspired to being officer of the Reserve after finishing military service. (One thinks here of the sympathetic figure of Rubehn, aspiring merchant and lieutenant of the Reserve in Fontane's novel *L'Adultera*.) Liberal Jews tended to acknowledge

---

[3] "Hep" derives from the initials of the Latin tag: [H]ierusalem est perdita! Devastation to Jerusalem!

the existence of vulgar anti-Semitism by associating it with fringe elements in society. But by the 1880s many student fraternities were closed to Jewish students, and the Berlin Anti-Semitic Conflict had dominated headlines in 1879–80, with the holder of the prestigious chair of history, Treitschke, playing a deeply ambivalent leading role. In 1892 the German Conservative party adopted the so-called Tivoli Program, with active discrimination against Jews as part of official policy. One year later the Anti-Semitic party won seventeen seats in the Reichstag elections. Anti-Semitism was by this time regarded by many as both intellectually respectable and socially acceptable, not least because the Kaiser himself, despite his friendship with individual Jews, such as the industrialist Emil Rathenau (1848–1915) and his son, Walther (1867–1922), was prone to vicious outbursts against the Jews.

However, for German Jews in 1900, looking back on the century that had just passed, their history was too persuasive a story of success against the odds not to inspire optimism and confidence in the future, even perhaps complacency. The Jewish community, taken in its broadest sense, could only congratulate itself on what had been achieved. Moreover, those liberal Jews who had long since ceased to practice their faith remained conscious of their obligations to fellow Jews less fortunate than themselves. Family bonds remained strong in this highly mobile society. The old, established families had augmented their wealth and connections in Europe and also overseas, particularly in the United States. The traditional orthodox communities in the east still lived a ghettolike existence, but they continued to produce clever children who won fame and even fortune in the world beyond. For those Jews occupying positions of trust and influence, as bankers and doctors, research scientists, artists, writers, musicians, university teachers, theater managers, and journalists, they knew their race had made an outstanding contribution to the life of the nation. While they retained a general pride in their racial origins, they felt and thought as Germans.

Chapter 14
Germany in 1900—A State to Be Proud of?

Germans' perception of their history in the nineteenth century was, like the century itself, one of overwhelming change. To observers of Germany, it seemed that the German national character had itself undergone a profound metamorphosis between the era of Napoleon and the age of imperialism. Germans used to be regarded by their neighbors with indulgence, even affection, but Germans rightly felt the patronizing tone with which, in particular, the English and the French habitually regarded them. All this had changed by the 1900s, including the Germans' own self-image.

In the early decades of the nineteenth century, articulate Germans had frequently given expression in their letters, diaries, and reminiscences to a sense of hurt and frustration at what they saw as the diminution of their public self, implicit in the fragmented and politically backward state of their country. When they compared themselves to their western neighbors, France, Britain, and the United States, they felt uncomfortable and even embarrassed. In the 1830s and 1840s, German writers and artists popularized a masochistic national stereotype in the figure of *der deutsche Michel*, poor Mick, ineffectual, passive, put upon by others. By contrast with Britain's self-image, John Bull, France's Marianne, or the United States's Uncle Sam, little German Michael was an extraordinarily negative self-image. By 1900, *der deutsche Michel* had faded from memory or had been reinvented as a thrusting, muscular type. In place of self-accusation, Germans liked to focus on what their country had done and become in the century that had just drawn to its close. Even Germany's many critics at home of the political system, social inequities, and embarrassing diplomatic gaffes of their Kaiser, even these Germans could not but share some sense of their country's achievements in the recent past.

Probably the achievement which afforded greatest satisfaction was national unity, but in so many other respects, modern Germany, broadly speaking, won the admiration of its citizens. Most obvious were the spectacular advances made by the economy, which underpinned Germany's status in 1900 as a world power. People took pride also in the provision, impressive by international standards, which the German state now made for the security, health, and mobility of its citizens, and for the education of the nation's children. Famine had haunted European society for centuries, and as late as the mid-1840s the Swiss novelist Gotthelf could paint a graphic picture of rural starvation in his haunting novel, *Käthe die Großmutter*. By the second half of the century, famine (though not severe malnutrition) had become a thing of the past. Where local harvests failed as a result of natural catastrophe, the transport revolution and the growth of the state as a regulatory agent made the market capable of succoring the victims in a way that had not been possible in earlier generations. True, the cholera epidemic in Hamburg in 1892 reminded the authorities as well as the populace of the limits of state (will?) power. But by the end of the decade, effective efforts were being made by many municipal authorities to provide clean water for the nation's city-dwellers, and in subsequent years to start work on modern sewage disposal systems.

Among other benefits of life in the first two decades of Wilhelm II's reign, particularly esteemed by the middle ranks of society, were stable prices, a stable currency, and low tax rates. The working man might rightly feel discriminated against, politically, when he tried to organize to improve his working conditions, socially in terms of his diet and accommodation. Yet by the century's end he, too, was experiencing many of the material benefits of being a German worker, with his steadily rising real wages and low rates of unemployment (around 3 percent) and, thanks to the Bismarckian legislation of the 1880s, the existence of some measure of invalid, accident, and old-age insurance. Between 1871 and 1912 the number of working hours dropped steadily, from something in the region of an average of seventy per week in 1871 to between fifty-four and sixty. Such change might seem cosmetic to us today, but an eight-hour working day was already a policy goal for the Social Democrats from the time of their 1891 Erfurt conference. By 1900 the notion of leisure, alien to most older generations of Germans, had already begun to make its impact on German society. Industry had begun to adapt to leisure, not least in helping to provide cheap transport into the countryside for a Sunday or holiday excursion. By the 1890s, mass production of rubber-tired bicycles was under way in Germany, for women as well as men, for workers as well as burghers.

True, very many Germans were deeply disturbed at the extraordinary rate of growth of German towns and cities in the decades immediately preceding the 1914 war. Wretched living and working conditions were found among the urban and also among the rural poor. But, by contrast with the industrial cities of, say, Great Britain, extensive parts of German cities in the Rhineland and Westphalia, the hub of German heavy industry, could be pleasant places to live in for those with modest incomes, as well as for the well-off. Thanks to Baron Stein's urban reform program back in the early nineteenth century, and rising local taxes in the later decades, Prussian cities had substantial budgets at their disposal, and they invested them in public utilities and in culture. The municipal transport system was well developed and cheap. Much entertainment, such as the parks and military bands, was free, and most major towns had their own subsidized concert halls, museums, and theaters. Because of the regional distribution of Germany's cities and the steady fall in the cost of transport, most urban dwellers had reasonable access to green spaces, both within and outside the city boundaries. City dwellers had their own newspapers and local culture. Even ordinary-sized towns could offer the public heated libraries and reading rooms (such as Fontane's Mathilde Möhring frequented as part of her plan to launch her captive husband on his career). The streets were paved and lit now, though properly organized rubbish disposal remained a dream for many. However, the visible impact of effective government, by the state and municipal authorities, was to be seen almost everywhere. A sense of material well-being was induced by the variety of shops—there were some 450,000 shopkeepers in Germany in the early twentieth century. The goods they offered were affordable to a growing proportion of the populace. They included life-enhancing and labor-saving devices in the home.

And so many things were "made in Germany." This very term became a symbol of material advance and of the change in public perception over the last two generations. At the beginning of the century, to say something was "made in Germany" would have implied that it was perhaps cheap, but certainly inferior. In those days, German manufacture could not hold a candle to that of Britain. As late as 1876, comment was passed on the poor quality of German exhibits at the Pennsylvanian international trade fair. However, by the beginning of the new century, as Germany challenged world competition in a whole variety of industrial goods, from steel, machine tools, and chemicals to precision instruments, pharmaceuticals, and household consumer durables, the label "made in Germany" was the hallmark of international quality. The witty *Simplicissimus* caricature of 1896 not only captured Germans' pride in their nation's achievement but also their characteristic need to reassure themselves by proving Germany better than its arch rival Britain.

The Wilhelmine era, like the emperor Wilhelm II, was a highly self-conscious era. This trend toward performance and metaphorical mirror-gazing, so typical of the Kaiser, was reflected and popularized, as it were, by the media explosion of the century's end. Whether in the form of reports on the debates in the Reichstag or Prussian state parliaments, in the advertisements of the daily and weekly press or the billboards on buildings promoting goods for sale, the hysterical pamphlets of this or that pressure group, the public was continually badgered to respond. Even old Dubslav Stechlin in his broken-down mansion two hours north of Berlin complains at the advertisements

"The English sword." "Oh if it had been 'made in Germany' it would have lasted better!" Drawing by Th. Th. Heine from *Simplicissimus*

which the daily post brings into his rural retreat. The Wilhelmine era marked the beginning of the age of mass democracy. Mass sport and mass entertainment, too, were the product of these years, typified in the new popular medium, the cinema, and in the fashion for the circus. Before the century's end, football had made its appearance as a new national sport. The German Football Federation was founded in 1899 and the first national championships staged in 1907. The end of a century seems to stimulate people's appetite for prophecy about the future, nostalgia for the past. German newspapers and journals cashed in by conducting an endless round of surveys, and canvassing writers (Fontane was one of them) for their views. In doing so, they clearly caught the public imagination. Some of their findings, such as those of the 1900 survey conducted by the popular newspaper, the *Berliner Illustrirte*, make fascinating reading, such as that "the greatest woman of the nineteenth century" was the Prussian queen Louise, who died in 1810, with the octogenarian but still living Queen Victoria coming only a poor second.

The modernization of the economy promoted information gathering at virtually every level. The introduction of regular censuses from 1869 onward marked a general trend of modern societies to solicit ever more information from the citizenry. The census also spawned a need for ever-growing numbers of minor officials to process the data. If the effect was to increase the regulatory powers of the state, such activities raised expectations among the public. They began to want more and more of their state. In early twentieth-century England, as A. J. P. Taylor wrote in the opening page of his *History of England 1914–1945* (Oxford 1965), the average citizen only noticed the state when he went to post a letter or saw a policeman on the street. In Germany it was quite different. For centuries Germans had been accustomed to the interference of the state in their lives. The system's critics were vociferous about the "nanny state," but probably a large proportion of the population took for granted and even appreciated the paternalist culture in which they had grown up. It made them feel safe.

However, as popular expectations grew and, when, after the outbreak of war in 1914, controls became more stringent, neither the public nor the state grasped a salient fact: namely, that the state's capacity to respond to major social and economic crises was limited, especially on the scale created by the war and its consequences. Not the least cause of the deep psychological crisis of post-1918 Germany, as the Nazis so intuitively and uniquely recognized, were the unrealistic expectations placed by ordinary Germans in the state's power to change and ameliorate their lot.

The Second German Empire and, in particular, the years of Wilhelm II's rule, have been for more than two generations the target of intensive analysis by historians and literary historians, largely because of the causal links postulated in the historiography of post-1945 Germany, between the failings of the Second Empire and the horrors of the Third Reich. In more recent years, historians, among them the authors of important general histories of nineteenth-century Germany, such as James J. Sheehan and David Blackbourn, have helped readers to begin to see the period more on its own terms, rather than primarily through the prism of post-Holocaust Germany. They too, like Gordon A. Craig, and Fritz Stern, American historians born in Europe, have made sensitive use of literature to help us understand the mind of the time.

For the student of literature, the Wilhelmine era is a fascinating period, but one full of contradictions. Why, for example, was it that the writers who in their day enjoyed great material success and even imperial patronage, are now so little regarded? The forgotten idols of their day include the first German Nobel Prize winner, Paul Heyse, the best-selling novelist Friedrich Spielhagen, and the court dramatist, Anton von Wildenbruch, himself an illegitimate scion of the ruling Prussian house of Hohenzollern. What was the appeal to German readers around 1900 of the hugely popular literary nostalgia industry, known as *Heimatliteratur* or literature about one's region? Why did Germans seem to want to reject or block out the process of urbanization and industrialization which they were witnessing, while still wishing to enjoy its many benefits?

More cogently for modern students of German literature, why is it that the writers of late imperial Germany whom we study today in our universities as the leading figures of the age, such as the naturalist dramatist Gerhart Hauptmann, the realist novelists Theodor Fontane or Wilhelm Raabe, or the Expressionist poets, made at the time much less impact on the public consciousness? These and others, such as Franz Wedekind, the Mann brothers, Carl Sternheim, Hermann Hesse, or Gottfried Benn (1886–1956), medical doctor and poet, offered an extraordinarily diverse critique of their world, marked by irony and satire, or, as in the case of the Expressionists, by anger and terror. These writers interacted continually with one another, and their works were vigorously read and debated in the columns of the great literary journals of the day, in the theater foyers, and in the cafés and bars of Berlin, Vienna, Munich, Leipzig, and Hamburg. But the public did not buy them in anything like the quantities they did the modish and now forgotten authors. Most of the writers we read today, and the great critics of that age, such as Maximilian Harden, Otto Brahm (1856–1912), or, in Vienna, Karl Kraus, felt outsiders in their own world. This was more marked in the German Empire than in the Austro-Hungarian monarchy, which had a long-established tradition of metropolitan satire, as in Vienna, Prague, and Budapest. As the Prussian novelist Fontane put it in his scathing essay of 1891, "The Situation of the Writer in Our Times," many writers felt and were excluded because they lacked the *staatliche Etikettierung*, the label of state approval, which guaranteed monetary reward along with social status. Broadly speaking, their more successful contemporaries tended to view them as critical eccentrics, regarding their views as exaggerated and themselves as out of touch with the times.

The fundamental difference between these two broad categories of literature, is that the one was socially and politically affirmative in character. It enduced and encouraged a passive readership or audience, who approved of the status quo, of the way things were. By contrast, the critical, reflective character of the second group aimed specifically to challenge and disturb the reader's certainties; active participation by the public was, in their view, a necessary prelude to change. Even the Prague-born poet Rainer Maria Rilke (1875–1926), who was neither ironic nor satiric nor angry, offered in the corpus of his poetry as well as in his philosophical novel *Malte Laurids Brigge* and in his letters, an alternative way of looking at society, which spoke to the minds and hearts of those disturbed by the values of contemporary society. Literature, like music and art, tried to mediate change in different ways. The affirmative artists appeared to provide their public with an alternative escape or 'safe haven' of the imagination, with the implied suggestion that the authorities would shield the people from the disturbing aspects of change. Modern, critical writers and artists demanded of their public that they actually engage with the very different world in which they were living; that they themselves develop strategies for dealing with it. It is hardly surprising that the second alternative was not popular. At the same time, the immense acceleration of the pace of change and awareness of it in the population created a restlessness among the populace generally, which is a key characteristic of Germany in the prewar years—and which makes this period one of the most fascinating for students of modern Germany, students of political, social, and economic history, and, not least, for students of literature and culture.

Some Suggestions for Further Reading

Students today are fortunate to have easy access to good general histories of nineteenth-century Germany in English (or English translation), with bibliographies, notably:

Berghahn, Volker R. *Germany and the Approach of War in 1914* Basingstoke: Macmillan 1993.

Blackbourn, David *The Long Nineteenth Century 1770-1918. The Fontana History of Germany* London: Fontana 1997. (Has a particularly good index.)

——— and Geoff Eley eds. *The Peculiarities of German History. Bourgeois Society and Politics in Nineteenth-Century Germany* Oxford: Oxford University Press 1984.

Chickering, Roger *Imperial Germany. A Historiographical Companion* Westport, Ct.: Greenwood Press 1996.

Craig, Gordon A. *The Germans* Harmondsworth: Penguin 1978.

———*Germany 1866-1945* Oxford: Clarendon Press 1981.

Fulbrook, Mary ed. *German History since 1800* London: Edward Arnold 1997.

Mommsen, Wolfgang J. *Imperial Germany 1870-1914. Politics, Culture and Society in an Authoritarian State* London, New York: Edward Arnold 1995.

Nipperdey, Thomas *Deutsche Geschichte 1866-1918* 2 vols (1: *Arbeitswelt und Bürgergeist*; 2: *Machtstaat vor der Demokratie*) Munich: C.H. Beck 1990-2.

——— *Germany from Napoleon to Bismarck, 1800-1866* Dublin: Gill and Macmillan 1995.

Ramm, Agatha *Germany 1789-1919. A Political History* London: Methuen 1967.

Sagarra, Eda *A Social History of Germany 1648-1914* London: Methuen 1977.

———and Peter Skrine *A Companion to German Literature* Oxford: Blackwell 1997.

Schröder, Paul *The Transformation of European Politics, 1763-1848* Oxford: Clarendon Press 1984.

Sheehan, James J. *German History, 1770-1866* Oxford: Clarendon Press 1989.

Simms, Brendan *The Struggle for Mastery in Europe, 1779-1850* (European History in Perspective) London: Macmillan Press 1998. (Has a well-focused, student-friendly bibliographical essay.)

Sked, Alan *The Decline and Fall of the Habsburg Empire 1815-1918* London: Longman 1989.

Watanabe-O'Kelly, Helen ed. *The Cambridge History of German Literature* Cambridge: Cambridge University Press 1997.

Wehler, Hans-Ulrich *The German Empire 1871-1918* Leamington Spa: Berg 1989.

———*Deutsche Gesellschaftsgeschichte* 3 vols Munich: C. H. Beck 1987-95. (Dense and not very well organized, but immensely informative.)

Chapters 1 & 2

Berdahl, Robert M. *The Politics of the Prussian Nobility. The Development of a Conservative Ideology, 1770-1848* Princeton NJ: Princeton University Press 1988.

Blanning, Timothy C. W. *The French Revolution in Germany. Occupation and Resistance in the Rhineland 1792-1802* Oxford: Clarendon Press 1983.

——*The French Revolutionary Wars 1787-1802* London: Arnold 1996.

Ingrao, Charles *The Habsburg Monarchy 1618-1815* (New Approaches to European History 3) Cambridge: Cambridge University Press 1984.

Kraehe, Enno E. *Metternich's German Policy*. Vol. 1: *The Contest with Napoleon* Princeton NJ: Princeton University Press 1963.

Saul, Nicholas D. B. "Aesthetic Humanism 1770-1830." In: Watanabe-O'Kelly ed. *The Cambridge History of German Literature*, 202-271. Cambridge: Cambridge University Press 1997.

Simms, Brendan *The Impact of Napoleon. Prussian High Politics, Foreign Policy and Executive Reform* Cambridge: Cambridge University Press 1997.

——*The Struggle for Mastery in Europe 1779-1850* (European History in Perspective) London: Macmillan Press 1998.

Whaley, Joachim "The Habsburg Legacy. National Identity in Historical Perspective." In: *Austrian Studies 5*, edited by Ritchie Robertson and Edward Timms, 2-12. Edinburgh: Edinburgh University Press 1994.

Chapters 3 & 4

Angermann, Erich "Germany's 'Peculiar Institution', the Beamtentum." In: *Oceans Apart? Comparing Germany and the United States*, edited by Erich Angermann and Marie-Luise Frings, 77-107. Stuttgart: Klett-Cotta 1981.

Bade, Klaus J. ed. *Population, Labour and Migration in 19th and 20th Century Germany* Leamington Spa: Berg 1987. (Especially chapters by Bade, Dieter Langewiesche/ Friedrich Lenger, and Peter Marschalck.)

Blackbourn, David and Richard J. Evans eds *The German Bourgeoisie. Essays on the Social History of the German Middle Class from the Eighteenth to the Early Twentieth Century* London: Routledge 1991.

Blanning, Timothy C. W. "Empire and State in Germany, 1648-1848." In: *German History* 12 (1994), 220-236.

Conze, Werner "Vom »Pöbel« zum »Proletariat«. Sozialgeschichtliche Voraussetzungen für den Sozialismus in Deutschland," 136-167. In: Hans-Ulrich Wehler ed. *Moderne deutsche Sozialgeschichte* (Neue Wissenschaftliche Bibliothek) Cologne: Kiepenheuer & Witsch 1966.

Evans, Richard J. ed. *The German Working Class. The Politics of Everyday Life* London: Croom Helm 1982.

——and W. R. Lee eds *The German Family. Essays on the Social History of the Family in Nineteenth- and Twentieth-Century Germany* London: Croom Helm 1981.

―――― *The German Peasantry. Conflict and Community in Rural Society from the Eighteenth to the Twentieth Centuries* London: Croom Helm 1986.

Fremdling, Rainer "Railroads and German Economic Growth." In: *Journal of Economic History* 37 (1977), 583-604.

Hull, Isabel *Sexuality, State and Civil Society in Germany, 1700-1815* Ithaca NY & London: Cornell University Press 1996.

Imhof, Arthur *Life Expectancies in Germany from the 17th to the 19th Century* Weinheim: VCH Acta Humaniorum 1990.

Katz, Jakob *Out of the Ghetto. the Social Background of Jewish Emancipation, 1770-1870* Cambridge MA: Harvard University Press 1974.

Kitchen, Martin *The Political Economy of Germany 1815-1914* London: Croom Helm 1978.

Lauster, Martina ed. *Vormärzliteratur in europäischer Perspektive*. 3 vols: I, Helmut Koopmann and Martina Lauster eds *Öffentlichkeit und nationale Identität*; II, Martina Lauster and Günter Oesterle eds *Politische Revolution—Industrielle Revolution—Ästhetische Revolution*; III, Martina Lauster ed. *Zwischen Daguerrotyp und Idee* Bielefeld: Aisthesis 1996, 1998, 2000.

Moeller, Robert G. ed. *Peasants and Lords in Modern Germany. Recents Studies in Agricultural History* Boston MA and London: Allen & Unwin 1986. (Especially introduction and chapters by Hanna Schissler, Hans-Jürgen Puhle, and Ian Farr.)

Ogilvie, Sheilagh and Markus Cerman eds *European Proto-industrialisation* Cambridge: Cambridge University Press 1996.

Pollard, Sidney *European Economic Integration, 1815-1970* London: Thames & Hudson 1974.

Pounds, Norman G. *An Historical Geography of Europe* Cambridge: Cambridge University Press 1990.

Sorkin, David *The Transformation of European Jewry 1780-1840* Oxford: Oxford University Press 1987.

Walker, Mack *German Home Towns. Community, State and General Estate, 1648-1871* Ithaca NY: Cornell University Press 1971.

Wülfing, Wulf "Bahnhofsperspektiven im Vormärz." In: Lauster and Oesterle (1998), 131-42.

Chapter 5

Blackbourn, David *The Long Nineteenth Century 1770-1918. The Fontana History of Germany* London: Fontana 1997.

Sheehan, James J. *German Liberalism in the Nineteenth Century* Chicago: University of Chicago Press 1978.

―――― *German History 1770-1866* Oxford: Oxford University Press 1989, 655-729.

Siemann, Wolfram *The German Revolution of 1848-49* London: Macmillan Press 1998. (With helpful bibliography.)

Sperber, Jonathan *Rhineland Radicals. The Democratic Movement and the Revolution of 1848-1849* Princeton NJ: Princeton University Press 1991.

―――― *The European Revolutions, 1848-1851* Cambridge: Cambridge University Press 1994.

Chapter 6

Berdahl, Robert M. "New Thoughts on German Nationalism." In: *American Historical Review* 77/1 (1972), 65-80.

Breuilly, John ed. *The State of Germany. the National Idea in the Making, Unmaking and Remaking of a Modern State* Basingstoke: Macmillan 1992.

Hobsbawm, Eric J. *The Age of Capital 1848-1875* London: Weidenfeld & Nicolson 1995.

Hughes, Michael *Nationalism and Society. Germany 1800-1945* London: Arnold 1988.

Paret, Peter *Art as History. Episodes in the Culture and Politics of Nineteenth Century Germany* Princeton NJ: Princeton University Press 1988.

Schleunes, Karl A. *Schooling and Society* New York: Berg 1989.

Schulze, Hagen ed. *Nation-building in Central Europe* Leamington Spa: Berg 1987.

—— *The Course of German Nationalism from Frederick the Great to Bismarck, 1763-1867* Cambridge: Cambridge University Press 1991.

Siemann, Wolfram *Gesellschaft im Aufbruch. Deutschland 1849-1871* (Neue Historische Bibliothek) Frankfurt/M: Suhrkamp 1990.

Chapter 7

Breuilly, John *The Formation of the First German Nation-State 1800-1871* (Studies in European History) New York and Basingstoke: Macmillan 1996. (Especially for its succinct overview of the German wars of unification in the European diplomatic context.)

Craig, Gordon A. *The Battle of Königgrätz. Prussia's Victory over Austria, 1866* London: Weidenfeld & Nicolson 1965.

Hamerow, Theodor S. *The Social Foundations of German Unification, 1858-71* 2 vols Princeton NJ: Princeton University Press 1969-72.

Mosse, Werner E. *The European Powers and the German Question, 1848-7, with Special Reference to England and Russia* Cambridge: Cambridge University Press 1958.

Pflanze, Otto *Bismarck and the Development of Modern Germany* 3 vols Princeton NJ: Princeton University Press 1990.

Sheehan, James J. *German History, 1770-1866* Oxford: Clarendon 1989.

Siemann, Wolfram *Gesellschaft im Aufbruch. Deutschland 1849-1871* (Neue Historische Bibliothek) Frankfurt/M: Suhrkamp 1990.

Tilly, Richard "The Take-off in Germany." In: Erich Angermann and Marie-Luise Frings eds *Oceans Apart? Comparing Germany and the United States*, 47-59 Stuttgart: Klett-Cotta 1981.

Chapter 8

Becker, Eva D. *Literarisches Leben. Umschreibungen der Literaturgeschichte* (Saarbrücker Beiträge zur Literaturwissenschaft) edited by Karl Richter, Gerhard Sauder, and Gerhard Schmidt-Henkel. St. Ingbert: Röhrig Universitätsverlag 1994.

——— "Literaturverbreitung." In: Edward McInnes and Gerhard Plumpe eds *Bürgerlicher Realismus und Gründerzeit 1848-1890*, 108-430. (Hansers Sozialgeschichte der deutschen Literatur vol. 6) Munich: Hanser 1996.

Boetcher-Joeres, Ellen and Mary Jo Maynes eds *German Women in the Eighteenth and Nineteenth Centuries* Bloomington: University of Indiana Press 1986.

Brinker-Gabler, Gisela ed. *Deutsche Literatur von Frauen*, vol. 2, Munich: C. H. Beck 1988.

Freydank, Ruth *Theater in Berlin. Von den Anfängen bis 1945* Berlin: Aufbau 1988.

Martino, Alberto *Die deutsche Leihbibliothek. Geschichte einer literarischen Institution (1756-1914)* (Beiträge zum Buch- und Bibliothekswesen vol. 29) Wiesbaden: Harrasowitz 1990.

Osborne, John *The Meiningen Court Theatre 1866-1890* Cambridge: Cambridge University Press 1988.

Rossbacher, Karlheinz *Literatur und Liberalismus. Zur Kultur der Ringstraßenzeit in Wien* (especially 79-113) Vienna: J&V 1993.

Sagarra, Eda *Tradition and Revolution. German Literature and Society 1830-1890* New York: Harper 1971.

——— "The German Woman Writer 1900-1933. Socio-Political Context and Literary Market." In: Brian Keith-Smith ed. *German Women Writers 1900-1933. Twelve Essays*, 1-22. Lewiston: Edwin Mellen Press 1993.

——— and Peter Skrine *A Companion to German Literature* (especially 123-183) Oxford: Blackwell 1997.

Schieth, Lydia *Die Entwicklung des deutschen Frauenromans im ausgehenden 18. Jahrhundert. Ein Beitrag zur Gattungsgeschichte* (Beiträge zur deutschen Literatur vol. 5) Frankfurt/ M.: Peter Lang 1987.

Wittmann, Reinhard *Buchmarkt und Lektüre im 18. und 19. Jahrhundert* Tübingen: Niemeyer 1982.

Yates, W. Edgar *Theatre in Vienna. A Critical History 1776-1995* Cambridge: Cambridge University Press 1996.

Chapter 9

Albisetti, James C. *Secondary School Reform in Wilhelmine Germany* Princeton NJ: Princeton University Press 1983.

Allen, A. T. *Feminism and Motherhood in Germany* New Brunswick NJ: Rutgers University Press 1991.

Bebel, August *Woman in the Past, Present, and the Future* London: Zwan 1988.

Boetcher-Joeres, Ellen and Mary Jo Maynes eds *German Women in the Eighteenth and Nineteenth Centuries* Bloomington: University of Indiana Press 1986.

Brinker-Gabler, Gisela ed. *Deutsche Literatur von Frauen* vol. 2 Munich: C. H. Beck 1988.

Evans, Richard J. *The German Feminist Movement 1894-1933* London: Sage 1976.

Fout, John C. ed. *German Women in the Nineteenth Century. A Social History* New York and London: Schocken Books 1984.

Frevert, Ute *Women in German History. From Bourgeois Emancipation to Sexual Liberation* Oxford and Providence: Berg 1990.

Hausen, Karin ed. *Frauen suchen ihre Geschichte* Munich: C. H. Beck 1987. (Especially the introduction by Hausen and essays by Regina Schulte, Dorothee Wierling, Ute Gerhard, and Irene Stoehr.)

——"Technical Progress and Women's Labor in the Nineteenth Century. The Social History of the Sewing Machine." In: George G. Iggers ed. *The German Conception of History*, 259-81. Middletown: Wesleyan University Press 1983.

Huber, Therese *Briefe. Band I: 1774-1803* Tübingen: Niemeyer 1999.

Kall, Alfred *Katholische Frauenbewegung in Deutschland. Eine Untersuchung zur Gründung katholischer Frauenvereine im 19. Jahrhundert* (Beiträge zur Katholizismusforschung) Paderborn: Schöningh 1983.

Sagarra, Eda "Rückert's *Kindertotenlieder*." In: Gillian Avery and Kimberley Reynolds eds, 154-167. London: Macmillan 1999.

Chapter 10

Anderson, Margaret L. "The Kulturkampf and the Course of German History." In: *Central European History* 19 (1986), 82-115.

Blackbourn, David *Populists and Patricians* London: Allen and Unwin 1987.

——— *Marpingen. Apparitions of the Virgin Mary in Bismarckian Germany* Oxford: Clarendon Press 1994. (Despite the seemingly narrow focus of the title, an outstanding book on Bismarckian Germany.)

Craig, Gordon A. *The Politics of the Prussian Army, 1640-1945* Oxford: Clarendon Press 1955.

Gall, Lothar *Bismarck, the White Revolutionary* 2 vols London: Allen & Unwin 1986.

Geiss, Imanuel *German Foreign Policy, 1871-1914* London: Routledge & Kegan Paul 1976.

Pflanze, Otto *Bismarck and the Development of Modern Germany*, 3 vols Princeton NJ: Princeton University Press 1990.

Sheehan, James J. *German History, 1770-1866* Oxford: Clarendon 1989.

Sperber, Jonathan *Popular Catholicism in Nineteenth-Century German* Princeton NJ: Princeton University Press 1984.

Stern, Fritz J. *Gold and Iron. Bismarck, Bleichröder and the Building of the German Empire* London: George Allen & Unwin 1977.

Chapter 11

(For this and the following chapter see bibliography in David Blackbourn *The Long Nineteenth Century 1770-1918. The Fontana History of Germany* London: Fontana 1997, 538-545.)

Anderson, Margaret Lavinia "Voter, Junker, *Landrat*, Priest. The Old Authorities and the New Franchise in Imperial Germany." In: *American Historical Journal* 98 (1993), 1448-74.

Berghahn, Volker R. *Germany and the Approach of War in 1914* Basingstoke: Macmillan 1993.

Burns, Rob ed. *German Cultural Studies. An Introduction* Oxford: Oxford University Press 1995.

Cecil, Lamar *Kaiser Wilhelm II* 2 vols Chapel Hill N. Carolina: University of North Carolina Press 1989-1996.

Eley, Geoff *Reshaping the German Right. Radical Nationalism and Politician Change after Bismarck:* Yale and New Haven: Yale University Press 1980.

Evans, Richard J. ed. *Society and Politics in Wilhelmine Germany* London: Croom Helm 1978.

——*Rethinking German History* London: Allen and Unwin 1987.

—— *The German Underworld. Deviants and Outcasts in German History* London: Routledge 1988.

Fischer, Fritz *War of Illusions. German Foreign Policy 1911 to 1914* London: Chatto & Windus 1975.

Frevert, Ute *Men of Honour. A Social and Cultural History of the Duel* Cambridge: Polity 1995.

Gay, Ruth *The Jews of Germany* New Haven: Yale University Press 1992.

Geary, Dick *Karl Kautsky* Manchester: Manchester University Press 1987. (This succinct study is also an informed source of information on the Social Democrats during the later Wilhelmine period.)

Hull, Isabel *The Entourage of Kaiser Wilhelm II* Cambridge: Cambridge University Press 1982.

Jones, Larry E. and James N. Retallack eds *Elections, Mass Politics and Social Change in Imperial Germany. New Perspectives* Cambridge and New York: Cambridge University Press 1992.

Miller, Susanne and Heinrich Potthoff *A History of the German Social Democracy from 1848 to the Present* Leamington Spa: Berghahn 1986. (Includes a useful document section.)

Mommsen, Wolfgang J. *Max Weber and German Politics* Chicago: Chicago University Press 1984.

——*Imperial Germany 1870-1914. Politics, Culture and Society in an Authoritarian State* London, New York: Edward Arnold 1995.

Retallack, James *Notables of the Right* London: Hyman 1988.

―― ed. *Germany in the Age of Kaiser Wilhelm II* (Studies in European History) New York: St Martin's Press 1996.

Röhl, John C. G. *The Kaiser and his Court. Wilhelm II and the Government of Germany* Cambridge and New York: Cambridge University Press 1994.

―― and Nicolaus Sombart eds *Kaiser Wilhelm II. New Interpretations* Cambridge: Cambridge University Press 1982.

Schorske, Carl E. *German Social Democracy 1905-1917* Cambridge Mass: Harvard University Press 1955.

Sperber, Jonathan *The Kaiser's Voters. Electors and Elections in Imperial Germany* Cambridge: Cambridge University Press 1997.

Suvall, Stanley *Electoral Politics in Wilhelmine Germany* Chapel Hill N. Carolina: University of North Carolina Press 1985.

Chapters 12, 13 & 14

See also bibliography under chapters 3 and 4.

Applegate, Celia *A Nation of Provincials. The German Idea of Heimat* Berkeley California: University of California 1990.

Beller, Steven *Vienna and the Jews, 1867-1938. A Cultural History* Cambridge: Cambridge University Press 1989.

Blessing, Werner K. "The Cult of Monarchy. Political Loyalty and the Workers' Movement in Imperial Germany." In: *Journal of Contemporary History* 13 (1978), 357-75.

Bucholz, Arden *Moltke, Schlieffen and Prussian War Planning* Providence and Oxford: Berg 1991.

Evans, Richard J. *Death in Hamburg. Society and Politics in the Cholera Years, 1830-1920* Oxford: Clarendon Press 1987.

―― "Proletarian mentalities. Pub conversations in Hamburg." In: *Proletarians and Politics. Socialism, Protest and the Working Class in Germany before the First World War* London: Harvest Wheatsheaf 1990.

Horne, John and Alan Kramer *German Atrocities in 1914. Meanings and Memories of War* Cambridge Mass: Harvard University Press 2001. (A pioneering study on mentalities, politics and the army.)

Jeismann, Michael *Das Vaterland der Feinde. Studien zum nationalen Feindbegriff und Selbstverständnis in Deutschland und Frankreich 1792-1918* Stuttgart: Klett-Cotta 1992.

Jones, Larry E. and James N. Retallack eds *Elections, Mass Politics and Social Change in Imperial Germany. New Perspectives* Cambridge and New York: Cambridge University Press 1992.

Kaplan, Marion A. *The Making of the Jewish Middle Class. Women, Family and Identity in Imperial Germany* New York: Oxford University Press 1991.

Klüger, Ruth *Katastrophen. Über deutsche Literatur* Göttingen: Wallstein Verlag 1994.

Kocka, Jürgen ed. *Bürger und Bürgerlichkeit im 19. Jahrhundert. Deutschland im europäischen Vergleich* 3 vols Munich: Deutscher Taschenbuchverlag 1988.

Ladd, Brian *Urban Planning and Civic Order in Germany, 1860-1914,* Cambridge Mass: Harvard University Press 1990.

Lee, W. R. ed. *German Industry and German Industrialisation* London: Routledge 1990.

Lütge, Fredrich *Die Geschichte der deutschen Agrarverfassung vom frühen Mittelalter bis zum 19. Jahrhundert* 2. ed. Stuttgart: Gustav Fischer 1967.

Mosse, Werner E. *Jews in the German Economy* Oxford: Clarendon Press 1987.

Nipperdey, Thomas *Deutsche Geschichte 1866-1918* Munich: C.H. Beck 1990. (See especially vol. I, 531-601.)

Pascal, Roy *From Naturalism to Expressionism. German Literature and Society 1880-1914* London: Weidenfeld and Nicolson 1978.

Pulzer, Peter G. J. *Jews and the German State 1848-1933* Oxford: Blackwell 1992.

Retallack, James *Notables of the Right* London: Hyman 1988.

Ringer, Fritz K. *The Decline of the German Mandarins. The German Academic Community, 1890-1933* Cambridge Mass and London: Harvard University Press 1969. (Classic work on universities and intellectuals.)

Roseman, Mark *Generations in Conflict. Youth Revolt and Generation Formation in Germany, 1770-1968* Cambridge: Cambridge University Press 1995.

Sagarra, Eda "Fürsorgliche Obrigkeit und Lebenswirklichkeit. Die katholischen Dienstbotenzeitschriften in Deutschland 1830-1900." In: Martin Huber and Gerhard Lauer eds *Bildung und Konfession. Politik, Religion und literarische Identitätsbildung 1850-1918.* (Studien und Texte zur Sozialgeschichte der Literatur vol. 59) (Festschrift für Wolfgang Frühwald), 95-106. Tübingen: Niemeyer 1996.

Stern, Fritz *The Politics of Cultural Despair* Berkeley California: University of California Press 1974.

Tipton, Frank B. *Regional Variations in the Economic Development of Germany during the Nineteenth Century* Middletown, Ct.: Wesleyan University Press 1976.

Walker, Mack *Germany and the Emigration 1816-85* Cambridge Mass: Cornell University Press 1964.

Wistrich, Robert S. *The Jews of Vienna in the Age of Franz-Joseph* Oxford: Published for the Littmann Library by Oxford University Press 1989.

Index

Aachen, 40, 256
Abitur, 62, 163
absolutism, 27, 49, 81, 87, 190
actors, 48
Agrarian League, 200, 210, 222f, 249
agriculture, 31, 33, 110, 116, 158, 207, 236–8, 250, 266-8
Albert, Prince Consort, 77, 197
Alexander I, Tsar, 19
Allgemeine deutsche Bibliothek, 144
Allgemeine Zeitung, 141, 147
Allgemeiner Arbeiterverein (General Workers' Association), 202
Allgemeiner Deutscher Frauenverein, 166
almanacs, 49, 58, 134, 145, 172
Alsace-Lorraine, 52, 130f, 183f, 190f, 203, 211
Altenberg, Peter, 143
Amsterdam, 61
  Jews in, 269
Anhalt, 184
anthropology, 133
anti-Semitism, 195, 215, 223, 255, 271f
aristocracy. See nobility
army. See military
Arndt, Ernst Moritz, 6, 100, 106
Arnim, Achim von, 6, 49, 54
Arnim, Bettine von, 54, 68f, 156, 173f
artisans, 13, 69, 75, 104, 155, 258f, 260
associations, 20, 71, 81, 86, 90, 92, 114, 118, 167, 185, 201f, 211, 222, 228f, 266
Aston, Louise, 57, 67, 92, 165
Athenäum, 144

Auer, Ludwig, 141
Auerbach, Berthold, 44, 61, 65, 146, 161, 234
Augsburg, 8, 55, 134, 241, 269
Auguste Viktoria, Empress, 169, 213
Austen, Jane, 50
Austerlitz, 12, 26
Baader, Franz von, 68
Bad Homburg, 202
Baden, 2, 4, 8, 20, 22f, 33, 44, 56, 59, 72, 80, 82f, 85, 89f, 93, 95, 108, 121, 128, 130, 162, 184, 197, 201, 241, 244, 249, 266f
Baden Aniline and Soda Factory (BASF), 241
Baden, Max von, 191
Balzac, Honoré de, 55
Bamberger, Ludwig, 108
banks, bankers, banking, 48, 122, 217, 240, 256, 267, 269, 272
Bassermann, Friedrich Daniel, 85, 108
Bavaria, 4, 20–5, 31, 52, 55, 59, 61, 76f, 85, 108, 117f, 125, 128, 130, 183–85, 196, 213, 235, 241, 249, 266–71
Bebel, August, 64, 91, 161, 189, 194, 200, 203, 205, 230f
Becker, Nikolaus, 105
Becker, Rudolf Zacharias, 138
Beethoven, Ludwig van, 14, 99, 271
Begas, Karl, 152
Belgium, 1, 12, 104, 119
Benn, Gottfried, 278
Bennigsen, Rudolf von, 126, 193, 198

Berlin, 5f, 24f, 34, 39, 44, 49, 52, 55, 60, 62, 69, 73, 77f, 82, 84f, 88, 92–5, 100, 111f, 121–3, 129, 133, 135, 141, 144–6, 159, 162f, 167, 179, 183, 197, 199, 204, 234f, 239, 241, 244, 247, 256, 258, 260, 265, 269, 271f, 278
Berlin, Congress of, 110
Berlin, University of, 6, 10
Berliner Illustrirte Zeitung, 148, 276
Berlinische Monatsschrift, 144
Bernstein, Elsa, 150
Bertuch, Friedrich Justus, 135
Besitzbürgertum, 255–7
  See also bourgeoisie
Bethmann-Hollweg, Theobald, 187, 195, 217, 231
Bible, 60, 134, 137
bicycles, 157, 179, 274
Biedermeier, 39, 49, 60, 61, 157, 161, 174, 176
Bildungsbürgertum, 255
  See also bourgeoisie
Binder, Robert, 140
Birch-Pfeiffer, Charlotte, 150
Bismarck, Otto von, x, 14, 19–21, 26, 40, 52, 86, 94, 96, 108–11, 113, 118f, 121–31, 133, 136, 141, 183, 185, 187f, 191–6, 198f, 201, 203–5, 207–10, 212, 215–7, 220, 228, 230f, 239, 242, 247, 250, 254, 256, 265, 269
Bleichröder, Gerson, 122, 254, 256, 269
Blücher, Gebhart Leberecht, 101
Blum, Robert, 87f, 164
Bohemia, 33, 39, 44, 52, 63, 67, 80f, 84, 94, 124
Böhlau, Helene, 143
Bonaparte. See Napoleon
book fair (Leipzig), 134, 144

book trade, 2, 133–5, 138, 140, 141
Bordeaux
  Jews in, 269
Born, Stephan, 64, 90, 91
Börne, Ludwig, 4, 103, 106
Börsenverein, 134
Borsig, August, 115, 256, 258
Bosch, Robert, 226
bourgeoisie, 3, 11, 17, 25f, 32, 49, 55f, 61, 67, 72, 90f, 110f, 118, 120, 122, 143, 156, 162f, 167, 169f, 177, 179, 187f, 195, 197, 202, 208, 211f, 214, 250f, 254f, 257, 261, 264f, 267, 270. See also *Besitzbürgertum*, *Bildungsbürgertum*, middle classes
Brahm, Otto, 278
Brandenburg, 3, 5, 24, 49, 54, 88, 200, 235
Bremen, xi, 2, 8, 20, 35, 37, 183, 226, 228, 241, 256, 270
Brentano, Clemens, 6, 48f, 54, 56, 150
Breslau, ix, 6, 12f, 59, 74, 100, 106, 202, 239, 241, 269, 270
Brockhaus Encyclopedia, 57
Brockhaus, Friedrich Arnold, 57f, 141f, 153
Brockhaus, publishing house, 171
Brontë, Charlotte, 35
Brunswick, 39, 184
Büchner, Georg, 7, 28, 63
Budapest, 59, 117, 278
Bülow, Bernard von, 191, 195, 205, 212, 216f, 223
Bundestag. See Federal Diet
Burckhardt, Jakob, 14, 102, 133
Bürger, Gottfried August, 137
Burgtheater, 53, 67, 81
Burschenschaften, 103, 105
Byron, Alfred Lord, 35, 103

Calendar für Damen, 138
Calvinism, Calvinists, 126, 256
Camarilla, 95
Campe, Joachim Heinrich, 174
Campe, Julius, 57, 59
Campe, publishers, 57
Camphausen, Ludolf, 89
canals, 35
Cannstadt, 141
capitalism, 202
Caprivi, Leo von, 210f, 223, 229, 250
cartels, 240
Castlereagh, Robert, Viscount, 19
Catholic church, Catholics, 23f, 60, 102, 111, 137, 141, 147, 155, 163, 169, 175, 189, 191, 195, 200f, 203, 207, 213, 223, 242f, 250, 255, 259, 263
Cauer, Minna, 167
Cavaignac, General, 89
CDI, 222–4
censorship, 20, 28, 59, 77, 136, 140, 144, 197
Center party, 191, 194f, 200f, 205, 213, 235, 244, 263
Chamisso, Adelbert von, 42
Charlemagne, 8, 40
Charles X, French king, 27
Chesterton, Gilbert Keith, 167
childcare, 169
children, childhood, 33, 44, 155, 158, 160f, 164, 172–4, 176f, 245, 261
Christmas, 88, 174, 177, 179
churches, 23f, 60, 91, 100, 141, 228, 263, 266, 269. *See also* Catholic church, Protestants
cinema, 180, 276
Civil Code, 135, 170, 251
civil servants, 10, 24, 59, 74, 81, 118, 192, 220, 252, 254f

civil service, 50, 62, 111, 159, 192, 252, 259
Clausewitz, Carl von, 6
clergy. *See* Catholics, Protestants
coal, 33, 39, 118, 238, 240, 242
Coburg, 117
Code Napoléon, 6, 252
Cologne, 1, 34, 40, 57, 90, 92, 102, 141, 169, 202, 244, 256, 269
Colonial League, 229
colporteurs, 138f
communications, 34f, 40, 139, 141, 236, 257. *See also* media, mass
Communist League, 90
Communist Manifesto, 72, 258
Confederation of the Rhine, 4, 8f, 13, 99
Confederation, North German, 125
Conrad, Michael Georg, 146
conscription, 11, 185
conservative parties, 91, 195, 199
constitution, 20, 22, 74, 79, 83–5, 88, 93f, 103, 122, 127, 151, 185f, 191f, 212, 220
Constitutional Conflict, 21, 116, 119f, 126, 185f, 197–9
Conversationslexikon, 58, 153
Cook, Captain, 99
copyright, 135f
Cosmos, 142
Cotta, Friedrich, 57f, 135, 141–5, 147
Cotta, publishing house, 142
counter-revolution, 71, 73, 84, 87–91, 95, 140, 164
Courths-Mahler, Hedwig, 172
craftsmen. *See* artisans
Customs Parliament (*Zollparlament*), 129
Customs Union (*Zollunion*), 37f, 90, 108, 117–9, 130

Czernowitz, 133
Daheim, 172
Dahlmann, Friedrich, 21, 74, 81
Dahn, Felix, 149
Danube, 26, 35, 84, 94, 102, 134, 198
Danzig, 2, 56, 117
Daumier, Henri, 28
day laborers, 66f, 266
Declaration of the Rights of Man, 7
Defense League, 114, 229
Delbrück, Rudolf, 130, 192
demography, 151
Denmark, 40, 76, 83, 85f, 123, 204
Der Kinderfreund, 138, 174
Der Sozialdemokrat, 204
Deutsche Rundschau, 146, 173
Deutscher Michel, 273
Deutschland, Deutschland über alles, 106
Deutschmark, 198
Deutz, 40
Dickens, Charles, 55
Die deutsche Frau, 172
Die Fackel, 146
Die Frau, 169
Die Frau und der Sozialismus, 161
Die Gartenlaube, 146
Die Gesellschaft, 146
Die Gleichheit, 170
Die Zukunft, 146
diet, 46, 154, 224, 236, 245
doctors, 244f, 255, 272
Dohm, Hedwig, 173
domestic servants. *See* servants
Donauwörth, 141, 213
Dorfdichtung (village tale), 65
Dortmund, 235
Dostoyevsky, Fyodor, 143
dowry, 156

Dresden, xi, 39f, 51, 89f, 118, 140, 149, 202
dress, 43, 56, 157, 187, 194, 251, 259
Dronke, Ernst, 69
Droste-Hülshoff, Annette von, 53, 157, 172
Droysen, Johann Gustav, 81, 85, 108
Dürer, Albrecht, 2
dynamo, invention of, 239
East Elbia, 40, 53, 210f, 216, 220, 237, 249, 266f
East Prussia, ix, 8, 11, 56, 98, 117, 120, 122, 234f, 249, 269
Ebers, Georg, 149
Ebert, Friedrich, 196
Ebner-Eschenbach, Marie von, 53, 146, 149, 172, 176, 252, 257
ecclesiastical princes, 7
economy, economic development, 14, 17, 31–42, 67, 74f, 85, 89–91, 93, 98, 104, 108–11, 114f, 117–9, 122f, 158, 192, 196f, 203, 209f, 215, 228f, 231, 233–46, 249, 256, 273, 276
Edict of Tolerance, 7, 270
education, 46f, 49, 54, 62f, 68, 81, 90, 92, 116, 137, 151–3, 242, 244. *See also* schools, teachers, universities, women
Edward VII, 218
Eichendorff, Josef von, 25, 49, 54
Eisen-Journal, 36, 145
Elbe, 2, 9, 32, 35, 64, 86, 117
emancipation, 6, 11, 32, 48, 67f, 93, 98, 100, 103, 120, 151, 154, 163, 167f, 198, 215, 269–71
emigration, 93, 214, 233
Engels, Friedrich, 7, 17, 57, 72, 75, 90f, 108, 187

Index

England, 4, 19, 50, 55, 57, 76, 83, 86, 104, 117, 161–3, 174f, 187, 217, 277
Enlightenment, 8, 26, 48, 56, 64, 98, 137, 141f, 144, 147, 151, 153f, 163, 270
Entente Cordiale, 217
Erbach, 51
Erfurt Party, 206
Erfurt Party congress, 167
Ernst August, king of Hanover, 20
Ernst II, duke of Saxe-Coburg-Gotha, 197
Erzgebirge, 67, 176
Eulenburg, Philipp von, 212
factory workers, 66f, 161, 225, 240, 260, 265. *See also* wage laborers
Familienzeitschriften, 146
family, 26, 31, 33, 43, 46, 48, 52–6, 64, 67, 80, 93, 113, 128, 142, 148f, 151, 155–8, 160, 167, 170, 172, 174, 176f, 179, 187, 200, 236f, 239, 241, 256
family size, 155
Federal Act, 19f, 22, 136
Federal Diet, 37, 83, 202
federal traditions, 109
Ferdinand, Austrian emperor, 84, 88
Feuerbach, Anselm, 239
feuilletons, 147, 149
Fichte, Johann Gottlieb, 6, 100, 135, 144, 163
Fischer, Samuel, 143
Fontainebleau, 14
Fontane, Emilie, 46, 156, 256
Fontane, Mete, 156
Fontane, Theodor, ix, x, 9, 22f, 28, 46, 52, 61f, 77f, 88, 93, 124, 128, 146f, 155f, 159, 162, 168, 180, 187, 193f, 212, 229, 234, 244, 250, 252, 255–7, 265, 271, 275, 278

food, food production, 32, 116, 161, 224, 236f, 245, 258
Forster, Georg, 99
Forster-Huber, Therese, 57, 171–3
fourth class, 47, 65, 66, 67
France, 2–5, 7, 9, 13, 15, 17, 19, 27, 33, 39f, 54f, 65f, 68, 72f, 76, 99, 104f, 109, 111, 113f, 118f, 128, 131, 162f, 180, 191, 200f, 216f, 233, 238, 241, 243, 271, 273
Francis I, Austrian emperor, 12, 21, 26, 84, 88
Francis II, Holy Roman emperor, 21
François, Louise von, 146, 172, 252
Franconia, 24, 108, 241, 269
Franco-Prussian trade agreement, 119
Frankfurt, ix, 4, 8, 20, 37, 55f, 74, 77, 79–96, 103, 106, 108, 118, 125, 130, 134, 145, 183, 196f, 202, 212, 269
Frankfurt Parliament, 79, 82–7, 93, 95
Franklin, Benjamin, 144
Franz Joseph I, 52
Franzos, Karl Emil, 133
Frauenfrage, 163, 167
Frauen-Zeitung, 67, 164
Frederick Barbarossa, medieval emperor, 8
Frederick II of Prussia, 56, 94, 179
Frederick Karl, margrave, later grand duke of Baden, 2
free trade, 117, 119, 120
freelancers, 66, 69
Freiburg, 8, 22, 163
Freiligrath, Ferdinand, 51f, 57, 69, 104
Freytag, Gustav, 74, 149, 252, 270
Friedrich III, German emperor, 120, 196, 209

Friedrich Wilhelm III, king of
  Prussia, 7, 9, 21, 24f, 59, 100
Friedrich Wilhelm IV, king of
  Prussia, 25, 51, 72, 85, 93, 95, 97,
  102, 118, 125, 162, 210, 250
Friends of Light, 163
Fröbel, Friedrich, 164, 174
Fürth, 39
Gagern, Friedrich von, 54, 80
Gagern, Heinrich von, 54, 74, 82, 85
Galicia, 72, 133, 271
Gaskell, Elizabeth, 173
Gastein, Treaty of, 124
Geiger, Theodor, 255
Gellert, Christian Fürchtegott, 154
gender stereotyping, 154
German Confederation, 19f, 22, 26,
  35f, 45, 50, 59, 76, 80, 83f, 86, 88,
  93, 123, 125–9, 185f, 192, 201, 203
German Shop Assistants
  Association, 260
German writers, 133. *See also under
  individuals' names*
Germanistik, 74, 103
Gervinus, Georg Gottfried, 81
Gessner, Salomon von, 64
Gneisenau, August Neithardt von,
  11, 101
Goethe, Johann Wolfgang von, 1, 3f,
  6, 20, 48, 50, 55–7, 98, 136, 138,
  142–4, 176, 252, 271
Görres, Joseph, 102
Göschen, Georg Joachim, 138, 142
Gotha, 91, 203
Gotthelf, Jeremias, 34, 60f, 65, 67,
  161, 273
Göttingen, 10, 20, 64, 74, 144, 145, 288
Göttingen Seven, 74
Grabbe, Christian Dietrich, 16

Graz, 82
Grillparzer, Franz, 16, 26, 48, 59,
  77, 127
Grimm, Hermann, 173
Grimm, Jacob, 6, 20, 74, 81, 102f, 261
Grimm, Wilhelm, 6, 20, 74, 81, 102f,
  173, 176, 261
Gründerzeit. See Promoters' Boom
guilds, 3, 47, 63, 66, 257
Gulbransson, Olaf, 218, 262
Gutzkow, Karl, 57, 61f, 69, 140, 145,
  149, 162, 252, 265
gypsies, 48
Haber, Fritz, 241
Halle, 141, 145
Haller, Albrecht von, 64
Hallische Jahrbücher, 145
Hambach, 104
Hamburg, ix, xi, 2, 8, 14, 20, 35–7,
  55–7, 77, 91f, 117, 134, 141, 144f,
  183f, 197, 202, 219, 223, 226, 228,
  241, 244, 256, 265, 269, 274, 278
Hanover, 10, 20, 59, 65, 74, 76, 85, 118,
  125f, 183, 194, 198, 202, 226, 234
Hansabund, 222, 228
Hanseatic cities. *See also* Bremen,
  Hamburg, Lübeck
Hansemann, David, 89
Hapag, 35
Harden, Maximilian, 146, 207, 278
Hardenberg, Friedrich Leopold von,
  49, 54, 103
Hardenberg, Karl August von, 10, 21,
  31, 49
Harkort, Friedrich, 68
Hauptmann, Gerhart, 143, 181, 244, 278
health, 118, 129, 155, 195, 213, 242,
  244, 273
Hebbel, Friedrich, 46, 67, 68

Index

Hecker, Friedrich, 79
Hegel, G.W.F., 6, 17, 148
Heidelberg, 5, 24, 49, 79, 163
Heimatliteratur, 260, 278
Heimburg, Wilhelmine, 172
Heimgarten, 136
Heine, Heinrich, 4f, 7, 14–7, 27f, 35, 44, 51, 56f, 59, 61, 67–9, 73, 75, 86, 92, 101f, 135, 147, 149, 164, 233, 263, 269
Heine, Thomas Theodor, 276
Helgoland, 105
Herder, Johann Gottfried, 98
Herder, publishing house, 234
Hermann the Cherusker, 114
Herwegh, Emma, 80
Herwegh, Georg, 51, 80, 104
Hess, Moses, 90
Hesse, Hermann, 143, 179, 242, 278
Hesse-Darmstadt, 4, 28, 74, 85, 108, 128, 130, 249
Hesse-Kassel, 74, 118, 125, 183, 196, 198
Heyse, Paul, 277
Hintze, Otto, 249
Hitler, Adolf, 7, 125, 131
HKT, 228
Hofer, Andreas, 13
Hoffmann von Fallersleben, Heinrich, 74, 105, 107
Hoffmann, Ernst Theodor Amadeus, 27, 59
Hofmannsthal, Hugo von, 143
Hohenlohe-Ingelfingen, Kraft von, 52
Hohenlohe-Schillingsfürst, Chlodwig von, 211
Holberg, Ludwig, 2
Hölderlin, Friedrich, 63

Holstein, 2, 68, 86, 124f.
See also Schleswig-Holstein
Holstein, Friedrich von, 216, 219
Holy Roman Empire, 1, 3, 5, 8f, 12, 21, 50, 86, 99, 125, 201
Hoverbeck, Leopold von, 122
Huber, Therese.
See Forster-Huber, Therese
Huch, Ricarda, 163
Humboldt, Alexander von, 142
Humboldt, Wilhelm von, 7, 10, 21, 62, 98, 100, 270
Hungry Forties, 33, 116, 233
Husum, 125
Ibsen, Henrik, 150
illegitimacy, 46, 156, 235, 277
Immermann, Karl, 25, 60
imperialism, 113, 179, 215, 219, 233, 273
Indemnity Bill, 126, 198
industrial revolution, ix, 33, 39, 233, 237f, 240f, 256, 258, 263
industrialization, 23, 33, 37, 39, 43, 60, 73, 140, 144, 202, 205, 215, 226, 238, 247, 260–3, 278
infant mortality, 155, 235, 244f
intellectual property, 135
Ireland, 11, 33, 113, 233
Italy, ix, 2, 118, 201, 215, 243
Jacobin republic, Jacobins, 1, 90, 100
Jahn, "Turnvater," 6, 106
Jean Paul (Richter), 176
Jefferson, Thomas, 144
Jena, 9, 105, 144f
    battle of, 9, 13, 252
    university of, 49, 103
Jérome, king of Westphalia, 9, 99, 252
Jesuits, 126, 207

Jews, 4, 7, 39, 43f, 48, 93, 102, 168f, 174, 189, 198, 207, 213, 256, 260, 268–72
 and education, 61f, 169, 243
 discrimination against, 111, 189, 213
 emancipation of, 48, 198
Johann, Archduke of Austria, 82, 84, 88
Johann, king of Saxony, 25
John Bull, 273
Jordan, Sylvester, 74
Jordan, Wilhelm, 106
Joseph II, Holy Roman emperor, 31, 50, 135, 242
journalists, 68, 136, 163, 179, 204, 228, 272
journeymen. *See* artisans
Junkers, 52, 53, 120, 237
Kaiser Wilhelm Gesellschaft, 242
Kaiser Wilhelm II. *See* Wilhelm II
Kalender, 147
Kant, Immanuel, 6, 98, 135, 142, 144, 163
Kardorff, Wilhelm von, 199
Karlsbad, 81
Karlsbad Decrees, 20, 28, 59, 76, 136, 140
Karlsruhe, 2, 56, 72, 91f, 197, 241, 244
Katholikentage, 92, 169, 201
Keil, Ernst, 146
Keller, Gottfried, 61, 133, 139, 146, 257
Ketteler, Wilhelm von, 263
Kiderlen-Wächter, Alfred von, 219
Kiel, 108, 145
Kindergarten, 164, 174
Kinkel, Gottfried, 60
Kinkel, Johanna, 60
Kladderadatsch, 247-8
Klaipeda. *See* Memel

Kleinbürgertum, 55, 90f, 137, 156–9, 197, 213, 229, 257–60, 264, 268
kleindeutsch, 108, 111, 119, 131
Kleist, Heinrich von, 6, 12, 15, 48, 54, 88, 99, 100, 134
Klopstock, Friedrich, 51
Kollwitz, Käthe, 244
Kolping, Adolf, 263
Kompert, Leopold, 44
König, Heinrich, 141
Königgrätz, 124, 126
Königsberg, ix, 55, 59, 117, 269
Konstanz, 8
Köppen, Luise, 172
Kossuth, Lajós, 95
Kotzebue, August von, 103, 150
Kraus, Karl, 146f, 278
Kreuz-Zeitung, 147, 199, 200
Kröner, Adolf von, 142
Krüger, Franz, 58
Krupp, Alfred Friedrich, 228, 241, 260
Krupp, Fritz von, 211
Kugler, Frank, 63
Kulturkampf, 111, 136, 147, 195, 201, 243
Kürnberger, Ferdinand, 147
Landrat, 229, 247
Landtag (Prussian parliament), 119–22, 126, 130, 190, 195, 198f, 211, 264
Lange, Helene, 163, 166f, 169
Lasker, Eduard, 198
Lassalle, Ferdinand, 197, 202f, 205, 269
Laube, Heinrich, 57, 62, 81, 103, 145
Law on Associations, 165, 166
Legien, Carl, 225-6
Leipzig, 2, 13, 16, 39, 40, 52, 55f, 81, 91f, 134f, 141–5, 154, 171, 202, 241, 278
Leipzig book fair, 134, 144
Lenau, Nikolaus von, 42, 57

lending libraries, 3, 46, 137–9, 145f, 172
Leopold II, Holy Roman emperor, 31
Lepel, Bernhard von, 62, 93
Lessing, Gotthold Ephraim, 3, 142, 154
Levin, Rahel. *See* Varnhagen, Rahel
Lewald, Fanny, 82, 87, 179, 269
liberalism, 89, 91, 93, 105, 117, 119, 122, 195, 202, 247
Liberals. *See also* National Liberal party, Progressive party, 42, 108, 125f, 147, 191, 193, 198f, 203
Liebig, Justus, 33
Liebig's *Fleischextrakt*, 245
Liebknecht, Karl, 170
Liebknecht, Wilhelm, 203f
Lippe, 183f
List, Friedrich, 36, 145
literacy, 46, 133, 137f, 140
literary market, 42, 56, 61, 133f, 142f, 148, 150f, 171f. *See also* book fair, book trade
Louis Ferdinand, 62, 101
Louis Napoleon. *See* Napoleon
Louis Philippe, king of France, 72
Louis XIV, king of France, 131
Louis XVI, king of France, 27
Louise, queen of Prussia, 101, 165f, 180
Lübeck, xi, 2, 8, 20, 55, 183f, 228, 256
Ludwig I, king of Bavaria, 24, 101
Ludwig, Otto, 67, 257
Luther, Lutheranism, 23, 103, 256. *See also* churches, Protestants
Luther, Martin, 242
Lützow Free Corps, 13
Luxemburg, Rosa, 163, 170
Maaßen, Karl Georg, 36
Magazin zur Erfahrungsseelenkunde, 174
Magdeburg, 13, 57, 92
Mahler, Gustav, 61, 176

Mainz, 1, 7, 8, 87
  Republic of, 1, 99
Malmö, 86
Manchester, 57, 116
Mann, Heinrich, 140, 242
Mann, Thomas, 49, 143, 173, 179, 242, 254
manorial estates, 11, 32
Manz, publishers, 234
March days, 20, 88
Maria Theresia, Empress, 31, 137, 162, 242
Marianne, symbol of France, 180, 273
Marie Louise, consort of Napoleon, 12
marketing, 57, 134, 138, 141–7, 215, 237, 240, 245. *See also* literary market
Marlitt, Eugenie, 172
marriage, 33, 44–7, 53, 55, 153, 155, 159, 165, 264, 266, 269
Marx, Karl, 7, 14, 17, 46, 57, 61, 66, 68, 72, 75, 90f, 96, 128, 147, 164, 190, 203, 206, 251, 258, 263
Märzerrungenschaften, 83
Mathy, Karl, 83, 85
Max Planck Society. *See* Kaiser Wilhelm Gesellschaft
Maximilian II, king of Bavaria, 51
Mazzini, Giuseppe, 83
Mecklenburg, xi, 2, 6, 15, 27, 37, 83, 101, 190, 199, 234, 249, 250
Mecklenburg-Schwerin, 184, 190
Mecklenburg-Strelitz, 184, 190
media, mass, 1, 3, 28, 42, 50–2, 57, 92, 108, 113, 124, 126, 133–50, 163, 166, 171f, 189, 193, 197, 199, 201, 208, 275f
Memel, 40, 117
Mendelssohn, Moses, 56, 142
Mendelssohn-Bartholdy, Abraham, 56
Mendelssohn-Bartholdy, Fanny, 56

Mendelssohn-Bartholdy, Felix, 56
Mennonites, 234
Menzel, Adolph (later von), 63, 78, 227
Menzel, Wolfgang, 106
Merckel, Wilhelm von, 63, 88
Mereau, Sophie, 150
metalworkers, metalworking, 33, 115, 226, 258
Metternich era, 21f, 26, 66f, 137–47
Metternich system, 19–23, 27–9, 72
Metternich, Clemens von, 13f, 19–21, 26, 28, 52, 63, 72, 77, 83f
Metzler, publishers, 141
Meyer, Conrad Ferdinand, 146
Meyerbeer, Giacomo, 269
Meysenburg, Malwida von, 164
middle classes, 2f, 23, 43, 46, 49f, 54f, 62, 65, 71f, 74f, 78f, 81, 86f, 101, 108–10, 120, 144, 153, 156–60, 166, 171, 176, 188, 213–6, 225, 247, 250–7, 259, 264. See also bourgeoisie, *Mittelstand*
military, 9, 11, 13, 38, 40, 54, 72, 77, 94, 106, 109–16, 120–3, 127, 129, 158, 179, 185–9, 192, 194, 196, 198, 201, 204, 211f, 220, 225, 236, 251, 264, 271, 275
Mill, John Stuart, 151
Miquel, Johannes, later von, 212, 216, 223
Mitteleuropa, 216
Mittelstand, 75, 251, 259f, 268
"new" *Mittelstand*, 259
Möbius, Paul, 181
modernization, 20, 35, 39, 59, 167, 190, 210, 260, 276
Mohl, Robert von, 22
Moltke, Helmut von, 40, 54, 113, 123, 129, 155, 186
Mommsen, Theodor, 197, 255

monarchy, ix, 22, 26f, 81, 84, 94, 127, 198, 235, 268f, 271, 278
Mönchen-Gladbach, 141
Moore, Thomas, 26
Moravia, 84, 237
Morgenblatt, 57, 145, 172
Mörike, Eduard, 57, 60, 61
Moritz, Karl Philipp, 174
Mosse, publishers, 143
Motley, John Lothrop, 55
Müller, Adam, 6
Müller, Max, 63, 179
Munich, ix, 24, 56, 101f, 117, 130, 146, 168, 173, 189, 241, 278
music, musicians, 25, 51, 59, 105, 112, 128, 256, 271, 279. See also under individual composers' names
Nachmärz, 23, 92f, 147, 166, 238
Napoleon, 1–26, 50, 52, 99–101, 105f, 120, 177, 180, 252, 270, 273
Napoleon III, 118f, 128–30
Nassau, 10, 20, 100, 118, 125
Nathusius, Marie, 261
Nathusius, Philipp, 261
National Liberal party, 126
nationalism, 5, 10, 14f, 91, 95, 98–102, 105f, 109, 111, 113, 124, 149, 162, 228, 247
Nationalverein, 117, 197
National-Zeitung, 147
naturalism, naturalists, 143, 278
Naumann, Friedrich, 208, 229
navy, 113, 185, 212–4, 255
Navy League, 114, 213, 222, 228, 255, 260
Nazi, Nazism, ix, 7, 61, 105, 131, 223, 277
Nestroy, Johann, 48, 63, 68, 87
Netherlands, 1, 12, 55

Neue Bahnen, 166
Neue Deutsche Rundschau, 146
Neue Rheinische Zeitung, 57, 147
Neuschwanstein, 130
newspapers, 57, 113, 126, 141, 143, 146–8, 197, 199, 255, 275f
Nicholas I, Tsar of Russia, 25
Nicolai, Friedrich, 142, 144
Nietzsche, Friedrich, 48, 115, 238, 250
nobility, 2, 7, 22, 47–55, 111, 190, 200, 209, 247–55, 267
Notburga, 213, 234
Noth- und Hülfsbüchlein für Bauersleute, 138
Novalis. *See* Hardenberg, Friedrich Leopold von
Nuremberg, 2, 39, 55, 145, 174, 176, 241, 269
Oder, ix, 35, 117
Oetker, Dr., 245
Offenburg, 92
Oldenburg, 99
Olmütz, 94
Otto(-Peters), Louise, 44, 57, 67, 92, 164–6
Overbeck, Friedrich, 97
Palácky, František, 84
Palatinate, Upper, 267
Paris, 3–7, 66, 72, 80, 89, 121, 142, 148
  Jews in, 269
parliament, parliamentary system, 21f, 60, 71, 79, 81f, 88f, 106, 116, 119–27, 170, 185–203, 224, 247, 264
Passau, 117
patrimonial jurisdiction, 93
Paulsen, Friedrich, 236
Paulskirche, 79, 82, 87
pauperism, 11, 23, 32, 44, 66
Peace Movement, 114, 228

peasantry, 2, 11, 31, 47f, 64, 71, 75, 93, 100, 267
Pennsylvania, 234
Pennsylvanian Dutch, 234
Perthes, Friedrich, 134, 142
Pestalozzi, Johann Heinrich, 174
petty bourgeoisie. *See Kleinbürgertum*
philosophy, 61, 133, 201
Pietism, 100
piracy, 134–6
Pius IX, Pope, 92
Piusvereine, 92
Poland, Poles, ix, 13, 94–8, 103, 105f, 111, 113, 133, 180, 195, 224, 237, 261, 269
Polish Partitions, 9
political parties, 191, 193, 196f, 199, 221.
  See also under individual parties
Pomerania, 234, 235
Pope, Alexander, 93
Popp, Adelheid, 161, 177
population, 21, 24, 85, 184
Posadowsky-Wehner, Arthur von, 212
Posen, 80, 228, 234f, 271
postal system, 184, 239, 259, 277
Potsdam, 39
Prague, 80, 84, 87, 95, 124, 278
Pre-Parliament, 79
preserves, 156
press, 53, 73, 74, 86, 104, 113, 136, 141–8, 172, 193, 201, 205, 223, 264, 275
pressure groups, 91, 189, 195, 199, 222, 228, 249f, 255, 260, 267, 275
Preußische Jahrbücher, 120, 146
professors, 20, 22, 60, 74, 100, 105, 163, 243, 254
Progressive party (*Fortschrittspartei*), 126, 186, 198, 202f
proletariat, 57, 68, 75, 205, 234, 244, 258, 270

Promoters' Boom, 239
protectionism, 37
protective tariffs. *See* tariffs
Protestants, 23f, 54, 60, 98, 100, 102, 108, 134–7, 141, 145, 147, 155, 163, 169, 172, 200f, 213, 223, 228, 243, 245, 250, 256, 263, 269
protoindustrialization, 33
Prussian Law on Associations, 165
publishers, publishing, 2, 133–5, 138, 140–4, 148, 171, 234.
   See also chapter 9
Punch, 207
Pustet, publishers, 234
Puttkamer, Robert von, 192
Raabe, Wilhelm, 67, 146, 162, 233, 252, 257, 278
Radowitz, General Joseph Maria, 97
railway, 32, 36–42, 86, 130, 141, 197, 238, 241, 248, 259
Raimund, Ferdinand, 137
Ranke, Leopold von, 71
Rathenau, Emil, 272
readers, 65, 103, 133, 139–41, 144, 172, 181, 278
reading revolution, 133, 134
Reich Law on Associations, 166
Reich League against Social Democracy, 260
Reich, Philipp Erasmus, 135
Reichsmark, 198
Reichspartei. *See also* conservative parties, 199
Reichstag, 108, 185f, 189, 191–5, 198–200, 203, 205, 209, 211, 215, 221, 224, 263, 272, 275
Reichsverweser (Regent of Germany, 1848), 82

Renner, Karl, 236
Restoration, 21, 23, 25f, 28, 32, 44, 51, 73, 103, 251–4
Reuss-Greiz, 184
Reuss-Schleiz, 184
Reuter, Fritz, 26, 157
Reuter, Gabriele, 143
Reutlingen, 138
Revolution, American, 22, 99
Revolution, French, 5–9, 14, 53, 65, 75f, 99, 144
Revolution, of 1830, German, 20f, 28, 34, 104, 136
Revolution, of 1848, German, 22, 28, 54, 60, 64, 68, 72, 76, 84, 93, 121, 136, 146, 163–6, 188, 196, 202, 254, 255, 269, 270
Rheinlieder, 105
Rhine, Rhineland, 1, 4, 7f, 14–19, 33, 35, 39f, 76, 79, 99f, 102, 105, 114f, 117, 128f, 141, 180, 199, 201, 204, 223f, 226, 234f, 240f, 250, 256, 263, 270, 274
Richter, Eugen, 194, 198
Richter, Jean Paul, 176
Riezler, Kurt von, 231
Rilke, Rainer Maria, 278
road network, 35
Robespierre, Maximilien de, 75
Roche, Sophie von la, 145
Rodenberg, Julius, 146, 173
Romanticism, 49, 98, 153f
Romantics, 61
Roon, Albrecht von, 119–23, 127
Rosegger, Peter, 65, 136, 176
Rosenzweig, Franz, 271
Rothschild family, 269
Rotteck, Karl, 22

Rotwelsch, 48
Rouanet-Kummer, Emilie.
   See Fontane, Emilie
Rousseau, Jean Jacques, 75
Rückert, Friedrich, 61, 176
Rüdesheim, 114
Ruge, Arnold, 81, 145
Ruhr, 39, 57, 115, 225f, 234, 256
Rumania, 133, 216
Russia, ix, 13, 19, 21, 52, 56, 83, 86, 100, 104, 109, 215–9, 238, 269, 271
Saar, Ferdinand von, 54, 149
Saarland, 115, 234
Sadowa. *See* Königgrätz
Sailer, Michael, 61
salons, 3, 62
Salzburg, 117
Sammlungspolitik, 212
Sattelzeit, 3
Savigny, Friedrich Karl von, 100
Saxe-Altenburg, 184
Saxe-Coburg-Gotha, 77, 184, 197
Saxe-Meiningen, 184
Saxe-Weimar, 20, 22, 55
Saxony, 15, 20–4, 31, 33, 37, 39, 51, 63, 65, 67, 76, 81, 85, 89f, 95, 108, 115, 118, 125, 134f, 137, 163f, 183f, 190, 202, 204, 221, 226, 228, 234, 241f, 252, 264
Scharnhorst, Gerhard, 11, 101
Schaumburg-Lippe, 184
Schill, Ferdinand von, 13
Schiller, Friedrich, 6, 49, 55, 57, 98, 103, 136–8, 142, 144, 150, 171, 176
Schinkel, Karl, 24
Schlegel, August Wilhelm, 48f, 99, 103
Schlegel, Friedrich, 48f, 99, 103, 144
Schlegel-Schelling, Caroline, 173
Schleiermacher, Friedrich, 6, 60, 100

Schleswig-Holstein, 82–8, 95, 106, 123f, 197
Schlögl, Friedrich, 136f, 147
Schmerling, Anton von, 84
Schmid, Christoph, later von, 61, 175
Schmidt, Auguste, 166
Schneckenburg, Max von, 105
Schnitzler, Arthur, 143
schools. *See also* education, 63, 159, 170, 243
Schopenhauer, Adele, 56
Schopenhauer, Arthur, 56, 181
Schopenhauer, Johanna, 56
Schumann, Robert, 105, 176
Schwarzburg-Rudolfstadt, 184
Schwarzburg-Sondershausen, 184
Schwarzenberg, Felix von, 52, 88, 94
Schwarzenberg, Karl von, 13, 52
seasonal workers, 266
Sedan Day, 113
Sedan, Battle of, 130
Septennat, 127, 185
serfs, 11, 32, 68
servants, 47, 66f, 81, 156, 162, 223, 264–7
service sector, 158, 237
Seume, Johann Gottfried, 99
sewing machine, 160, 239
Shaw, George Bernard, 143
shipping, 35, 236
Siebenpfeiffer, Philipp Jakob, 105
Siemens, Werner, 116, 189, 197, 238f, 256f
Silesia, ix, 33, 52, 59, 94, 100, 115, 164, 199, 201f, 228, 234f, 261, 269
Simmel, Georg, 136
Simon, Heinrich, 269
Simplicissimus, 146, 189, 218, 231, 262, 275f

Smith, Adam, 10
Social Democratic party, 64, 161, 167, 170, 191, 196, 206, 213, 221, 225, 228, 255, 264, 266
social imperialism, 113
social welfare, 8, 161, 204, 220
socialism, socialists, 64, 69, 91, 104, 111, 136, 140f, 147, 167, 169f, 177, 189, 194, 200, 202–6, 213, 215, 221, 224–6, 236f, 258, 263f, 269
Socialist party, 195f, 202, 205
Socialist Workers Party, 202f
Spielhagen, Friedrich, 110, 149, 252, 277
Spitzer, Daniel, 147
sport, 276
Staatslexikon, 22
Standesherren (mediatized princes), 50f
Ständestaat, 2
Steffens, Henrik, 12, 13, 25
Stein, Baron Karl, 10f, 13, 20, 31, 100f, 125, 274
Sternheim, Carl, 179, 278
Stettin, 117
Stifter, Adalbert, 34, 52, 61, 63, 176, 257
stock exchange collapse, 109
Stollwerck (chocolate manufacturer), 245
Storm and Stress, 64
Storm, Theodor, 49, 60f, 125, 146, 176, 252, 257
Stosch, Albrecht von, 214
Strasbourg, 243
strikes, strike-breaking, 66, 90, 177, 186, 203, 225, 261
Struve, Gustav von, 79
Stumm-Halberg, Karl von, 211
Stuttgart, 56, 82, 89, 95, 141f, 145f, 226, 241
Styria, 82

suffrage, universal (male), 81, 88, 190–2, 203
Switzerland, 1, 33, 66f, 130, 133, 141, 198, 204
Talleyrand, Charles Maurice de, 26
tariffs, 37, 40, 192, 210, 216, 220, 224, 237
teachers, teaching, 3, 23, 47, 49, 60, 63, 79, 91, 106, 159, 162, 167f, 200, 244, 246, 254, 263
technology, ix, 34, 116, 140, 142, 157, 236, 238, 242, 245
telegraph, 34, 126, 238
Telegraph für Deutschland, 145
Telegraphenbüro, 148
textile manufacture, 33, 260
Thackeray, William, 35, 55
Thaer, Albrecht, 33
Thalia, 144
theater, x, 25, 51, 53, 67, 81, 87, 137, 147, 149, 272, 278
theology, 8, 60, 61, 133
Third Reich, 105
Thoma, Hans, 130
Thomas à Kempis, 61
Thomasius, Christian, 154
three-class franchise, 120, 190, 221
Thuringia, 98, 226
Tieck, Ludwig, 25, 29, 99, 142
Tilsit, treaty of, 9
Tirpitz, Alfred von, 212–5, 228
Tivoli Program, 272
Tocqueville, Alexis de, 76
Tolstoy, Leo, Count, 143
toys, 174, 176, 177
trade unions, 213, 224f
  Christian, 223–6
  Free, 222–4
  Hirsch-Duncker, 224

Index 305

transport. *See also* canals, railways, road network, waterways, 32, 35, 39f, 190, 213, 221, 257, 259, 274f
Trattner, Johann Thomas von, 135
Treitschke, Heinrich von, 108, 254f, 272
Trier, 1
Tübingen, 22, 60, 142, 144, 249
Tunnel over the River Spree (club), 62
Twesten, Karl, 120, 122, 125
Uhland, Ludwig, 60, 81
Ullstein, publishers, 143
Uncle Sam, 273
unification, ix, 37, 40, 52, 54, 74, 83, 95, 108f, 115, 117, 119, 123–5, 127, 131, 139, 155, 177, 183, 186, 192, 197, 238, 244, 255, 270
universal suffrage (male), 81, 88, 190–2, 203
universities. *See also* education, 6, 49, 60, 100, 140, 163, 241–4, 278
university teachers. *See also* professors, 105, 272
Unter den Linden, 58, 79, 87, 179
Urania, 58
urbanization, 147, 247, 278
Usedom, Gustav von, 85
Valhalla, 102
Varnhagen, Rahel, née Levin, 62
Versailles, 2, 110f, 130
Victoria, later empress, 196
Victoria, queen of England, 116, 196, 276
Victorian England, 187
Victorian fiction, 173
Viebig, Clara, 143, 234
Vienna, xi, 13f, 21f, 52–5, 59, 62, 68, 76f, 83f, 87f, 92f, 117, 133f, 136, 143, 146, 162, 234–7, 269, 271, 278

Vienna, Congress of, 14, 19, 21, 24, 135, 136, 270
village tale (*Dorfdichtung*), 65
Virchow, Rudolph, 152
Vischer, Friedrich Theodor, 81f
Volksverein (Prussian Conservative Organization), 197, 223
Volksverein für das katholische Deutschland, 201, 213, 223
Vollmar, Georg von, 224
Vormärz or "pre-March," 21, 28, 43, 51, 60, 63, 66f, 73f, 141, 147, 254
Vorparlament, 79
Vorwärts, 147
Voß, Johann Heinrich, 11, 48f, 64
Vossische Zeitung, 147
wage laborers, 161, 213, 260, 263f
wages, 65, 142, 144, 156, 221, 226, 235, 261, 267, 274
Wagner, Richard, 89
Waldeck, Benedikt, 122
Waldeck, principality of, 184
Waldmüller, Ferdinand, 176
War
  Austro-Prussian, 124
  Danish, 123f
  First World, 40, 53, 155, 169, 213, 229, 231
  Franco-Prussian, 105, 124, 128, 131, 203, 229, 238
  Napoleonic. *See* Wars of Liberation
  Thirty Years, 126, 138
war veterans, 114, 229
Wars of Liberation (*Befreiungskriege*), 12f, 25, 100, 101
water, 154, 156, 274
Waterloo, Battle of, 14, 19, 89, 103
waterways, 1, 35, 259
Weavers' Revolt of 1844, 44, 73

Weber, Marianne, 170
Weber, Max, 170, 246, 250, 266
Wedekind, Franz, 179, 181, 208, 242, 278
Weerth, Georg, 57
Weimar, 56, 135, 196
Weiße, Christian Felix, 138, 174
Weitling, Wilhelm, 64
Welcker, Karl, 22
Werner, Anton von, 110
West Prussia, 1, 228, 234, 271
Westphalia, 9, 19, 31, 53, 99, 223f, 235, 240f, 250, 252, 266, 270, 274
white collar workers, 259
Wieland, Christoph Martin, 141
Wigand, Otto, publisher, 142
Wildermuth, Ottilie, 172
Wilhelm I, German emperor, 25, 114, 116, 120, 127f, 130, 186
Wilhelm II, German emperor, 66, 123, 140, 143, 167, 186–9, 200, 208–11, 216, 218, 220f, 229, 241, 247, 259, 274f, 277
Wilhelmine (definition), 209
William I, king of Württemberg, 22
William the Founder. *See* Wilhelm I
Willkomm, Ernst, 67
Windischgrätz, Alfred Fürst zu, 84, 87, 95, 106
Windthorst, Ludwig, 194, 201, 203, 244
Wolfenbüttel, 39
Wollstonecraft, Mary, 163
women, 151–206
  civil service, 159
  domestic service, 162
  dress, 157
  education, 153, 162f
  emancipation, 92, 154, 163–70
  employment, 67, 69, 158–62, 169, 234, 239, 260
  farming, 157, 159, 161
  fashion, 151, 158
  health, 155
  life expectancy, 154, 233
  marriage, 46
  organization, 204, 222, 225
  poverty, 157
  vote, 171
  wages, 156
  working class, 155
  writers, 53, 69, 138, 143, 145, 149f, 171f
  writing, 173
Wrangel, Friedrich von, 85, 88
Wrocław, ix, 13, 269
Württemberg, 3f, 8, 20f, 50, 56, 59f, 65, 76f, 85, 108, 118, 125, 128, 130, 137, 183–5, 226, 241, 249, 259
Yiddish, 48
Young Germans, 7, 51, 57, 59, 140
Young Hegelians, 7, 140
Zabern Affair, 189
Zeiss (optics), 241
Zeiss, Carl, 256
Zeitung für die elegante Welt, 145
Zentrum. *See* Center party, 201
Zetkin, Clara, 170
Zille, Heinrich, 244
Zola, Émile, 130, 143
Zollunion. *See* Customs Union
Zschokke, Heinrich, 67